W9-CNN-385

Buying Stocks Without A Broker

Buying Stocks Without A Broker

Charles B. Carlson, CFA
Dow Theory Forecasts, Inc.

McGraw-Hill, Inc.

New York   St. Louis   San Francisco   Auckland   Bogotá
Caracas   Lisbon   London   Madrid   Mexico   Milan
Montreal   New Delhi   Paris   San Juan   São Paulo
Singapore   Sydney   Tokyo   Toronto

Library of Congress Catalog Card Number: 91-32447

1 2 3 4 5 6 7 8 9 0   DOC/DOC   9 7 6 5 4 3 2 1

ISBN   0-07-009951-0   {HC}
ISBN   0-07-009952-9   {PBK}

The sponsoring editor for this book was David J. Conti, the editing supervisor
was Joseph Bertuna, and the production supervisor was Donald F. Schmidt. It
was set in Baskerville by McGraw-Hill's Professional Book Group composition
unit.

Printed and bound by R. R. Donnelley & Sons Company.

This publication is designed to provide accurate and authoritative information in
regard to the subject matter covered. It is sold with the understanding that the
publisher is not engaged in rendering legal, accounting, or other professional
service. If legal advice or other expert assistance is required, the services of a
competent professional person should be sought.
—from a declaration of principles jointly adopted by a committee
of the American Bar Association and a committee of publishers

To my parents, whose love and support have meant more to me than they will ever know.

Contents

Preface

It's probably the last remaining break for the small investor in the stock market—but don't expect to hear about it from your broker. Indeed, as you will soon discover in these pages, there are programs which permit investors to purchase stocks directly through the issuing companies, sometimes at a discount, without ever calling a broker and paying brokerage commissions. The programs are called dividend reinvestment plans (DRIPs), and they are the subject of this book.

Contrary to what you may be thinking, I have no axe to grind with brokers, who often have thankless jobs with customers taking all of the credit when things go well and dumping all of the blame when things go badly. I will not attempt to discuss the relative merits of brokers in this book. I trust that those brokers who have been successful for their clients have nothing to fear from these pages.

My point—and this is indisputable—is that brokers don't work for nothing. They cost you money in the form of commissions. And these commissions can take a toll on a portfolio's performance. Thus, if a way exists in which individual investors can hold down or eliminate commission costs, it seems to me investors have a right to know about it.

Yet, many investors are simply not aware of the commission-free investing possibilities available with DRIPs. When this subject appears as a feature in *Dow Theory Forecasts*, the investment newsletter published by our firm, it always generates many calls and letters from individuals who had never heard of the programs prior to our report. I suppose that's no surprise—it's not as though brokers beat the drums for these plans, for obvious reasons.

Hence, the reason for writing this book is to make investors aware of these plans and to provide guidance in using them. With information being everything in the investment game, you owe it to yourself to be informed about all options in stock investing. DRIPs are one option you can ill-afford not to at least consider, given their many benefits.

Acknowledgments

Putting together a book of this magnitude is by no means a one-man show. Many people deserve credit for their efforts. I'd like to thank the entire staff of *Dow Theory Forecasts*, especially Tim Waggoner, Avis Beitz, and Sandy Spisak, for their support and encouragement. Thanks also go to the companies who responded to our verbal and written inquiries concerning their DRIPs. The Federal Reserve Bank of Richmond and Potomac Electric Power deserve special thanks for permitting me to use some of their materials in the book. And to the readers of *Dow Theory Forecasts*, whose interest in this subject was the primary impulse for this book, many thanks for your comments and suggestions.

Finally, I would be remiss if I didn't give special recognition to my two assistants, Robin Sikora and Monica Taylor. Without their tireless efforts in helping to compile the DRIP directory, this book would still be in my head instead of in your hands.

Charles B. Carlson

Introduction

Right up front, I'm pretty sure I already know two things about you. First, your stockbroker didn't tell you about this book. Second, you're probably fed up with what's happening on Wall Street these days.

Now, I realize I'm no clairvoyant. But, my position as editor of *Dow Theory Forecasts* gives me a good idea of what's on the minds of individual investors. Currently, you're a disgruntled lot. Indeed, individual investors—the "little guys," according to Wall Street—are fed up. You're fed up with insider trading scandals; fed up with computer program trading and other tactics used by the "big boys" that increase market volatility; fed up with "junk bonds" that have lived up to their name; and finally, fed up with skyrocketing brokerage commissions and service fees.

The result has been an exodus from the stock market of literally hundreds of thousands of individual investors. However, there is another way—and one guaranteed to save you money while keeping it out of your broker's hands. DRIPs provide a powerful way to keep individual investors in the stock market game—and to keep them winning. Briefly, around 900 public corporations and closed-end funds have DRIPs that allow individuals to purchase stock by reinvesting dividends in new shares. In most cases, investors may also send optional cash payments directly to the companies to purchase additional shares.

The primary appeal of these plans is that most firms charge no commissions or fees for these services. Let me say that one more time.

No commissions.

In fact, many companies permit investors to buy stock through the plans at discounts of up to 10 percent of the prevailing price in the stock market. Further, DRIPs allow individuals to invest in expensive, blue-chip issues, such as IBM, for as little as $10 at a time.

And the benefits of DRIPs don't stop with commission-free investing. As this book will show, DRIPs are much more than a gimmick. Investing through DRIPs provides an ideal avenue for long-term investing—an approach that, by the end of this book, I hope you'll agree is the best way to profit in the stock market, especially during the volatile times ahead.

Certainly, knowing about DRIPs and who offers them are important, and you'll learn about that inside these pages. However, to stop there without providing strategies and specific stock recommendations would shortchange the reader. Thus, this book goes several steps further:

- Just because a company offers a DRIP does not make it a worthwhile investment. This book explores which companies are best suited for investing via DRIPs—and which ones aren't—and highlights especially attractive issues.

- Investment objectives differ among individuals. Therefore, it's important to structure DRIP investments to meet these objectives. This book provides model portfolios for a variety of investors—those interested in maximum capital gains as well as those looking for safety, those who have a lot of money and those with a little.

- There are plenty of positive aspects of DRIPs, but what are the negatives? You'll find a full review of potential pitfalls of the programs as well as investor "don'ts" concerning DRIP investing.

In short, it's all here—the nuts and bolts of DRIPs as well as various strategies, specific recommendations, and a comprehensive directory of corporate DRIPs.

Thus, whether you're a novice investor or a sophisticated stock market jockey, familiar with DRIPs or just thinking that they frequent boring dinner parties, this book has something for you. In the pages before you is a blueprint for the do-it-yourself investor—a well-marked path to building a profitable investment portfolio while saving hundreds and thousands of dollars in commissions in the process.

1

What's a DRIP?

Quick & Reilly, one of the largest discount brokerage firms in the country, runs an advertisement that appears frequently in financial newspapers. The ad's headline reads: "Why YOU Probably Need TWO Brokers."

I'm here to tell you—that might be two brokers too many. Indeed, there is a way to purchase stocks, in many cases at a discount to prevailing market prices, without paying brokerage commissions.

Though it seems too good to be true, you can bypass the broker's bite when buying stocks by using corporate dividend reinvestment plans (DRIPs). Never heard of DRIPs? That's not surprising. Even though they've been around for years, DRIPs remain a secret to many individual investors. One reason is that your broker isn't likely to speak highly of DRIPs or to comment at all about them. That's because investing via DRIPs takes commission dollars out of your broker's pocket and puts them in yours.

What's a DRIP?

What are DRIPs? They are programs, sponsored by around 900 firms and closed-end funds, which permit current shareholders of these companies to purchase additional shares by going directly to the firms, thereby bypassing the broker and commission fees. Investors purchase the stock with cash dividends that the company reinvests for them in additional shares. In addition, most plans permit investors to make voluntary cash payments directly into the plans to purchase shares.

DRIPs have several attractive features:

- Most companies charge no commissions for purchasing stocks through their DRIPs, and those that do only charge a nominal fee.

- Over 100 firms have DRIPs which permit participants to purchase stock at discounts to prevailing market prices. These discounts are usually 3 to 5 percent and may be as high as 10 percent.

- Most plans permit investors to send optional cash payments (OCPs), in many cases for as little as $10, directly to the company to purchase additional shares. Thus, it's possible to purchase a stock (or a fraction of one) such as IBM for as little as $10 at a crack—an especially attractive feature for small investors who otherwise may not be able to afford expensive, blue-chip issues.

- DRIPs are an excellent tool for "dollar-cost averaging," a powerful long-term investment strategy that will be explored further in subsequent chapters.

Read the Prospectus

Starting an investment program using DRIPs is quite simple, but it requires some up-front homework. Not all companies offer DRIPs, so it is important to find out first if a company in which you are interested has a DRIP. Fortunately, the corporate directory in Chapter 7 lists addresses and phone numbers for around 900 companies offering DRIPs. Since companies drop plans periodically and others initiate them, it pays to double check with the investor relations department of the company to make sure the firm offers a DRIP.

Once you find out the firm offers a DRIP, the next step is to find out the specifics of the plan. Not all DRIPS are alike. For example:

- Although many DRIPs offer discounts on shares purchased through the plans, most do not; and those firms that do have discounts may only offer them on shares purchased through reinvested dividends and not on OCPs.

- Some firms permit the reinvestment of preferred dividends for common shares, while others may not.

- Some companies allow partial reinvestment of dividends, while others require that all dividends be reinvested.

- A number of firms permit OCPs only if the shareholder participates in the DRIP, although some firms allow shareholders to receive all dividend payments and still participate only in the optional payment feature of the plan.

- Companies differ on the timing of stock purchases for shareholders. Some will enter the market only around the dividend payment dates—once every 3 months—while others will enter the market more frequently.

- The amount of OCPs that may be made into plans differs among DRIPs. For example, IBM allows OCPs of $10 up to $5000 every 3 months, while shareholders in Citicorp's DRIP may make optional cash payments of up to $20,000 per month.

- Costs of the plans differ, especially fees shareholders pay to sell stocks from the plans.

- A host of other differences may arise among plans, such as the availability of safekeeping services for shareholders' certificates and the number of shares required to enroll in the plan.

How does an investor learn about the plans? Once again, the directory in this book provides a wealth of information concerning the individual plans. However, it still pays to obtain a prospectus providing information and eligibility requirements of the DRIP.

I think that the term *prospectus* often creates anxiety in individual investors who believe they won't understand a prospectus. Not true. Sure, there are some prospectuses that require a law degree to decipher. But most are straightforward and easy to understand. To take some of the fear out of a prospectus, I have reprinted most of the prospectus for the DRIP of Potomac Electric Power (see Figure 1-1). This example should not be construed as a solicitation of Potomac Electric Power's DRIP. Rather, it is an example of the type of vital information available in a prospectus.

DRIP Nuts and Bolts

Here is a summary of some of the nuts and bolts of DRIPs:

Purchasing Fees. In most cases, firms do not charge brokerage commissions or service fees for purchasing stock through the plans. However, there are a few companies that do charge participants their pro rata share of brokerage fees. These fees are usually nominal since firms can obtain favorable brokerage rates because of the large quantities they invest. Companies may also have various service charges, such as safekeeping fees. Again, these fees are usually $5 or less.

POTOMAC ELECTRIC POWER COMPANY

SHAREHOLDER DIVIDEND REINVESTMENT PLAN

4,000,000 SHARES OF
COMMON STOCK

(Par Value $1 Per Share)

Potomac Electric Power Company (the "Company") is continuing to offer to holders of its Common Stock an opportunity to reinvest their cash dividends on Common Stock in additional shares of the Company's Common Stock. Under the Plan, holders of the Company's Common Stock have the option of reinvesting dividends on all shares held by them both of record and in the Plan or only on shares held by the Plan (while continuing to receive cash dividends on all other shares). A participant may also purchase additional shares of the Company's Common Stock through the Plan by making a voluntary cash payment in an amount of not less than $25 nor more than $5,000 each month. **If a shareholder is already a participant in the Plan, it is not necessary to take any action in order to continue to have Common Stock dividends reinvested.**

The Company at its option may elect to sell newly issued shares of its Common Stock to meet the requirements of the Plan or, if the Company does not elect to do so, the Plan Agent will purchase shares for the Plan on the open market. The purchase price of shares of Common Stock purchased from the Company will be the average of the reported high and low sale prices for the Company's Common Stock on the New York Stock Exchange, Inc. on the pricing date. The purchase price of shares purchased on the open market will be the market price. Brokerage fees in connection with all such open market purchases will be paid by the Company.

Participants do not pay any fees or commissions when they acquire shares under the Plan. The Company bears the cost of administering the Plan. Participants may be subject to charges for certain requested services. See Question 8 under "Description of Plan."

Although the Plan contemplates the continuation of quarterly dividend payments, the payment of dividends will depend upon future earnings, the financial condition of the Company and other factors. The Company reserves the right to modify, suspend or terminate the Plan at any time.

The Riggs National Bank of Washington, D.C. acts as Agent for shareholders under the Plan.

THESE SECURITIES HAVE NOT BEEN APPROVED OR DISAPPROVED BY THE SECURITIES AND EXCHANGE COMMISSION OR ANY STATE SECURITIES COMMISSION NOR HAS THE SECURITIES AND EXCHANGE COMMISSION OR ANY STATE SECURITIES COMMISSION PASSED UPON THE ACCURACY OR ADEQUACY OF THIS PROSPECTUS. ANY REPRESENTATION TO THE CONTRARY IS A CRIMINAL OFFENSE.

November 27, 1990

Figure 1-1. Sample of DRIP prospectus. (*From Potomac Electric Power Company*)

Selling Fees. DRIPs handle selling in one of two ways. Some companies permit shareholders to sell directly through the DRIP. Usually a participant must put his or her sell request in writing and submit it to the DRIP. After the DRIP receives the sell request, it may take as long

SUMMARY OF PLAN

The following summary is qualified in its entirety by the detailed information describing the Plan and the Company appearing elsewhere in this Prospectus. Readers should review that information with care, and it is suggested that this Prospectus be retained for future reference. Reference numbers refer to detailed information found in questions and answers on pages 5 through 14.

		Question References
Name of Plan:	Potomac Electric Power Company Shareholder Dividend Reinvestment Plan.	
Purpose:	The Plan provides holders of the Company's Common Stock the opportunity to reinvest quarterly dividends and the option to purchase additional shares of the Company's Common Stock. The purchase of shares from the Company provides the Company cash to support its ongoing capital requirements including its ongoing utility construction program and operations. The Company retains the option of meeting share purchase requirements of the Plan by instructing the Plan Agent to purchase shares of Common Stock on the open market.	1, 2
Benefits:	Dividends are reinvested free of charge. Participants may elect to receive cash dividends on shares held by them of record rather than having such dividends reinvested (the "Limited Dividend Reinvestment" option). An optional cash investment of not less than $25 nor more than $5,000 may be made each month. All brokerage fees or commissions will be paid by the Company. Purchase transactions, custodial service and certificate issuance are free to Plan participants.	2, 8, 11, 13, 16
Eligibility:	The Plan is open to any recordholder of Common Stock.	3
Costs to Participant:	All administrative costs of the Plan are paid by the Company. The participant will be charged $3 plus any applicable brokerage commission if the participant directs the Agent to sell Plan shares.	1, 8, 21
Joining the Plan or Changing Participation:	The shareholder completes a special authorization form and delivers it to the Plan Agent. The Plan Agent must receive the Plan authorization form prior to the record date for a dividend in order for such dividend to be reinvested under the Plan or otherwise to effect a change in participation.	5, 6, 7, 23
Termination of Participation:	Termination of participation is permitted at any time.	22, 31
Limitations:	The Plan invests, issues certificates, provides custodial service and sells shares only as specified herein. The participant continues to bear the risk of market price fluctuations.	13, 26, 32, 33
Voting Rights:	All voting rights are retained by the participant.	29
Administration:	The Riggs National Bank of Washington, D.C., as Agent for participants, administers the Plan.	4
Tax Consequences:	Summarized in answer to Question 30.	

4

Figure 1-1. (*Continued*) Sample of DRIP prospectus. (*From Potomac Electric Power Company*)

as 10 business days before the sale is made. In a few cases, the firms pick up selling costs. However, the majority of companies charge brokerage fees; however, these rates are usually less than the individual would pay if going through a broker. Investors should note that not all companies

---

SHAREHOLDER DIVIDEND REINVESTMENT PLAN

DESCRIPTION OF PLAN

Purpose

1. *What is the purpose of the Plan?*

The Plan provides the holders of Common Stock of Potomac Electric Power Company (the
· "Company") a convenient method for investing their quarterly dividends in shares of the Company's
Common Stock. In addition, the Plan permits participants to make voluntary cash payments for the
purchase of additional shares of the Company's Common Stock. Shares of Common Stock purchased
through operation of the Plan may be newly issued shares or, at the option of the Company, may be
purchased on the open market by the Plan Agent. All commissions and fees incurred in connection
with the purchase of shares by the Plan will be paid by the Company. The proceeds from the sale to
the Plan of newly issued shares will be used to fund ongoing capital requirements of the Company
including its ongoing utility construction program and operations. Dividends reinvested under this
Plan are includable in taxable income.

Advantages

2. *What are the advantages of the Plan to participants?*

Full Dividend Reinvestment—If this option is chosen, cash dividends on all of the full and
fractional shares of Common Stock owned by Plan participants, whether held in the Plan or
registered in the name of the participant, are reinvested in additional shares of the Company's
Common Stock. See Questions 10, 11 and 12.

Limited Dividend Reinvestment—If this option is chosen, only dividends on shares held by the
Plan are reinvested in additional shares of the Company's Common Stock. Cash dividends on shares
registered in the name of the participant and held outside the Plan are paid to the participant. See
Questions 10, 11 and 12.

Additional Investment Option—Participants may make voluntary cash payments to purchase
shares of Common Stock. A single voluntary cash payment of not less than $25 nor more than $5,000
may be made each month. See Questions 10, 11, 13, 16, 17 and 24.

Custodial Service—Shares credited to a participant's account receive complimentary
safekeeping. In addition, a participant can transfer shares held of record to the Plan Agent, which
will credit such shares to the participant's Plan account share balance. Regular statements of account
will be mailed to each participant as soon as practicable after each investment. See Questions 18, 25
and 26.

Transaction Costs—Plan participants pay no brokerage fees or commissions either on shares
newly issued by the Company or on shares purchased by the Plan Agent on the open market. See
Question 8.

5

Figure 1-1. *(Continued)* Sample of DRIP prospectus. *(From Potomac Electric Power Company)*

will sell shares in the plan. Some firms send certificates to shareholders
who want to sell. The participant must then go through a broker to sell
shares.

Partial Dividend Reinvestment.   This option, found in many DRIPs,
permits participants to receive some cash dividends while having a por-

---

Eligibility

3. *Who is eligible to participate in the Plan?*

Any holder of record of the Company's Common Stock is eligible to participate in the Plan. Beneficial owners of Common Stock whose only shares are held for them in registered names other than their own, such as in the names of brokers, banks or trustees, must take such steps as they deem appropriate to become a holder of record in order to qualify for Plan participation. A shareholder who has separately registered accounts, for example "John Smith" and "John Q. Smith," must complete separate authorization forms in order to enroll both accounts in the Plan.

Administration

4. *Who administers the Plan?*

The Riggs National Bank of Washington, D.C. (the "Bank" or "Agent") acts as agent for the participating shareholders under the Plan. See Question 32.

The Agent's address is The Riggs National Bank of Washington, D.C., Corporate Trust Division, Dividend Reinvestment Unit, P.O. Box 96213, Washington, D.C. 20090-6213. For the convenience of Plan participants, a toll free number for any questions concerning a Plan account is available during business hours (8 a.m.-5 p.m.) at 1-800-642-7365.

Participation

5. *How does an eligible shareholder participate?*

To participate in the Plan, an eligible shareholder is required to complete an authorization form and to send it to the Bank at the address given in Question 4, above. Authorization forms are available from Potomac Electric Power Company, Shareholder Service Department, P.O. Box 1936, Washington, D.C., 20013-1936, or by telephoning the Shareholder Service Department at 1-800-527-3726 or, in the Washington, D.C. area, at 202-872-3183.

6. *What does the authorization form provide?*

The authorization form enables each eligible shareholder to designate for reinvestment either:

(a) all cash dividends paid **both** on shares of Common Stock registered in the shareholder's name and on shares held for the shareholder in the Plan; or

(b) all cash dividends paid **only** on shares of Common Stock held in the Plan, while continuing to receive in cash the dividends paid on shares registered in the shareholder's name.

The authorization form also appoints the Bank as the agent for the shareholder to receive dividends on the shares designated by the shareholder and to apply such dividends, and any voluntary cash payments made by the participant, to purchase shares of the Company's Common Stock for the participant in accordance with the Plan's terms and conditions. See Question 32.

6

Figure 1-1. *(Continued)* Sample of DRIP prospectus. *(From Potomac Electric Power Company)*

tion of their dividends reinvested for additional shares. This feature is especially attractive for individuals who may need at least a share of their dividends to supplement other income.

Discounts. Over 100 firms offer discounts on stocks purchased through the plans. These discounts reach as high as 10 percent off the

---

7. *When may a shareholder join the Plan or change participation?*

Eligible shareholders may join the Plan at any time. Participants also may change their participation at any time. If a new or changed authorization form is received by the Bank on or before the record date for the payment of the next dividend (approximately 30 days in advance of the payment date), such dividend will be invested in additional shares of Common Stock for the participant's Plan account in accordance with the shareholder's choice of Full or Limited Dividend Reinvestment. If a new authorization form is received after any dividend record date but before the payment date, that dividend will be paid in cash and the shareholder's new dividend reinvestment will begin with the following dividend. An authorization form requesting a change which is received between a dividend record date and payment date will become effective with the next dividend following such payment date. Voluntary cash payments may be made when joining the Plan or at any time while participating in the Plan. See Questions 10 and 13.

Costs

8. *What costs do participants pay?*

Participating shareholders bear none of the costs of administering the Plan. Upon written request of a participant, the Agent will sell Plan shares in the open market for the account of the participant, for which the participant will be assessed a charge of $3.00 plus any applicable brokerage commission. See Questions 19 and 21. Otherwise, the Company bears Plan costs, including brokerage commissions for shares being purchased by the Plan Agent on the open market. The expense to the Company of the Plan, including the fees of the Bank, is estimated at approximately $224,000 per year.

Purchases

9. *What is the source of the shares purchased under the Plan?*

Shares acquired from the Company will be legally authorized but unissued shares of Common Stock of the Company. Shares acquired on the open market will be purchased by the Agent for the participant on any securities exchange where shares of the Company's Common Stock are traded, in the over-the-counter market or in negotiated transactions.

10. *When will the funds be invested?*

Dividends will be reinvested as of each dividend payment date which is usually the last business day of the calendar quarter. Voluntary cash payments will be invested as of the dividend payment date in any month in which a cash dividend on Common Stock is paid. In all other months, voluntary cash payments will be invested as of the last business day of the month. When shares are to be acquired by the Agent on the open market such shares will be purchased on or promptly after each investment date (i.e., the dividend payment date or the last business day of the month). See Questions 11, 16 and 17.

Plan participants making voluntary cash payments to purchase additional shares are urged to mail such payments so that they reach The Riggs National Bank of Washington, D.C. not less than five days before the date such payments are to be invested. A participant may obtain the return of any voluntary cash payment at any time upon written request received by the Agent not less than two business days prior to its investment.

7

Figure 1-1. (*Continued*) Sample of DRIP prospectus. (*From Potomac Electric Power Company*)

prevailing market price. In most cases, the discounts apply only to shares purchased through reinvested dividends, although some companies apply the discount to stock purchased through OCPs as well. Chapter 2 discusses discounts further and provides a complete list of companies offering discounts.

Participants' funds held by the Agent will not earn interest.

11. *What price will participants pay for shares?*

The price of shares of Common Stock purchased from the Company is the average of the high and low sale prices for the Company's Common Stock on the New York Stock Exchange, Inc. on the pricing date. The pricing date with respect to a dividend payment date is the last business day preceding such dividend payment date. The pricing date in months when no dividends are paid on Common Stock is the business day preceding the last business day of the month. If the New York Stock Exchange, Inc. is open on the pricing date but no trading occurs in the Company's Common Stock, the price will be the average of the bid and asked prices on that date. If the New York Stock Exchange, Inc. is closed on the pricing date, prices on the next preceding trading date will be used.

The price of shares purchased in open market transactions is determined by dividing the sum of the cost (excluding brokerage commissions) of all such shares purchased to meet Plan requirements as of the investment date (including shares purchased with both reinvested dividends and voluntary cash contributions) by the number of shares purchased. See Question 10.

It should be recognized that since purchase prices are determined as of the dates specified above, a participant in the Plan loses any advantage otherwise available from being able to select the timing of his investment.

If for any reason funds cannot be invested in shares of Company Common Stock, the funds will be promptly remitted to the participant. See Question 31.

12. *How many shares may be acquired with a participant's dividend?*

The full amount of the dividend to be reinvested for each participating shareholder, less any required tax withholding, and the full amount of each voluntary cash payment, will be used to purchase as many full and fractional shares (calculated to three decimal places, without rounding) as can be acquired based upon the price of the shares purchased. See Question 11.

When a dividend payment is reduced by required tax withholding, only the remainder of such dividend payment will be reinvested in shares of Common Stock.

13. *What are the limitations on voluntary cash payments?*

A participant may make one voluntary cash payment each month of not less than $25 nor more than $5,000. The Agent will not fulfill orders to purchase a specific number of shares and remit any difference to the participant. Payments which do not conform to these limitations will be promptly returned. Question 10 describes when voluntary cash payments will be invested.

Statements

14. *How will participants be advised of their purchase of stock?*

Following each transaction a participant will receive a statement from the Agent showing the latest transaction and all prior transactions for the year. These statements are the participant's continuing record of cost information and should be retained for tax purposes.

8

Figure 1-1. (*Continued*) Sample of DRIP prospectus. (*From Potomac Electric Power Company*)

Optional Cash Payments. Nearly every plan permits participants to make OCPs into the plan. The maximum and minimum amounts of these payments vary from plan to plan, as does the frequency with which these funds are invested by the firm. Also, many firms allow investors to enroll in the DRIPs to make OCPs, even if they don't reinvest their dividends. Chapter 3 goes into the OCP option in more depth.

15. *What other communications will a participant receive?*

Each participant will receive a copy of this Plan prospectus and any amendments thereto. Each participant in the Plan also will receive copies of the Company's annual and interim reports to shareholders, as well as proxy statements, and any tax notices distributed with respect to shares held in the Plan. Where more than one shareholder has the same address, only one copy of certain materials will be sent to that address if shareholders to whom such materials would otherwise be sent agree thereto in writing.

Each participant for whom shares are purchased in the open market will receive a statement shortly after the end of the year separately listing the fees and commissions referred to in Question 30 under "Special Rules Concerning Shares Purchased on the Open Market."

Dividends

16. *How will a participant's cash dividends be treated?*

All dividends paid on shares held of record by each participant who elects Full Dividend Reinvestment and all dividends paid on shares held by the Plan will be delivered directly to the Agent (or its nominee) who will invest such dividends in additional shares of Common Stock. See Question 11. All such shares purchased will be immediately credited to the accounts of participants.

Participants who have elected the Limited Dividend Reinvestment option will receive from the Company a check for cash dividends on shares of which the participant is the holder of record.

17. *When will dividends be earned on voluntary cash payments?*

Shares purchased through voluntary cash payments made during the first month of a calendar quarter will normally be entitled to any dividend payable at the end of that quarter. Shares purchased through voluntary cash payments made during the second or third month of a quarter will normally not be entitled to any dividend payable at the end of that quarter since those shares will normally be purchased subsequent to the record date for such dividend.

Certificates

18. *Are certificates issued for the shares purchased?*

Certificates for shares held in the Plan are issued in the name of the Agent (or its nominee) and held for the accounts of participants. This provides protection against loss, theft or inadvertent destruction of stock certificates and facilitates the ownership by participants of fractional shares.

No certificates will be issued for shares held for a participant's account unless a written request for a certificate is sent to the Agent, or until the participant's account is terminated. A participant may at any time request the Agent to send a certificate for any full shares credited to the participant's account. Certificates for fractional shares will not be issued.

19. *What happens to a fractional share when a participant requests a certificate for whole shares but wishes to remain in the Plan, when a participant's account is terminated, or when the Plan is terminated?*

9

Figure 1-1. (*Continued*) Sample of DRIP prospectus. (*From Potomac Electric Power Company*)

Purchase Price. The pricing of shares differs among plans. For example, for some companies, the purchase price is the price of the stock on the last trading day prior to the investment date. In other instances, it might be the average price of all shares purchased in a 5-day period preceding the investment date. Obviously, when the stock is purchased and how the purchase price is determined have a big impact on your cost basis. Make sure you check the prospectus on this one.

A request for a certificate for whole shares does not terminate participation in the Plan so long as a participant remains in the Plan and owns, either directly or under the Plan, at least one full share. Any fractional share balance will continue to be maintained to the credit of the participant's account.

In the case of termination of participation or termination of the Plan, a cash payment will be made representing the participant's interest in any fractional share. The cash payment will be based on the market price of shares of the Company's Common Stock on the New York Stock Exchange, Inc. at the time of sale of the fractional share.

20. *In whose name will certificates for whole shares be issued?*

Each account in the Plan will be maintained in the name of the participant as shown by the Company's shareholder records at the time the participant entered the Plan. When issued, certificates for full shares will be registered in the same name.

Upon written request, certificates can be registered in names other than that of the participant subject to compliance with any applicable laws and the payment by the participant of any applicable transfer taxes.

Sale of Shares

21. *Will the Plan Agent sell shares held by the Plan for a participant?*

Yes. At any time, a participant may request in writing that the Agent sell shares held for the participant by the Plan (but not shares that are directly held by the participant). Upon such sale, the Agent will distribute the proceeds to the participant, less a charge of $3.00 and any applicable brokerage commission or charge. The participant must separately negotiate the sale of shares held of record.

Termination of Participation

22. *How may a Plan account be terminated by a participant?*

A participant may terminate participation in the Plan at any time by a notice given in writing to The Riggs National Bank of Washington, D.C., Corporate Trust Division, Dividend Reinvestment Unit, P.O. Box 96213, Washington, D.C. 20090-6213. Upon such termination, the participant will receive at no cost a certificate for all full shares, and cash for any fractional share, held in the participant's account.

If a termination request is received by the Agent between the record date and the dividend payment date, the dividend attributable to the shares will be paid in cash. If the request is received by the Agent after a dividend payment date, the dividend paid on such date will be reinvested in additional shares and will be reflected in the termination distribution.

Whenever a participant no longer owns shares held of record and owns less than one full share under the Plan, the Agent is authorized to terminate the participant's Plan account and send the participant a cash settlement as outlined under Question 19 for the fractional share.

10

Figure 1-1. (*Continued*) Sample of DRIP prospectus. (*From Potomac Electric Power Company*)

Safekeeping Services. Shares purchased under most DRIPs are held in the participant's plan account by the company, and certificates for these shares are not usually issued unless requested. Most companies do not charge any fee for this service, and those firms that do usually set the charge at $5 or less.

23. *When may a shareholder rejoin the Plan?*

Generally, an eligible shareholder may again become a participant at any time. However, the Company and the Agent reserve the right to reject any authorization form from a previous participant on grounds of excessive joining and termination. Such reservation is intended to minimize unnecessary administrative expense and to encourage use of the Plan as a long-term shareholder investment service.

Other Information

24. *Is a participant obligated to make voluntary cash payments?*

No, a participant is not required to make such cash payments.

25. *What is the effect on a participant's Plan account if the participant transfers all shares held of record?*

None, as long as the participant has at least one full share in the Plan account. Dividends on Plan shares and any voluntary cash payments would continue to be invested under the Plan in additional shares of Common Stock.

If a shareholder participating in the Plan chooses to dispose of all Company Common Stock, the shareholder must make separate arrangements to dispose of shares held in the Plan, as described under Questions 21 and 22, and shares held of record. The transfer of stock certificates representing shares held of record will have no effect on shares held in a participant's Plan account, except if the Plan account has less than one full share. See Questions 19 and 22.

A participant may elect to transfer all shares held of record to the participant's Plan account for safekeeping and convenience.

26. *What limitations are imposed on a participant with regard to the assets held by the Bank as Agent under the Plan?*

The participant has no right to draw checks or drafts against a Plan account or to give instructions to the Agent with respect to any shares or cash held therein except as expressly provided herein.

The participant may not assign as collateral any shares held by the Agent. In order to assign any such shares as collateral, the participant must request delivery of a certificate for shares as provided in Question 18.

27. *If the Company has a Common Stock rights offering, how will the rights on Plan shares be handled?*

All rights on shares registered in the name of the Agent (or its nominee) will be issued to the Agent. If such rights have a market value, the Agent will sell such rights, apply the proceeds to the purchase of additional shares of the Company's Common Stock, and credit such Common Stock to each participant's account in proportion to the full and fractional shares held therein as of the record date for such rights. Alternatively, any participant who wishes to exercise stock purchase rights on

11

Figure 1-1. (*Continued*) Sample of DRIP prospectus. (*From Potomac Electric Power Company*)

Eligibility Requirements. Most companies permit those who hold only one share to enroll in the DRIP, although a few require more shares. The corporate directory in Chapter 7 provides information on firms requiring more than one share for enrollment. Another eligibility requirement for most DRIPs is that the shares be registered in the shareholder's name, not the "street name" or brokerage name. This may

Plan shares must request, prior to the record date for any such rights, that the Agent deliver a certificate for full shares as provided in Question 18. Rights on shares held of record by a participant will be mailed directly to the participant in the same manner as to shareholders not participating in the Plan.

28. *What happens if the Company issues a stock dividend or declares a stock split?*

Any shares distributed by the Company in respect of shares held in the Plan as a result of a stock dividend or stock split will be credited to the participants' accounts. Stock dividends or stock split shares distributed on shares held of record by a participant will be mailed directly to the participant in the same manner as to shareholders not participating in the Plan.

29. *How will a participant's Plan shares be voted at annual or special meetings of shareholders?*

Full shares held in the Plan for a shareholder will be voted as the shareholder directs. Fractional shares cannot be voted.

A proxy covering shares held of record, if any, and full (but not fractional) shares held in a participant's Plan account will be sent to the Plan participant. Such shares will be voted in accordance with the shareholder's proper instructions. If no instructions are indicated on a properly signed and returned proxy, such shares will be voted in accordance with the recommendations of the Company's management.

30. *What are the federal income tax consequences of participation in the Plan?*

The following tax information is provided solely as a guide to participants. The rules in this area are complex and, therefore, participants are advised to consult their own tax advisors as to the federal and state income tax effects of participation in the Plan.

General Rules Concerning
Taxation of Plan Dividends

A participant will be treated for federal income tax purposes as having received on each dividend payment date the full amount of the cash dividend payable on that date with respect to shares registered in the participant's name and shares held for the participant's account under the Plan, even though the amount of the dividend was not actually received by the participant in cash, but instead was applied to the purchase of new shares for the participant's account. See Question 11.

Participants will not realize any taxable income when they receive certificates for whole shares of stock credited to their accounts, either upon their requests or upon withdrawal from or termination of the Plan. Participants will, however, realize capital gain or loss when whole shares acquired under the Plan are sold or exchanged either by the Agent, or by participants themselves. Participants also realize capital gain or loss when they receive cash payments from the sale of any fractional share upon withdrawal from or termination of the Plan. Such gain or loss on the sale of whole or fractional shares will be long-term or short-term depending on the holding period of the shares. The amount of any such capital gain or loss will be the difference between the amount realized by a participant from the sale of the shares and the shareholder's adjusted basis in such shares.

12

Figure 1-1. (*Continued*) Sample of DRIP prospectus. (*From Potomac Electric Power Company*)

require changing the registration on shares you already hold if you plan to enroll in the company's DRIP. Contact your broker on this one.

Fractional Shares. If dividends or OCPs aren't large enough to purchase whole shares, DRIPs will purchase fractional shares for plan par-

---

Special Rules Concerning Shares Purchased on the Open Market

If shares are purchased under the Plan in the open market, a participant will be treated for federal income tax purposes as having received an additional dividend in an amount equal to the brokerage fees or commissions paid by the Company with respect to such purchases. For purposes of establishing the basis and holding period of shares of stock purchased on the open market under the Plan, such shares will be treated in the same manner as shares of stock purchased outside the Plan. Thus, the amount paid, increased by the brokerage fees and commissions paid by the Company with respect to such shares, will be the adjusted basis of such shares and the holding period will begin on the day following the purchase date.

31. *May the Plan be modified or discontinued, or may the purchase or sale of Common Stock be suspended by the Plan?*

The Company reserves the right to suspend or terminate the Plan at any time. It also reserves the right to make modifications to the Plan. Participating shareholders will be informed of any such suspension, termination or modification.

Purchases and sales of Common Stock may be suspended by the Agent at any time if such purchases or sales would, in the judgment of the Agent, contravene or be restricted by applicable regulations, orders or interpretations of the Securities and Exchange Commission, any other governmental agency or instrumentality, or any court or securities exchange. The Agent shall not be liable for its failure to make purchases or sales at such times or under such circumstances.

32. *What is the responsibility of the Agent under the Plan?*

The Agent receives the participants' dividends and voluntary cash payments with which it purchases additional shares of the Company's Common Stock, maintains records of each participant's account, holds in a nominee name all shares purchased for participants, and advises participants as to all transactions for, and the status of, their accounts. The Agent selects the broker or brokers through which to make any open market transactions under the Plan.

All notices from the Agent to a participant will be addressed to the participant's last address as shown by records of the Agent. The participant should notify the Agent promptly in writing of any change of address.

Neither the Agent nor its nominee has any responsibility beyond the exercise of ordinary care for any reasonable and prudent actions taken or omitted pursuant to the Plan nor shall they have any duties, responsibilities or liabilities except as are expressly set forth in the Plan.

The Agent may not create a lien on any funds, securities or other property held under the Plan.

33. *Who bears the risk of market price fluctuations in the Company's Common Stock?*

A participant's investment risk in shares held in the Plan is no different than the investment risk in shares held of record. Participants bear the risk of loss and the benefits of gain from market price changes with respect to all of their shares.

13

Figure 1-1. (*Continued*) Sample of DRIP prospectus. (*From Potomac Electric Power Company*)

ticipants. And these fractional shares participate proportionately in future dividends.

DRIP Statements. One downside of DRIPs is that they increase paperwork for participants, particularly those in several DRIPs. Companies attempt to help participants by sending regular statements, usually

Neither the Company nor the Agent can guarantee that shares purchased under the Plan will, at any particular time, be worth more or less than their purchase price and make no representation in this regard.

34. *What has been the level of participation in the Plan?*

At August 30, 1990, approximately 23,700 holders of record of Common Stock, representing 27% of all holders of Common Stock, were participants in the Plan. These participants owned approximately 16,700,000 shares, or 17%, of Common Stock outstanding. During the 12 months ended September 30, 1990, Plan participants invested approximately $28,300,000 to purchase approximately 1,350,000 shares of Common Stock.

DESCRIPTION OF COMMON STOCK

The authorized capital stock of the Company consists of Common Stock, Serial Preferred Stock and Preference Stock. As of September 30, 1990, the Company had a total of 200,000,000 authorized shares of Common Stock, par value $1.00 per share ("Common Stock"), of which 99,186,703 shares were outstanding (and 92,705 shares were reserved for issuance upon conversion of the Company's Serial Preferred Stock, $2.44 Convertible Series of 1966 (the "Convertible Preferred Stock"), 202,583 shares were reserved for issuance under the Company's Shareholder Dividend Reinvestment Plan, 1,474,600 shares were reserved for issuance under the Company's Savings Plans for employees and 2,777,703 shares were reserved for issuance upon conversion of the Company's 7% Convertible Debentures due 2018 (the "Debentures")), 6,616,166 authorized shares of cumulative Serial Preferred Stock, par value $50 per share ("Serial Preferred Stock"), divided into seven outstanding series and of which a total of 3,515,683 shares were outstanding, and 8,800,000 authorized shares of cumulative Preference Stock, par value $25 per share ("Preference Stock"), of which no shares were outstanding.

The outstanding Common Stock of the Company is, and the Common Stock into which the Convertible Preferred Stock and the Debentures may be converted will be upon issuance, fully paid and nonassessable.

The following statements with respect to the Common Stock of the Company are a summary of certain rights and privileges attaching to the stock under the laws of the District of Columbia and the Commonwealth of Virginia and pursuant to the Company's Articles of Incorporation and By-Laws which are incorporated by reference as exhibits to the Company's Annual Report on Form 10-K.

Dividends. Dividends on the Common Stock may be declared and paid, out of funds legally available therefor, at the discretion of the Board of Directors, provided all dividends for the past and current quarters, and any sinking fund requirements, with respect to outstanding Serial Preferred Stock and any outstanding Preference Stock have been paid or provided for.

So long as Serial Preferred Stock is outstanding, if, at the end of the calendar month preceding the declaration of a dividend on the Common Stock, the ratio of Common Stock capital, plus surplus (less the proposed dividend), to total capital (including long-term debt), plus such surplus, is less than 20%, dividends on Common Stock for the year ending on the date of such declaration (including the proposed dividend) may not exceed 50% (or 75% if the above ratio is 20% or more but less than 25%) of net earnings (less dividends on other stock) for the 12 calendar months preceding the declaration. If the above ratio exceeds 25%, any dividends on the Common Stock may not reduce the ratio below 25% (or 20%) except in accordance with the foregoing restrictions.

14

Figure 1-1. (*Continued*) Sample of DRIP prospectus. (*From Potomac Electric Power Company*)

on a quarterly basis. The statements show amounts invested, purchase prices, shares purchased, account maintenance fees charged, if any, and other relevant information.

Voting Rights. Participants don't sacrifice their say in the company because they use DRIPs. Voting rights are granted to whole shares in a DRIP, although fractional shares may not have voting rights in all cases.

Termination of the Plan.   Terminating a DRIP is usually quite simple. Most plans require written notification stating your intention to terminate your participation. If you request it, many firms will sell your shares on the open market. Companies that do not sell shares for participants will send the stock certificates to participants along with cash for fractional shares.

Stock Splits and Stock Dividends.   Your DRIP holdings are not adversely affected by stock splits or stock dividends. New shares will be added to the participant's account reflecting the split or dividend.

Taxes.   Although DRIPs let you dodge the broker, they won't let you dodge the tax collector. Even though your dividends are reinvested, they are subject to income taxes as if you received them. This wasn't always the case. As recently as the early 1980s, DRIPs in certain electric utilities were exempt from taxation on up to $750 ($1500 for joint filers) of dividends reinvested in the plans. However, that exemption expired midway through the decade. In addition to taxes on reinvested dividends, investors must pay taxes on the amount of commissions and service fees picked up by the firm, although these amounts are usually quite nominal. Also, these service fees may be deducted by investors who itemize. In DRIPs which provide discounts, participants are taxed on the amount of the discount. This point is explored further in Chapter 2. DRIPs send participants 1099 information forms, which come in handy during tax preparation time. Consult with your tax adviser concerning DRIPs so you don't get any surprises on April 15.

Who Do You Call?

O.K. So you've picked out a stock you like, the company has a DRIP that meets your objectives, you've gone over the prospectus, and you're ready to take the plunge. What do you do? Call a broker.
   Call a broker!
   Well, the fact is that the only way to enroll in DRIPs is to be a current shareholder. Thus, with a few exceptions (which are covered in Chapter 3), initial purchases of the stock must be made through a broker.
   Nevertheless, ways exist to limit the broker's bite. Although some DRIPs require shareholders to own 50 shares or more before enrolling, most firms permit shareholders to enroll with only one share. Thus, investors should consider purchasing only the minimum number of shares needed to enroll in the plan to keep initial brokerage costs down.

A frequent question I hear is, "Which is the best brokerage firm?" What the question usually means is, "Who has the cheapest commissions?" Though full-service brokers will argue that their rates are competitive with discounters—and in some instances this may be true—as a rule you'll probably pay lower brokerage costs with a discount firm. Investors who do their own research will probably choose a discount broker, while others, who feel less secure in their own investment judgments, may appreciate a full-service broker.

Since this book gives you practical guidance on DRIPs, complete with specific recommendations and model portfolios (Chapters 5 and 6), as well as performance ratings on the stocks in the company directory (Chapter 7), you probably don't need a full-service broker, unless he or she is willing to cut commission rates.

Which firm has the cheapest commission rates? It's hard to say. Many brokers will discount their commissions if they believe that the individual will throw a lot of business their way. Also, while one firm may have a lower minimum commission charge than another, the latter firm may have cheaper rates for round-lot purchases. As I was putting this book together, I called some discount and full-service brokers to see how much they'd charge me to purchase five shares of McDonald's, which at the time was trading in the mid-$20s. The rates varied substantially. Interestingly, Dean Witter, a full-service broker, actually had the lowest quote—$14 in commissions. This rate was lower than several discounters.

Does that make Dean Witter the best choice since its commissions are the lowest? Not necessarily. Rates may vary among brokers depending on the amount of stock you purchase, and, in fact, Dean Witter's rates for a 100-share purchase were higher than those of the discount firms. I suggest that when you're ready to purchase stock, contact three or four brokers in order to compare rates. Below are some of the more prominent discount brokers:

Andrew Peck (800-221-5873)

Burke, Christensen & Lewis Sec. (800-621-0392)

Charles Schwab & Co. (800-435-4000)

Fidelity Brokerage Services (800-225-1799)

Muriel Siebert & Co. (800-872-7865)

Quick & Reilly (800-221-5220)

StockCross (800-225-6196)

Vanguard Brokerage Services (800-662-7447)

Don't forget to try some full-service brokers as well. Depending on how desperate they are for business, you may be able to drive a bargain. Chances are most major full-service brokers have a branch in your neighborhood. Check the *Yellow Pages.*

One important thing to remember is that regardless of the brokerage firm you use, most DRIPs require that shares be held in the name of the individual investor rather than in street name accounts. For this reason, it is important to make sure your broker knows that the stock should be registered in your name to avoid any problems later.

Once you have purchased the stock, contact the firm concerning enrollment in the DRIP. Quite likely, the company will send you a prospectus and application form once it receives your name as a shareholder of record. Once enrolled in the DRIP, you may begin your investment program.

It's that simple—and you'll never need to call a broker again.

Commissions Matter

While we're on the subject of brokerage commissions, I think it's important to discuss how significant these fees can be in eating away at your investment dollars. I could recite a litany of academic articles emphasizing how harmful transaction costs can be on a portfolio, especially for small investors. But a personal experience may drive this point home even more.

Although I don't advise investing in stock or index options, I sometimes don't take my own advice. August 1990 was one of those times. On August 21, I purchased a put option on the S&P 100 index. A put option is a bet on lower stock prices.

Fortunately, the market dropped sharply, and my strategy worked, at least I thought so. I sold the put at a nice "paper" profit. Indeed, I bought the option for $350, and I sold it at $575. A profit of 64 percent. A pretty sweet gain for just a few days, right?

Not exactly. When I received my brokerage confirmation statement, I was stunned. To purchase the option, the commission and fees were $87. Likewise the commission for selling the option was $87. Thus, on an investment of $350, the round-trip commissions were a whopping $174, or roughly 50 percent of the investment value. After commissions, my profits nearly disappeared.

When I called my broker, he stated that the firm's minimum commission on options was $87 (he lowered the commission to $53 after my complaint). Of course, had I purchased five or ten options instead of one, the commissions would have represented a smaller percentage of the investment. Nevertheless, the point is that small investors, who may not have big bucks to invest, are punished disproportionately.

I admit that option commissions are generally higher than stock commissions. However, the same scenario is possible for stock investments. Of course, you might get lucky and find a broker who will buy for you a small number of shares in a company for $15 to $25. However, higher minimum commissions are commonplace in the brokerage industry.

Take the following example. Say you want to purchase 50 shares of a $10 stock—a $500 investment. Assuming a round-trip commission of $100—$50 to get in and $50 to get out—your investment has to rise $100, or 20 percent, just to break even after commissions. The investment game is tough enough without stacking the odds that badly against the small investor.

Now, take the same situation using a DRIP. Let's say you made an OCP of $500. Your commissions were zero. And when it comes time to sell these 50 shares, you'll pay a commission that is much lower than $50 if they are sold through the DRIP, perhaps as low as $5 to $10. Thus, to break even, the stock needs to increase just 2 percent. It's easy to figure out that your chances for investment success are increased greatly.

Keep in mind that this is just one trade. Multiply this four or five times a year, 40 or 50 trades over the course of 10 years. That isn't a great deal of activity for an investor. But even at this modest level, the commission savings, assuming a minimum commission of $50 at your broker, are $2000. And if you're more active, your savings are greater.

For example, let's say you enroll in the DRIP for IBM. In addition to reinvesting dividends, you make monthly OCPs of $50. Thus, you are purchasing IBM stock at least 12 times a year. Let's assume a minimum commission of $50. In this scenario, your commission savings on the buy side alone are $600 annually.

Another way to look at the commission break is if you have deep pockets and make OCPs of, not $50 per month, but $5000 per month. On a $5000 investment, it's not unusual to pay commissions of $100 or more at a full-service broker. Multiply that number 12 times a year and the savings are around $1200; over 10 years, the savings are $12,000— and that doesn't take into account rising brokerage commission rates over that time period. Nor does it take into account administrative fees for things like monthly account statements that more and more brokers are charging customers.

As you can see, we're not talking about saving a few dollars through DRIPs but about some serious cash. The bottom line is that commissions matter, and they matter a lot in terms of portfolio performance and real, out-of-pocket dollars.

Downside to DRIPs

We've discussed the many pluses of DRIPs:

- Commission-free investing
- Moderate commissions for selling in many instances
- Modest capital requirements because of small minimums in most OCP plans
- Discounts on shares purchased
- Full investment of funds because of purchase of fractional shares
- Safekeeping of shares

However, there are some minuses associated with DRIPs. A minor headache is the increased paperwork associated with the plans. True, the companies do their best to simplify things by issuing regular statements. Still, if you're in 25 or 30 DRIPs, the record keeping could become a bit onerous. Thus, DRIPs do require some discipline in terms of record keeping. Therefore, it's probably not worth it to join more than 20 DRIPs. You'll achieve adequate portfolio diversification with 13 to 20.

The biggest downside to DRIPs is the lack of control over the price at which shares are bought and sold. For example, let's say that you are in the DRIP for Hershey Foods. The stock has recently fallen and you want to purchase shares. However, in order to invest in the stock via the DRIP, you'll have to wait until the next investment date, which may be 2 weeks or more away, before you can buy. By the time you send in your OCP and the stock is purchased by the company, the issue has jumped up three points. Likewise, on the sell side, you decide to sell a stock at $50. You inform the DRIP that you would like to sell 50 shares. However, as is the case with many DRIPs, the sale doesn't take place until 10 business days after your request to sell, and the stock has fallen to $45.

As you can see, the time lag between buy and sell decisions could have an impact on your portfolio. However, as we'll see in upcoming chapters, investing via DRIPs is a long-term strategy and not geared toward frequent trading. Over time, this lack of control of exact buy and sell executions should wash and have a minimal impact on a portfolio. However, on a short-term basis, the impact might be large. Thus, traders need not apply when it comes to DRIPs.

There are some ways to improve on this situation. One is to focus investments on companies in which OCPs are invested weekly or twice a month, as in the case of Eastman Kodak and McDonald's, respectively. How do you find out when companies invest OCPs? Each directory listing in Chapter 7 includes the frequency with which OCPs are invested.

Another strategy is to have possession of a portion of your shares. This way, once you've decided to sell, you can move quickly by going through a discount broker.

What's in It for the Companies?

You may be wondering at this point what's in it for the companies which offer DRIPs. First, many investors who have come to love the commission-free investing aspects of DRIPs buy stock only in firms that offer DRIPs. So companies who feel it is important to have individual investors represented among their shareholders will offer the plans.

Companies usually like having individual investors owning their shares. As a group, small investors are more loyal than institutional holders and generally invest for the long term. Thus, individual investors aren't likely to be actively trading the issue and increasing the stock's volatility. Also, a large representation of individual investors makes it more difficult for a corporate raider or unfriendly suitor to accumulate shares for a proxy battle or hostile takeover.

Another reason firms offer the plans is that DRIPs provide a potential source of equity capital. Some companies purchase shares for DRIP participants on the open market. Purchases in this manner do not add to the firm's capital base. Rather, the company acts merely as an intermediary for shareholders. However, many companies issue to shareholders in the DRIP "original issue shares." Proceeds from shares purchased in this way expand the firm's capital base and may be used for such corporate purposes as research and development spending or capital improvements. This method of raising capital carries little cost to the company relative to the large fees and administrative costs of making a public offering of stock through an investment bank. Raising equity capital via DRIPs does not increase the firm's debt burden and interest expense. The implications of raising equity capital via DRIPs are explored further in Chapter 2.

2
Free Lunch: Buying Stocks at a Discount

When I first learned about DRIPs, it was hard for me to believe that in some DRIPs it was possible to buy stocks at discounts to the prevailing market price. In other words, you were guaranteed an instant profit on your holdings. A sham, I thought. No way can you actually buy stocks more cheaply than in the market. However, as I discovered, this feature is the closest thing to a free lunch that you can get in the stock market.

More than 100 companies offer discounts on stock purchased through their DRIPs. Most of the discounts apply only to shares purchased through reinvested dividends. A few firms also permit optional cash payments (OCPs) to receive the discount, although this number is dwindling for reasons discussed later in this chapter.

While most discounts are in the 3 to 5 percent range, some are higher. For example, York Financial offers a 10 percent discount on stock purchased through reinvested dividends. Think about that for a moment. That means you can buy $100 worth of stock with your dividends for just $90. And because of the way the math works, your "instant profit" is actually greater than the 10 percent discount—more like 11.1 percent (profit of $10 divided by your cost of $90). Actually, your profit is a bit less after taxes. Nevertheless, you are still getting "free" money. Sure, you could lose this profit if the stock falls below your discounted purchase price. But your losses aren't nearly as great as are someone's who purchased the stock at the market price.

Why Do Companies Offer a Discount?

One reason for my initial skepticism concerning discounts was that I couldn't see what companies got out of the deal. After all, weren't they losing money?

Not really. As the list at the end of this chapter indicates, many of the firms offering discounts are in capital-intensive industries—primarily banks and utilities. These businesses require constant cash flow to conduct business.

Companies have a number of ways to raise capital. First, they can go to a friendly banker and take out a loan. Firms can float bonds. This method is basically the same thing as taking out a loan, except the creditor isn't the bank but institutional and individual investors who purchase the bonds. A company can raise money by issuing stock. The attraction of stock is that a firm doesn't make interest payments on stock as it does on bank debt or bonds. The downside is that the firm might have to pay dividends on the stock. Also, while interest payments receive favorable tax treatment for the corporation—hence the reason many companies issue debt—dividends do not.

There are two popular ways to issue stock. The most traditional method is to sell shares to the public or institutional investors via a public offering or private placement. In most cases, the firm uses an investment banker, such as Salomon Brothers, Merrill Lynch, Morgan Stanley, or Goldman Sachs, to make the offering. The investment banker, in turn, has a syndicate of other investment houses that helps to sell the offering. For their efforts, the investment banks take a piece of the action. In addition to the investment bankers' take, substantial administrative, clerical, legal, and accounting fees may be incurred. In some cases, all of these fees can be 5 percent of the offering value and as high as 10 to 15 percent, particularly if the issuer is small and the investment bank foresees potential problems in moving the stock. As you can see, this avenue for raising equity has its share of hassles.

Another way to sell stock is via a DRIP. Herein is a major reason why so many companies offer the plans. Indeed, with DRIPs, there are no investment banking fees. Companies that offer stock at a discount are not really shorting themselves of cash. If they went through an investment bank to raise funds, they would have to pay for services that potentially would cost more than the 3 or 5 percent discounts offered in DRIPs. Therefore, these firms pass on the savings to DRIP participants.

The company benefits in that the discount makes the firm's DRIP more attractive to investors.

Raising Capital Quickly

The power of a DRIP with a discount to pull in cash can be impressive. Just ask South Jersey Industries, a natural gas utility serving portions of southern New Jersey, including Atlantic City. In April 1990, the firm's Board of Directors amended the company's DRIP to provide for the purchase of newly issued shares at a 5 percent discount from the market price. South Jersey stipulated that, in addition to reinvested dividends, OCPs of up to $30,000 annually qualified for the discount. A generous program, to say the least, and rather surprising since South Jersey Industries is a pretty good company, with a three-star rating, and would have ample investor interest in its DRIP regardless of a discount.

As it turned out, investors jumped all over the new plan. In fact, in June 1990, plan participants purchased approximately 479,000 new shares of common stock for almost $8 million. While companies like to raise capital through DRIPs, there is a point at which too much capital too fast isn't a good thing since the company cannot profitability use it to benefit shareholders. Such was the case with South Jersey Industries. To slow down the stream of new capital, the firm amended the DRIP again in August 1990, this time lowering the discount to 3 percent on reinvested dividends and OCPs and setting a maximum on OCPs of $1000 per quarter.

Drawbacks to a Discount

If there is a drawback to the discounts, it is that issuing shares in a DRIP, especially at a discount, has a dilutive impact on shares currently outstanding. This was probably another factor influencing South Jersey Industries' decision to trim the discount.

This dilutive aspect is the major reason First Interstate Bancorp suspended its discount in August 1990. As mentioned, DRIPs offer capital-intensive firms such as banks an easy and low-cost way to replenish their capital base. Under its DRIP, First Interstate offered a 2.5 percent discount on shares purchased through reinvested dividends. However, as was the case with most bank stocks in 1990, First Interstate's stock price hit the skids.

The dramatic drop in the stock price presented a catch-22 for First Interstate. On the one hand, First Interstate needed equity, and the discount was an effective way of generating equity capital via the DRIP. Yet, issuing shares via the DRIP at such cut-rate prices didn't serve the best interests of existing shareholders, who were having their current holdings diluted by the DRIP. The firm chose to discontinue the discount as well as the OCP portion of the plan.

Another drawback is when the discount is really no discount at all. This could happen under certain circumstances, depending on how the company classifies the purchase price that receives the discount. For example, let's say that a firm, which offers a 5 percent discount on reinvested dividends and OCPs, considers the purchase price for OCPs to be 95 percent of the average of the closing stock prices for the 5 consecutive business days preceding the investment date. Say the stock drops steadily during this 5-day period, closing on the fifth day at $7. However, the average price for the 5-day period was $8. Thus, the purchase price would be 95 percent of $8, or around $7.60—a price actually higher than the last trading price. You'd be better off purchasing the stock in the market at full price than at a 5 percent discount in the DRIP. In some DRIPs, it is possible to request the return of your funds prior to the investment date. In this instance, it would obviously be in your best interest to get your money back.

Interestingly, such a scenario, if reversed, would actually increase the amount of the discount for investors. For example, let's say that the average price for the 5-day period was still $8, but the closing price on the fifth day is now $10. Your purchase price of around $7.60 (95 percent of $8) now represents a 24 percent discount from the last price of $10—considerably higher than the 5 percent stated discount in the plan.

Abusing the Benefit

The number of DRIPs offering discounts has been shrinking over the last several years. One of the reasons appears to be the manipulation of the plans by big investors. Wall Streeters don't miss a trick, and the fact that free money was available in DRIPs with discounts sent them scurrying to take advantage of it.

The scheme works something like this: Let's say you join a DRIP that offers a 5 percent discount on stock purchased with reinvested dividends as well as OCPs. And let's say that the maximum OCP that can be made into the plan on a monthly basis is $5000. Thus, every month, you can accumulate $5000 worth of stock for $4750. Now, while you're buying the stock, you are simultaneously selling the stock for the full market price. This can be done by selling the stock short in the market on the investment date or selling shares in which you have taken possession of the certificates. By simultaneously buying stock for $4750 and selling the same stock at $5000, you lock up a risk-free return of $250. Do this each month and your risk-free gains for the year are roughly $3000.

One hitch that lowers the return somewhat is the tax implications of DRIPs with discounts. For example, you are taxed at your current rate on the difference between the discounted price and the market value. In our example, assuming you are in the 28 percent tax bracket, the taxes on the annual $3000 profit generated by the discount would be $840. You would also be taxed on the short-term gains generated by this strategy, which would be another $840 (28 percent times $3000 in capital gains). Thus, your total tax bill comes to $1680, reducing your yearly take to $1320. Remember though, you incurred no risk to earn this $1320.

Now, what some investors and brokers do is to open multiple accounts in which to take advantage of the discount. It's not too difficult to see how lucrative this strategy can be. Take this $1320 risk-free profit times 10 to 15 accounts in the names of various relatives or friends, and the gains are huge. Or, if you're an investor with access to an even larger number of accounts, the gains can be downright obscene.

An interesting study on profiting from the discounts was conducted by Myron S. Scholes, best known for his option pricing model, and Mark A. Wolfson. The two college professors wanted to determine if, in fact, exploiting the discount would yield abnormal returns. From 1984 to 1988, the individuals purchased, via DRIPs, shares in companies that offered discounts on OCPs, with 90 percent of their activity occurring in a period of less than 2 years.

What were the results? Staggering, to say the least. With an investment of $200,000, the two realized a profit of $421,000, consisting of $163,800 of net discount income (the sum of all gross discounts less transaction costs), $182,600 of return on investment from a general increase in stock prices, and $74,600 of abnormal return on investment beyond the net discount income. This profit was net of all costs.

Are Scholes, Wolfson, and others who capitalize on these discounts villains or savvy investors merely taking advantage of an inefficiency in the market? Both, depending on your viewpoint. What they did was perfectly legal, and the two were fortunate enough to possess enough capital to generate major gains. Still, such manipulation of the discount is one reason that the number of plans offering discounts is shrinking, which hurts all investors.

Because of the abuse of the discount, firms offering discounts reserve the right to terminate a shareholder account in which they believe such manipulation is taking place. First Commerce Corp., a Louisiana-based bank with a 5 percent discount on reinvested dividends, states it clearly in its DRIP prospectus:

The objective of the Plan is to encourage long-term investment by allowing Security Holders to accumulate FCC (First Commerce Corp.) Common Stock at a favorable price over a long period of time, thus providing benefits to Security Holders and FCC. Excessive activity in a Participant's account, especially activity suggesting the Plan is being used to acquire shares at a discount and sell such shares at market price does not serve these objectives and may cause the Plan Administrator to terminate the eligibility of a Participant.

The abuse of the discount is one reason that there are very few firms which offer discounts on both reinvested dividends and OCPs. Taking advantage of the difference between the discount price and the market price, or arbitrage as it is known on Wall Street, is more lucrative if done through OCPs. The sums of money are larger and the frequency of investment greater because of monthly investment of OCPs by many companies.

Summary

Here are some things to remember concerning discounts:

- The ability to purchase stock at a discount under the DRIP is truly one of the few benefits the small investor has in the market. Don't abuse it by excessive trading. This defeats the purpose of DRIPs and could cause the company to eliminate the discount.

- Don't invest in a company merely because it offers a discount. Although there are quality companies with DRIPs that offer discounts, there are also plenty of companies that offer discounts because they would otherwise have trouble drawing investors' dollars because of their poor prospects and track record. Stay with quality.

- Most of the companies that offer discounts are banks and utilities — two areas, especially the former, where extra care must be taken when making investments.

- You can't dodge the tax collector when it comes to discounts, since you will be taxed on the difference between the discount and the market price.

The following is a list of companies offering discounts. Each listing is accompanied by our performance rating, with a four-star rating being the highest. *NR* means not rated. For a full explanation of the ratings, see the introduction to the company directory (Chapter 7). Companies offering discounts on both reinvested dividends and optional cash payments are indicated by bold type. Investors should note that while a company may have a policy of offering a discount on reinvested dividends, it is not uncommon to find some of these companies not currently paying a dividend because of profit setbacks. Once again, it pays to check with the company before investing.

Acme Electric Corp. (**)
10 percent discount on reinvested dividends

American Express Co. (***)
3 percent discount on reinvested dividends

American Water Works Co., Inc. (***)
5 percent discount on reinvested dividends

Aquarion Co. (**)
5 percent discount on reinvested dividends

Ball Corp. (***)
5 percent discount on reinvested dividends

Baltimore Bancorp (**)
5 percent discount on reinvested dividends

Bancorp Hawaii, Inc. (****)
5 percent discount on reinvested dividends

Bank of Boston Corp. (**)
3 percent discount on reinvested dividends

BankAmerica Corp. (**)
1 percent discount on reinvested dividends and on OCPs

Bankers First Corp. (NR)
5 percent discount on reinvested dividends

Banks of Mid-America, Inc. (**)
5 percent discount on both reinvested dividends and OCPs

Bay State Gas Co. (***)
2 percent discount on reinvested dividends and OCPs on shares made available from the company

BB&T Financial Corp. (***)
5 percent discount on reinvested dividends

Beverly Enterprises (*)
5 percent discount on reinvested dividends

Blount, Inc. (**)
5 percent discount on reinvested dividends

BMJ Financial Corp. (**)
5 percent discount on both reinvested dividends and OCPs

Bow Valley Industries Ltd. (**)
5 percent discount on reinvested dividends

Burnham Pacific Properties, Inc. (**)
5 percent discount on reinvested dividends

C & S/Sovran Corp. (**)
5 percent discount on reinvested dividends

California Real Estate Investment Trust (**)
5 percent discount on reinvested dividends

CCNB Corp. (***)
5 percent discount on reinvested dividends

Chase Manhattan Corp. (**)
5 percent discount on reinvested dividends

Chittenden Corp. (NR)
5 percent discount on reinvested dividends

Citicorp (**)
3 percent discount on reinvested dividends

Colonial Gas Co. (***)
5 percent discount on reinvested dividends

Colorado National Bankshares, Inc. (**)
5 percent discount on reinvested dividends

Connecticut Water Service, Inc. (***)
5 percent discount on reinvested dividends

Constellation Bancorp (**)
5 percent discount on reinvested dividends

Crestar Financial Corp. (**)
5 percent discount on reinvested dividends

Dominion Bankshares Corp. (**)
5 percent discount on reinvested dividends

E'Town Corp. (**)
5 percent discount on both OCPs and reinvested dividends

Eastern Utilities Associates (**)
5 percent discount on reinvested dividends

Empire District Electric Co. (***)
5 percent discount on reinvested dividends (*doesn't* apply to shares purchased on open market)

EnergyNorth, Inc. (***)
5 percent discount on reinvested dividends

F & M National Corp. (VA) (NR)
5 percent discount on reinvested dividends

FB & T Corp. (NR)
5 percent discount on reinvested dividends and OCPs

First American Corp. (TN) (*)
5 percent discount on reinvested dividends

First Bank System, Inc. (**)
3 percent discount on reinvested dividends

First Chicago Corp. (**)
4 percent discount on reinvested dividends

First Commerce Corp. (**)
5 percent discount on reinvested dividends

First Eastern Corp. (NR)
5 percent discount on reinvested dividends

First Fidelity Bancorp. (**)
5 percent discount on reinvested dividends

First Michigan Bank Corp. (***)
5 percent discount on reinvested dividends

First Midwest Bancorp, Inc. (**)
3 percent discount on reinvested dividends

First of America Bank Corp. (***)
5 percent discount on reinvested dividends

First Union Corp. (***)
5 percent discount on reinvested dividends; 3 percent on OCPs

Fleet/Norstar Financial Group, Inc. (**)
5 percent discount on reinvested dividends

Fleming Cos. Inc. (***)
5 percent discount on reinvested dividends

Great Western Financial Corp. (**)
3 percent discount on reinvested dividends

Green Mountain Power Corp. (**)
5 percent discount on reinvested dividends

Health Care REIT, Inc. (**)
4 percent discount on both reinvested dividends and OCPs

Heritage Financial Corp. (NR)
5 percent discount on both reinvested
dividends and OCPs

Hexcel Corp. (**)
5 percent discount on reinvested dividends

Hibernia Corp. (**)
5 percent discount on reinvested dividends

Huntington Bancshares, Inc. (***)
5 percent discount on reinvested dividends

Inco Ltd. (**)
5 percent discount on reinvested dividends

Independence Bancorp (PA) (**)
5 percent discount on reinvested dividends

Independent Bank Corp. (MA) (*)
5 percent discount on reinvested dividends

Independent Bank Corp. (MI) (NR)
5 percent discount on reinvested dividends

IRT Property Co. (**)
5 percent discount on reinvested dividends

Jefferson Bankshares, Inc. (NR)
5 percent discount on reinvested dividends

Kemper Corp. (**)
5 percent discount on reinvested dividends

Kennametal, Inc. (**)
5 percent discount on reinvested dividends

Lafarge Corp. (**)
5 percent discount on reinvested dividends

Landmark Bancshares Corp. (**)
5 percent discount on reinvested dividends

Manufacturers Hanover Corp. (**)
3 percent discount on reinvested dividends

Manufacturers National Corp. (***)
5 percent discount on reinvested dividends

Mercantile Bankshares Corp. (***)
5 percent discount on reinvested dividends

Meridian Bancorp, Inc. (**)
5 percent discount on reinvested dividends

Merry Land & Investment Co., Inc.
(*)
5 percent discount on reinvested dividends

MNC Financial Corp. (*)
5 percent discount on reinvested dividends

Moore Corp. Ltd. (***)
5 percent discount on reinvested dividends

Morgan, J. P., & Co., Inc. (****)
3 percent discount on reinvested dividends

Multibank Financial Corp. (*)
5 percent discount on reinvested dividends

Napa Valley Bancorp (NR)
5 percent discount on reinvested dividends

NCNB Corp. (**)
5 percent discount on reinvested dividends

New Plan Realty Trust (**)
5 percent discount on reinvested dividends

North Carolina Natural Gas Corp.
(***)
5 percent discount on reinvested dividends

North Fork Bancorporation, Inc. (**)
5 percent discount on reinvested dividends

Northern Telecom Ltd. (***)
5 percent discount on reinvested dividends

NUI Corp. (**)
5 percent discount on reinvested dividends

Oneida Ltd. (**)
5 percent discount on reinvested dividends

Pacific Western Bancshares, Inc. (**)
5 percent discount on reinvested dividends and OCPs

Panhandle Eastern Corp. (**)
5 percent discount on reinvested dividends

Philadelphia Suburban Corp. (**)
5 percent discount on reinvested dividends

Piccadilly Cafeterias, Inc. (**)
5 percent discount on reinvested dividends

Piedmont Natural Gas Co. (***)
5 percent discount on reinvested dividends

Presidential Realty Corp. (*)
5 percent discount on reinvested dividends

Public Service Co. of Colorado (**)
3 percent discount on reinvested dividends

Public Service Co. of North Carolina (***)
5 percent discount on reinvested dividends

Puget Sound Bancorp (NR)
5 percent discount on reinvested dividends

Santa Anita Companies (**)
5 percent discount on reinvested dividends

Security Pacific Corp. (**)
3 percent discount on reinvested dividends; 2½ percent discount on OCPs

Seibels Bruce Group, Inc. (**)
5 percent discount on reinvested dividends

Signet Banking Corp. (**)
5 percent discount on reinvested dividends

South Jersey Industries, Inc. (***)
3 percent discount on both reinvested dividends and OCPs

Southeast Banking Corp. (FL) (*)
5 percent discount on reinvested dividends

Southwest Water Co. (***)
5 percent discount on reinvested dividends

Southwestern Electric Service Co. (***)
5 percent discount on reinvested dividends

Suffolk Bancorp (NR)
3 percent discount on reinvested dividends and OCPs

Sunwest Financial Services, Inc. (NR)
5 percent discount on reinvested dividends

Telephone & Data Systems, Inc. (***)
5 percent discount on reinvested dividends

Texas Utilities Co. (***)
5 percent discount on reinvested dividends

Timken Co. (**)
5 percent discount on reinvested dividends

Total Petroleum (North America) Ltd. (**)
5 percent discount on reinvested dividends

TransCanada Pipelines Ltd. (**)
5 percent discount on reinvested dividends

UGI Corp. (**)
5 percent discount on reinvested dividends

Union Bank (***)
5 percent discount on reinvested dividends

Union Planters Corp. (**)
5 percent discount on reinvested dividends

United Cities Gas Co. (***)
5 percent discount on reinvested dividends

United Water Resources, Inc. (***)
5 percent discount on reinvested dividends

Universal Foods Corp. (***)
5 percent discount on reinvested dividends

UST Corp. (**)
10 percent discount on reinvested dividends

UtiliCorp United, Inc. (***)
5 percent discount on reinvested dividends

Valley Resources, Inc. (***)
5 percent discount on reinvested dividends

Volunteer Bancshares, Inc. (NR)
5 percent discount on reinvested dividends

Washington Energy Co. (***)
5 percent discount on reinvested dividends

Washington National Corp. (**)
5 percent discount on reinvested dividends

Westcoast Energy, Inc. (**)
5 percent discount on reinvested dividends

York Financial Corp. (NR)
10 percent discount on reinvested dividends

3

Buying IBM at $10 a Crack: Optional Cash Payment Plans

A popular excuse for many individuals who don't invest in the stock market is, "I just don't have enough money, especially to buy the blue chips." That excuse doesn't hold up when you look at dividend reinvestment plans (DRIPs). For example, with a DRIP, you can invest as little as $10 per payment to buy such high-priced, blue-chip issues as IBM, GE, and Bristol-Myers Squibb. What makes investing in these issues possible for the average investor is the optional cash payment (OCP) plans of DRIPs.

How OCPs Work

OCPs are available with most DRIPs. Investing via OCPs is simple. Once enrolled in the DRIP, and usually after the first dividend has been reinvested, an investor is eligible to send voluntary cash payments directly to the company to accumulate additional shares. Companies differ on the minimum and maximum payments permitted under the plans. For example, IBM permits OCPs of $10 to $5000 every quarter. BellSouth has a minimum OCP of $50 per year, with a maximum of $50,000 per year. In the case of Procter & Gamble, a shareholder in the DRIP can make an OCP of just $2 to accumulate additional shares. For those with deeper pockets, P&G permits OCPs of up to $120,000.

Investors should note that an OCP is strictly voluntary — shareholders in DRIPs are not obligated to send in money. Nor are shareholders obligated to send in the same amount of money each time. For example, let's say you get a bonus at work and drop $1000 in the OCP one month. You don't have to make another $1000 payment in the following month. In fact, you don't necessarily have to make another payment into the plan again.

One of the beauties of OCP is that fractional shares are purchased for investors. For example, let's say you send in $10 to purchase a stock that sells for $60 per share. Obviously, your payment isn't enough to buy a single share. However, your investment buys fractional shares. In this example, the investor would be credited with purchasing 0.167 share if taken to three decimals. Your fractional share receives a fractional portion of the dividend as well. While this may not seem like much, it can add up over a period of months and years.

Some other factors to consider include:

1. *When the OCP is invested.* Companies usually invest the money quarterly — at the same time that the firm reinvests the dividends — or monthly, usually around the first or last business day of the month. The more often the firm purchases stock with OCPs, the increased opportunities you have to "dollar-cost average," an investment strategy discussed in Chapter 4 which is ideal for long-term investing. Briefly, dollar-cost averaging relies on regular investments in a stock with the same dollar amount each investment period. All things considered, a firm that invests OCPs monthly is a better choice for investors who plan to use OCPs extensively in order to dollar-cost average.

One firm that makes monthly OCPs hassle-free is Pacific Telesis. This regional telephone issue, the result of the breakup of AT&T in 1984, permits "automatic supplemental contributions" of at least $50 per month via direct electronic funds transfer from a participant's account with his or her financial institution.

2. *The applicability of discounts.* As discussed in the previous chapter, most companies that offer discounts on reinvested dividends do not offer them on OCPs. Thus, if you want to invest in an issue that offers a discount on OCPs, check first with the company.

3. *The OCP "option."* Many companies permit investors who do not want to reinvest dividends to enroll in the DRIP and make voluntary cash payments. This feature is especially attractive for investors who may need to receive their quarterly dividends for one reason or another but would like to make purchases of additional shares through OCPs. Again, look in the prospectus to see if this option is available.

4. *The timing of OCP payments.* It's important not to send the money too far ahead of the investment date—the date the firm enters the market to purchase stock. That's because companies do not pay interest on funds awaiting reinvestment. Therefore, funds should be sent as close as possible prior to the investment date, which is given in the prospectus. Many companies provide a window of opportunity for investors to have OCPs returned prior to reinvestment. For example, let's say you sent $2000 to purchase stock via a company's OCP option, with the money arriving 10 days prior to the investment date. However, immediately after sending the cash, your refrigerator goes on the blink and you have to replace it. In most cases, as long as you notify the plan a few days before the investment date, you can have the money returned to you.

5. *Fees charged for purchasing stock with OCPs.* Although most companies don't charge any brokerage fees or service charges when purchasing stocks with reinvested dividends or OCPs, there are those companies that charge a nominal brokerage fee. Brokerage commissions are based, to some extent, on the size of the purchase, and big orders will usually command substantial discounts in brokerage fees. Thus, in order to keep down any pro rata brokerage fees you'll have to pay in certain plans, you should plan to send your money at times when the company is making its biggest purchases. This is usually at the dividend payment date, when the firm is reinvesting dividends.

"Rich Person's" Portfolio

As mentioned, the OCP is one of the best friends an individual investor, particularly one working with limited resources, has in the market. Through OCPs, investors need not necessarily eliminate any issue from their investment program, regardless of price. As an example, an investor can purchase stock in each of the high-priced issues in the following rich person's portfolio for a total minimum monthly payment of less than $50:

	Stock price	Min. OCP
Atlantic Richfield Co.	$123	$10
Bristol-Myers Squibb Co.	80	10
International Business Machines Corp.	106	10
Philip Morris Companies, Inc.	68	10
Procter & Gamble Co.	85	2
Monthly OCP payment		*$42*

   Here's a sampling of some issues which permit minimum OCP investments of $10 or less per payment:

AAR Corp.

Abbott Laboratories

Acme-Cleveland Corp.

Albany International Corp.

AMCORE Financial, Inc.

Ameribanc, Inc.

American Brands, Inc.

American Business Products, Inc.

American Cyanamid Co.

American Electric Power Co., Inc.

American Recreation Centers, Inc.

Ameritrust Corp.

AMP, Inc.

AmSouth Bancorp

Aquarion Co.

ARCO Chemical Co.

Arkla, Inc.

Ashland Oil, Inc.

Atlantic Energy, Inc.

Atlantic Richfield Co.

Atmos Energy Corp.

Avnet, Inc.

Avon Products, Inc.

Baker Hughes, Inc.

Baltimore Gas & Electric Co.

Banc One Corp.

Banta Corp.

Bard, C. R., Inc.

Barnes Group, Inc.

Bay State Gas Co.

BayBanks, Inc.

BCE, Inc.

Beneficial Corp.

Bethlehem Steel Corp.

Black & Decker Corp.

Blount, Inc.

Bob Evans Farms, Inc.

Boise Cascade Corp.

Borden, Inc.

Boston Edison Co.

Bristol-Myers Squibb Co.

British Airways Plc

British Petroleum Co. Plc

Brooklyn Union Gas Co.

Brunswick Corp.

Brush Wellman, Inc.

BSB Bancorp, Inc.

Cabot Corp.

Capital Holding Corp.

Carlisle Companies, Inc.

Carolina Freight Corp.

Carpenter Technology Corp.

Caterpillar, Inc.

CCB Financial Corp.

Centerior Energy Corp.

Central & South West Corp.

Central Jersey Bancorp
Central Maine Power Co.
Champion International Corp.
Charter One Financial, Inc.
Chemed Corp.
Chemical Financial Corp.
Chesapeake Corp.
Chubb Corp.
CIGNA Corp.
Cincinnati Bell, Inc.
CIPSCO, Inc.
Citizens First Bancorp, Inc.
Cleveland-Cliffs, Inc.
Clorox Co.
Coca-Cola Bottling Co. Consolidated
Coca-Cola Co.
Coca-Cola Enterprises, Inc.
Colonial BancGroup
Colonial Gas Co.
Columbia Gas System, Inc.
Comerica, Inc.
Commonwealth Energy System
ConAgra, Inc.
Consolidated Rail Corp.
Consumers Water Co.
Control Data Corp.
Corning, Inc.
Countrywide Mortgage Investments, Inc.
CPC International, Inc.
Crane Co.
Crestar Financial Corp.
CRSS, Inc.
Cummins Engine Co., Inc.
Curtice Burns Foods, Inc.
Dana Corp.
Dayton Hudson Corp.
Deere & Co.
Delmarva Power & Light Co.

Dial Corp.
Dominion Resources, Inc.
Donaldson Co., Inc.
Donnelley, R. R., & Sons Co.
Dow Chemical Co.
DQE, Inc.
Du Pont E. I., de Nemours & Co.
Eagle-Picher Industries, Inc.
Eastern Enterprises
Eastern Utilities Associates
Eastman Kodak Co.
Eaton Corp.
Ecolab, Inc.
EG&G, Inc.
Engelhard Corp.
Enron Corp.
Enserch Corp.
Equifax, Inc.
Equitable Resources, Inc.
Exxon Corp.
Federal National Mortgage Assn.
Federal Paper Board Co., Inc.
Federal-Mogul Corp.
Figgie International, Inc.
Fina, Inc.
Fleet/Norstar Financial Group, Inc.
Florida Progress Corp.
Ford Motor Co.
Foster Wheeler Corp.
Freeport-McMoRan, Inc.
Fuller, H. B., Co.
Gannett Co., Inc.
GenCorp, Inc.
General Electric Co.
General Mills, Inc.
General Re Corp.
Genuine Parts Co.
Giant Food, Inc.

Gillette Co.

Goodyear Tire & Rubber Co.

Goulds Pumps, Inc.

Handleman Co.

Handy & Harman

Harris Corp.

Harsco Corp.

Hartford Steam Boiler Inspection & Insurance Company

Health Care REIT, Inc.

Hercules, Inc.

Heritage Financial Corp.

Household International, Inc.

Huffy Corp.

IBP, Inc.

Idaho Power Co.

IMCERA Group, Inc.

Ingersoll-Rand Co.

Inland Steel Industries, Inc.

Intermark, Inc.

International Business Machines Corp.

International Multifoods Corp.

Interpublic Group of Companies, Inc.

K N Energy, Inc.

Kemper Corp.

Kerr-McGee Corp.

KeyCorp

Keystone Heritage Group, Inc.

Kuhlman Corp.

Lance, Inc.

Lowe's Companies, Inc.

McGraw-Hill, Inc.

McKesson Corp.

Madison Gas & Electric Co.

Manufacturers National Corp.

MAPCO, Inc.

Marion Merrell Dow, Inc.

Mark Twain Bancshares, Inc.

Marsh & McLennan Cos., Inc.

Marsh Supermarkets, Inc.

MCN Corp.

Medalist Industries, Inc.

Mercantile Bancorp, Inc.

Meridian Bancorp, Inc.

Midlantic Corp.

Minnesota Mining & Manufacturing Co.

Minnesota Power & Light Co.

Mobil Corp.

Modine Manufacturing Co.

Monsanto Co.

Montana Power Co.

Nash-Finch Co.

National Medical Enterprises, Inc.

National Service Industries, Inc.

National-Standard Co.

NBD Bancorp, Inc.

New York State Electric & Gas Corp.

New York Times Co.

Nordson Corp.

Norfolk Southern Corp.

Northern States Power Co.

Northwestern Public Service Co.

Nucor Corp.

NYNEX Corp.

Occidental Petroleum Corp.

Ohio Casualty Corp.

Ohio Edison Co.

Omnicare, Inc.

Otter Tail Power Co.

PaineWebber Group, Inc.

Pall Corp.

Paramount Communications, Inc.

Parker Hannifin Corp.

Peerless Tube Co.

Penney, J. C., Co.

Pennsylvania Power & Light Co.

Pentair, Inc.

PepsiCo, Inc.

Pfizer, Inc.

Phelps Dodge Corp.

Philip Morris Companies, Inc.

Phillips Petroleum Co.

Pinnacle West Capital Corp.

Pittston Co.

Polaroid Corp.

PPG Industries, Inc.

Premier Industrial Corp.

Procter & Gamble Co.

Quaker Oats Co.

Quaker State Corp.

Quanex Corp.

Ralston Purina Co.

Raymond Corp.

Raytheon Co.

Roadway Services, Inc.

Rochester Gas & Electric Corp.

Rockwell International Corp.

Rose's Stores, Inc.

RPM, Inc.

Rubbermaid, Inc.

Russell Corp.

Ryder System, Inc.

St. Paul Companies, Inc.

Salomon, Inc.

Sara Lee Corp.

Savannah Foods & Industries, Inc.

SCEcorp

Scott Paper Co.

Security Bancorp, Inc.

Sherwin-Williams Co.

Signet Banking Corp.

Simpson Industries, Inc.

Smith, A. O., Corp.

Sonoco Products Co.

Southern New England Telecommunications

Southwest Gas Corp.

Square D Co.

Stanhome, Inc.

Stanley Works

State Street Boston Corp.

Stone & Webster, Inc.

Stride Rite Corp.

Sun Co., Inc.

SunTrust Banks, Inc.

Super Valu Stores, Inc.

Synovus Financial Corp.

Talley Industries, Inc.

Telephone & Data Systems, Inc.

Tenneco, Inc.

Thomas & Betts Corp.

Toro Co.

Total System Services, Inc.

Transamerica Corp.

Travelers Corp.

Trinova Corp.

TRW, Inc.

Twin Disc, Inc.

UJB Financial Corp.

U S West, Inc.

Union Electric Co.

Union Pacific Corp.

Union Planters Corp.

United Illuminating Co.

United Telecommunications, Inc.

Universal Corp.

USLIFE Corp.

USP Real Estate Investment Trust

UST Corp.

UtiliCorp United, Inc.

Valley Bancorporation

Van Dorn Co.

Varian Associates, Inc.

Westvaco Corp.

Vermont Financial Services Corp.

Wetterau, Inc.

VF Corp.

Whirlpool Corp.

Voplex Corp.

Whitman Corp.

Vulcan Materials Co.

Wilmington Trust Co.

Walgreen Co.

Winn-Dixie Stores, Inc.

Warner-Lambert Co.

Witco Corp.

Washington Water Power Co.

Xerox Corp.

Weingarten Realty Investors

Zions Bancorporation

Weis Markets, Inc.

Zurn Industries, Inc.

Commission Breaks for Big Spenders

I have focused on OCPs as an avenue for the little investor to purchase stock in high-quality, big-ticket issues by taking advantage of the low minimum OCP payments. However, investors who may be able to afford bigger voluntary cash payments can reap large benefits in the way of commission savings.

For example, the maximum OCP for Citicorp is $20,000 per month, or a whopping $240,000 per year. Let's say that you like Citicorp stock a lot and have the cash to take a major position of $150,000 in the stock over the course of the year. Commissions on an investment of that magnitude could run well into four figures. However, if you make the purchases via OCPs, your commissions are zero.

The following big spender DRIP stocks permit OCPs of $60,000 or more per year:

Aetna Life & Casualty Co.

Anheuser-Busch Companies, Inc.

Albany International Corp.

Arkla, Inc.

Allied Group, Inc.

Atlanta Gas Light Co.

Allied-Signal, Inc.

Atlantic Richfield Co.

Aluminum Company of America

Atmos Energy Corp.

American Express Co.

Avnet, Inc.

American Family Corp.

Avon Products, Inc.

American Home Products Corp.

Bank of Boston Corp.

American Southwest Mortgage Investments

Bank South Corp.

Amoco Corp.

BankAmerica Corp.

Angeles Mortgage Investment Trust

Bankers Trust New York Corp.

Angeles Participating Mortgage Trust

Banks of Mid-America, Inc.

Barnett Banks, Inc.
Bausch & Lomb, Inc.
Bob Evans Farms, Inc.
Boise Cascade Corp.
Bowater, Inc.
British Airways Plc
British Petroleum Plc
Brooklyn Union Gas Co.
Browning-Ferris Industries, Inc.
Capital Holding Corp.
Carolina Freight Corp.
Caterpillar, Inc.
Central Fidelity Banks, Inc.
Central Louisiana Electric Co., Inc.
Champion International Corp.
CIGNA Corp.
CIPSCO, Inc.
Citicorp
Citizens First Bancorp, Inc.
Clorox Co.
CMS Energy Corp.
Coca-Cola Co.
Coca-Cola Enterprises, Inc.
Colgate-Palmolive Co.
Control Data Corp.
Copley Properties, Inc.
Corning, Inc.
Crane Co.
Curtice Burns Foods, Inc.
Deere & Co.
Delmarva Power & Light Co.
Diamond Shamrock Offshore
  Partners LP
Dominion Resources, Inc.
Donnelley, R. R., & Sons Co.
Dow Chemical Co.
DQE, Inc.
Eastman Kodak Co.
Eaton Corp.

Ecolab, Inc.
Enserch Corp.
Enserch Exploration Partners Ltd.
Exxon Corp.
Fay's, Inc.
Federal Realty Investment Trust
First Chicago Corp.
First Fidelity Bancorp.
First of America Bank Corp.
First Security Corp.
First Union Corp.
First Union Real Estate Invest-
  ments
Firstar Corp.
Foster Wheeler Corp.
Gannett Co., Inc.
General Electric Co.
Georgia-Pacific Corp.
Goodyear Tire & Rubber Co.
Goulds Pumps, Inc.
Grace, W. R., & Co.
Great American Bank
Handy & Harman
Harsco Corp.
Idaho Power Co.
IE Industries, Inc.
International Multifoods Corp.
ITT Corp.
Johnson Controls, Inc.
Kelley Oil & Gas Partners Ltd.
KeyCorp
Kroger Co.
Lukens, Inc.
MacDermid, Inc.
McDermott International, Inc.
McDonald's Corp.
McKesson Corp.
Magna Group, Inc.
Manufacturers Hanover Corp.

Martin Marietta Corp.

Maytag Corp.

Media General, Inc.

Michigan National Corp.

Mobil Corp.

Modine Manufacturing Co.

Morgan, J. P., & Co., Inc.

Nalco Chemical Co.

National Community Banks, Inc.

National Fuel Gas Co.

New England Electric System

NICOR, Inc.

Nooney Realty Trust, Inc.

Northeast Utilities

Norwest Corp.

Ohio Casualty Corp.

Olin Corp.

Pacific Enterprises

PacifiCorp

Pall Corp.

Panhandle Eastern Corp.

Pennsylvania Power & Light Co.

PepsiCo, Inc.

Pfizer, Inc.

Philip Morris Companies, Inc.

Phillips Petroleum Co.

Potomac Electric Power Co.

Procter & Gamble Co.

PSI Resources, Inc.

Public Service Co. of Colorado

Public Service Enterprise Group, Inc.

Questar Corp.

Rochester Gas & Electric Corp.

Rochester Telephone Corp.

Rockefeller Center Properties, Inc.

St. Paul Companies, Inc.

SCEcorp

Security Bancorp, Inc.

Signet Banking Corp.

Southeast Banking Corp. (FL)

Southern Indiana Gas & Electric Co.

SouthTrust Corp.

Stanley Works

Summit Bancorporation (NJ)

Summit Tax Exempt Bond Fund L.P.

SunTrust Banks

Texaco, Inc.

Transamerica Corp.

Travelers Corp.

Union Electric Co.

Union Pacific Corp.

United Carolina Bancshares Corp.

Universal Health Realty Income Trust

USP Real Estate Investment Trust

UST, Inc.

Valley Bancorporation (WI)

Valley Resources, Inc.

Weingarten Realty Investors

Whitman Corp.

Woolworth Corp.

Wrigley (William) Jr. Co.

Xerox Corp.

Zero Corp.

Bypass the Broker Altogether

As mentioned in Chapter 1, investors usually have to be shareholders in the company before they can join a DRIP. However, there are a few companies that permit a type of optional cash payment whereby investors can avoid the broker altogether. The following issues permit initial investments to be made directly through the company; the minimum for each is in parentheses:

Central Vermont Public Service Corp.—initial purchases permitted for residents in over half of the states ($50)

Citizens First Bancorp, Inc. ($10)

Grace, W. R., & Co., Inc. ($50)

Johnson Controls, Inc. ($50)

Kroger Co. ($20)

Madison Gas & Electric Co. ($10)

Manufacturers Hanover Corp. ($1000)

Mobil Corp. ($10)

Procter & Gamble Co. (one share)

Questar Corp. ($50)

Texaco, Inc. ($250)

The following firms, primarily banks and utilities, permit initial purchases directly through the company for customers of the corporation or, in some cases, residents of the state in which the company is headquartered; the minimum for each is in parentheses:

Bancorp Hawaii, Inc. ($250)

Centerior Energy Corp. ($10)

Central Maine Power Co. ($25)

Duke Power Co. ($25)

Hawaiian Electric Industries, Inc. ($100)

Minnesota Power & Light Co. ($10)

National Community Banks, Inc. ($100)

Nevada Power Co. ($25)

Philadelphia Electric Co. ($25)

Puget Sound Power & Light Co. ($25)

Southwest Gas Corp. ($10)

Union Electric Co. (no min.)

Keep in mind that just because a firm will allow you to bypass the broker altogether doesn't make it a good buy. Check the performance ratings before investing.

4

What's Dollar-Cost Averaging and How Can It Make Me Rich?

Investment Strategies Using DRIPs

You've probably been inundated with a lot of horror stories concerning the stock market.

"My broker gave me a bum tip that lost me thousands."

"The game's stacked against the little guys."

"You're better off putting your money in CDs or a money market fund and taking your 7 or 8 percent."

However, it pays to know the facts so you can judge if stocks are for you. For example:

- From 1926 to 1990, stocks, as measured by the Standard & Poor's 500, achieved an average annual total return of 10 percent, including appreciation and dividends. This outpaced the performance of long-term corporate bonds (average annual total return of 5.2 percent) and U.S. Treasury Bills (3.7 percent). These numbers come from Ibbotson Associates, a Chicago-based research firm.

- Even more significant for long-term investors, Ibbotson Associates found that investors who held stocks for 5 years at a time would have lost money in only 7 of the 60 rolling 5-year periods since 1926, and 4 of those 7 periods encompassed the 1929 crash.

- To put it in simple terms, stocks have risen in more than 2 out of every 3 years since 1926, according to Ibbotson Associates.

- Money manager David Dreman, who writes a regular column in *Forbes* magazine, conducted an interesting study regarding "crisis investing." He found that in 10 major crises since World War II, including the Cuban missile crisis, 1979–1980 oil crisis, and 1987 market crash (but not covering the period of the war in the Persian Gulf), stocks rallied from the market low of each crisis 1 year later in 9 out of the 10 crises and showed big gains in the 2-year period following the crisis.

However, such impressive statistics lose something in translation. Let's look at some simple computations to show just how money can build over time, assuming a buy-and-hold strategy.

- Let's assume you invest $1000 in a stock, hold for 10 years, and earn an average annual return of 10 percent (around the average since 1926). That $1000 would more than double to nearly $2600.

- Now, invest $1000 and hold for 20 years, earning an average 10 percent return on your stock. Your investment would grow to $6727—an increase of 572 percent.

- Finally, let's say you invest $1000 each year for 20 years—a total investment of $20,000—and you average a 10 percent return per year. Your sum at the end of 20 years would be around $63,000.

Of course, there's no assurance that you'll achieve 10 percent returns. However, there are individuals who do better than 10 percent. If you're among these investors, your results can be especially impressive. For example:

- A $1000 investment, earning an average annual rate of 12 percent for 10 years, would grow to over $3100.

- And if you keep up this pace for 20 years, your $1000 investment would grow to over $9600.

- Finally, an annual $1000 investment, earning an average of 12 percent for 20 years, would result in a sum of nearly $80,700.

Now let's look at real returns from a variety of stocks over different time periods:

- A $10,000 investment in PepsiCo in 1965 was worth $380,000 on December 29, 1990, assuming reinvestment of dividends.

- Rubbermaid was an impressive performer for its shareholders, with a $10,000 investment in 1980 growing to over $210,000 at year-end 1990.

- H. J. Heinz satisfied the appetites of its profit-hungry shareholders. Indeed, shares purchased at the beginning of calender year 1981 for a split-adjusted price of $3.78 were worth almost $35 at the end of 1990.

- Walgreen, a leading drugstore chain and one of my favorite DRIP investments, made lots of money for its shareholders in the 1980s. In fact, 100 shares of stock valued at $3787 on August 29, 1980, grew to 800 shares valued at $36,500 10 years later.

- Even a cyclical company such as Stanley Works, which produces tools and household accessories, can turn in impressive gains over an extended period of time. Indeed, an investment in Stanley Works has grown at a compound annual rate of 12.4 percent over the last 23 years.

- Utility stocks are often perceived as stodgy investments suited primarily for income. However, Southeastern Michigan Gas Enterprises, a natural gas utility, turned in not-so-stodgy results in the second half of the 1980s, with a $16,500 investment increasing to $66,330 at the end of 1989 — a 302 percent increase in value.

I picked these issues not because they were the most impressive. Rather, they show that all types of stocks — growth and income, cyclicals, and recession-resistant companies — can achieve fairly impressive gains over time. Granted, the 1980s were good for most stocks. Still, I think the examples provide a look at the possible returns available for investors with a long-term focus.

Focus on the Long Term

Long-term results can be impressive. However, while stocks have been the best investments over an extended period of time, they have also been among the most volatile. In any given year, stock prices can fall sharply, as evident by the price drop shown on Figure 4-1. Thus, the temptation is great to try to time the market, trying to get in at the bottom and out at the top.

But such trading is difficult to do successfully for an extended period of time. For the average investor — and many academicians would argue all investors — timing the market is a losing proposition. Textbooks are

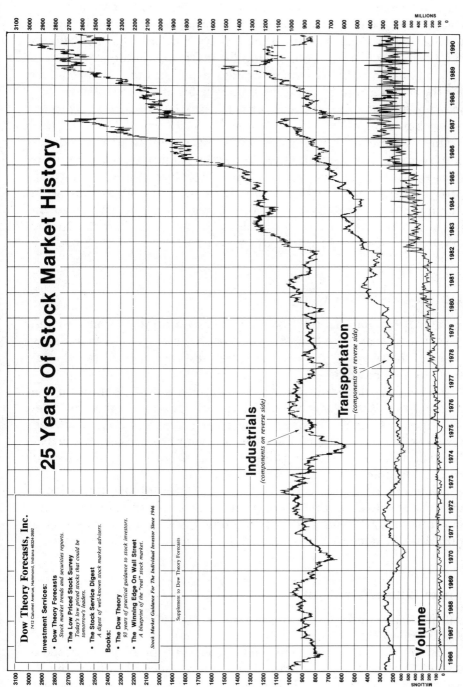

Figure 4-1. Twenty-five years of stock market history.

filled with many research studies indicating the futility of attempting to trade the market. True, some investors have made fortunes being able to time the market. My firm, Dow Theory Forecasts, has had success, since being founded in 1946, timing the market using the Dow Theory. Still, a buy-and-hold investment strategy is perhaps the one best suited for the widest group of investors, especially for individual investors who may not have the time or the energy to track holdings on a day-to-day or week-to-week basis.

One of the most attractive long-term investment strategies is dollar-cost averaging. In a nutshell, dollar-cost averaging removes all of the guesswork of market timing and replaces it with an easy, disciplined approach to investing. The beauty of dollar-cost averaging, as you'll see, is that it guarantees that you buy more shares when a stock is cheap and less shares when a stock is richly valued. And best of all, dollar-cost averaging is tailor-made for investments via DRIPs.

Dollar-Cost Averaging

What if I told you that there was an investment strategy which guaranteed that your average cost of a stock would always be less than the average of the prices at the time the purchases were made? Read this last sentence one more time.

It doesn't say that your cost basis will always be less than the current market price of the stock. No market strategy guarantees this. However, what it does mean is this: Say you purchase shares in IBM on three different occasions. I can guarantee you that your average cost per share is less than the average selling price of the stock at the time of your purchases. Still interested? Read on.

Dollar-cost averaging is one of the most powerful investment strategies available to investors. It works on the principle that, instead of trying to time market purchases, you simply institute a policy of regular purchases of stock with the same cash amounts at specific intervals.

Time Diversification

All of us are familiar with the notion of diversification across investments and stocks, and this diversification is important. Fortunately, adequate portfolio diversification can be achieved with a stock portfolio of 13 to 17 stocks from a variety of industries, especially when coupled with other investments such as money markets, bonds, real estate, etc. Since the capital requirements of DRIP investments are not that onerous, investors should be able to achieve a decent level of diversification through investment in a number of issues.

However, this is not the only diversification that can affect a portfolio's performance. Indeed, say you purchased your entire portfolio at once and hoped for the best. Perhaps you'd get lucky and buy at the bottom of a market. However, chances are just as likely that you'd buy close to the top and see your investment evaporate. Why not spread out your investments over time? That's where dollar-cost averaging is especially appropriate. In effect, it provides time diversification. Since your investments are done over time, you are assured of not always buying at the top.

Let's look at an example of dollar-cost averaging. In this example, you purchase $1000 worth of stock near the beginning of the month for a 5-month period (the number of shares purchased was rounded off in this example, although fractional shares would be purchased with investments made via a DRIP):

Investment	Market price	No. shares purchased
$1000	$ 25.00	40
1000	17.50	57
1000	17.50	57
1000	31.00	32
1000	25.00	40
$5000	$116.00 ÷ 5 = $23.20	226

In this scenario, the average share price at which you purchased the stock is $23.20 ($116.00 divided by 5). However, the average cost of the shares you purchased was just slightly over $22 per share ($5000 divided by 226 shares). How can this be? It's because the magic of dollar-cost averaging makes you buy more shares at the cheaper price with your fixed investment and fewer shares at the higher price. In fact, with this strategy, it pays to have the stock drop in price early in your investment program so that you accumulate more shares prior to any price rise. Also interesting is that despite the fact that the stock over this time period did not generate any capital gains ($25 per share at the beginning of the period and $25 at the end of the period), you are sitting with a profit of almost $3 per share (the current trading price of $25 minus your cost per share of just over $22) since you were dollar-cost averaging during this time frame. The key is that you invest the same dollar amount at the same time each month or each quarter. Keep in mind also that the more frequent your investments in a dollar-cost average program, the more opportunity to maximize your results by increasing the probability of buying at or near the bottom.

As you can see, dollar-cost averaging is a mechanical strategy that takes all of the guesswork out of market timing. How many times have you avoided investing in a stock because you thought it was too high only to see the stock race off to even higher levels? Or how many times do you wish you had bought more shares of a particular stock when it fell momentarily on some temporary bad news only to see the stock soar to high prices?

Dollar-cost averaging takes the emotion out of investing. This is a critical point. Investing is a highly emotional activity. However, emotion can be deadly in the stock market. It causes us to make investment decisions based on the "herd mentality." We get spooked out of stocks when the market drops and everybody is selling. Yet, these instances are when we should be buying, not selling. Dollar-cost averaging helps eliminate some of these emotions. It automatically makes your buy decisions for you and does so in a way which should help you buy low over time. It also provides a strategy for regular investments every month or quarter, not just when you get a few extra bucks or are feeling lucky.

Benefit From Market Volatility

Another plus is that dollar-cost averaging is the perfect way to beat Wall Street at its own game. I receive countless letters from investors each year deploring program trading and other antics by institutional investors which heighten market volatility. Program trading is the use of computerized trading strategies to take advantage of discrepancies between the selling prices of stock futures and options and baskets of underlying stocks, such as the S&P 500. When these discrepancies occur, institutional investors crank up their computers to perform computer-driven trading instantaneously to capture the differences. Such trading can occur at a moment's notice and have a huge impact on trading prices on a short-term basis. Obviously, for a small investor who holds a position in a company such as IBM or GM, it's disconcerting to see the stock price jumping around, up three points one hour, only to fall two points the next. However, if you are dollar-cost averaging, you don't care about such short-term volatility. Indeed, your focus isn't the next week or next month with this strategy, but 3 to 4 years down the road at a minimum and usually much longer. Thus, it doesn't make any difference what the stock does on a day-to-day basis because of, in part, gyrations caused by program trading.

In fact, such gyrations can be a plus for investors. If a stock such as McDonald's falls because of program trading or some other institutional gimmickry, but its fundamentals are still strong, the price break allows you to buy additional shares of the stock through dollar-cost averaging at a lower price. And as we've already seen, a price drop is not the worst thing in the world for an investor using dollar-cost averaging. As long as the stock eventually rebounds, you are actually better off when the stock falls when you are dollar-cost averaging.

DRIPs Perfect for Dollar-Cost Averaging

Implementing a dollar-cost averaging program is not difficult. You could do it with any stock, even for a company which doesn't have a DRIP. However, the beauty of DRIPs for dollar-cost averaging is that the programs, since they reinvest dividends quarterly for participants, assure that you will automatically dollar-cost average at least every 3 months. Outside of a DRIP program, you could still make quarterly investments to dollar-cost average, but you might be more apt to forget a payment or skip one because you're a little short that quarter. With a DRIP, this doesn't happen. In addition, the optional cash payment (OCP) portion of most DRIPs permits an avenue to increase the frequency of your dollar-cost averaging via monthly cash payments. Best of all, DRIPs permit you to dollar-cost average without incurring the sizable commissions you otherwise would pay for dollar-cost averaging.

What Industry Groups? What Stocks?

Of course, dollar-cost averaging doesn't guarantee a profit. It does guarantee disaster if you dollar-cost average in a stock that goes from $30 to $20 to $5 and never rebounds. Thus, as in any investment program, the critical factor for success is proper stock selection.

What industry groups and stocks are best suited for a dollar-cost averaging via DRIPs? Since DRIP investments are long-term oriented, an essential characteristic is the ability to stay in business for a long time. No kidding. Yet, how many of us insist on finding the next "Horatio Alger stock" in high-risk, penny stocks or dead-end businesses where growth prospects are weak at best and competition keen. It doesn't take a genius to figure out that the prospects for failure are highest in these industries. Thus, investors should be careful when investing in certain industry groups.

Banking

The banking and savings and loan groups are easy targets for criticism these days given the sorry state of these industries. However, much of the damage has been self-inflicted. In its purest form, banking is basically a commodity-type business: loan money to creditworthy customers at high rates, take in money at low rates, pocket the difference. Now I'm sure a banker would take exception to this simplistic view of the business. However, I would argue that attempts to complicate the business have led to much of its trouble. Indeed, exotic loans for exotic ventures in foreign lands led to rather exotic loan-loss provisions for many banks. Bad real estate loans haven't helped matters either. All of which leads me to my point—if the people running these shows don't have a clue, how's the average investor supposed to know what's going on in these businesses. Sure, there are good banks, mostly small regional banks you've probably never heard of, that are turning nice profits and increasing the wealth of shareholders. These banks have three- or four-star performance ratings and are suitable for modest investments in DRIPs. But in the main, the group has been a disaster area for investors. Some of the stocks have and will continue to rebound, and in those few cases, sizable profits will be made. However, chances are great you'll probably choose the runt if you go picking in this litter. Steer clear of most major money center banks, don't chase the ones with the high yields, and check the performance ratings before investing in any banks.

REITs

Real estate investment trusts, better known as REITs, are publicly traded trusts which pool investors' funds to invest in various types of properties, from commercial retail and office space to REITs that invest solely in medical-related facilities. The cash flows from the real estate are passed to the shareholders of the REIT. Indeed, 95 percent of REIT taxable income must be passed on in the form of dividends in the year in which they are earned.

Part of the selling pitch for REITs is that they provide a low-cost way to participate in the commercial real estate market. Also, many REITs offer high yields. Sound pretty good, don't they?

Except REITs rarely have delivered in the last several years what they promised. Part of the reason is that empty commercial office space and overbuilding in many markets created cash flow problems for REITs. The group's price appreciation has been spotty at best, and there have been some real disasters. For example, L&N Housing, after peaking at over $34 in 1986, fell to below $5 in 1990, and MGI Properties fell from around $24 in 1987 to under $7 in 1990. And what about those great yields? Of the 11 REITs followed in the *Value Line Investment Survey*, 6, or over half, have cut their dividends within the last 5 years.

As with the banks, there are exceptions. Washington REIT has increased its dividend at a double-digit rate for the last 2 decades and is the only REIT rated better than two stars in the performance ratings. Outside of this one, I'd be hard-pressed to find another I'm comfortable with for a DRIP investment. With the real estate market, especially on the commercial side, continuing to look rather sluggish, I don't look for great things from REITs and would suggest treading lightly in this area.

Limited Partnerships

An "evil twin" of the REIT is the publicly traded limited partnership (LP). Publicly traded LPs exist in such industries as oil, gas, real estate, and forest products. These partnerships are formed primarily as tax dodges to avoid paying higher corporate tax rates.

LPs have had their share of problems in the last few years. Oil and gas LPs were hit with heavy selling when oil prices fell for much of the 1980s. And certain hotel limited partnerships were hurt when overcapacity in the industry hammered profits and cash flow. Dividend cuts have been commonplace among LPs and may continue. With so many other attractive areas for DRIP investments available, don't waste your time or money investing in LPs.

Gold

Gold stocks have their ardent followers among the freeze-dried food crowd who feel that one of these days gold will have its day. Of course, they've been saying that for the last 10 years, but it hasn't happened. I suppose every dog has its day, and gold will eventually undergo a sustained rally. Nevertheless, by that time, the Dow could be at 5000 or more, and people who had their eye on gold stocks will look like gold fools (or is that fool's gold?).

What's with gold? One problem seems to be an oversupply of the metal. Also, South Africa, a major gold supplier, isn't the most liked country in the world these days, and the negativism generated by apartheid has spilled over to Wall Street. Many pension funds and institutional money avoid South African stocks, which means limited demand for South African gold shares. Gold is often seen as an inflation hedge, and inflation has been held pretty much in check over the last several years. The thought at Dow Theory Forecasts concerning gold stocks has been twofold: first, a small portion in a portfolio, say no more than 5 percent, is acceptable for diversification purposes, but big holdings aren't needed. Second, if you must invest in gold, consider diversified natural resources firms with gold representation rather than pure plays.

Fortunately, only a couple of gold issues have DRIPs, so it's not likely you'll be tempted too greatly to jump into this group.

Other Industry Groups

The four areas given above are by no means the only industries where extra care is required. Other groups that may not be appropriate for aggressive DRIP investments include:

- *Technology.* I know that some of the fastest-growing companies are in this area. Still, in an industry where technological obsolescence occurs weekly and where secondary players are squashed by the likes of IBM and Microsoft, it pays to be extra cautious when considering DRIPs in this group.
- *Toys.* The futures of firms in this industry depend on the whims of your average 8-year-old. Enough said.
- *Autos.* This industry is too cyclical and too exposed to foreign competition.
- *Steel.* Aside from the specialty steel producers, it's tough to get too excited about this group's long-term prospects in light of new alternative materials and perpetual labor strife.
- *Insurance.* Many insurance firms got caught up in the same mess as the banks—bad real estate holdings, bad investments (i.e., junk bonds), etc. It'll be a while before most of these stocks come back to former levels.

So What Groups Are Good DRIP Investments?

We've just run through some groups that aren't good DRIP investments. Here are some that are:

Drug Companies

Dow Theory Forecasts readers are well aware of my fondness for drug firms. Indeed, a slew of them—Warner-Lambert, American Home Products, Johnson & Johnson, Merck & Co., and Bristol-Myers Squibb, just to name a few—are on our recommended lists. Here are some reasons why I like pharmaceutical stocks:

- *Consistent earnings growth.* Ultimately, earnings drive stock prices, and few groups match the drug sector when it comes to steady earnings gains. The recession-resistant nature of the group is a big reason for the steady performance. Further, demographics play into the industry's hands. Walgreen, the drugstore chain and a major filler of prescription drugs, estimates that the median age of baby boomers will be 63 in 2020. Obviously, the graying of America has major implications for demand for drugs and health-care services.

- *Outstanding dividend growth.* A by-product of strong earnings growth is a rapidly rising dividend, and several drug companies have achieved double-digit dividend growth over the last several years. Since dividends are important in a DRIP program, drug stocks are that much more appealing for investment via DRIPs.

- *Product development.* Critics argue that one reason the United States has lost its luster in many markets is that corporations have scrimped on research and development. This criticism cannot be directed at pharmaceutical companies. It's common for these firms to have R&D outlays anywhere from 6 to over 10 percent of annual sales. In dollar terms, the numbers are huge. Merck alone spends around $1 billion a year on R&D — outlays that dwarf the annual sales of nearly one-third of the Fortune 500. Such dynamic product development keeps the United States on top in worldwide markets, a point that is extremely important in light of the new global markets.

- *Healthy finances.* Pharmaceutical companies eschewed the growth-by-debt strategy that now has many companies in a difficult pickle. It's difficult to find any of the top-tier drug companies with long-term debt levels over 50 percent of capital. Such strong finances ensure that the companies will be around for a while and leave them ample flexibility to make acquisitions, fund R&D, and make capital expenditures.

If there are any downsides to the group, it's that the stocks are rarely cheap. However, remember that DRIPs are 5-year propositions at a minimum, and dollar-cost averaging over a period of time smoothens out periods when you may be buying the stock on the high side. If you do any DRIP investing at all, you should have at least a couple of good drug stocks.

Food Stocks

Another attractive area for DRIP investments is the food group. Like the drugs, food stocks are recession resistant and generally post steady earnings growth. Another similarity is the dividend growth in the major food issues. Food companies are also poised to exploit the growing demand in Eastern Europe as well as underdeveloped nations. Finally, strong brand names provide major barriers to entry, keeping competition limited in many markets. H. J. Heinz and Kellogg are just two of the many attractive issues in the group which have DRIPs.

The Market Makers

No, I'm not talking about the people on the floors of the various financial exchanges making markets in stocks. I'm talking about marketing-driven firms in various consumer-products industries, names such as PepsiCo, Philip Morris, and Procter & Gamble, where marketing acumen has established their products as leaders and, in fact, helped define the market. Such market dominance translates into impressive earnings growth for these firms. Marketing expertise will be especially important as companies make an even bigger push in overseas markets. These companies have the ability to weather economic downturns and generally have upwardly trending earnings and dividends.

Utilities

One of the more attractive DRIP investment areas for conservative investors is the utility group. Electric utilities meet many of the criteria that are important in DRIP investments: market-leading positions (remember, utilities, with few exceptions, are monopolies), healthy dividend records in many cases, longevity, and minimal volatility. This last characteristic isn't necessarily that critical for investors with a long-term time horizon to spread out the price swings of more volatile issues. However, for conservative investors nearing retirement, it's important that investments, even DRIP investments, have moderate volatility. Electric utilities fit the bill. Natural gas utilities are attractive as well, especially in light of the push for clean air and the emphasis on cleaner-burning fuels.

Despite the appeal of utilities, some pitfalls must be avoided. The biggest mistake investors make when considering an electric utility is to chase the ones with the highest yields. However, the many dividend cuts and omissions by utilities over the last several years indicate that all utilities aren't alike. How can you tell the good ones from the bad ones? One quick way is to check the yield. An electric utility that yields 2 to 4 percentage points more than the group in general is one for which Wall Street has some concerns about the safety of the dividend. Thus, an extremely high yield should be a giant red flag for investors and reason to explore more fully before buying.

Another pitfall is to eliminate from consideration electric utilities merely because of nuclear energy exposure. I'll grant you that nuclear energy doesn't have the best reputation. However, there are many quality utilities that have made this energy source work to their advantage. It'd be a shame to exclude one of these quality companies because of a "no-nukes" bias.

One last word about electric utilities. I've seen a lot of portfolios in which investors have 10 or 15 utility stocks and little else. I don't care if utilities are fairly conservative. Having a lot of them in a portfolio, and little else, is not prudent portfolio allocation. Electric utilities are interest-rate sensitive, and during periods of rising interest rates, they generally will not behave well. A portfolio overly stocked with utilities is not the best portfolio-building strategy. Four to six quality utilities are ample for any size portfolio.

Telephone Companies

Another fairly conservative sector for DRIP investments is the regional telephone industry. These issues, a result of the 1984 breakup of AT&T, combine the attributes of monopolies with growth opportunities in unregulated markets, such as cellular telephone and paging services as well as data transmission services. Our favorites in the group are BellSouth and Southwestern Bell. Enhancing their appeal are above-average yields and decent dividend growth. Telecommunications — voice and especially data transmission — will enjoy steady growth over the next several years, and the "Baby Bells" will have a major stake in these developments. This industry is well suited for DRIP investments.

Some More Industry Groups

The groups given above are not the only attractive sectors for DRIP investments. The following industry groups have appeal for more aggressive investors:

- *Pollution control.* Can you imagine a better growth market in the 1990s and beyond, especially with the increased emphasis on the environment and recent regulation?

- *Database and informational services.* These companies will continue to feed off our insatiable appetite for information of every kind. Clean balance sheets and healthy profit margins highlight the leaders in these fields.

- *Consumer and commercial services.* Companies that make life easier for individuals and corporations should find growing markets in this decade and beyond and represent attractive growth areas for DRIP investments.

Happy Hunting

Now that we've discussed the right hunting ground for DRIP investments, it's time to focus on important characteristics for DRIP investments within these favored groups. We've already mentioned many of the attributes of good DRIP investments:

- Longevity
- Market dominance, aided by strong brand names, patents, technological strength, etc.
- Strong finances, with manageable debt levels and good cash flow
- Steady earnings growth over a period of several years and at least a couple of economic cycles
- Decent growth prospects for the industry
- Attractive dividend-growth potential

Dividends Matter

This last characteristic often gets shortchanged in an investment program. However, it's tough to overestimate the impact dividends can have on a portfolio, especially if you're reinvesting your dividends for additional shares as is the case with DRIPs.

The following is an excellent example that shows that dividends, indeed, matter: For the 1980s, the Dow Jones Industrial Average and S&P 500 produced a total return, including dividends reinvested, of 427 and 403 percent, respectively, according to Lipper Analytical Services, Inc. But if you wash out the dividend effect, the results cool to a gain of 228 and 227 percent, respectively. To drive the point home even further, if you go back another 5 years, to the beginning of 1975, the Dow Jones Industrial Average and S&P 500 in the 15-year period through 1989 achieved a total return of 831 and 905 percent, respectively. Without dividends, the gains would be reduced dramatically, to 346 percent for the Dow Jones Industrial Average and 415 percent for the S&P 500. Clearly, dividends matter, and they matter in a big way.

Why such a big difference in investment results when dividends are considered? The magic of compounding.

Compounding is a powerful force, especially over a long period of time. For example, let's say you own two stocks of equal price. One pays a dividend that yields 7 percent; the other pays no dividend at all. You hold each of the stocks for 10 years, through up and down markets. At the end of the 10-year period—a period that has been brutal on stocks in general—both stocks are still the same price they were when you bought them. A bummer, to be sure. However, your total return on each of these investments is decidedly different. On the stock that paid no dividend, your return is zilch. However, on the one that provided a 7 percent yield, your total investment about doubled because of your dividends, even though you had no capital gains. And if, by chance, the company increased its dividend during that time, the total return would have been even greater. Thus, dividends can be a very potent fuel for portfolio performance, especially during times when stock prices may be standing still. In addition, yields provide a cushion during price drops.

I'm not saying that all investors should focus exclusively on high-yielding, low-growth issues for DRIP investments. However, to ignore yield in portfolio selection could have long-term consequences. It's wise to combine income with growth when making investment decisions, especially in a DRIP investment. And it's especially important that the issue raises its dividend on a regular basis.

The following list comprises companies—all offering DRIPs—that have raised their dividends annually for at least the last decade. Make sure to check the performance ratings before investing.

Abbott Laboratories

Alco Standard Corp.

Allegheny Power System, Inc.

American Brands, Inc.

American Business Products, Inc.

American Heritage Life Investment Corp.

American Home Products Corp.

American Water Works Co., Inc.

AMP, Inc.

AmSouth Bancorp

Anheuser-Busch Companies, Inc.

Aon Corp.

Aquarion Co.

Atlanta Gas Light Co.

Atlantic Energy, Inc.

Ball Corp.

Baltimore Gas & Electric Co.

Banc One Corp.

Bank South Corp.

Bankers Trust New York Corp.

Banta Corp.

Bard, C. R., Inc.

Barnett Banks, Inc.

Baxter International, Inc.

BB&T Financial Corp.

Becton, Dickinson & Co.

Black Hills Corp.

Block, H & R, Inc.

Boatmen's Bancshares, Inc.

Bob Evans Farms, Inc.

Borden, Inc.

Bristol-Myers Squibb Co.

Brooklyn Union Gas Co.

Browning-Ferris Industries

Brush Wellman, Inc.

California Water Service Co.

Campbell Soup Co.

Capital Holding Corp.

Carlisle Companies, Inc.

CCB Financial Corp.

Central & South West Corp.

Central Fidelity Banks, Inc.

Century Telephone Enterprises, Inc.

Chemed Corp.

Chubb Corp.

Cincinnati Bell, Inc.

Cincinnati Financial Corp.

Clorox Co.

Coca-Cola Co.

Colgate-Palmolive Co.

Colonial Gas Co.

Comerica, Inc.

ConAgra, Inc.

Connecticut Water Service, Inc.

Consolidated Edison Co. of New York

Consolidated Natural Gas Co.

Consumers Water Co.

CoreStates Financial Corp.

Crompton & Knowles Corp.

Curtice Burns Foods, Inc.

Dayton Hudson Corp.

Dean Foods Co.

Delmarva Power & Light Co.

Dominion Resources, Inc.

Donnelley, R. R., & Sons Co.

Dow Jones & Co., Inc.

Duke Power Co.

E'town Corp.

EG&G, Inc.

Emerson Electric Co.

EnergyNorth, Inc.

Equifax, Inc.

Federal Realty Investment Trust

Fifth Third Bancorp

First Alabama Bancshares, Inc.

First Bancorporation of Ohio

First Michigan Bank Corp.

First Tennessee National Corp.

First Union Corp.

First Virginia Banks, Inc.

Firstar Corp.

Florida Progress Corp.

Flowers Industries, Inc.

Fourth Financial Corp.

FPL Group, Inc.

Fuller, H. B., Co.

Gannett Co., Inc.

General Cinema Corp.

General Electric Co.

General Re Corp.

Gillette Co.

Gorman-Rupp Co.

Green Mountain Power Corp.

GTE Corp.

Hannaford Brothers Co.

Hartford Steam Boiler Inspection & Insurance

Hawaiian Electric Industries, Inc.

Heinz, H. J., Co.

Hershey Foods Corp.

Honeywell, Inc.

Hormel, Geo. A., & Co.

Hubbell, Inc.

Humana, Inc.

Huntington Bancshares, Inc.

IE Industries, Inc.

Indiana Energy, Inc.

Iowa-Illinois Gas & Electric Co.

Jefferson-Pilot Corp.

Johnson & Johnson

Johnson Controls, Inc.

Jostens, Inc.

Kansas Power & Light Co.

Kellogg Co.

KeyCorp

Keystone International, Inc.

Kimberly-Clark Corp.

Knight-Ridder, Inc.

La-Z-Boy Chair Co.

Laclede Gas Co.

Lance, Inc.

LG&E Energy Corp.

Lilly, Eli, & Co.

Louisiana-Pacific Corp.

Luby's Cafeterias, Inc.

McDonald's Corp.

McGraw-Hill, Inc.

Madison Gas & Electric Co.

Mark Twain Bancshares, Inc.

Marsh & McLennan Companies, Inc.

Marshall & Ilsley Corp.

Martin Marietta Corp.

Mercantile Bankshares Corp.

Merck & Co., Inc.

Meridian Bancorp, Inc.

Middlesex Water Co.

Millipore Corp.

Minnesota Mining & Manufacturing Co.

Minnesota Power & Light Co.

Monsanto Co.

Morgan, J. P., & Co., Inc.

National Medical Enterprises, Inc.

National Service Industries, Inc.

NCNB Corp.

Nevada Power Co.

New Jersey Resources Corp.

New Plan Realty Trust

New York Times Co.

Nordson Corp.

North Carolina Natural Gas Corp.

Northern States Power Co.

Northwest Natural Gas Co.

Nucor Corp.

Ohio Casualty Corp.

Oklahoma Gas & Electric Co.

Olin Corp.

Orange & Rockland Utilities, Inc.

Otter Tail Power Co.

Pall Corp.

Pennsylvania Power & Light Co.

Pentair, Inc.

PepsiCo, Inc.

Pfizer, Inc.

Philip Morris Companies, Inc.

Piedmont Natural Gas Co.

PNC Financial Corp.

Potomac Electric Power Co.

PPG Industries, Inc.

Premier Industrial Corp.

Procter & Gamble Co.

Public Service Enterprise Group, Inc.

Quaker Oats Co.

Questar Corp.

Ralston Purina Co.

Rochester Telephone Corp.

Rockwell International Corp.

Rouse Co.

RPM

Rubbermaid, Inc.

St. Joseph Light & Power Co.

Sara Lee Corp.

SCANA Corp.

SCEcorp

Security Bancorp, Inc. (MI)

Security Pacific Corp.

Selective Insurance Group, Inc.

Sherwin-Williams Co.

Smucker, J. M., Co.

Society Corp.

South Carolina National Corp.

South Jersey Industries, Inc.

Southern California Water Co.

Southern Indiana Gas & Electric Co.

Southern New England Telecommunications

SouthTrust Corp.

Southwest Water Co.

Stanley Works

Star Banc Corp.

State Street Boston Corp.

Summit Bancorporation (NJ)

Super Valu Stores, Inc.

Synovus Financial Corp.

Telephone & Data Systems, Inc.

Texas Utilities Co.

Thomas & Betts Corp.

TNP Enterprises, Inc.

Union Electric Co.

Universal Corp.

USLIFE Corp.

UST, Inc.

UtiliCorp United, Inc.

Valley Bancorporation (WI)

Valley National Bancorp (NJ)

VF Corp.

Wachovia Corp.

Walgreen Co.

Warner-Lambert Co.

Washington Energy Co.

Washington Gas Light Co.

Washington Real Estate Investment Trust

Waste Management, Inc.

Weis Markets, Inc.

Winn-Dixie Stores, Inc.

Wisconsin Energy Corp.

Witco Corp.

Worthington Industries, Inc.

WPL Holdings, Inc.

Zero Corp.

Selling Strategies

No discussion about investment strategy is complete without a few choice words about selling. Fortunately, in a long-term investment program such as a DRIP, selling loses some of its importance. Sure, holding onto a dog that goes into a free fall and never recovers can hurt, and we'll take a look at some ways to keep this from happening. Perhaps the best way to approach this difficult topic is to look at reasons *not* to sell.

My Broker Made Me Do It

Countless times I have heard investors bemoaning the fact that they sold stock on their broker's advice only to see the stock rise rapidly. My rebuttal is usually the same. How does a broker make money? By performing transactions for clients. Thus, the only way the broker makes a buck is if you do something. Does this seem like a conflict of interest? Sure it is, although it's not the broker's fault. It's a problem with the system. I'm not saying that all brokers suggest frequent buying and selling just to make a living. I am saying that the temptation to do this is built into the system. Thus, it's critical that you don't react to a broker's suggestion on blind faith. You should ask yourself some questions. What are my broker's reasons for selling, and do they make sense? How well have I done with this broker's recommendations in the past? Fortunately, if your investment program is done primarily through DRIPs, you won't be getting calls from your broker to sell.

Sell on Bad News

Wall Street's myopic tendencies dictate that a stock that is hit with bad news needs to be sold pronto to avoid further bloodshed. There are several reasons for this short-term thinking. First, the mutual fund business has become quite competitive, and the ability to advertise excellent short-term investment results is crucial to garnering more cash from investors. Thus, investment portfolios have become more and more focused on short-term performance. That is why when bad news hits a company, institutional investors are quick to drop a stock. Related to this is the notion of "window dressing" which occurs in the mutual fund field. This is the process by which portfolio managers weed out dogs and laggards prior to the end of the quarter so that they don't show a position in the stock in the quarterly reports that are sent to shareholders.

What this short-term focus does is to trash good companies that have had temporary problems. Individual investors are often tempted to follow suit and sell, but this may not be the best strategy. Indeed, shareholders who were spooked out of Johnson & Johnson during its Tylenol tampering disasters abandoned a quality company whose stock bounced back dramatically once the smoke cleared. In fact, product tamperings, particularly in industry-leading product lines, are reasons to *buy*, not sell. Other instances in which investors should probably avoid dumping stocks are strike news, lawsuits, and regulatory problems. Granted, each of these things can evolve into a long-term mess for the company. But in more cases than not, the stock discounts the problems, and the shares rise once the problems have been resolved. Thus, staying the course with your DRIP investments, particularly if the holdings are in market-leading firms, is the best strategy.

Sell on "Hot Tips" That You Read About in the Paper

Reacting to news that's in the newspapers is natural. However, by the time you see the news, it's already too late to sell in most cases. The *Wall*

Street Journal and other financial newspapers and magazines frequently discuss companies that are supposedly takeover stocks. Invariably I'll receive a call from investors wishing to buy the stock. My advice is that by the time the person on the street hears of a potential takeover deal, insiders and those close to Wall Street have already bid the stock to a level reflecting the news. This scenario works on the downside as well. By the time you see bad news about your company in the paper, the stock has already fallen and is discounting the news. Should you still sell, especially if the news has long-term ramifications? Perhaps. But it pays to do some homework to judge whether the condition is terminal. Remember, with DRIP investments and a long-term strategy, time is on your side.

Tax-Loss Selling

One common mistake is to let taxes drive sell decisions. It's understandable. The end of the year comes, you've taken some capital gains, and you want to offset them with some losses. So you sell some of your losers. Unfortunately, all too often those same stocks move up sharply in January. Why? Analysts call this the "January Effect." Many reasons have been given for this phenomenon. The one that makes the most sense to me is that stocks that have been weak during the year are beaten down during December by investors selling to establish losses for tax purposes. Thus, when January rolls around, all of the selling has been wrung out of the stocks, so any buying drives prices up sharply.

Tax selling makes sense if the stock's fundamentals have deteriorated to a point where a rebound is unlikely in any reasonable period of time. However, with a long-term investment program such as DRIPs, tax-loss selling probably does more harm than good.

So When Do I Sell?

Intuitively, it makes sense to sell stocks in which fundamentals are poor and long-term prospects are limited. Sounds pretty simple, right? But how can you tell if prospects are limited? Although selling is anything but an exact science, here are some tips that may help to discern if a stock merits dumping.

Watch Those Debt Levels

A long-term investment strategy can go up in smoke if the company goes bankrupt. Thus, perhaps the most crucial reason to consider selling a stock is if the company's debt levels have risen rapidly. Such increases may be caused by funding an acquisition, paying out a "special" one-time dividend, or—and this can be especially disastrous—taking on debt to pay the dividend.

How much is too much debt? One important ratio is long-term debt as a percentage of total capital (total capital is shareholders' equity + long-term debt). These numbers can be found easily on the company's balance sheet. Generally speaking, any amount over 50 percent is cause for concern, and levels approaching 65 to 70 percent are downright scary. Average debt levels will vary depending on the industry. For example, capital-intensive industries will probably have higher debt levels than service firms. Further, an industry with high cash flow and inventory turnover, such as fast food and consumer products, can support higher-than-average debt levels. Nevertheless, debt is probably the biggest factor affecting corporate livelihood, and high debt levels may be as good a reason as there is to sell a stock.

Failure to Keep Pace With Changing Industry Conditions

This reason is what makes investing in technology issues so dicey. The failure of certain mainframe computer manufacturers to respond to the increased demand for desktop power is a perfect example of the failure to change with the industry.

What companies are likely to fall victims to these developments? Those with limited R&D budgets. One sign that a firm is a candidate to fall behind is that its R&D spending fails to increase on an annual basis either in absolute dollar terms or as a percentage of annual revenues. R&D is the lifeblood of industries in fields such as drugs and computers, and scrimping on research is likely to lead to an early exit for the company.

The Stupid Acquisition or Expansion Move

In the go-go 1980s, many acquisitions took place in which you didn't have to be a rocket scientist to figure that they probably wouldn't work. Firms attempted to combine apples with oranges and ended up with lemons in most cases. The bottom line is that it pays to stick with what you know and do best. Academics call it a company's "core competency." If you make cars, don't buy an aerospace firm. If your position in an industry is already weak, don't hurt it even more by taking on more debt to buy an even weaker sister with a different technological strategy. *Synergy* was one of the most overused and misused words in the investment field in the last 10 years, and many companies that professed synergy in a merger had nothing but problems. If a company in which you own stock never buys another company, it may not be the worst thing.

Notice I haven't said anything about falling earnings or sales as reasons to sell. These are the results of some of the things addressed above. If you address the causes and take action accordingly, you'll be ahead of the game.

5

My Favorite DRIPs

I've discussed some of the factors that make an issue a good DRIP investment. Now it's time to look at some real-life examples. This chapter features 20 of my favorite DRIP issues. The stocks cut across many industries and investment objectives. Thus, whether you're a growth or income investor, you should find an issue among these 20 that meets your objective.

Abbott Laboratories

The long-term nature of DRIPs lends itself perfectly to investments in the health-care sector. An aging population points to increased demand for health-care products over the next several years. One of the best investments in the health-care market is Abbott Laboratories.

Abbott Laboratories provides products and services in a variety of markets. Its most profitable sector is the pharmaceutical and nutritional products operation. Pharmaceuticals include Erythrocin antibiotics, Hytrin antihypertensives, and Abbokinase, a clot-dissolving agent. Nutritional products include Similac and Isomil infant formulas. Abbott's remaining operations are in hospital and laboratory products, including intravenous and irrigating fluids, anesthetics, and critical-care products. The firm has built a major position in diagnostic tests. The company is the leader in supplying diagnostic products for blood banks and was the first firm to market a diagnostic test to detect AIDS (HIV) antigens.

Several things stand out right away when you look at Abbott Laboratories. One is the fact that sales and earnings have set records for nearly 2 consecutive decades. Even more impressive is that for the decade of

the 1980s, average return on shareholders' investment was 27.6 percent—among the top performances of any company in any industry. Financially, the firm has always been first rate, with modest debt levels
and ample cash flow. The financial position has provided ample resources for healthy research and development spending, which increased more than fivefold in the 1980s. One of the other main factors
to consider for a DRIP is the dividend record, and Abbott's has been
stellar. Dividends have risen each year for more than a decade and are
expected to rise at an annual double-digit rate for the foreseeable future.

Any potential pitfalls in these shares? Certainly spiraling health-care
costs could force more dramatic regulation of product pricing in the
health-care industry, and such a development would obviously affect
profit margins for Abbott. However, it's not clear, at least to me, if strict
regulation is really the most efficient route to controlling costs. It could
hinder the dynamic nature of the industry, especially from a product
development standpoint. Even if price competition increases in the
field, Abbott's efficient operations should keep it in good shape. It's
hard for me to see these shares do anything but trend higher over the
next 5 to 10 years and beyond.

BellSouth Corp.

The breakup of AT&T at the beginning of 1984 created confusion and
uncertainty in the investment community. How would the Baby Bells
handle being out from under Ma Bell's wing? The answer turned out to
be very well, as the seven Baby Bell regionals have posted outstanding
gains. While all of the regionals are good investments, as reflected by
four-star ratings for all of them, my favorite is BellSouth.

Headquartered in Atlanta, BellSouth serves 70 percent of the population and 51 percent of the territory within Alabama, Kentucky, Louisiana, Mississippi, Florida, Georgia, North Carolina, and South Carolina. The firm had some advantages over its Baby Bell brethren when
the breakup occurred. While the other Baby Bells were made up of a
mishmash of operating companies under the old Bell system, BellSouth
evolved pretty much intact after the breakup and predictably had a
smoother transition than some of the other regionals. Another advantage is the firm's service region, which holds 6 of the 10 fastest-growing
counties in the United States.

On the surface, BellSouth's earnings growth would seem to be limited
given the regulated nature of some of its markets. Not to worry. For
starters, certain changes in how the local telephone markets are regulated now allow firms to share the benefits of their ability to lower costs.
Second, certain markets that were off-limits to the regionals initially fol-

lowing the breakup are beginning to open up to the firms. Finally, local telephone service is only part of the story for the regionals. The other is cellular and paging activities. BellSouth has been building these businesses in recent years.

Fundamentally, BellSouth is in good shape. Finances are probably the best among the regionals. Dividends have been expanding at a 6 to 8 percent rate, and annual increases should continue. BellSouth's yield is decent and makes this issue especially attractive from a DRIP standpoint. The stock's expected low volatility makes these shares appropriate for conservative investors.

Bristol-Myers Squibb Co.

As you've probably noticed, I like health-care companies. What's there not to like? Few industries have such well-defined growth prospects as health care, and few industries have as many quality firms. Bristol-Myers Squibb is one of those quality firms.

Chances are that even if you've never heard of Bristol-Myers Squibb, you've probably used one of their products. Its major pharmaceuticals include Capoten, one of the three biggest-selling drugs in the world with over $1 billion in annual sales; VePesid, one of the fast-growing anticancer medications; and BuSpar, an antianxiety drug. Over-the-counter products include Enfamil infant formula; Bufferin, Excedrin, and Nuprin analgesics; and Comtrex cough and cold remedies. Consumer products range from Drano drain cleaner and Windex window cleaner to Clairol hair-care products and Ban deodorant.

In an era when mergers often make about as much sense as a Franz Kafka novel, Bristol-Myers Squibb is the exception. The firm is the result of the 1989 marriage of Bristol-Myers and Squibb. Each firm brought specific strengths to the union. Bristol-Myers has long been regarded as a marketing powerhouse. Squibb had a strong reputation in research and product development. The benefits from the merger have come even faster than most analysts had expected. Profits should post 15 to 20 percent annual growth over the next several years. Such growth should keep the dividend rising at a rapid rate.

New products are the lifeblood of any health-care company, so research and development is vital to continued success in the industry. But the costs of new products are high. Bristol-Myers Squibb estimates that it takes up to 10 years and an average of $125 million to get a new pharmaceutical to market. For this reason, size matters in the drug industry. Bristol-Myers Squibb, as the second-largest drug company in the world, is in position to spend the dollars needed to stay on the cutting edge. Research and development outlays increased around fourfold in the 1980s, and R&D spending will probably be around $1 billion in 1991.

Bristol-Myers Squibb's recession-resistant businesses should allow it to post earnings gains even during slow economic periods. For this reason, the stock should hold up better than most stocks during periods of market weakness. The stock has demonstrated an upward trend in price over the last decade, and favorable price action should continue. The issue is appropriate for conservative growth investors.

Browning-Ferris Industries, Inc.

It's a dirty job, but somebody's got to do it—and Browning-Ferris Industries does it as well as any firm in the business. This leading provider of solid waste collection and processing services serves some 350 locations in North America and over 100 locations outside of the continent. In addition to residential, commercial, and industrial collection, the firm has been expanding into a variety of other waste-management markets. Medical waste is a burgeoning business, and Browning-Ferris has been staking out a place in this market. Recycling is another growing area for the firm. Waste-to-energy is another technology the firm is exploring.

Browning-Ferris has grown rapidly since being founded just over 2 decades ago. Revenues will approach $3.5 billion in fiscal 1991. Profits have generally moved higher. Dividends have increased annually since 1976, and that record should continue. One key to Browning-Ferris' position in its industry is its ownership of landfills. With landfill space becoming more limited because of political and public concerns, Browning-Ferris' landfill acquisition program in recent years should pay hefty dividends.

The pollution problem in this country seems only to be getting worse, and the problem is not exclusive to the United States. Many opportunities exist for Browning-Ferris over the next 5 to 10 years and longer. For that reason, the stock is well suited for DRIPs. There are some downsides. Alleged antitrust activities and problems related to waste sites periodically cause some price volatility in the group, and these factors have hurt the stock over the last year. Browning-Ferris Industries' risk level is higher than, say, an electric utility or a drug issue. For that reason, investors with time on their side to ride out the price swings are the best candidates for DRIP investments in Browning-Ferris Industries.

Equifax, Inc.

You don't usually hear Equifax mentioned in the same breath as IBM, GE, GM, and other well-known corporate acronyms. You may never have heard of the firm. But if you have a mortgage, life insurance, a credit card, or checking account, chances are Equifax has heard of you.

The company is the world's leading source of information services and systems to facilitate consumer-initiated financial transactions. Customers include banks, mortgage lenders, insurance companies, government agencies, retailers, and any firms that extend credit to consumers.

Equifax has made this information niche pay off handsomely. Per-share earnings have been rising, and the 1990s hold even greater potential. The growing demand for informational services puts the company in the right place at the right time. Equifax has not been standing still. New products have been developed, and the firm's massive database should fuel additional products. Expansion via acquisitions is another growth avenue. The acquisition of Telecredit, a provider of credit-card processing, check authorization, and other payment services to retail merchants and financial institutions, meshes well with Equifax's existing businesses.

Equifax is one of the smallest firms among the 20 appraised in this chapter, and price volatility could be above average given the premium P-E ratio the issue traditionally sports. Thus, this issue may not be appropriate for an investor who has a limited time horizon. However, more aggressive growth investors should score big gains with these shares via investments in the firm's DRIP.

Exxon Corp.

Oil stocks have been all over the map through the years. The late 1970s saw oil issues soar as oil suppliers cried shortage and getting a tank of gas took just slightly less time than reading *War and Peace* in Russian. But the early 1980s saw the exact opposite, with a glut in the market and stock prices of oil producers and drillers dropping dramatically. The down period in the industry created problems for the poorly financed companies and opportunities for those with financial muscle. Exxon was in the latter category and used the industry slump to enhance its stature in the industry.

It's no secret that the prospects for oil companies rise and fall with oil prices. But predicting oil prices accurately is akin to shooting skeet blindfolded—you may get lucky every now and again but you'll miss much more than you'll hit. Investors need to concentrate on quality when investing in the group. Exxon ranks high in nearly every category. Finances are top-notch, with moderate debt levels and ample cash flow. Operations are nicely divided between domestic and international markets. Such a diversified business portfolio is essential in such volatile markets. Dividend growth has been excellent, with annual payout hikes the norm.

Oil stocks present their own set of risks for investors. Obviously, the erratic history of oil prices heightens the volatility of these stocks. Environmental concerns are never far away from the group, and the Exxon Valdez tanker incident in 1989 reflects these risks. However, Exxon's ability to rebound following this incident—the stock moved to all-time highs in 1990—reflects the quality of these shares. Given the issue's above-average yield, good dividend-growth prospects, and outstanding finances, the stock is an appropriate DRIP investment for investors who are willing to accept a moderate risk level.

General Electric Co.

Ask your neighbor what GE does, and he or she will probably tell you the company makes light bulbs. What he or she isn't likely to tell you is that GE is also NBC, or GE is Kidder Peabody brokerage services. And that's GE's biggest problem—investors have a hard time getting a handle on the company. Is it an electrical-equipment firm? Is it a broadcasting company? Is it a financial-services concern?

GE is all of these things and much more. And while many firms have attempted to duplicate GE's diversified business portfolio with little success, GE has made it work. That's because the common thread between these operations is that they all have the potential to be market leaders. Market dominance is the driving strategy behind GE. This was not always the case. The company entered the 1980s with some 350 business and product lines. The firm closed the decade with a much different look. Gone were natural resources, housewares, consumer electronics, and many more marginal operations. During the period the firm spent $17 billion in acquisitions, adding NBC; Kidder, Peabody investment firm; aerospace businesses; chemical operations; and medical systems— all with the potential to be one of the top two in their respective industries.

The company's bottom line benefited handsomely from the restructuring, with per-share profits and dividends more than doubling from 1980 to 1989 and rising again in 1990. Shareholders didn't do too badly either, with the stock price rising from a split-adjusted $11 per share in 1980 to over $75 per share in 1990.

The 1990s hold more exciting opportunities for the firm. The company is poised to capitalize on the opening of overseas markets. Dividend growth should keep pace with the 9 percent growth rate established during the 1980s. Markets, such as power generation systems, should be especially strong, with the rebirth of nuclear energy in this country—yes, nuclear energy (remember, you heard it here first). And the stock should find additional backers on Wall Street as more investors begin to understand and appreciate the firm's growth strategy. The stock is a suitable DRIP investment for nearly every investor.

H. J. Heinz Co.

The sign of a good company is how well it pays attention to both sides of the profit equation. Most firms are pretty good at watching the revenue side. Few are equally skilled in keeping an eye on costs. Heinz's vision is 20-20. Revenues climbed from nearly $3 billion in 1980 to over $6 billion in 1990. Even more impressive is the near doubling of net profit margins in that time to over 8 percent. And the impressive statistics don't stop there. Earnings have moved higher annually for more than a quarter century, annual dividend growth has been in double digits, and where it counts most — in shareholders' pocketbooks — Heinz scores big. From the beginning of 1981 to the end of 1990, Heinz's stock price increased by 800 percent.

The 1990s certainly have a tough act to follow, but Heinz is up to the challenge. A cornerstone of the company's long-term strategy is the international sector. Foreign operations already account for around 40 percent of total sales and operating income, and those figures will grow. The company estimates that the European Community is a market of 320 million people, and the integration of these markets in 1992 presents many opportunities for the firm. Developing countries represent another growth avenue, especially as standards of living improve. Certainly carving out a share of these markets will be no easy task. However, Heinz's popular brand names, ranging from Star-Kist to Weight Watchers, give it a leg up in penetrating overseas markets and maintaining market share in more mature domestic markets.

On nearly every score Heinz comes out a winner. If a downside exists, it's Heinz's popularity on Wall Street and the premium P-E ratio accorded to these shares. This rich valuation does leave the stock vulnerable to sell-offs in line with market corrections. However, for investors whose time horizon is 5 to 10 years, these shares are excellent holdings for accumulation via a DRIP.

Indiana Energy, Inc.

Coal pollutes. Oil pollutes. Nuclear power means Chernobyl, Three Mile Island, and the China Syndrome. So what's left? Natural gas.

The greening of America has put natural gas center stage. Investors can go a number of ways to capitalize on the expected surge in demand for natural gas. Natural gas pipeline issues are one route, although these stocks have been a bit too erratic through the years for my liking. A more conservative area is natural gas utilities. Indiana Energy is one of the best of the bunch.

Indiana Energy distributes natural gas in the north central, central, and southern portions of Indiana. Its service region has been expanding at a healthy rate. Growth in industrial customers has been a plus, and acquisitions have boosted its presence throughout the state. Although earnings have been somewhat volatile over the last decade, the trend has been upward in the last few years. The company has been especially prolific in boosting the dividend, with the payout rising annually for nearly 2 decades.

Regulatory considerations remain a major risk factor for the utility industry. Fortunately, Indiana Energy's regulatory climate has generally been accommodating. Keep in mind that weather patterns affect quarterly profits, and unseasonably warm winter weather will hurt profits and fuel some selling pressures. Also, it's not unusual for the company to post losses in the June and September quarters because of seasonal factors. However, minor price pullbacks aside, the stock's price trend has had an upward bias over the last decade, and that pattern should continue. The healthy yield enhances the appeal of these shares as a DRIP investment.

Johnson & Johnson

If the measure of a person is his or her ability to overcome adversity, I suppose the same can be said for a corporation. And none has done it any better than Johnson & Johnson.

Twice the firm faced the ultimate in crisis management—the Tylenol tampering incidents. Both times the stock sold off immediately following the news. Both times analysts rang the death knell for Tylenol's market dominance. Both times Johnson & Johnson proved them wrong. Tylenol is still the biggest-selling analgesic, and Johnson & Johnson is still one of the premier companies in the health-care markets.

Johnson & Johnson is far from being a one-trick pony. In its consumer segment, which includes such popular names as Stayfree, Carefree, Band-Aid, and Sure, 70 percent of sales come from products that are number one worldwide. Its stable of pharmaceuticals is just as impressive. Products include Ortho-Novum oral contraceptives, Haldol tranquilizer, and Retin-A acne medication. Research and development outlays of more than $800 million annually keep the new product pipeline well stocked.

The recession-resistant nature of Johnson & Johnson's markets makes the company especially appropriate for a long-term investment strategy. The strong dividend record, with the payout tripling in the 1980s, is just one more reason investors should take a good look at the stock. These shares are suitable for any investment portfolio.

McDonald's Corp.

Wall Street analysts love to take potshots at McDonald's. A saturated domestic market for fast-food restaurants, higher labor costs, increased emphasis on healthy eating habits, and the increasing number of dishes prepared for microwave cooking spell a slow demise for Big Mac, say the experts.

Don't believe them. True, few industries are as competitive as the fast-food industry, and McDonald's sheer size in the industry makes it difficult for the firm to maintain its torrid growth pace in the United States. But there are other worlds to conquer for McDonald's, and overseas expansion is the real kicker behind these shares.

Not that its domestic business requires life support. Aside from the heavy discounting which pervades the industry periodically, U.S. operations are in relatively good shape. Its huge network of some 8000 franchised outlets provides a stable base of revenues for the firm relative to other fast-food chains. An important aspect of the franchise system is McDonald's fee structure with its franchisees, which is based on a percentage of sales, not profits. This payment scheme assures a steady stream of revenues back to McDonald's and helps shield the firm from higher food and labor costs.

McDonald's is attempting to duplicate its U.S. success throughout the world. Currently, foreign outlets number around 3000, or roughly 26 percent of all units. Concentrations have been primarily in Australia, France, Canada, Japan, West Germany, and the United Kingdom. Recently, Golden Arches have been popping up in Russia and China. Forays abroad will not initially be as profitable as U.S. outlets since the firm incurs sizable start-up costs. However, as these costs subside and economies of scale take over with a greater concentration of outlets, profitability should rise sharply. The lack of any real competition overseas makes McDonald's look even more attractive.

McDonald's has all the ingredients for a DRIP investment—consistency of earnings growth, outstanding finances, a rising dividend, and market leadership. These shares have already been outstanding holdings for shareholders over the last decade, with the stock making higher highs every year except one and rising from a split-adjusted price of under $4 in 1980 to more than $38 in 1990. There's no reason that this stock should go on a diet at this point, and I recommend these shares for conservative growth investors.

Merck & Co., Inc.

From a drug company's laboratory springs its future, and firms that make the big R&D outlays usually are at the top of the industry. No firm spends more money on R&D than Merck. The company spent around $4.5 billion on R&D in the 1980s, and 1991 will be a billion-dollar year for R&D outlays.

What has Merck received for its big spending?

- Some 18 products selling $100 million or more on an annual basis
- Over 9 percent of the United States market for prescription drugs
- A billion-dollar drug in Vasotec, an antihypertensive drug
- Pioneering positions in a variety of exciting long-term growth markets

And Merck is not standing still. The firm formed a joint venture with Du Pont to develop and market new drugs. Another joint venture with Johnson & Johnson expands its presence in over-the-counter medications. AIDS research is a major priority, and it is hard to conceive of a breakthrough in this area not involving Merck. Any company that can afford to spend around $1 billion in R&D annually obviously has its financial house in order. A strong financial position is also one reason the dividend increased nearly fivefold in the 1980s.

Merck's strengths have not been lost on Wall Street and the business community. The company has been among the most admired firms in America for the last 5 years, according to an annual *Fortune* magazine survey. Merck gets high marks as one of the best places to work for minorities and women. Such popularity may, ironically, work to the stock's disadvantage from time to time, since the rich P-E ratio leaves ample downside potential during shakeouts in the stock market. However, for investors willing to ride through intermittent volatility, these shares offer exceptional opportunities for DRIP investments.

Minnesota Mining & Manufacturing Co.

Many companies give lip service to product development. 3M mandates it. One of the firm's corporate goals is to generate at least 25 percent of annual sales from products introduced within the last 5 years.

One of its better-known products is the Post-it self-stick removable notes. How the Post-it was developed is one of the more popular stories in business literature and exemplifies the innovation at 3M. The idea was hatched by a 3M scientist who was frustrated by page markers that constantly fell out of his church hymnals. The scientist recalled a discovery by another 3M scientist of a barely sticky adhesive. The scientist applied the adhesive to pieces of paper, and the material worked perfectly — sticky enough to hold a piece of paper to nearly any surface, yet not so strong that the paper couldn't be removed easily. To be sure, championing the product through 3M and to the marketplace presented its own set of problems for developers, but the product eventually reached the market and was a success.

The product would never have evolved if one scientist didn't know what the other had discovered. Communication is the cornerstone of the firm's innovation. Corporate buildings are laid out so that engineers, scientists, and marketing people are readily accessible to each other. 3M also provides the time and resources for innovation. The company's "15 percent rule" permits technical people to spend 15 percent of their time pursuing their own ideas, and its Genesis and Alpha programs provide employees time and money to develop ideas.

On every count, 3M rates high marks. The company sports stellar finances; strong and growing overseas representation; a diversified business portfolio, including life sciences, consumer products, and imaging markets, that helps shield the firm from downturns in any one market; and a record of annual dividend increases spanning more than 3 decades. The stock has excellent total-return potential over a 5 to 10 year time horizon and would be a worthwhile DRIP investment for any investor.

Nalco Chemical Co.

Water shortages in the United States were a rarity 2 decades ago. Now they are commonplace. This development poses opportunities for firms in the water treatment market. A leader in this industry is Nalco Chemical.

Nalco is the world's largest producer of specialty chemicals and services for water and waste treatment, pollution control, petroleum production, papermaking, and other basic industries. The company's products help reduce water corrosion in manufacturing processes, recover and recycle heavy metals from waste streams in order to prevent waste disposal problems, and extend the life of equipment used in these industries as well as in the automotive industry and oil drilling.

Spurring demand for products is the increased legislation concerning wastewater disposal. The growth in environmental regulations abroad offers additional expansion opportunities. The continued push for efficiency in corporate America is yet another positive development for the company since its products help improve the quality of manufacturing processes and the end products. This factor should keep demand relatively steady even during down periods in some of the firm's more cyclical markets.

Nalco may not have the blue-chip pedigree of the other issues appraised in this chapter, and its earnings history, especially in the early 1980s, has been erratic. However, profit growth has picked up nicely in recent years, and environmental concerns should keep the bottom line moving higher. Finances are in good shape, returns on equity have been in the 20 to 30 percent range in the last few years, and net profit margins are in double-digit figures. Except for a period in the mid-1980s, dividends have risen annually, and the rate of growth in the payout should accelerate as profits rise. The stock's risk level, given the cyclical nature of some of its markets, is higher than the other issues reviewed in this chapter. For that reason, DRIP investments in these shares are suited primarily for long-term growth investors.

PepsiCo, Inc.

If I asked you what is the world's largest restaurant company in terms of number of outlets, you'd probably say McDonald's. Good guess—but you'd be wrong. And you probably would be even more surprised to discover that the world's largest restaurant company is also the world's largest snack food company.

Still don't know who it is? O.K. last try. The largest restaurant and snack food company is also the world's second-largest soft-drink company.

By now you've probably guessed that the company is PepsiCo. Interestingly, the business it's best known for is the only one in which it is not number one in its markets. But that doesn't mean that the company runs a distant second. Just ask Coca-Cola (which, by the way, is another four-star issue). Indeed, these two powerhouses have waged aggressive campaigns for market share in recent years. PepsiCo has won in some key markets. For example, Pepsi is the largest-selling food product of any type in U.S. supermarkets.

PepsiCo's restaurant operations include the Pizza Hut, Taco Bell, and Kentucky Fried Chicken chains. Each of these chains is the leader in its respective niche in the fast-food field. Menu innovations and aggressive promotional campaigns have helped growth in the restaurant operations far outpace that of the industry.

Snack foods are under the Frito-Lay banner. This unit dominates the

U.S. market for snack chips, with market share more than 4 times that of its nearest competitor. Overseas expansion via acquisitions has put the firm in position to capitalize on the opportunities in this market.

Fundamentally, PepsiCo is sound. Debt is higher than I would like to see in most companies, but PepsiCo's operations throw off plenty of cash, and interest payments are easily handled. The trend of earnings and dividends has been to move higher through the years, and growth should continue for the foreseeable future. Fueling future gains will be an expanded overseas presence. PepsiCo receives only around one-fifth of total sales from foreign operations, so there is plenty of room to expand. Because of its market leadership and steady track record, the stock is rarely cheap. But a long-term investment program via the firm's DRIP should produce attractive returns.

Philip Morris Companies, Inc.

Strong brand names are to consumer-products concerns what patents are to drug companies—licenses to print money. And Philip Morris Companies, with its powerful brand names in the tobacco, food, and brewing industries, has its money machine in high gear. Paced by such popular brands as Marlboro, Bensen & Hedges, Miller, Lowenbrau, Oscar Mayer, Maxwell House, Jell-O, Kraft, and Kool-Aid, Philip Morris has charted an impressive growth course. Profits have been growing at a 20 percent plus clip in recent years. This performance is especially impressive considering that the firm is posting such growth on top of a revenue base of some $50 billion.

Philip Morris' business profile looks much different than it was at the beginning of the 1980s. Indeed, tobacco was its primary activity, supplemented with operations in soft drinks (7-Up). However, Philip Morris embarked on an intensive restructuring program, shedding operations while moving aggressively into the food sector via acquisitions. First was the acquisition of General Foods in 1985. The firm followed up with the purchase of Kraft at the end of 1988.

Not only did these purchases bring on board a number of attractive brand names, but they also helped lessen dependence on the tobacco sector. The tobacco segment continues to be the company's major profit center. However, Philip Morris realizes the possible problems for the tobacco sector down the road—escalating excise taxes, public sentiment against smoking, and potential liability issues. True, the inelastic demand of cigarettes and the burgeoning overseas markets should continue to keep profits rising from this sector. However, Philip Morris saw the need to diversify, and its choice of the food industry has been quite profitable.

Fundamentally, Philip Morris is sound. Dividends have increased for more than 2 decades, rising 525 percent in the decade of the 1980s. Long-term debt, although above 50 percent of total capital, is manageable given the firm's huge cash flow. In fact, it wouldn't be surprising to see Philip Morris add to its business portfolio via a major acquisition. Tobacco stocks may be volatile because of liability litigation that looms over manufacturers, and Philip Morris has had some fairly wide price swings in the past. However, the stock combines excellent capital-gains potential with healthy dividend-growth prospects and is appropriate for investment via DRIPs.

Procter & Gamble Co.

Marketing expertise will be more important than ever in the 1990s and beyond, especially if U.S. firms hope to capitalize on the opening of European markets. Few firms match the marketing muscle of Procter & Gamble. The company is often regarded as tops in brand management, and its brand managers are hotly recruited by other consumer-products companies. Procter & Gamble has managed to retain enough good managers to keep its profits growing at a healthy rate in recent years — an especially impressive performance considering the many mature markets the company serves.

A common theme among many of the companies highlighted in this chapter is strength via brand names, and Procter & Gamble certainly has its share of top names in a variety of consumer-products markets — Bounce, Ivory, Cheer, Pampers, Crest, Head & Shoulders, Pepto-Bismol, Crisco, Duncan Hines, Folger's, and Old Spice. Most of these names have been home grown, although the firm has benefited from selected niche acquisitions. The November 1989 acquisition of Noxell is a good example. This leading maker of cosmetics, including the industry-leading Cover Girl line, brought on board an already strong brand name, and Procter & Gamble's marketing muscle should strengthen it even more.

With the advent of the global market, Procter & Gamble should reap sizable profits. Financially, the firm has more than enough resources to support its growth plans. Long-term debt is manageable, and its products generate large amounts of cash. Strong finances, along with steady earnings growth, have funded regular hikes in the dividend, and growth in the payout has accelerated in the last 3 years.

Procter & Gamble offers some interesting wrinkles for DRIP investors. First, investors are able to bypass the broker altogether by making initial investments in the stock directly through the company. Second, the minimum optional cash payment that can be made in the DRIP is only $2. This high-quality issue is suitable for conservative growth investors.

Rubbermaid, Inc.

The 1980s saw unparalleled merger activity in this country, spawned by deregulation, cheap money, and an influx of foreign investors. But the benefits to corporate America have been rather illusory. Sure, merger mania made investment bankers, takeover lawyers, and deal makers wealthy. It elevated the likes of Donald Trump, who used debt like a contractor uses bricks to build his financial empire, to celebrity status. But in the final analysis, many of these corporate marriages failed, leaving behind corporate corpses with big debt loads and little hope. And those financial empires turned out to be nothing more than houses of cards.

Nevertheless, there were some exceptions. One of them was Rubbermaid. I'm sure most of you have used a Rubbermaid product. The firm makes those plastic and rubber products that are omnipresent in homes and offices—household containers, food storage products, plastic food preparation utensils, and the like.

What sets Rubbermaid apart from the pack is its ability to make acquisitions work. The firm was an active player in the acquisition arena in the 1980s. The firm acquired Con-Tact decorative coverings in 1981, Little Tikes children's toys in 1984, Gott coolers in 1985, SECO Industries floor-care products and MicroComputer Accessories office products in 1986, Viking Brush brushes in 1987, and Eldon Industries office products in 1990.

On the surface, it would seem that such a diverse portfolio of companies would lead to nothing but headaches. But if you look closely, all of the deals made sense. They played off Rubbermaid's strength in consumer and office markets. Many of the acquisitions involved products that were made from raw materials that were similar to what Rubbermaid was already using in its rubber and plastic markets. This point is especially critical since it allowed the firm to boost resin capacity, increasing economies of scale.

The bottom line, however, is how did shareholders benefit from the deals? Not bad, if you think that turning a $10,000 investment in Rubbermaid at the beginning of 1980 into $210,000 by the end of 1990 is an acceptable return. I think more gains are ahead and recommend these shares for growth-oriented investors.

SCEcorp

Electric utilities are popular DRIP vehicles as evidenced by the big numbers of shareholders in most plans. Utilities are appropriate for DRIP investments on several counts. The companies have virtual monopolies in their service regions. Utilities traditionally pay above-average dividends. Utility stocks tend to be less volatile and therefore appeal to conservative income investors. Investors who desire a DRIP in the electric utility group should consider SCEcorp.

Before I go any further, you probably should know that, yes, SCEcorp has stakes in several nuclear plants. But contrary to popular belief, having nuclear energy isn't all bad. In fact, I predict a rebirth of nuclear energy in this country over the next 20 years. Think about it — clean-air concerns, increasingly expensive natural resources, and a growing need for capacity additions in the industry play into the hands of nuclear energy. Admittedly, the history of the nuclear industry hasn't been all smiles. Still, I think we'll see this energy option become more accepted as we move into the next century.

A big plus for SCEcorp is its service region. The company provides electricity to a population of over 10 million people in southern California. Growth in this region has been strong and is expected to continue at a steady rate. Obviously, SCEcorp will have to support this growth, and finances are more than up to the task. On the nonutility side, operations in alternative energy sources, real estate development, and financial investments provide avenues for additional growth.

When you look at what really counts with utility investments — dividend growth — SCEcorp shines. The dividend has been increased annually since 1976, and further hikes are expected. These shares may turn off some investors who are concerned about the nuclear exposure and traditionally tough California regulatory climate. However, investors who are willing to accept some moderate price volatility may consider these shares for DRIP investments. If you're looking for attractive electric utilities without nuclear exposure, consider such four-star firms as Potomac Electric Power, Orange & Rockland Utilities, and Southern Indiana Gas & Electric.

Walgreen Co.

As has been argued throughout this book, one of the best long-term growth markets is health care, as an aging population guarantees strong demand for pharmaceutical products. Attractive offshoots of the health-care sector are those firms which serve as the intermediaries between the drug companies and the customers — retail drugstores. The leader in this sector is Walgreen.

Walgreen operates more than 1500 stores throughout the nation. Approximately 80 percent of its current outlets have been opened or remodeled in the last 5 years. Its stores serve nearly 2 million customers daily.

Walgreen's competitive strengths lie primarily in its use of technology and its focus on cost cutting. The company has been increasing its use of scanning technology, which provides such benefits as faster checkout, more accurate and automatic ad pricing, reduced labor costs, and better inventory control. The firm's satellite data network provides faster and more reliable communications between stores.

Another competitive advantage is its lucrative position as the nation's leading filler of prescription drugs. Walgreen fills more than 6 percent of all U.S. retail prescriptions. Pharmacy sales are around one-third of total revenues for the company, and that figure is likely to grow in the years ahead.

Fundamentally, Walgreen is sound. Profits have risen annually for well over the last decade, and dividends increased fourfold from 1980 to 1990. Strong finances should continue the company's aggressive growth strategy. The stock was an excellent performer from 1980 to 1990, increasing 863 percent. While the firm has a tough act to follow, the 1990s should be another solid decade. Conservative growth investors may consider these shares for investment via the firm's DRIP.

6
Model Portfolios Using DRIPs

This book attempts to construct from the ground up an investment strategy using DRIPs. Chapters 1, 2, 3, and 4 lay the foundation. Chapter 5 provides the building blocks.

Now it's time to build the model. But an appropriate model portfolio for a single, 28-year-old is not necessarily the right one for a married couple 5 years from retirement.

What are some factors to consider when building a portfolio?

- *Investment time horizon.* Obviously, an investor with 30 years or more has ample time to make up for a multitude of investment sins. He or she can be more aggressive than an investor who is retired and cannot afford to take a big loss in any one year.

- *Portfolio diversification.* An individual who has assets in several investments—real estate, fixed-income investments, tax-exempts, life insurance, and common stocks—will have a different portfolio objective than an individual beginning an investment program and having only a few investments. The proper number of stocks in a portfolio is a much debated topic in the financial community. Probably most academicians would agree that a portfolio of 13 to 17 stocks, representing a variety of industries, is sufficient to achieve decent diversification. Given the small financial requirements for DRIP investments, building a portfolio, over time, of 13 to 17 stocks shouldn't be too daunting for most investors.

- *Financial responsibilities and restraints.* A married couple facing college bills only 5 years down the road has certain financial obligations to consider when investing, unlike empty nesters whose houses are paid for and consumer debt is minimal or nonexistent. Also, a doctor making $200,000 a year will have different investment objectives than a young single parent.

- *Risk aversion.* Some investors just flat out do not like to take risks with their investments, even assuming such risk is prudent given long time horizons and ample financial assets. And then there are those investors who should be cautious, but they like the action and are comfortable with a higher level of risk.

Only after you consider these factors are you ready to build a portfolio. This chapter features model portfolios—each consisting of at least 13 stocks—to meet a variety of investment objectives. All of the companies in these portfolios offer DRIPs.

The Golden Years Portfolio

Investors near or at retirement age have definite investment objectives, not the least of which is preservation of capital. Thus, stocks with a relatively low volatility are appropriate for this portfolio. In addition, high yields are an important consideration, especially since these investors are at a point when they probably will begin to want to take at least some of their dividends in order to supplement Social Security and pension payments. Industry groups which are suitable hunting grounds for conservative stocks are water, electric, and natural gas utilities and telephone issues. These areas are well represented in the portfolio below:

BellSouth Corp.	SCEcorp
Brooklyn Union Gas Co.	South Jersey Industries, Inc.
Exxon Corp.	Southern Indiana Gas & Electric Co.
Indiana Energy, Inc.	Southwest Water Co.
Northern States Power Co.	Southwestern Bell Corp.
Orange & Rockland Utilities, Inc.	WPL Holdings, Inc.
Potomac Electric Power Co.	

Indiana Energy, BellSouth, SCEcorp, and Exxon were reviewed in Chapter 5 and are among the more attractive conservative issues in the market.

Southwest Water is an interesting issue in this group. The firm, whose stock trades on the NASDAQ National Market, provides water, sewage disposal, and wastewater treatment services in portions of California, New Mexico, Texas, and Mississippi. It's no secret that water is in demand in the western part of this country, and Southwest Water is in a good position. The firm derives much of its water supply from over 50 company-owned wells. Operations in sewage disposal and wastewater treatment give this company representation in the pollution-control field. Dividends have more than doubled since 1982, and growth in the payout should be in the 4 to 7 percent range.

South Jersey Industries has appeal on several fronts. Its natural gas business should realize increased demand as natural gas becomes more popular as a clean-burning fuel. Participants in South Jersey Industries' DRIP receive a bonus with the 3 percent discount on reinvested dividends and optional cash payments. Brooklyn Union Gas, which provides natural gas services to the boroughs of Queens and Brooklyn, offers another attractive natural gas issue.

Southwestern Bell is one of the top regional Bell companies. The firm's position in the Southwest provides an interesting way to play further economic revival in the oil-patch states. Rising dividends and operations in the growing cellular telephone market enhance appeal.

Potomac Electric Power, Orange & Rockland Utilities, Northern States Power, and WPL Holdings, along with SCEcorp and Southern Indiana Gas & Electric, give the portfolio a healthy representation in electric utilities. All of these utilities have good finances, solid dividend-growth prospects, and favorable growth prospects relative to most utility issues. None of these utilities has been plagued by problems with nuclear energy. Potomac Electric Power, Orange & Rockland Utilities, and Southern Indiana Gas & Electric have no nuclear exposure. Northern States Power, WPL Holdings, and SCEcorp have had no major incidents with nuclear power and have used this energy source successfully. With the rash of dividend cuts and omissions among utilities over the last several years, investors should be able to sleep well holding these issues.

The Bluest-of-the-Blue-Chips Portfolio

Investing in corporate America's elite has its advantages. Indeed, you'd expect these stocks to be here today, tomorrow, and 20 years from now. Such longevity is critical when undertaking a long-term investment strategy such as DRIPs. Further, these industry leaders, because of pricing flexibility, large research and development programs, strong brand names, and other competitive advantages, should be able to hold up better during periods of market or economic weakness. The following portfolio contains many familiar names and would be suitable for investors who desire decent appreciation potential, steady dividend growth, and an above-average degree of safety.

American Telephone & Telegraph Co.	Johnson & Johnson
	Kellogg Co.
Bristol-Myers Squibb Co.	Merck & Co., Inc.
Colgate-Palmolive Co.	Minnesota Mining & Manufacturing Co.
General Electric Co.	
Heinz, H. J., Co.	Morgan, J. P., & Co., Inc.
International Business Machines Corp.	Philip Morris Companies, Inc.
	Procter & Gamble Co.

Bristol-Myers Squibb, H. J. Heinz, Philip Morris Companies, Johnson & Johnson, Procter & Gamble, 3M, GE, and Merck & Co. were highlighted in Chapter 5 as some of my favorites for DRIP investments.

AT&T was missing from the list of my top 20 selections, but it is not far behind. One reason for my reluctance to put the issue in my upper echelon is that it is still feeling its way around to a certain extent in its markets. AT&T is a relatively new company, having only been in existence in its present corporate form since the breakup of the Bell system in 1984. However, AT&T has come a long way in a short period of time. The firm remains the unqualified leader in the long-distance market and appears to be strengthening its position. Its equipment and computer businesses have been fairly erratic but, over time, should be able to provide additional avenues for growth. The addition of NCR should give a lift to computer operations given time. AT&T still faces some uphill battles on the regulatory front. But the trend appears to be leaning toward less regulatory restrictions in the telecommunications sector, and this will work to AT&T's advantage. Looking down the road, it's tough to conceive of an area filled with more growth promise than telecommunications, both in this country and throughout the globe. It's tough to see AT&T not being at the forefront of this dynamic market.

J. P. Morgan & Co. probably brought a few shudders and gasps from you. After all, it is — I almost hate to say it — a bank, and we all know what kind of problems have befallen this industry in the last few years. However, Morgan isn't your run-of-the-mill, free-wheeling, bad-loan-accumulating financial institution. Its client base consists of the elite of corporate America, which helps shield it from deadbeats that have helped force closings and government takeovers of some banks and S&Ls. The firm didn't overexpose itself to loans to developing countries. It didn't try to make a killing in real estate and thus avoided getting killed by bad real estate deals. An indication of the quality of this institution is that it is the only bank that the Federal Reserve Board has allowed to underwrite securities. The stock is appropriate for investment-grade accounts.

Kellogg's record of earnings and dividend growth stacks up against nearly any firm. Prior to 1989, earnings had risen annually for more than 3 decades. Following the dip in 1989 caused, in part, by intense competition, profits rebounded in 1990 and should stay on the growth track for the foreseeable future. Dividend growth has been even more impressive, with the payout rising annually since 1956. Kellogg's stable of top brand names—Corn Flakes, Rice Krispies, Special K, Frosted Flakes, Froot Loops, Product 19, and Eggo waffles—ensures strong profit margins and return on equity.

Colgate-Palmolive has its own profitable brand names—Dynamo, Fab, Ajax, Palmolive, Colgate, Ultra Brite, and Irish Spring. While domestic business remains decent, Colgate-Palmolive's star is hitched to international markets. The firm has been aggressive in bringing new brands to overseas markets. Overall, international operations account for over 65 percent of sales. Given the improved living standards in many developing countries and the opening of markets in Europe in 1992, foreign business will no doubt expand even more. The stock's performance over the last decade has been impressive, and further capital gains are expected.

If you want representation in the technology sector, stick with IBM. The company's marketing acumen should help it remain among the leaders in nearly every computer market. New products have been well received, and the firm seems ready to embark on a sustained upward trend in profitability. Of all of the stocks in this portfolio, IBM is probably the one that will be the most volatile in line with the action of its industry group. Nevertheless, the issue provides excellent appreciation potential over a 3- to 5-year time frame. The fact that the company offers a DRIP opens the door for nearly any investor to purchase this otherwise high-priced stock.

Conservative Growth Portfolio

The title of this portfolio seems oxymoronic. However, it is possible to have a portfolio of stocks invested primarily for growth that doesn't leave you exposed to large risk levels. Granted, any growth-oriented portfolio will carry a slightly higher risk level than, say, an income portfolio. Nevertheless, the following conservative growth portfolio shouldn't turn your hair gray (unless it is already) and should pay off handsomely over a 5-year time frame and beyond:

Abbott Laboratories	Browning-Ferris Industries,
Bausch & Lomb, Inc.	Inc.
Baxter International, Inc.	Donnelley, R. R., & Sons Co.

Emerson Electric Co.

Equifax, Inc.

Gannett Co., Inc.

Humana, Inc.

McDonald's Corp.

PepsiCo, Inc.

Rubbermaid, Inc.

Walgreen Co.

Many of these issues are already familiar to you from Chapter 5—Abbott Laboratories, Browning-Ferris Industries, Equifax, McDonald's, PepsiCo, Rubbermaid, and Walgreen. Each of these firms has a growth rate far in excess of the growth of the economy, and, with minor exceptions, has managed to post a long history of higher annual profits. Given the expected growth of some of the industries represented among these stocks—pollution control, informational services, consumer products, and health care—these stocks should continue to post healthy profits.

One could argue that Emerson Electric's operations in a variety of electrical equipment and electronics markets are anything but traditional growth markets. But nobody told Emerson Electric. Profits have risen annually for more than 3 decades. This record takes into account several recessionary periods and indicates the quality of these shares. Emerson Electric hasn't done it with smoke and mirrors but old-fashioned cost controls and industry-leading products. The percentage of the company's products that are first or second in their domestic markets is around 86 percent, up from 78 percent at the beginning of the 1980s. Continued overseas expansion, strategic acquisitions, and over 3 decades of higher dividends enhance long-term appeal of this issue.

R. R. Donnelley & Sons, the world's largest commercial printer, doesn't have permission to print money. But you couldn't tell it from its bottom line. The firm has its hand in nearly every printing market—catalogs, tabloids, directories, magazines, books, and financial documents. Despite being in an industry that is sometimes cyclical and always price competitive, Donnelley's per-share profits more than tripled in the 1980s and continued to grow in 1990. Strong finances have allowed the firm to expand market share at the expense of poorly financed competitors. The stock's trend has been up, and investors should continue to enjoy good returns from these shares.

Baxter International's appeal lies in its strong market position. The firm offers "one-stop" shopping for hospitals in need of basic medical supplies. Baxter's long-term prospects are keyed by growing positions in diagnostic and pharmaceutical markets. Baxter also has a leading position in home health care through its Caremark division. As hospitals continue to release patients earlier, in part because of cost considerations, this market should grow rapidly. Profitability took a breather in the mid-1980s while it digested the acquisition of American Hospital

Supply. However, the firm is now reaping the benefits from this deal. Steadily rising profits should fuel a rising stock price.

Humana prospers in an industry that has had its share of casualties in the last several years. The firm is one of the largest hospital-management firms in the country. After strong profits in the 1970s and early 1980s, Humana registered an earnings decline in 1986. Problems with its health plans and emergency medical outlets crimped results. However, Humana's restructuring put profits on the right track. HMO operations provide a steady stream of patients for the company's hospitals. Thus, Humana's patient numbers have been steady. With managed health care becoming more popular in light of rising medical costs, Humana is situated to maintain its growth record.

Bausch & Lomb is an interesting way to play a variety of health-care markets. The firm commands a strong market position in contact lenses, and this area should remain the bread-and-butter sector for the company. The firm is also a major provider of laboratory animals via its Charles River breeding unit. This segment has excellent long-term potential given the continued heavy research spending in the drug industry. On the consumer side, Bausch & Lomb has generated major profits from its sunglasses business. The contact lens business is competitive, which affects margins periodically. Nevertheless, profits are on a nice upward trend, which should continue to fuel capital gains.

Not many companies could absorb start-up costs of a new venture and continue to post strong earnings. But Gannett isn't most companies. This leading newspaper publisher showed its mettle by bringing out the first true national newspaper, *USA Today*. Although quarterly results from the paper have been erratic, *USA Today* represents an important profit center down the road. Especially impressive was that the firm managed to keep its profits healthy despite the huge drain caused by the start-up of *USA Today*. The company's network of small regional newspapers generates big profits. Its strategy is to enter small- to medium-sized towns where there is little or no competition, control the market, and hold the line on costs. This strategy plays extremely well with shareholders. Gannett's stock rose from a split-adjusted price of less than $9 per share in 1980 to a high in 1990 of over $44 per share. Although economic downturns will limit advertising revenues and profitability from time to time, the upward trend in the bottom line and stock price is intact.

Light-Blue Chip Portfolio

I suppose you could call the stocks in this portfolio blue-chip "wannabees." Light-blue chips are issues that lack the size and seasoning of consensus blue chips, such as GE, PepsiCo, and Heinz, but have the potential to become tomorrow's blue-chip stocks.

What makes a light-blue chip?

- Leadership in a profitable and growing market niche
- The ability to weather economic cycles
- Strong finances, highlighted by little long-term debt and ample cash flow
- Steady earnings and dividend growth
- Annual revenues of $1 billion or less, with a focus on issues with revenues below $500 million
- Outstanding shares totaling no more than 60 million, with a preference toward firms with less than 25 million shares outstanding.

Stocks that meet these criteria usually have several things in common. First, they traditionally aren't institutional favorites because of their size and moderate number of shares outstanding. This is a plus since the stocks can generate substantial returns once they are discovered by Wall Street. Second, since the firms are working from a smaller base than larger companies, the opportunity for substantial earnings gains is greater for these issues. Since earnings surprises are a major fuel to superior stock performance, the odds improve on finding such stocks among light-blue chips. Finally, because of their size, light-blue chips tend to be more volatile than investment-grade and conservative-growth stocks. However, investors with long time horizons or an aggressive approach to portfolio management should find the following stocks attractive:

American Business Products, Inc.	Pall Corp.
Crompton & Knowles Corp.	Rollins, Inc.
Hubbell, Inc.	RPM, Inc.
Jostens, Inc.	Russell Corp.
Keystone International, Inc.	Thomas & Betts Corp.
Loctite Corp.	Zurn Industries, Inc.
Nalco Chemical Co.	

You've probably either never heard of most of these companies or know very little about them. That's O.K. — Wall Street doesn't know much about many of them either. But that situation won't last forever, especially as these firms grow and their track records become better publicized. Thus, investors who take positions now should be in excellent shape 5, 10, or 15 years from now when these issues are more popular—and more expensive.

Perhaps the quintessential light-blue chip issue is Rollins. The firm meets our criteria for light-blue chips in convincing style. Rollins is the leader in extermination services under its Orkin unit. In addition, it has expanded into lawn-care and protective security services. Clean finances, rising profits and dividends, and well-defined growth prospects give this issue outstanding capital-gains potential. If there is a drawback, it's that Rollins' DRIP doesn't permit optional cash payments, and a minimum of 50 shares is needed before enrolling in the DRIP. Nevertheless, investors should be pleased with the long-term performance of these shares.

We have been stressing the excellent growth prospects of the pollution-control field. Nalco Chemical, highlighted in Chapter 5, holds a strong position in water-treatment chemicals. Another light-blue chip that provides representation in several pollution-control markets is Zurn Industries. The company is a leader in the market for water quality-control systems. Zurn also has a growing position in waste-to-energy plants. With landfill space becoming increasingly difficult to find, plants that convert waste to energy should have a large market. Profitability has generally demonstrated an upward trend and should continue to do so for the foreseeable future.

The one company that you might have heard of is Jostens. In fact, if you have high-school age children, chances are you've contributed to Jostens' profitability via a class ring for your son or daughter. Jostens is the leading manufacturer of school rings, pictures, and recognition awards. Other products include computer-based instructional materials. Profits have risen annually for more than 3 decades, and that streak should continue. Pacing long-term growth is its computer instructional materials, which should find strong demand at the elementary level.

Loctite, a producer of adhesives, sealants, coatings, and other specialty chemicals, generates the majority of sales and profits from overseas markets. This international reach has allowed the firm to offset some of the cyclical aspects of its domestic markets. Dividend growth has been especially attractive, with the payout increasing more than fourfold in the last 10 years.

Two American Stock Exchange issues—Hubbell, Inc. and Pall Corp.—are in our portfolio of light-blue chip stocks. Hubbell manufactures electrical equipment, such as power distribution equipment and wiring devices—rather mundane stuff and equipment that is usually susceptible to economic cycles. However, you couldn't tell by looking at Hubbell's results: profits and dividends have risen every year since 1960. Financially, the firm is sound, with minimal debt and rising profit margins and return on equity. Pall produces disposable filters and fluid-clarification equipment for health-care, aerospace, and processing industries. The company's growth record has been impressive, and a focus on fast-growing markets, such as health care, should help the bottom line accelerate.

Over-the-counter stocks sometimes suffer from guilt by association. True, it would be hard to classify many OTC stocks as stable and steady. However, RPM has a record that stands up well against any company listed on any exchange. This manufacturer of wall coverings, specialty chemicals, hobby crafts, and sealants has achieved higher sales and earnings for over 40 consecutive years. Acquisitions have been a major cog behind this growth. Dividend growth has been impressive as well, and further hikes are expected. Debt, because of its acquisitions, is a bit higher than I would normally like for light-blue chips. However, strong cash flow allows the firm to handle this debt load well.

Thomas & Betts and Keystone International hold strong market positions in relatively cyclical markets. However, the firms have managed to hold up relatively well during down periods in the economy. Thomas & Betts produces electrical connector equipment. A key to its resiliency is its productive research and development program. Keystone International's diversified customer base for its various valve and flow-control products helps shield the firm from downturns in any one sector. Acquisitions have expanded overseas business dramatically. Both companies are financially strong and leaders in their respective markets.

Corporate restructurings often offer fertile ground for bargain hunting. Crompton & Knowles was one restructuring situation that turned into a bonanza for shareholders. In the second half of the 1980s, this producer of specialty chemicals and food ingredients sold off marginal areas to concentrate on its primary businesses. The move has paid off beautifully. Profits, which had been stagnant for much of the late 1970s and well into the 1980s, took off, and earnings momentum still looks strong. The stock benefited from the improvement in profitability, with the issue rising from a split-adjusted low of $5 per share in 1988 to a high of over $23 in 1990. The stock still has plenty of upside left in it, especially as increased production capacity comes on line and boosts profits.

American Business Products offers light-blue chip representation in the office-supplies market. Products include business forms, specialty mailers, and envelopes, as well as books, catalogs, and brochures. Earnings have generally moved higher on an annual basis. Occasionally, pricing will become tight in this competitive market. However, American Business Products' profits and stock price have held up better than its competitors' during past industry slowdowns. Rising dividends complement an attractive capital-gains outlook.

If you ever played competitive sports, you're probably familiar with Russell. The company is a leading maker of athletic uniforms and recreational apparel, including sweatpants, sweatshirts, and T-shirts. The apparel sector has had its share of casualties over the years, as the fickle fashion-minded have caused some former highfliers to crash when fashion moved on to the next fad. However, Russell's clothes have a timelessness to them. More importantly, the company's vertical integration provides a tight reign on costs. A major capital spending program should improve manufacturing efficiencies even more. Apparel stocks exhibit high volatility, and Russell won't be an exception. Still, the stock price should have an upward bias over the next several years.

The Playschool Portfolio

For several reasons, not the least of which are minimal start-up dollars and a long-term focus, DRIPs have become an investment vehicle of choice for many parents saving for their children's college education. One interesting side benefit of investing in this manner is that you can teach your children about stocks and even have them kick in a few dollars from their piggy banks each month toward their college educations.

A good case could be made that any of the portfolios we have covered up to this point would be appropriate for a program geared toward meeting college tuition bills and teaching children about money management. However, I think it's important that, in the case of a portfolio in which your son or daughter will likely have an active interest, you invest in stocks that might mean something to your child. I'm not advocating that you throw out all good stock-picking rules and choose a stock strictly because the company makes a product that's the rage with preschoolers. However, if you can find stocks in quality firms with products or services that your child knows, I think it makes for a much more enjoyable and profitable venture for child and parent. This goes for you grandparents, too.

The notion of investing in companies that are familiar because you use their products or have a familiarity with the company is one of the most underrated methods of stock selection. All of us tend to make stock investing too complicated. We have to use the latest technical and fundamental indicators. We have to have the latest investment gadgets and equipment. However, I have had the most success with companies in which I'm familiar with their products and can understand their business. Applying this strategy to a child's portfolio is especially appropriate since your son or daughter could lose interest fast if he or she doesn't relate to the company. The following companies have interesting business segments or popular products that give their stocks a place in a child's portfolio. Note that these companies span the interests and needs of children of all ages. So you should be able to find an issue or two that would appeal to your child.

American Telephone and Telegraph Co.	McDonald's Corp.
	PepsiCo, Inc.
Baby Bells	Procter & Gamble Co.
Coca-Cola Co.	Rubbermaid, Inc.
Gerber Products Co.	Smucker, J. M., Co.
Hershey Foods Corp.	VF Corp.
Kimberly-Clark Corp.	Woolworth Corp.
Limited, The, Inc.	Wrigley, William, Jr. Co.

An obvious selection for a child's portfolio is a toy company. However, I have generally avoided this group over the years since the stocks are too volatile. Remember when demand for Cabbage Patch Dolls was driving prices so high that they were costing just slightly less than a condo? When near riots were breaking out at your local toy store to gobble up the limited supply? What happened to Coleco? It filed for bankruptcy in 1988.

It's essential to invest in toys that have stood the test of time if you plan to invest in the toy group. One popular line of toys is produced by Little Tikes, a division of Rubbermaid. I sang the praises of Rubbermaid in Chapter 5 as a top-notch growth issue. Little Tikes is just one of its many operating units. As with its other operations, new-product development has been the key to success in its toy operations. Little Tikes is situated nicely in the market for infant, toddler, and pre-school toys—a business that should continue to be strong.

It probably makes no difference to a baby what stocks are purchased for him or her in an investment program. But by owning the following companies, you may not feel so bad dropping big bucks during your next shopping trip. First, it seems you can't buy enough diapers when you have a baby, even when you buy them in those packages that are about the size of Sputnik. One way to see some benefits of this spending, other than in unsoiled living room furniture, is via investment in the two leading diaper manufacturers—Procter & Gamble (Pampers) and Kimberly-Clark (Huggies). P&G has special appeal for an investment program involving a youngster. Its minimum optional cash amount is just $2, small enough to allow your youngster to be an active participant in the plan without busting the piggy bank. And if you have a financial interest in one end of your baby, why not have a stake in the other? Gerber Products is the major player in baby food and has been posting impressive earnings. A corporate restructuring toward the end of the 1980s eliminated marginal products and returned the firm's focus to its most profitable lines. Earnings should remain on an upward trend in the 1990s.

A number of foods and drinks are staples among our teens. For example, hanging out at McDonald's after a Friday night high school football game certainly is universal among teens. Why not own a piece of the Golden Arches? Or perhaps you never see your child without a Pepsi or Coke. Why not have some of those quarters go toward your dividends by owning some of these shares? Peanut-butter-and-jelly sandwiches are part of every person's childhood, and Smucker, the leading producer of jellies and preservatives, is the blue chip in the group. Finally, who doesn't remember finding a wad of chewing gum under a desk in school (or, for that matter, putting one there). Chances are, the gum was one of the brands manufactured by William Wrigley Jr., the world's largest chewing gum producer. Apparently a lot of us still buy the firm's products since the trend of Wrigley's profits has been upward over the years and has accelerated in recent periods. No long-term debt, return on equity in the 30 percent range, and double-digit profit margins reflect the quality of these shares. And what other product defined our early teens (and complexions) more than Hershey's chocolates? You could do a lot worse than buy shares in Hershey Foods for your child. Rising profits and healthy dividend growth should help propel the stock price higher.

Our childhood and teen years are defined not only by what we eat and drink but also by what we wear. Jeans remain a popular wardrobe choice for our youth, and VF Corp., through its Wrangler and Lee brands, has a strong position in this market. If you have a teenaged daughter or granddaughter, you're probably more than a little familiar with The Limited, a chain of fashionable women's clothing stores. The company has broadened its presence through new store formats, such as its Limited Express, Victoria's Secret, and Henri Bendel outlets. Earnings have grown from just $0.03 per share in 1980 to $1.10 in fiscal 1990. Although this stock has a history of large price swings, the issue is a suitable holding for a portfolio with a long-term view. Distinctive footwear, especially high-priced athletic shoes, have gained a foothold (no pun intended) with today's youngsters and teens. A leader in retail shoe stores is Woolworth. Most of you probably know Woolworth by its discount stores. However, the company's transformation over the last decade has made it into one of the biggest factors in the footwear market through its Kinney, Foot Locker, and Lady Foot Locker outlets. In addition, Woolworth has Kids Mart, Richman, and Anderson-Little clothes stores. A strong overseas presence, especially in West Germany, makes it one of the retailers best situated to exploit the opportunities in opening markets in Europe.

Finally, what would our teen years have been without the permanent attachment of a telephone to our ears? Now, when your children are following in your footsteps and churning out huge phone bills, at least you can find solace if you have investments in AT&T or your regional bell company—Ameritech, BellSouth, NYNEX, Bell Atlantic, U S West, Pacific Telesis, or Southwestern Bell. Each of these companies has attractive long-term growth prospects and decent dividend-growth potential.

We have had some fun with this portfolio. Nevertheless, let's not forget its basic point—to achieve long-term growth via sound, high-quality stocks and to focus on those companies in which your children may be familiar or have some attraction. All of these issues have three- and four-star ratings and meet demanding criteria concerning finances, growth potential, market leadership, and rising dividends. And best of all, they all offer DRIPs.

7

Directory of Company Dividend Reinvestment Plans

You've now read the book. You buy the concept of DRIPs and the power of dollar-cost averaging. The dollar amounts to get started don't scare you. And you're fired up to get going.

But you have some questions and concerns. You wonder if PepsiCo's minimum optional cash payment amount fits with your investment budget of $25 a month. You'd like to find an electric utility with a DRIP that lets you reinvest some of your dividends while pocketing some of the cash. You want to know which top-rated issues offer DRIPs with discounts.

Relax. These and a thousand other questions and concerns are addressed in the following pages.

About the Directory

The directory listings provide a plethora of information—addresses, phone numbers, stock symbols, business profiles, and DRIP specifics. Nearly all of the listings provide a performance rating to help steer you toward the best stocks and away from the worst.

Here are some things to consider when using the directory:

- The performance ratings range from the highest (****) to the lowest (*). In the case of a few firms—primarily small regional banks—I

98

lacked sufficient corporate information and financial data on which to rate the companies. These firms were not rated (NR).

- Each listing features the stock exchange on which the issue trades (NYSE: New York Stock Exchange; ASE: American Stock Exchange; NASDAQ: NASDAQ National Market and the Over-the-Counter Markets) and the stock symbol.

- Unless specified in the company's Plan Specifics, you can assume that a company picks up all costs and fees for purchasing stock in its DRIP.

- Nearly all companies allow shareholders to enroll in the plans with only one share. For those few firms in which more shares are required, the number is stated in the Plan Specifics.

- OCP is the abbreviation used for optional cash payments — the voluntary payments that shareholders may make directly into the DRIP in order to purchase additional shares. For example, in the case of Abbott Laboratories, the OCPs allowed under the plan are a minimum of $10 to a maximum of $1000 per quarter. Each listing indicates how frequently OCPs are invested by the company. If a DRIP doesn't offer OCPs, this is indicated by "not available" in the Plan Specifics.

- Some plans permit partial dividend reinvestment. This option allows participants to receive dividends on part of the shares held in the plan while reinvesting dividends on the remainder. This option is addressed in the Plan Specifics.

- When possible, specific selling costs for shares from a DRIP are given. Plans in which investors must go through their own broker to sell stock are highlighted in the Plan Specifics.

- Often, the best source of information about a particular plan is the plan administrator. For that reason, many listings contain the address of the agent administering the plan. In addition, two phone numbers are often provided — the company's and the administrator's. If you call the company for information, ask for either the investor relations or shareholder services department.

- Each listing will indicate if a discount is available and, if so, the amount of the discount and whether it applies to just reinvested dividends or both reinvested dividends and OCPs.

About the Ratings

Any ratings — I don't care if it's the weekly Associated Press college football poll, Siskel & Ebert's movie reviews, or Mr. Blackwell's List of the 10

Worst-Dressed Women — always have an element of controversy. After all, you can't please everyone. However, I can assure you that these ratings were not given lightly but resulted from examining and evaluating several factors.

Financial strength was one of the major determinants of the ratings. Companies with high debt levels usually found themselves receiving one or two stars. Does that mean all companies with large debt loads are bad? Certainly not. But bankruptcy files are filled with highly leveraged firms that ran into problems when business dried up and interest payments were missed. Since investing with DRIPs is a long-term proposition, you want companies that will be able to stay in the game. Heavy debt burdens often make for an early exit. Am I painting all debt-heavy firms with too broad a brush? Perhaps. But my aim is to protect you from danger spots. If I err on the conservative side, so be it.

Earnings, sales, and dividend records were also important in assigning ratings. Firms with consistent sales and earnings growth were rated higher than firms where profitability has been inconsistent. Companies with records of steadily increasing dividends usually fared better in the ratings than those in which dividend growth has been erratic or where dividend cuts or omissions have occurred. Safety of the dividend was a key point.

The company's industry weighed heavily in the ratings. As you know from Chapter 4, real estate investment trusts and oil and gas limited partnerships leave a lot to be desired, in my opinion. Thus, I had a hard time giving any REITs or limited partnerships ratings higher than two stars.

Banking and utility stocks came under close scrutiny as well. The well-publicized problems in the banking system dictate a cautious approach when investing in banks. My ratings on banks reflect this conservatism. Utility stocks are often the refuge for the most conservative investors — people who depend on dividends to supplement their fixed income and who can't afford to have dividend cuts or omissions. Therefore, these issues faced a tougher test than other issues when it came to the ratings.

The long-term prospects of the industry were important. Cyclical industries, such as steel, precious metals, and autos, didn't do as well in the ratings as growth-oriented, recession-resistant sectors, such as food, drugs, and consumer products.

Finally, the ratings were based on the issue's overall suitability for investment via a DRIP. This analysis considered such factors as the competitive nature of the industry, the potential for technological obsolescence, and the projected volatility of the stock.

How should you use the ratings? Obviously, new investments should be focused on three- and four-star issues. However, because a stock you own has a two-star rating doesn't automatically make it a sell. A two-star rating should force you to take a closer look at the firm and its prospects. Does the stock still meet your objectives? Does it have the favorable prospects that led you to invest in it in the first place? If the answers are "yes," then maintain your position. Remember that these ratings are on the conservative side. Frankly, there are some recommendations of *Dow Theory Forecasts* that received two-star ratings, not because they are bad stocks, but because they may not be well suited for an investment program using DRIPs.

With that said about the ratings, I still expect to hear from companies moaning about their ratings. As I said, you can't please everyone.

A Reminder

Although I have said this throughout the book, it bears repeating. Companies frequently change certain aspects of their plans. For example, firms might drop the discount, lower the maximum amount of OCPs, or implement a service charge for administering the plan. In fact, when I was putting this book together, I was surprised by the number of firms that discontinued plans over the last year. Thus, it is critical that investors consult with the company and obtain a prospectus before investing.

AAR Corp. (NYSE:AIR)
1111 Nicholas Blvd.
Elk Grove Vlg., IL 60007
(708) 439-3939

Business Profile: Leading provider of services for commercial aviation markets.

Plan Specifics:
- Partial dividend reinvestment is not available.
- No Discount.
- OCP: $10 to $3000 per quarter.
- Selling costs are brokerage commissions.
- Company purchases stock quarterly with OCPs.

Performance Rating: ***

Abbott Laboratories (NYSE:ABT)
c/o First Nat'l Bank of Boston
P.O. Box 1681
Boston, MA 02105
(617) 575-2900   (708) 937-3923

Business Profile: Major manufacturer of health care and nutritional products for hospitals and laboratories. Maintains leading position in AIDS testing.

Plan Specifics:
- Partial dividend reinvestment is not available.
- No Discount.
- OCP: $10 to $1000 per quarter.
- Stock is purchased approximately eight times a year with OCPs.
- Selling cost is approximately 15 cents per share.
- Approximately 9269 shareholders in plan.

Performance Rating: ****

Acme-Cleveland Corp. (NYSE:AMT)
c/o AmeriTrust Co.
P.O. Box 6477
Cleveland, OH 44101
(216) 737-5742   (216) 292-2100

Business Profile: Provides products and services to improve productivity and quality of telecommunication and metal-working equipment.

Plan Specifics:
- Partial dividend reinvestment is not available.
- No Discount.
- OCP: $10 to $5000 per quarter.
- Selling costs are brokerage commissions.
- Company purchases stock quarterly with OCPs.

Performance Rating: **

Acme Electric Corp. (NYSE:ACE)
20 Water St.
Cuba, NY 14727
(716) 968-2400

Business Profile: Produces power conversion equipment for electrical systems such as computers, test systems, and other electronics.

Plan Specifics:
- Partial dividend reinvestment is not available.
- 10 percent discount on reinvested dividends.
- OCP: $100 to $1000 per quarter.
- Selling costs are small brokerage fees.
- Company purchases stock quarterly with OCPs.
- Approximately 950 shareholders in the plan.

Performance Rating: **

Aetna Life and Casualty Co. (NYSE:AET)
151 Farmington Ave.
Hartford, CT 06156
(203) 273-3977

Business Profile: Largest investor-owned insurance company providing business and personal insurance.

Plan Specifics:
- Partial dividend reinvestment is not available.
- No Discount.
- OCP: $50 to $5000 per month.
- Selling costs are brokerage fees.
- Company purchases stock monthly with OCPs.

Performance Rating: ***

Air Products & Chemicals, Inc. (NYSE:APD)
c/o Chase Manhattan Bank
P.O. Box 283, Bowling Green Sta.
New York, NY 10274
(215) 481-7067   (201) 296-4002

Business Profile: Manufactures industrial chemicals, equipment, and gases.

Plan Specifics:
- Partial dividend reinvestment is not available.
- No Discount.
- OCP: $50 to $3000 per quarter.
- Company purchases stock monthly with OCPs.
- Service charge for depositing previously acquired certificates is $5.
- Selling costs include brokerage commissions, applicable taxes, and a $5 service charge.

Performance Rating: ****

Albany International Corp.
(NYSE:AIN)
P.O. Box 1907
Albany, NY 12201
(518) 445-2200

Business Profile: World's largest manu-facturer of engineered fabrics essential to papermaking machines.

Plan Specifics:

* Partial dividend reinvestment is available.
* No Discount.
* OCP: $10 to $5000 per month.
* Selling costs are brokerage commission and any other costs of sale.
* Company usually purchases stock around the 1st of the month with OCPs.

Performance Rating: **

Alcan Aluminium Ltd. (NYSE:AL)
Shareholder Services
P.O. Box 6077
Montreal, Quebec H3C 3A7 Canada
(514) 848-8050

Business Profile: Largest aluminum man-ufacturer in the world primarily serv-ing the United States, Europe, and the Pacific.

Plan Specifics:

* Partial dividend reinvestment is available.
* No Discount.
* OCP: $100 to $6500 (United States) per year.
* Must go through own broker to sell shares.
* Stock is purchased around the 15th of the month with OCPs.

Performance Rating: ***

Alco Standard Corp. (NYSE:ASN)
c/o National City Bank
P.O. Box 92301
Cleveland, OH 44101-9957
(215) 296-8000

Business Profile: Distributes and manu-factures paper products, office prod-ucts, and food service equipment.

Plan Specifics:

* Partial dividend reinvestment is not available.
* No Discount.
* OCP: $25 to $1000 per month.
* Fees for purchasing stock include proportionate share of brokerage commissions.
* Stock is purchased around the 10th of the month with OCPs.
* Selling costs include brokerage com-missions and a service charge of $2.

Performance Rating: ***

Allegheny Ludlum Corp.
(NYSE:ALS)
c/o Mellon Bank
P.O. Box 444
Pittsburgh, PA 15230
(412) 391-5210

Business Profile: Major manufacturer of stainless steel, specialty metals, and steel alloys.

Plan Specifics:

* Partial dividend reinvestment is not available.
* No Discount.
* OCP: $25 to $3000 per quarter.
* Stock is purchased monthly with OCPs.
* Selling costs are $5 service charge and brokerage commission.

Performance Rating: **

**Allegheny Power System, Inc.
(NYSE:AYP)**
320 Park Ave.
New York, NY 10022
(212) 752-2121

Business Profile: Electric utility operating in Pennsylvania, Ohio, West Virginia, and Maryland areas.

Plan Specifics:
- Partial dividend reinvestment is available.
- No Discount.
- OCP: $50 to $10,000 per quarter.
- Selling costs are $15 charge and brokerage fees.
- Safekeeping feature is available for one-time fee of $3.
- Company purchases stock quarterly with OCPs.
- Approximately 25,000 shareholders in the plan.

Performance Rating: ***

**Allied Group, Inc.
(NASDAQ:ALGR)**
P.O. Box 974
701 Fifth Ave.
Des Moines, IA 50309-0974
(800) 247-5001   (312) 461-2569

Business Profile: Provides property-casualty insurance. Performs financial services for other insurance companies.

Plan Specifics:
- Partial dividend reinvestment is available.
- No Discount.
- OCP: $25 to $5000 per month.
- Fees for purchasing shares include brokerage fees.
- Selling costs include brokerage commission and any Harris Trust handling charge.

- Company purchases stock each month with OCPs.

Performance Rating: **

Allied-Signal, Inc. (NYSE:ALD)
P.O. Box 50,000 R
Morristown, NJ 07962
(201) 455-2127

Business Profile: Manufactures aerospace and automotive products as well as plastics and synthetic fibers.

Plan Specifics:
- Partial dividend reinvestment is available.
- No Discount.
- OCP: $25 to $5000 per month.
- Stock is purchased monthly with OCPs.
- Selling costs are approximately 15 cents per share brokerage fees or commissions and any transfer tax.
- Approximately 14,000 shareholders in the plan.

Performance Rating: ***

**Aluminum Company of America
(NYSE:AA)**
1501 Alcoa Building
Pittsburgh, PA 15219
(412) 553-4708   (412) 762-3678

Business Profile: Largest aluminum producer in the United States.

Plan Specifics:
- Partial dividend reinvestment is not available.
- No Discount.
- OCP: $25 to $5000 per month.
- Stock is purchased monthly with OCPs.
- Preferred dividends are eligible for reinvestment for additional common shares under the plan.

- Participants may incur brokerage fees when selling shares.

Performance Rating: *******

AMAX, Inc. (NYSE:AMX)
200 Park Ave.
New York, NY 10166
(800) 243-4000

Business Profile: Producer of natural resources such as aluminum, coal, and gold. Third-leading aluminum producer in North America.

Plan Specifics:
- Partial dividend reinvestment is available.
- No Discount.
- OCP: $100 to $5000 per quarter.
- Selling costs are brokerage charges and handling charges.
- Company purchases stock monthly with OCPs.
- About 42 percent of the shareholders are enrolled in the plan.

Performance Rating: ******

Amcast Industrial Corp. (NYSE:AIZ)
P.O. Box 98
Dayton, OH 45401-0098
(513) 298-5251

Business Profile: Manufactures metal products and specializes in flow control products and engineered components for manufacturers of original equipment.

Plan Specifics:
- Partial dividend reinvestment is not available.
- No Discount.
- OCP: $25 to $1000 per month.
- Selling costs include brokerage fees and $1 service charge.
- Company purchases stock with

OCPs at least quarterly and more often if enough funds accumulate to purchase a 100 share lot.

Performance Rating: ******

AMCORE Financial, Inc.
(NASDAQ:AMFI)
P.O. Box 1537
501 7th St.
Rockford, IL 61110-0037
(815) 968-2241

Business Profile: Multibank holding company located in Illinois.

Plan Specifics:
- Partial dividend reinvestment is available.
- No Discount.
- OCP: $10 to $3000 per quarter, after initial payment of $100.
- Must go through own broker to sell shares.
- Company purchases stock around the 1st business day of the month with OCPs.
- Approximately 350 shareholders in the plan.
- Minimum to open an OCP account is $100.

Performance Rating: ******

Amerada Hess Corp. (NYSE:AHC)
c/o Manufacturers Hanover
P.O. Box 24850, Church St. Sta.
New York, NY 10249
(212) 613-7147   (212) 997-8500

Business Profile: Explores, refines, and markets oil and natural gas.

Plan Specifics:
- Partial dividend reinvestment is available.
- No Discount.
- OCP: $50 to $5000 per quarter.

- Stock is purchased monthly with OCPs.
- Selling costs include brokerage fees and $1 service charge.

Performance Rating: **

Ameribanc, Inc. (NASDAQ:ABNK)
One Robidoux Center
St. Joseph, MO 64501-1704
(816) 233-2000

Business Profile: Multibank holding company located in Missouri.

Plan Specifics:
- Partial dividend reinvestment is not available.
- No Discount.
- OCP: $10 to $8000 per year.
- Purchases stock with OCPs within 30 days upon receipt.
- Purchasing and selling fees are nominal.

Performance Rating: **

American Brands, Inc. (NYSE:AMB)
c/o Bank of New York
P.O. Box 11002, Church St. Sta.
New York, NY 10277
(800) 524-4458

Business Profile: Important manufacturer of tobacco products and liquor with operations in life insurance and office products.

Plan Specifics:
- Partial dividend reinvestment is not available.
- No Discount.
- OCP: $10 to $10,000 per quarter.
- Selling fees are very nominal.
- Stock is purchased approximately 8 times a year with OCPs.

Performance Rating: ****

American Business Products, Inc.
(NYSE:ABP)
P.O. Box 105684
Atlanta, GA 30348
(404) 953-8300

Business Profile: Important producer of business forms and printed business supplies.

Plan Specifics:
- Partial dividend reinvestment is not available.
- No Discount.
- OCP: $10 to $1000 per month.
- Stock is purchased monthly with OCPs.
- Selling costs are brokerage commissions.
- Small fee for issuance of certificates.
- Approximately 350 shareholders in the plan.
- 100 shares needed to enroll.

Performance Rating: ***

American Colloid Company
(NASDAQ:ACOL)
1500 West Shure Dr.
Arlington Hgts., IL 60004-1434
(708) 392-4600

Business Profile: One of the world's principal producers of bentonite, a nonmetallic clay used in many different industries and products.

Plan Specifics:
- Partial dividend reinvestment is not available.
- No Discount.
- OCP: $25 to $1000 per quarter.
- Purchases made quarterly with OCPs.
- Selling costs are brokerage commission and transfer tax.
- Less than 250 shareholders in plan.

- Charges moderate brokerage fee for purchases under the plan.

Performance Rating: **

American Cyanamid Co.
(NYSE:ACY)
One Cyanamid Plaza
Wayne, NJ 07470
(201) 831-3586

Business Profile: Manufactures medical and pharmaceutical products, agricultural products, and chemicals.

Plan Specifics:
- Partial dividend reinvestment is not available.
- No Discount.
- OCP: $10 to $1000 per month.
- Stock purchased around the 15th of the month with OCPs.
- Selling costs are brokerage commissions plus $1.50 service charge.
- Over 5000 shareholders in the plan.

Performance Rating: ****

American Electric Power Co., Inc.
(NYSE:AEP)
P.O. Box 16631
1 Riverside Plaza
Columbus, OH 43216-6631
(800) 237-2667

Business Profile: Major electric utility holding company serving portions of Indiana, Kentucky, Michigan, Ohio, Tennessee, Virginia, and West Virginia.

Plan Specifics:
- Partial dividend reinvestment is available.
- No Discount.
- OCP: no minimum to $5000 per quarter.

- Stock is purchased around the 10th of the month with OCPs.
- Approximately 63,000 shareholders in the plan.
- Selling fees include nominal brokerage commission and transfer tax.

Performance Rating: **

American Express Co. (NYSE:AXP)
American Express Tower
World Financial Center
New York, NY 10285-4775
(212) 640-5693

Business Profile: Specializes in travel-related services with operations in investment services and international banking.

Plan Specifics:
- Partial dividend reinvestment is available.
- 3 percent discount on reinvested dividends.
- OCP: $50 to $5000 per month.
- Stock is purchased with OCPs around the 10th of every month.
- Selling costs are brokerage commission and applicable stock transfer tax.
- Approximately 11,500 shareholders in plan.
- Safekeeping for certified shares is available.

Performance Rating: ***

American Family Corp. (NYSE:AFL)
American Family Center
Columbus, GA 31999
(800) 235-2667

Business Profile: Major provider of supplemental cancer insurance in addition to accident and health cover-

age. Derives over 70 percent of revenues from Japan.

Plan Specifics:

- Partial dividend reinvestment is
available.
- No Discount.
- OCP: $20 to $5000 per month.
- Selling fees are about 5 to 20 cents
per share.
- Stock is purchased with OCPs
around the 1st of the month.
- Approximately 12,500 shareholders
in the plan.

Performance Rating: ★★★

American Filtrona Corp.
  (NASDAQ:AFIL)
P.O. Box 31640
Richmond, VA 23294
(804) 346-2400

Business Profile: Manufactures specialty
bonded fiber products, plastic products,
and industrial filtration products.

Plan Specifics:

- Partial dividend reinvestment is not
available.
- No Discount.
- OCP: $25 to $1000 per month.
- Nominal broker fees for purchases.
- Selling costs include brokerage fees.
- Stock is purchased monthly with
OCPs.

Performance Rating: ★★

American General Corp.
  (NYSE:AGC)
Shareholder Services
P.O. Box 4743
Houston, TX 77210
(800) 231-6327

Business Profile: A consumer-financial

services organization with operations
in life insurance, retirement annuities,
and consumer loans.

Plan Specifics:

- Partial dividend reinvestment is
available.
- No Discount.
- OCP: $25 to $6000 per quarter.
- Selling costs include brokerage fees
and applicable transfer taxes.
- Purchases with OCPs made around
the 1st of each month.

Performance Rating: ★★★

American Greetings Corp.
  (NASDAQ:AGREA)
c/o Ameritrust Co.
P.O. Box 6477
Cleveland, OH 44101
(216) 737-5742   (216) 252-7300

Business Profile: Leading supplier of
greeting cards and gift wrap.

Plan Specifics:

- Partial dividend reinvestment is not
available.
- No Discount.
- OCP: not available.
- Selling costs may include any bro-
kerage fees and $5 termination.

Performance Rating: ★★★

American Health Properties, Inc.
  (NYSE:AHE)
11150 Santa Monica Blvd. #800
Los Angeles, CA 90025
(213) 477-9399

Business Profile: Real estate investment
trust invests in broad range of health-
care-related facilities throughout the
country.

Plan Specifics:
- Partial dividend reinvestment is available.
- No Discount.
- OCP: $50 to $3000 per quarter.
- Must go through own broker to sell shares.
- Stock is purchased monthly with OCPs.
- Approximately 528 shareholders in the plan.

Performance Rating: **

American Heritage Life Investment Corp. (NYSE:AHL)
Investment Corporation
Eleven East Forsyth St.
Jacksonville, FL 32202
(904) 359-2545   (904) 354-1776

Business Profile: Insurance-based holding firm offers life, accident, and health insurance and annuities.

Plan Specifics:
- Partial dividend reinvestment is not available.
- No Discount.
- OCP: not available.
- Selling costs are brokerage commission and any taxes.

Performance Rating: ***

American Home Products Corp. (NYSE:AHP)
c/o Manufacturers Hanover
P.O. Box 24850, Church St. Sta.
New York, NY 10249
(212) 878-5000   (212) 613-7147

Business Profile: Produces prescription drugs, medical supplies, health care items, food and household products.

Plan Specifics:
- Partial dividend reinvestment is available.
- No Discount.
- OCP: $50 to $10,000 per month.
- Fees for purchasing stock under the plan include proportionate brokerage fees, $1.50 service charge for each quarterly dividend reinvestment, and $5 fee for each investment of OCPs.
- Selling fees include brokerage costs, and there is a termination fee of $15.
- Stock is purchased monthly with OCPs.

Performance Rating: ****

American Real Estate Partners, LP (NYSE:ACP)
10 Union Square East
New York, NY 10003
(800) 423-2737

Business Profile: Partnership involved in management and acquisition of real estate for office, retail, and industrial properties.

Plan Specifics:
- Partial dividend reinvestment is not available.
- No Discount.
- OCP: not available.
- Purchasing fees are 5 percent on each amount invested—not less than 75 cents or more than $2.50—plus proportionate brokerage commissions for each investment transaction.
- Selling fees are brokerage commission plus termination fee of $2.50.

Performance Rating: **

American Recreation Centers, Inc.
  (NASDAQ:AMRC)
P.O. Box 60729
Sacramento, CA 95860
(916) 362-2695   (415) 624-2486

Business Profile: Owns bowling centers, primarily in California and Texas, and is involved in direct-mail marketing of children's specialty products.

Plan Specifics:
* Partial dividend reinvestment is not available.
* No Discount.
* OCP: $10 to $500 per month.
* Stock purchased monthly with OCPs.
* No selling costs.
* One of the few plans where initial purchases may be made directly through the company—initial minimum investment is $50.

Performance Rating: **

American Southwest Mortgage
  Investments (ASE:ASR)
c/o Manufacturers Hanover
P.O. Box 24850, Church St. Sta.
New York, NY 10249
(602) 748-2111

Business Profile: Real estate investment trust.

Plan Specifics:
* Partial dividend reinvestment is available.
* No Discount.
* OCP: $250 to $100,000 per quarter.
* Stock purchased quarterly with OCPs.
* Selling costs are brokerage costs and $15 fee.
* $5 fee for issuing certificates.
* $3 certificate safekeeping fee.

Performance Rating: **

American Telephone & Telegraph
  Co. (NYSE:T)
c/o American Transtech
P.O. Box 45048
Jacksonville, FL 32232
(800) 348-8288

Business Profile: Major services include long-distance calling and international telecommunications with operations in manufacturing and marketing telecommunications equipment.

Plan Specifics:
* Partial dividend reinvestment is available.
* No Discount.
* OCP: $100 to $50,000 per year.
* Purchases stock with OCPs every month.
* An account activity fee of the lesser of $1 or 10 percent of the amount invested during the month will be charged for each month during which a plan investment is made.
* Selling costs are about 10 cents per share.
* Need 10 shares to enroll in the plan.

Performance Rating: ****

American Water Works Co., Inc.
  (NYSE:AWK)
c/o First Nat'l Bank Boston
P O Box 1681
Boston, MA 02105
(609) 346-8200   (617) 575-2900

Business Profile: Utility holding company provides water services in 20 states.

Plan Specifics:
* Partial dividend reinvestment is available.
* 5 percent discount on reinvested dividends.

- OCP: not available.
- Selling costs include brokerage fees, transfer taxes, and a handling charge.

Performance Rating: ***

Ameritech (NYSE:AIT)
c/o American Transtech
P.O. Box 44025
Jacksonville, FL 32231-4025
(800) 233-1342

Business Profile: Major telephone holding company for upper-Midwestern states.

Plan Specifics:
- Partial dividend reinvestment is available.
- No Discount.
- OCP: $50 to $25,000 per year.
- Fees for purchasing stock in the open market are nominal brokerage commission.
- Transfer agent will sell up to 99 shares for individual; selling costs are approximately 8 cents per share.
- Purchases are made around the 25th of the month with OCPs.

Performance Rating: ****

Ameritrust Corp. (NASDAQ:AMTR)
P.O. Box 6477
Cleveland, OH 44101
(216) 737-5742

Business Profile: Major Midwestern multibank holding company with principal headquarters in Ohio and Indiana.

Plan Specifics:
- Partial dividend reinvestment is not available.
- No Discount.
- OCP: $10 to $5000 per quarter.

- Stock is purchased monthly with OCPs.
- Selling costs are a 10 to 25 cents brokerage commission and a $5 termination fee.
- Approximately 2500 shareholders in the plan.

Performance Rating: **

Amoco Corp. (NYSE:AN)
c/o Chase Manhattan
P.O. Box 283, Bowling Green Sta.
New York, NY 10004
(312) 856-7986

Business Profile: Largest holder of natural gas reserves in North America. Refines, markets, and transports crude oil and natural gas worldwide.

Plan Specifics:
- Partial dividend reinvestment is not available.
- No Discount.
- OCP: $50 to $5000 per month.
- Purchasing fees are 5 percent of amount invested up to a maximum of $3 plus brokerage commission, which is about 1 percent of amount invested.
- Selling costs are $1 service charge plus broker commissions and transfer taxes.
- Stock purchased monthly with OCPs.

Performance Rating: ****

AMP, Inc. (NYSE:AMP)
c/o Manufacturers Hanover
P.O. Box 24935, Church St. Sta.
New York, NY 10249
(717) 780-6498

Business Profile: World's largest supplier of electrical and electronic connection devices.

Plan Specifics:
- Partial dividend reinvestment is not available.
- No Discount.
- OCP: $10 to $2000 per month.
- Selling costs may include brokerage fees.
- Company purchases stock monthly with OCPs.

Performance Rating: ****

AmSouth Bancorp. (NYSE:ASO)
P.O. Box 11007
Birmingham, AL 35288
(205) 583-4439

Business Profile: Alabama's largest bank holding company providing financial services to commercial and retail clients.

Plan Specifics:
- Partial dividend reinvestment is available.
- No Discount.
- OCP: $10 to $5000 per quarter.
- $5 fee for each sale of shares from account as well as small broker fees.
- Purchases stock quarterly with OCPs.
- Approximately 3000 shareholders in the plan.

Performance Rating: ***

AmVestors Financial Corp.
(NASDAQ:AVFC)
c/o Commerce Bank & Trust
P.O. Box 5049
Topeka, KS 66605-9990
(913) 232-6945

Business Profile: Insurance holding company selling single-premium deferred annuities and single-premium whole life insurance.

Plan Specifics:
- Partial dividend reinvestment is not available.
- No Discount.
- OCP: $25 to $2500 per quarter.
- Purchasing fees are very nominal brokerage fees.
- Selling costs are very nominal brokerage commission and $1 service fee for withdrawal.
- Stock is purchased quarterly with the OCPs.
- Approximately 4000 shareholders in the plan.

Performance Rating: **

Angeles Mortgage Investment Trust (ASE:ANM)
P.O. Box 366
Boston, MA 02101
(800) 426-5523   (800) 421-4374

Business Profile: Real estate investment trust.

Plan Specifics:
- Partial dividend reinvestment is available.
- No Discount.
- OCP: $25 to no maximum per month.
- Purchasing costs are nominal brokerage fees.
- Selling costs are brokerage commissions plus a $2.50 fee.
- Approximately 4000 shareholders in the plan.

Performance Rating: **

Angeles Participating Mortgage Trust (ASE:APT)
P.O. Box 366
Boston, MA 02101
(800) 426-5523   (800) 421-4374

Business Profile: Real estate investment trust making participating mortgage loans on factory-direct shopping malls.

Plan Specifics:

- Partial dividend reinvestment is available.
- No Discount.
- OCP: $25 to no maximum per month.
- Purchasing fees are the pro rata portion of the brokerage commissions.
- Selling fees include brokerage commission plus $2.50 service fee.
- Approximately 4000 shareholders in the plan.

Performance Rating: **

Anheuser-Busch Companies, Inc. (NYSE:BUD)
c/o First Chicago Trust-NY
P.O. Box 3506, Church St. Sta.
New York, NY 10008-3506
(212) 791-6422 (314) 577-2039

Business Profile: Largest brewer of beer in United States. Significant operations in bakery items and theme parks.

Plan Specifics:

- Partial dividend reinvestment is not available.
- No Discount.
- OCP: $25 to $5000 per month.
- Stock is purchased around the 9th of the month with OCPs.
- Selling costs are brokerage commission and any other costs of sale, if incurred.

Performance Rating: ****

Aon Corp. (NYSE:AOC)
c/o First Nat'l Bank Chicago
1 First Nat'l Plaza, Suite 0128
Chicago, IL 60670
(312) 407-4660

Business Profile: Insurance holding company writing accident and health, life, and specialty property-casualty insurance.

Plan Specifics:

- Partial dividend reinvestment is not available.
- No Discount.
- OCP: $20 to $1000 per month.
- Stock is purchased monthly with OCPs.
- Selling costs are broker fees.

Performance Rating: ***

Apache Corp. (NYSE:APA)
1700 Lincoln St. #1900
Denver, CO 80203-4519
(303) 837-5000

Business Profile: Independent oil and gas company occupied in exploration, production, and marketing crude oil and natural gas.

Plan Specifics:

- Partial dividend reinvestment is available.
- No Discount.
- OCP: $50 to $5000 per quarter.
- Stock is purchased monthly with OCPs.
- Company will buy back from shareholders less than 100 shares without charging a fee, otherwise participant pays normal brokerage fees.
- Approximately 4148 shareholders in the plan.

Performance Rating: **

Aquarion Co. (NYSE:WTR)
835 Main St.
Bridgeport, CT 06601
(203) 367-6621

Business Profile: Holding company providing water service to parts of Connecticut. Operations in forest products and real estate.

Plan Specifics:
- Partial dividend reinvestment is not available.
- 5 percent discount on reinvested dividends.
- OCP: $10 to $5000 per quarter.
- No selling costs.
- Company purchases stock at least quarterly, and most likely more frequently, with OCPs.
- Approximately 2300 shareholders in the plan.

Performance Rating: **

ARCO Chemical Co. (NYSE:RCM)
c/o First Chicago Trust-NY
P.O. Box 3506, Church St. Sta.
New York, NY 10008-3506
(212) 791-6422   (215) 359-2000

Business Profile: Produces specialty chemicals including propylene oxide, styrene monomer and polymers, and oxygenated fuels.

Plan Specifics:
- Partial dividend reinvestment is not available.
- No Discount.
- OCP: $10 to $3000 per quarter.
- Stock is purchased quarterly with OCPs.
- Selling costs are a $5 handling charge, brokerage commission, and any other cost of sale.

Performance Rating: ***

Arkla, Inc. (NYSE:ALG)
c/o Ameritrust
P.O. Box 2320
Dallas, TX 75221-2320
(318) 429-2925

Business Profile: Explores for, produces, transports, and distributes natural gas in south central United States.

Plan Specifics:
- Partial dividend reinvestment is not available.
- No Discount.
- OCP: $10 to no maximum.
- Purchasing fees include brokerage fees plus 5 percent on each investment up to $2.50 maximum.
- Selling costs include $1 service fee plus 5 to 6 cents per share.
- Stock is purchased quarterly with OCPs and more often if enough funds accumulate to purchase on a more regular basis.

Performance Rating: **

Armstrong World Industries, Inc.
 (NYSE:ACK)
P.O. Box 3001
Lancaster, PA 17604
(717) 396-2810

Business Profile: Leading residential and commercial manufacturer of interior furnishings, including floor coverings, building products, and furniture.

Plan Specifics:
- Partial dividend reinvestment is not available.
- No Discount.
- OCP: $50 to $3000 per quarter.
- Stock is purchased quarterly with OCPs.
- Selling costs are approximately 9

cents per share and a $3 handling fee.

- Approximately 2300 shareholders in the plan.

Performance Rating: ***

Arrow Financial Corp. (NASDAQ:AROW)
250 Glen St.
Glens Falls, NY 12801
(518) 793-4121

Business Profile: Regional banking company with offices in New York and Vermont.

Plan Specifics:
- Partial dividend reinvestment is not available.
- No Discount.
- OCP: $1000 to $3000 per quarter.
- Selling costs are brokerage commission.
- Company purchases stock monthly with OCPs.

Performance Rating: **

Arvin Industries, Inc. (NYSE:ARV)
c/o Harris Trust & Savings
P.O. Box 755
Chicago, IL 60690
(812) 379-3000   (312) 461-2339

Business Profile: Manufacturer of automotive parts to original equipment and replacement markets.

Plan Specifics:
- Partial dividend reinvestment is not available.
- No Discount.
- OCP: $25 to $1000 per month.
- Purchasing fees include 5 percent service charge for each amount invested up to a maximum $2.50 plus pro rata brokerage fees.

- Selling fees are brokerage fees and commissions.

Performance Rating: **

ASARCO, Inc. (NYSE:AR)
c/o First Chicago Trust-NY
P.O. Box 3506
New York, NY 10008-3506
(212) 791-6422

Business Profile: Operations in copper, silver, and other metals, as well as specialty chemicals.

Plan Specifics:
- Partial dividend reinvestment is available.
- No Discount.
- OCP: $25 to $1000 per month.
- Stock is purchased monthly with OCPs.
- Selling costs are brokerage commission and any other cost of sale.

Performance Rating: **

Ashland Oil, Inc. (NYSE:ASH)
Attn: Stock Transfer Dept.
P.O. Box 12328
Lexington, KY 40582
(606) 264-7165   (606) 329-3333

Business Profile: Leading petroleum refiner providing motor oil and chemicals.

Plan Specifics:
- Partial dividend reinvestment is not available.
- No Discount.
- OCP: $10 to $5000 per quarter.
- Stock is purchased about eight times a year with OCPs.
- Selling costs are brokerage commissions.
- 9900 shareholders in plan.

Performance Rating: **

Asset Investors Corp. (NYSE:AIC)
3600 South Yosemite
Denver, CO 80237
(303) 793-2703

Business Profile: Real estate investment trust.

Plan Specifics:
- Partial dividend reinvestment is not available.
- No Discount.
- OCP: $50 to $10,000 per quarter, in increments of $10.
- Fees for purchasing include service charge of 5 percent of the amount reinvested and 5 percent of each OCP with a maximum of $2.50 per transaction, plus broker's fee.
- Selling costs are brokerage commissions and a $5 termination charge.
- Company will reinvest OCPs within 30 days of receipt.

Performance Rating: **

Associated Banc-Corp.
 (NASDAQ:ASBC)
c/o Harris Trust & Savings Bank
P.O. Box A3309
Chicago, IL 60690
(312) 461-5545   (414) 433-3166

Business Profile: Fourth largest bank holding company in Wisconsin controlling commercial banks in Illinois and Wisconsin.

Plan Specifics:
- Partial dividend reinvestment is available.
- No Discount.
- OCP: not available.
- No selling fees.
- Approximately 1800 shareholders in the plan.

Performance Rating: ***

Atlanta Gas Light Co. (NYSE:ATG)
c/o Wachovia Bank & Trust Co.
P.O. Box 3001
Winston-Salem, NC 27102
(404) 584-3794

Business Profile: Largest natural gas utility in the southeastern portion of the United States.

Plan Specifics:
- Partial dividend reinvestment is available.
- No Discount.
- OCP: $25 to $5000 per month.
- Stock is generally purchased monthly on the 1st business day of the month with OCPs.
- Selling costs include broker fees and transfer taxes.

Performance Rating: ***

Atlantic Energy, Inc. (NYSE:ATE)
P.O. Box 1334
1199 Black Horse Pike
Pleasantville, NJ 08232
(609) 645-4506

Business Profile: Public utility holding company located in New Jersey.

Plan Specifics:
- Partial dividend reinvestment is not available.
- No Discount.
- OCP: no minimum to $30,000 per year.
- Fees include small brokerage commissions when stock purchased on open market.
- Stock is purchased monthly with OCPs.
- Selling costs are brokerage fees if sold on open market but not for shares sold to other participants in plan.

- Approximately 15,073 shareholders in the plan.

Performance Rating: ***

Atlantic Richfield Co. (NYSE:ARC)
c/o First Chicago Trust-NY
P.O. Box 3506, Church St. Sta.
New York, NY 10008-3506
(212) 791-6422   (213) 486-3593

Business Profile: Refines, produces, and markets crude oil and natural gas.

Plan Specifics:
- Partial dividend reinvestment is available.
- No Discount.
- OCP: $10 to $60,000 per year.
- Stock is purchased around the 20th day of the month with OCPs.
- Selling costs are brokerage commission, transfer taxes, and any other costs of sale.
- Preferred stock dividends are eligible for reinvestment for additional common under the plan.

Performance Rating: ****

Atmos Energy Corp. (NYSE:ATO)
P.O. Box 650205
Dallas, TX 75265-0205
(214) 934-9227

Business Profile: Supplies natural gas to residential, industrial, agricultural, and commercial users in parts of Kentucky, Louisiana, and Texas.

Plan Specifics:
- Partial dividend reinvestment is available.
- No Discount.
- OCP: $10 to $60,000 per year.
- Stock is purchased monthly with OCPs.

- Selling costs are brokerage commissions and any other costs of sale.
- Approximately 1945 shareholders in plan.

Performance Rating: ***

Avery Dennison Corp. (NYSE:AVY)
c/o Security Pacific
P.O. Box 3546
Los Angeles, CA 90051-9933
(800) 752-9833

Business Profile: Worldwide leader in self-adhesive base materials, labels, and office products.

Plan Specifics:
- Partial dividend reinvestment is not available.
- No Discount.
- OCP: $25 to $3000 per month.
- Company purchases stock monthly with OCPs.
- No selling costs.
- Approximately 1900 shareholders in the plan.

Performance Rating: **

Avnet, Inc. (NYSE:AVT)
80 Cutter Mill Rd.
Great Neck, NY 11021
(516) 466-7000   (800) 524-4458

Business Profile: Distributes electronic components and computer parts. Manufactures and distributes television antennas and electrical motors.

Plan Specifics:
- Partial dividend reinvestment is not available.
- No Discount.
- OCP: $10 to no maximum, in increments of $10 per payment.

- Stock is purchased eight times a year with OCPs.
- Selling costs are $1 handling charge, brokerage commissions, and any other cost of sale.

Performance Rating: *******

Avon Products, Inc. (NYSE:AVP)
c/o First Chicago Trust-NY
P.O. Box 3506
New York, NY 10008-3506
(212) 791-6422   (212) 546-6015

Business Profile: Door-to-door marketer of cosmetics, perfumes, and toiletries.

Plan Specifics:
- Partial dividend reinvestment is not available.
- No Discount.
- OCP: $10 to $5000 per month.
- Stock is purchased on the 1st business day of the month with OCPs.
- Selling costs are brokerage commission and any other cost of sale.

Performance Rating: ******

Baker Hughes, Inc. (NYSE:BHI)
c/o First Chicago Trust Co.-NY
P.O. Box 3506, Church St. Sta.
New York, NY 10008-3506
(212) 791-6422   (713) 439-8668

Business Profile: Manufactures equipment used in drilling oil and gas wells. Produces equipment for pumping and treating liquids.

Plan Specifics:
- Partial dividend reinvestment is not available.
- No Discount.
- OCP: $10 to $1000 per quarter.
- Stock is purchased quarterly with OCPs.

- Selling costs are approximately 10 cents per share plus a $5 service charge.

Performance Rating: ******

Ball Corp. (NYSE:BLL)
P.O. Box 2407
Muncie, IN 47307-0407
(317) 747-6472

Business Profile: Manufactures and markets packaging, industrial and consumer products, and provides aerospace systems and professional services to the federal sector.

Plan Specifics:
- Partial dividend reinvestment is not available.
- 5 percent discount on reinvested dividends.
- OCP: $25 to $3000 per quarter.
- Stock is purchased quarterly with OCPs.
- Selling costs are brokerage commissions plus transfer taxes.
- Approximately 2350 shareholders in plan.

Performance Rating: *******

Baltimore Bancorp (NYSE:BBB)
c/o Manufacturers Hanover
P.O. Box 24850, Church St. Sta.
New York, NY 10249
(301) 244-3360

Business Profile: Maryland bank holding company operating commercial and retail banking.

Plan Specifics:
- Partial dividend reinvestment is not available.
- 5 percent discount on reinvested dividends.
- OCP: $50 to $5000 per quarter.

- Stock is purchased monthly with OCPs.
- Must go through own broker to sell shares.

Performance Rating: **

Baltimore Gas and Electric Co. (NYSE:BGE)
Shareholder Services
P.O. Box 1642, Charles Center
Baltimore, MD 21203-1642
(800) 258-0499

Business Profile: Electric and gas utility serving central Maryland.

Plan Specifics:
- Partial dividend reinvestment is available.
- No Discount.
- OCP: $10 to $6000 per quarter.
- Stock is purchased monthly with OCPs.
- Purchasing fees are generally around 5 cents per share.
- Must go through own broker to sell shares.
- One third of common shareholders are in the plan.

Performance Rating: ****

Banc One Corp. (NYSE:ONE)
111 Monument Circle
Indianapolis, IN 46277
(317) 639-8110

Business Profile: Major bank holding company in Ohio deals in retail banking, including extensive credit card processing operations.

Plan Specifics:
- Partial dividend reinvestment is not available.
- No Discount.
- OCP: $10 to $5000 per quarter.

- Selling costs may include brokerage fees and $1 liquidation fee.
- Company purchases stock quarterly with OCPs.

Performance Rating: ****

Bancorp Hawaii, Inc. (NYSE:BOH)
P.O. Box 2900
Honolulu, HI 96846-6000
(808) 537-8239

Business Profile: Holding company for the largest commercial bank in Hawaii.

Plan Specifics:
- Partial dividend reinvestment is available.
- 5 percent discount on reinvested dividends.
- OCP: $25 to $5000 per quarter.
- Company purchases stock on the 10th business day of each month with OCPs.
- Approximately 2700 shareholders in the plan.
- Selling costs include brokerage commissions, applicable taxes, and service charges.
- Hawaii state residents may make initial purchases of stock directly through the company (minimum initial investment $250).

Performance Rating: ****

Bangor Hydro-Electric Co. (NASDAQ:BANG)
P.O. Box 1599
33 State St.
Bangor, ME 04401-1599
(207) 945-5621

Business Profile: Second largest electric utility in Maine, serving the eastern portion of the state.

Plan Specifics:
* Partial dividend reinvestment is available.
* No Discount.
* OCP: $25 to $25,000 per year.
* Selling cost is brokerage commission.
* Stock is purchased quarterly with OCPs.
* Preferred dividends may be reinvested for additional common shares under the plan.
* Approximately 3000 shareholders in the plan.

Performance Rating: **

Bank of Boston Corp. (NYSE:BKB)
c/o Bank of Boston
P.O. Box 1681
Boston, MA 02105
(617) 929-5445   (617) 575-2900

Business Profile: Bank holding company in New England region.

Plan Specifics:
* Partial dividend reinvestment is available.
* 3 percent discount on reinvested dividends.
* OCP: $25 to $5000 per month.
* Stock is purchased monthly with OCPs.
* Selling costs are brokerage commission and transfer taxes.
* Company will only sell up to 1000 shares and will sell roughly within 10 trading days after receiving request to sell.
* Approximately 6974 shareholders in the plan.
* Preferred stock dividends may be reinvested for additional common shares under the plan.

Performance Rating: **

Bank of Granite Corp.
(NASDAQ:GRAN)
Investor Relations Dept.
P.O. Box 128
Granite Falls, NC 28630
(704) 396-3141

Business Profile: North Carolina bank holding company.

Plan Specifics:
* Partial dividend reinvestment is not available.
* No Discount.
* OCP: not available.
* Must go through own broker to sell shares.
* Approximately 650 shareholders in the plan.

Performance Rating: NR

Bank of New England Corp.
(NYSE:NEB)
28 State Street
Boston, MA 02109
(617) 742-4000

Business Profile: New England regional bank holding company.

Plan Specifics:
* Partial dividend reinvestment is available.
* No Discount.
* OCP: $50 to $5000 per quarter.
* Selling costs include brokerage commissions.
* Company purchases stock monthly with OCPs.

Performance Rating: *

**Bank of New York Co., Inc.
(NYSE:BK)
Attn: Dividend Reinvestment
P.O. Box 11260, Church St. Sta.
New York, NY 10277-0760
(800) 524-4458**

Business Profile: Commercial and retail banking in New York City and suburbs. Active in securities clearing and processing.

Plan Specifics:
- Partial dividend reinvestment is not available.
- No Discount.
- OCP: $25 to $3000 per quarter.
- Selling costs include brokerage fees and $2.50 service fee per transaction.
- Company purchases stock monthly with OCPs.
- Interest on debt securities is eligible for reinvestment for additional common shares under the plan.

Performance Rating: **

**Bank South Corp. (NASDAQ:BKSO)
P.O. Box 3144, MC 47
Atlanta, GA 30302
(404) 529-4238   (404) 521-7071**

Business Profile: Multibank holding company headquartered in Atlanta with offices throughout Georgia.

Plan Specifics:
- Partial dividend reinvestment is not available.
- No Discount.
- OCP: $25 to $5000 per month.
- No selling fees associated with the plan.
- Company purchases stock monthly with OCPs.

Performance Rating: **

**BankAmerica Corp. (NYSE:BAC)
Bank of America Corporate
Service Center, P.O. Box 37002
San Francisco, CA 94137
(415) 624-4100**

Business Profile: Holding company for two banks in California and Washington.

Plan Specifics:
- Partial dividend reinvestment is available.
- 1 percent discount on reinvested dividends and OCPs.
- OCP: $100 to $20,000 per month.
- Stock is purchased monthly with OCPs.
- Selling cost is approximately 6 cents a share.

Performance Rating: **

**Bankers First Corp.
(NASDAQ:BNKF)
Attn: Office of the Secretary
945 Broad St.
Augusta, GA 30901
(404) 823-3200   (212) 791-6422**

Business Profile: Georgia-based savings and loan institution.

Plan Specifics:
- Partial dividend reinvestment is not available.
- 5 percent discount on reinvested dividends.
- OCP: $50 to $5000 per quarter.
- Stock is purchased around the 15th day of the month with OCPs.
- Selling costs are brokerage commission and any transfer taxes.

Performance Rating: NR

**Bankers Trust New York Corp.
(NYSE:BT)
P.O. Box 9050
Church Street Sta.
New York, NY 10249
(800) 221-4096**

Business Profile: Bank holding company. Concentrates efforts on commercial services with significant international business.

Plan Specifics:
- Partial dividend reinvestment is available.
- No Discount.
- OCP: $25 to $5000 per month.
- Stock is purchased monthly with OCPs.
- Selling costs are brokerage fees and transfer taxes.
- Approximately 10,000 shareholders in the plan.

Performance Rating: *****

**Banks of Mid-America, Inc.
(NASDAQ:BOMA)
c/o Liberty Nat'l Bank
P.O. Box 25848
Oklahoma City, OK 73125
(405) 231-6711**

Business Profile: Oklahoma-based multibank holding company.

Plan Specifics:
- Partial dividend reinvestment is available.
- 5 percent discount on both reinvested dividends and OCPs.
- OCP: $200 to $20,000 per quarter.
- Stock is purchased monthly with OCPs.
- Selling costs are brokerage commissions and any transfer taxes.

Performance Rating: ******

**Banta Corp. (NASDAQ:BNTA)
c/o First Wisconsin Trust Co.
P.O. Box 2054
Milwaukee, WI 53201
(414) 765-5000   (414) 722-7777**

Business Profile: Provides printing and graphic arts services.

Plan Specifics:
- Partial dividend reinvestment is not available.
- No Discount.
- OCP: $10 to $1000 per month.
- Stock is purchased quarterly with OCPs. If they have enough payments to purchase 100 shares, they will purchase mid-quarter.
- Minimal, if any, charges for selling shares.

Performance Rating: *******

**Banyan Short Term Income Trust
(ASE:VST)
c/o Mellon Bank Transfer Svcs.
P.O. Box 444
Pittsburgh, PA 15230
(412) 236-8000   (800) 637-3820**

Business Profile: Real estate investment trust.

Plan Specifics:
- Partial dividend reinvestment is not available.
- No Discount.
- OCP: not available.
- Purchasing fees are approximately 10 cents per share.
- Must sell shares through own broker.

Performance Rating: *****

Bard, C. R., Inc. (NYSE:BCR)
c/o First Chicago Trust Co.-NY
P.O. Box 3506, Church St. Sta.
New York, NY 10008-3506
(201) 277-8000

Business Profile: Supplies medical, diagnostic, and surgical products and is the largest manufacturer of urological products.

Plan Specifics:
- Partial dividend reinvestment is available.
- No Discount.
- OCP: $10 to $2500 per month.
- Stock is purchased monthly with OCPs.
- Selling costs are brokerage costs and any other costs of sale.
- Approximately 1992 shareholders in plan.

Performance Rating: ****

Barnes Group, Inc. (NYSE:B)
123 Main St.
Bristol, CT 06010
(203) 583-7070   (800) 288-9541

Business Profile: World's largest producer of precision mechanical springs with significant operations in replacement parts distribution.

Plan Specifics:
- Partial dividend reinvestment is not available.
- No Discount.
- OCP: $10 to $10,000 per quarter.
- Stock is purchased at least quarterly with OCPs.
- Selling costs may include brokerage fees.

Performance Rating: ***

Barnett Banks, Inc. (NYSE:BBI)
c/o Investor Relations Dept.
P.O. Box 40789
Jacksonville, FL 32203-0789
(904) 791-7720

Business Profile: Largest bank holding company in Florida.

Plan Specifics:
- Partial dividend reinvestment is not available.
- No Discount.
- OCP: $25 to $10,000 per month.
- Selling costs are brokerage fees plus any transfer tax.
- Company purchases stock around the 1st business day of the month with OCPs.
- Approximately 7123 shareholders in the plan.

Performance Rating: ***

Bausch & Lomb, Inc. (NYSE:BOL)
Shareholder Relations
P.O. Box 54, 1 Lincoln First Sq.
Rochester, NY 14601-0054
(716) 338-6025

Business Profile: Manufacturer of health-care products and optical devices. Leading producer of contact lenses and related accessories.

Plan Specifics:
- Partial dividend reinvestment is not available.
- No Discount.
- OCP: $25 to $5000 per month.
- Stock is purchased on the 1st business day of each month with OCPs.
- Selling costs are brokerage fees and

transfer taxes plus a nominal service fee.
- Approximately 1700 shareholders in the plan.

Performance Rating: ********

Baxter International, Inc.
(NYSE:BAX)
Stockholder Services Dept.
One Baxter Parkway
Deerfield, IL 60015
(708) 948-4913

Business Profile: Worldwide leading supplier and marketer of hospital products and medical specialties.

Plan Specifics:
- Partial dividend reinvestment is not available.
- No Discount.
- OCP: $25 to $1000 per month.
- Stock is purchased monthly with OCPs.
- Cost of selling shares purchased with dividends or OCPs is 10 cents.

Performance Rating: ********

Bay State Gas Co. (NYSE:BGC)
c/o 1st Nat'l Bank of Boston
P.O. Box 1681
Boston, MA 02105
(617) 828-8650

Business Profile: Natural gas distributor in Massachusetts and neighboring areas.

Plan Specifics:
- Partial dividend reinvestment is available.
- 2 percent discount on reinvested dividends and OCPs on shares made available from the company.
- OCP: $10 to $5000 per quarter.
- Selling costs are brokerage fees.

- Company purchases stock monthly with OCPs.
- Approximately 2800 shareholders in the plan.

Performance Rating: *******

BayBanks, Inc. (NASDAQ:BBNK)
Shareholder Relations
175 Federal Street
Boston, MA 02110
(617) 482-1040

Business Profile: Multibank holding company headquartered in Boston.

Plan Specifics:
- Partial dividend reinvestment is not available.
- No Discount.
- OCP: $10 to $1000 per month.
- Stock is purchased monthly with OCPs.
- Purchasing fees are low brokerage commissions.
- Selling costs are approximately 15 cents per share plus a handling fee of 5 percent on net proceeds not to exceed $2.50.

Performance Rating: ******

BB&T Financial Corp.
(NASDAQ:BBTF)
P.O. Box 1847
Wilson, NC 27894-1847
(919) 399-4291

Business Profile: Bank holding company serving clients in North and South Carolinas.

Plan Specifics:
- Partial dividend reinvestment is available.
- 5 percent discount on reinvested dividends; company is reexamining the discount policy.

- OCP: $25 to $2000 per month.
- Stock is purchased once a month with OCPs.
- Selling costs are brokerage commission, transfer taxes, and other associated costs.
- Company will sell shares within 10 business days of receipt of sell request.
- Approximately 6157 shareholders in the plan.

Performance Rating: ***

BCE, Inc. (NYSE:BCE)
c/o Montreal Trust Co.
P.O. Box 310, Sta. B
Montreal, Quebec H3B 3J7 Canada
(514) 982-7555

Business Profile: Holding company for leading provider of telecommunication services in Canada.

Plan Specifics:
- Partial dividend reinvestment is not available.
- No Discount.
- OCP: no minimum to $20,000 (Canadian) per year.
- Stock is purchased monthly with OCPs.
- Selling fee is roughly 3 cents per share.
- Dividends paid on preferred shares of BCE and interest paid on Bell Canada bonds may be used to purchase additional common.
- Approximately 132,841 shareholders in the plan.

Performance Rating: ****

Becton, Dickinson & Co.
(NYSE:BDX)
c/o First Chicago Trust-NY
P.O. Box 3506, Church St. Sta.
New York, NY 10008-3506
(212) 791-6422   (201) 848-6800

Business Profile: Produces and markets medical and diagnostic products.

Plan Specifics:
- Partial dividend reinvestment is not available.
- No Discount.
- OCP: $25 to $3000 per quarter.
- Stock is purchased approximately every 45 days with OCPs.
- Selling costs are brokerage commission and related expenses.

Performance Rating: ****

Bell Atlantic Corp. (NYSE:BEL)
c/o American Transtech
P.O. Box 44027
Jacksonville, FL 32232-4027
(800) 631-2355

Business Profile: Telephone holding company supplying exchange telephone service to mid-Atlantic states.

Plan Specifics:
- Partial dividend reinvestment is available.
- No Discount.
- OCP: $100 to $50,000 per year.
- Stock is purchased on 1st business day of every month with OCPs.
- 50-share minimum in order to enter plan.
- Selling costs are 6 to 10 cents per share broker fees.
- Participants are charged $1 fee per quarter.
- Company will sell up to 99 shares

and any fractional shares for shareholders.

Performance Rating: ****

BellSouth Corp. (NYSE:BLS)
c/o American Transtech
P.O. Box 44029
Jacksonville, FL 32231
(800) 631-6001

Business Profile: Second-largest telephone holding company providing local exchange service to southeastern states.

Plan Specifics:
- Partial dividend reinvestment is available.
- No Discount.
- OCP: $50 to $50,000 per year.
- Selling costs include brokerage fees and any transfer taxes.
- Will sell up to 99 shares and any fractional shares for shareholders.
- Company purchases stock monthly with OCPs.

Performance Rating: ****

Bemis Co., Inc. (NYSE:BMS)
c/o Norwest Bank Minnesota
P.O. Box 738
South St. Paul, MN 55075-0738
(612) 340-6000

Business Profile: Manufactures consumer and industrial flexible packaging products and pressure-sensitive materials.

Plan Specifics:
- Partial dividend reinvestment is not available.
- No Discount.
- OCP: $25 to $10,000 per quarter.
- Company purchases stock quarterly with OCPs.

Performance Rating: ***

Beneficial Corp. (NYSE:BNL)
First Chicago Trust-NY
P.O. Box 3506, Church St. Sta.
New York, NY 10008-3506
(212) 791-6422   (302) 798-0800

Business Profile: Consumer-oriented financial institution providing loans to citizens for education, home improvement, and debt consolidation.

Plan Specifics:
- Partial dividend reinvestment is not available.
- No Discount.
- OCP: $10 to $1000 per month.
- Stock is purchased monthly with OCPs.
- Selling costs are brokerage commission and other costs of sale.
- Preferred dividends are eligible for reinvestment for additional common shares under the plan.

Performance Rating: ***

Berkshire Gas Co. (NASDAQ:BGAS)
Attn: Sec. of Dividend Reinvestment
115 Cheshire Rd.
Pittsfield, MA 01201
(413) 442-1511

Business Profile: Massachusetts public utility produces and markets natural gas for residential, commercial, and industrial markets.

Plan Specifics:
- Partial dividend reinvestment is available.
- No Discount.
- OCP: $15 per month to $3000 per quarter.
- Stock is purchased on 15th of each month with OCPs.
- Selling costs are 5 percent on amount invested with a $5 maximum plus brokerage commissions.
- 10 shares to enroll.

Performance Rating: **

Bethlehem Steel Corp. (NYSE:BS)
c/o First Chicago Trust-NY
P.O. Box 3506, Church St. Sta.
New York, NY 10008-3506
(212) 791-6422   (215) 694-2424

Business Profile: Produces steel and steel-related products.

Plan Specifics:
- Partial dividend reinvestment is not available.
- No Discount.
- OCP: $10 to $3000 per month.
- Stock is purchased around the 1st day of the month with OCPs.
- Selling costs are brokerage commission and any other cost of sale.

Performance Rating: **

Beverly Enterprises (NYSE:BEV)
c/o First Interstate of CA
P.O. Box 60975, Terminal Annex
Los Angeles, CA 90060
(818) 577-6111   (501) 452-6712

Business Profile: Largest owner of nursing homes in United States. Involvements in retirement living and home health care units.

Plan Specifics:
- Partial dividend reinvestment is available.
- 5 percent discount on reinvested dividends (company is not currently paying a dividend).
- OCP: not available.
- Must go through a broker to sell shares.

Performance Rating: **

Black & Decker Corp. (NYSE:BDK)
c/o First Chicago Trust Co.-NY
P.O. Box 3506, Church St. Sta.
New York, NY 10008-3506
(212) 791-6422

Business Profile: Leading maker of power tools and household products.

Plan Specifics:
- Partial dividend reinvestment is not available.
- No Discount.
- OCP: $10 to $3000 per month.
- Stock is purchased monthly with OCPs.
- Selling costs are a $5 handling charge, brokerage commissions, and any other costs of sale.
- Approximately 5823 shareholders in the plan.

Performance Rating: **

Black Hills Corp. (NYSE:BKH)
c/o Manufacturers Hanover
P.O. Box 24850, Church St. Sta.
New York, NY 10249
(605) 348-1700

Business Profile: Supplies electricity to customers in South Dakota, Wyoming, and Montana.

Plan Specifics:
- Partial dividend reinvestment is not available.
- No Discount.
- OCP: $100 to $3000 per quarter.
- Purchasing fees include brokerage commissions plus a charge of $1.50 per dividend reinvestment and $5 per OCPs.
- Company purchases stock quarterly with OCPs.
- Selling costs are brokerage commissions and $15 termination fee.

Performance Rating: ***

Block, H & R, Inc. (NYSE:HRB)
c/o Boatmen's Trust Co.
P.O. Box 14768, 510 Locust St.
St. Louis, MO 63178
(816) 753-6900

Business Profile: Largest preparer of federal income tax returns. Provides temporary personnel throughout offices in the United States.

Plan Specifics:

* Partial dividend reinvestment is not available.
* No Discount.
* OCP: $25 to $2500 per quarter.
* Stock is purchased quarterly with OCPs.
* Purchasing fee is very nominal broker commission.
* Selling cost is brokerage fees.

Performance Rating: ***

Blount, Inc. (ASE:BLT.A)
c/o The Bank of Boston
P.O. Box 644
Boston, MA 02102-9976
(205) 244-4000   (617) 929-5445

Business Profile: International construction company. Manufactures cutting chain for chain saws and tree harvesting equipment.

Plan Specifics:

* Partial dividend reinvestment is available.
* 5 percent discount on reinvested dividends.
* OCP: $10 to $25,000 per year.
* Stock is purchased around the 1st business day of the month with OCPs.
* Selling cost is brokerage fees.
* Approximately 500 shareholders in the plan.

Performance Rating: **

BMJ Financial Corp.
(NASDAQ:BMJF)
P.O. Box 1001
243 Route 130
Bordentown, NJ 08505
(609) 298-5500

Business Profile: New Jersey-based bank holding company.

Plan Specifics:

* Partial dividend reinvestment is available.
* 5 percent discount on both reinvested dividends and OCPs.
* OCP: $100 to $2500 per quarter.
* Company invests OCPs around the 10th day of the month.
* Must go through own broker to sell shares.
* 848 shareholders in the plan.

Performance Rating: **

Boatmen's Bancshares, Inc.
(NASDAQ:BOAT)
c/o Boatmen's Trust Co.
P.O. Box 14764
St. Louis, MO 63178-9926
(314) 554-7713

Business Profile: Multibank holding company headquartered in St. Louis. Largest commercial banking firm in Missouri.

Plan Specifics:

* Partial dividend reinvestment is not available.
* No Discount.
* OCP: $100 to $5000 per quarter.
* Stock is purchased quarterly with OCPs.
* Investors must sell full shares through own broker.

Performance Rating: ***

Bob Evans Farms, Inc.
(NASDAQ:BOBE)
Stock Transfer Dept.
P.O. Box 07863
3776 South High St.
Columbus, OH 43207
(614) 491-2225

Business Profile: Owns and operates family-style restaurants concentrated in Ohio, Indiana, Illinois, Michigan, and Florida. Produces pork sausage food items.

Plan Specifics:
- Partial dividend reinvestment is not available.
- No Discount.
- OCP: $10 to no maximum per payment.
- Stock is purchased bimonthly (1st and 15th) with OCPs.
- Purchasing fee is the pro rata share of brokerage commission.
- Selling cost is brokerage commission.
- Approximately 10,000 shareholders in plan.

Performance Rating: *******

Boddie-Noell Restaurant Properties (ASE:BNP)
P.O. Box 1908
Rocky Mount, NC 27802
(919) 937-2000

Business Profile: Real estate investment trust created to acquire Hardee's restaurant properties in North Carolina and Virginia areas.

Plan Specifics:
- Partial dividend reinvestment is not available.
- No Discount.
- OCP: $25 to $3000 per quarter.
- Stock is purchased quarterly with OCPs.
- Purchasing costs include brokerage fees.
- Must sell through a broker.
- About 21 percent of all shareholders are enrolled in the plan.

Performance Rating: ******

Boise Cascade Corp. (NYSE:BCC)
One Jefferson Square
Boise, ID 83728
(208) 384-7590

Business Profile: Important manufacturer of paper, wood products, and building materials.

Plan Specifics:
- Partial dividend reinvestment is not available.
- No Discount.
- OCP: $10 to no maximum per month.
- Purchasing and selling costs are less than 10 cents a share.
- Stock is purchased monthly with OCPs.
- Approximately 11,000 shareholders in the plan.

Performance Rating: *******

Borden, Inc. (NYSE:BN)
277 Park Ave.
New York, NY 10172
(212) 573-4000

Business Profile: Nation's largest supplier of dairy and pasta items. Manufactures food products, nonfood consumer goods, and specialty chemicals.

Plan Specifics:
- Partial dividend reinvestment is not available.
- No Discount.
- OCP: $10 to $10,000 per quarter.
- Selling costs include brokerage commissions, transfer taxes, and banker's fee of $2.50.
- Stock is purchased monthly with OCPs.
- Approximately 4500 shareholders in the plan.

Performance Rating: ********

Boston Bancorp (NASDAQ:SBOS)
460 W. Broadway
Boston, MA 02127
(800) 524-4458

Business Profile: Savings institution serving clients in Boston, MA.

Plan Specifics:
- Partial dividend reinvestment is available.
- No Discount.
- OCP: $100 to $5000 per quarter.
- Minimal, if any, selling costs.
- Stock is purchased quarterly with OCPs.

Performance Rating: **

Boston Edison Co. (NYSE:BSE)
800 Boylston St.
Boston, MA 02199
(617) 424-2000

Business Profile: Electric utility provides electricity to residential, commercial, and industrial customers in Boston and neighboring cities.

Plan Specifics:
- Partial dividend reinvestment is available.
- No Discount.
- OCP: no minimum to $5000 per quarter.
- Stock is purchased quarterly with OCPs.
- Approximately 14,208 shareholders in the plan.
- Selling costs include brokerage fees and transfer tax.
- Selling will be done within 10 trading days after receipt of request.

Performance Rating: **

Bow Valley Industries Ltd.
(ASE:BVI)
P.O. Box 6610
Station D
Calgary, Alberta T2P 3R2 Canada
(403) 261-6100

Business Profile: International natural resource business. Explores and produces oil and natural gas.

Plan Specifics:
- Partial dividend reinvestment is not available.
- 5 percent discount on reinvested dividends (firm is not currently paying a dividend).
- OCP: $250 to $5000 (Canadian) per quarter.
- Must go through own broker to sell.
- Approximately 800 shareholders in the plan.
- Stock is purchased quarterly with OCPs.
- Dividends on preferred shares are also eligible for reinvestment in the plan.
- United States residents will be hit with a 15 percent withholding tax.

Performance Rating: **

Bowater, Inc. (NYSE:BOW)
P.O. Box 4012
One Parklands Dr.
Darien, CT 06820
(203) 656-7200

Business Profile: Major supplier of newsprint in the United States. Also manufactures coated publication paper, market pulp, and computer forms.

Plan Specifics:
- Partial dividend reinvestment is available.

- No Discount.
- OCP: $100 to $5000 per month.
- Stock is purchased monthly with OCPs.
- Approximately 2400 shareholders in plan.
- Selling costs include brokerage fees and transfer tax.

Performance Rating: **

Braintree Savings Bank, The
(NASDAQ:BTSB)
865 Washington St.
Braintree, MA 02184
(617) 843-9100

Business Profile: Massachusetts savings institution.

Plan Specifics:
- Partial dividend reinvestment is available.
- No Discount.
- OCP: $100 to $5000 per quarter.
- Selling costs are broker fees.
- Approximately 400 shareholders in the plan.
- Company purchases stock roughly every 45 days as long as enough funds have accumulated to purchase 100 shares.

Performance Rating: **

Briggs & Stratton Corp.
(NYSE:BGG)
P.O. Box 702
Milwaukee, WI 53201-0702
(414) 259-5333

Business Profile: Worldwide leading producer of gasoline engines for lawn and garden equipment and locks for automobiles and trucks.

Plan Specifics:
- Partial dividend reinvestment is not available.
- No Discount.
- OCP: $25 to $5000 per quarter.
- Selling cost is very nominal.
- Stock is purchased quarterly with OCPs and more frequently if sufficient money is received from shareholders.
- 2927 shareholders in the plan.

Performance Rating: **

Bristol-Myers Squibb Co.
(NYSE:BMY)
345 Park Ave.
New York, NY 10154
(212) 546-4000

Business Profile: Leading producer of pharmaceuticals, including cardiovasculars and antibiotics. Supplier of medical devices and nonprescription health products.

Plan Specifics:
- Partial dividend reinvestment is available.
- No Discount.
- OCP: $10 to $2500 per month.
- Selling fees include brokerage commission and handling charge.
- Stock is purchased around the 1st business day of the month with OCPs.

Performance Rating: ****

British Airways Plc (NYSE:BAB)
c/o First Chicago Trust-NY
P.O. Box 3506, Church St. Sta.
New York, NY 10008-3506
(212) 791-6422   (718) 397-4225

Business Profile: Major international airline.

Plan Specifics:
- Partial dividend reinvestment is not available.
- No Discount.
- OCP: $10 to $60,000 per year.
- Stock is purchased on 6th day of the month with OCPs.
- Purchasing fees are proportionate share of brokerage commission and 5 percent of total funds invested ($2.50 maximum).
- Selling costs are $5 handling fee, brokerage commission.

Performance Rating: ****

**British Petroleum Co. Plc
(NYSE:BP)
200 Public Square
Cleveland, OH 44114-2375
(216) 586-6077**

Business Profile: Major worldwide oil company.

Plan Specifics:
- Partial dividend reinvestment is not available.
- No Discount.
- OCP: $10 to $15,000 per quarter.
- Stock is purchased monthly with OCPs.
- Purchasing and selling fees are brokerage costs.
- Approximately 1850 shareholders in the plan.

Performance Rating: ****

**Brooklyn Union Gas Co. (NYSE:BU)
195 Montague St.
Brooklyn, NY 11201
(718) 403-3334**

Business Profile: Distributor of natural gas in New York City.

Plan Specifics:
- Partial dividend reinvestment is available.

- No Discount.
- OCP: $10 to $5000 per month.
- Selling costs are roughly 6 cents a share.
- Stock is purchased monthly with OCPs.
- Approximately 8000 shareholders in the plan.
- Shareholders of preferred stock and registered bonds may reinvest dividends and interest payments in additional common shares.

Performance Rating: ****

**Brown-Forman Corp. (ASE:BF.B)
P.O. Box 1080
Louisville, KY 40201
(502) 585-1100**

Business Profile: Major provider and importer of wine and spirits with operations in china and crystal.

Plan Specifics:
- Partial dividend reinvestment is not available.
- No Discount.
- OCP: $50 to $3000 per month.
- Purchasing fees include brokerage costs.
- Stock is purchased monthly with OCPs.
- Selling fee includes nominal brokerage commission and $5 service fee.

Performance Rating: ***

**Brown Group, Inc. (NYSE:BG)
P.O. Box 29
8400 Maryland Ave.
St. Louis, MO 63166
(314) 854-4000**

Business Profile: Supplier and retailer of branded footwear and fabric.

Plan Specifics:
- Partial dividend reinvestment is not available.

- No Discount.
- OCP: $25 to $1000 per month.
- Selling costs are brokerage fees.
- Stock is purchased monthly with OCPs.

Performance Rating: **

Browning-Ferris Industries, Inc. (NYSE:BFI)
c/o First Chicago Trust Co.-NY
P.O. Box 3506, Church St. Sta.
New York, NY 10008-3506
(713) 870-7827   (212) 587-6515

Business Profile: Collects, processes, and disposes of solid and liquid waste material for commercial, industrial, and residential customers.

Plan Specifics:
- Partial dividend reinvestment is available.
- No Discount.
- OCP: $25 to $60,000 per year.
- Selling costs are approximately 10 cents per share.
- Company purchases stock around the 10th of the month with OCPs.
- Approximately 4215 shareholders in the plan.

Performance Rating: ****

Brunswick Corp. (NYSE:BC)
One Brunswick Plaza
Skokie, IL 60077-9986
(708) 470-4293

Business Profile: Leading manufacturer of pleasure boats and marine engines. Provides recreation, industrial, and defense products.

Plan Specifics:
- Partial dividend reinvestment is not available.
- No Discount.
- OCP: $10 to $1000 per month.

- Selling costs are approximately 5 cents a share.
- Company purchases stock monthly with OCPs.
- Approximately 10,000 shareholders in the plan.

Performance Rating: **

Brush Wellman, Inc. (NYSE:BW)
1200 Hanna Building
Cleveland, OH 44115
(216) 443-1000

Business Profile: Major worldwide provider of beryllium alloys for electronic market and aerospace applications.

Plan Specifics:
- Partial dividend reinvestment is not available.
- No Discount.
- OCP: $10 to $5000 per quarter.
- Selling costs are a $5 termination charge and brokerage fees.
- Company purchases stock with OCPs within 30 days of receipt if any amount sufficient to purchase at least 100 shares of Brush Wellman stock, or a lesser number if the bank deems practicable, is received.

Performance Rating: ***

BSB Bancorp, Inc. (NASDAQ:BSBN)
58-68 Exchange St.
Binghampton, NY 13902
(607) 779-2525

Business Profile: Multibank holding company based in New York.

Plan Specifics:
- Partial dividend reinvestment is available.
- No Discount.
- OCP: $10 to $5000 per month.

- Stock is purchased monthly with OCPs.
- Selling costs are brokerage commissions.
- Approximately 500 shareholders in the plan.

Performance Rating: NR

Burnham Pacific Properties, Inc. (NYSE:BPP)
610 West Ash St.
San Diego, CA 92101
(619) 236-1555

Business Profile: Real estate investment trust with properties, primarily shopping centers, in Southern California.

Plan Specifics:
- Partial dividend reinvestment is available.
- 5 percent discount on reinvested dividends.
- OCP: not available.
- Must go through own broker to sell.
- 15 percent of shares outstanding are enrolled in the plan.

Performance Rating: **

C & S/Sovran Corp. (NYSE:CVN)
C & S/Sovran Trust Co.
P.O. Box 105555
Atlanta, GA 30348-5555
(800) 772-5564

Business Profile: Provides banking services in the Southeast.

Plan Specifics:
- Partial dividend reinvestment is available.
- 5 percent discount on reinvested dividends.
- OCP: $25 to $36,000 per year.
- Selling costs are brokerage fees.

- Company purchases stock monthly with OCPs.

Performance Rating: **

Cabot Corp. (NYSE:CBT)
P.O. Box 9073
950 Winter St.
Waltham, MA 02254
(617) 890-0200

Business Profile: Provides energy and specialty chemicals, including natural gas, oil, black carbon, and fumed silica.

Plan Specifics:
- Partial dividend reinvestment is available.
- No Discount.
- OCP: $10 to $5000 per quarter.
- Stock is purchased quarterly with OCPs.
- Selling cost is roughly 15 cents a share.
- Approximately 607 shareholders in the plan.

Performance Rating: **

California Real Estate Investment Trust (NYSE:CT)
705 University Ave. #A
Sacramento, CA 95825
(916) 929-5433   (415) 954-9500

Business Profile: Equity real estate investment trust involved in acquisition and management of income-producing properties primarily in Phoenix.

Plan Specifics:
- Partial dividend reinvestment is available.
- 5 percent discount on reinvested dividends.
- OCP: $25 to $3000 per quarter.
- Selling costs are brokerage fees.

- Stock purchased quarterly with OCPs.
- Approximately 800 shareholders in the plan.
- Shareholders may elect participation through IRAs, Keogh Plans, and 401(k) Plans.

Performance Rating: *

California Water Service Co. (NASDAQ:CWTR)
1720 N. First St.
San Jose, CA 95112
(408) 453-8414

Business Profile: Public utility providing water service to California communities.

Plan Specifics:
- Partial dividend reinvestment is available.
- No Discount.
- OCP: not available.
- Must go through own broker to sell.

Performance Rating: ***

Campbell Soup Co. (NYSE:CPB)
First Chicago Trust-NY
P.O. Box 3506, Church St. Sta.
New York, NY 10008-3506
(212) 791-6422

Business Profile: Leading producer of soup, spaghetti sauce, frozen dinners, and bakery products.

Plan Specifics:
- Partial dividend reinvestment is available.
- No Discount.
- OCP: $25 to $1000 per month.
- Stock is purchased around the last business day of the month with OCPs.
- Selling costs are brokerage commis-

sion, $5 handling charge, and any transfer taxes.
- Approximately 8000 shareholders in the plan.

Performance Rating: ****

Canadian Pacific Ltd. (NYSE:CP)
P.O. Box/CP 6042
Station A
Montreal, Quebec H3C 3E4 Canada
(514) 395-5151

Business Profile: Interests in forest products, hotels, oil and gas, and transportation services.

Plan Specifics:
- Partial dividend reinvestment is not available.
- No Discount.
- OCP: not available.
- Must sell through own broker.
- Approximately 25,000 to 30,000 shareholders in the plan.

Performance Rating: **

Capital Holding Corp. (NYSE:CPH)
P.O. Box 32830
Louisville, KY 40232
(502) 560-2000

Business Profile: Life insurance holding company. Writes accident and health, annuity, life, and property-casualty insurance.

Plan Specifics:
- Partial dividend reinvestment is available.
- No Discount.
- OCP: $10 to $5000 per month.
- Company purchases stock monthly with OCPs.
- Selling fees are very nominal, 10 to 12 cents per share.

Performance Rating: ***

Carlisle Companies, Inc.
(NYSE:CSL)
Suite 800
101 S. Salina St.
Syracuse, NY 13202-1330
(315) 474-2500

Business Profile: Operates in a variety of areas ranging from automotive and industrial products to data communications and electronics products.

Plan Specifics:
- Partial dividend reinvestment is not available.
- No Discount.
- OCP: $10 to $3000 per quarter.
- Selling costs are brokerage fees and handling charges.
- Stock is purchased monthly with OCPs.
- Approximately 300 shareholders in the plan.

Performance Rating: ***

Carolina Freight Corp. (NYSE:CAO)
Dividend Reinvestment
P.O. Box 1000
Cherryville, NC 28021
(704) 435-6811

Business Profile: Holding company whose primary operations are for-hire trucking companies providing surface freight hauling services.

Plan Specifics:
- Partial dividend reinvestment is not available.
- No Discount.
- OCP: no minimum or maximum.
- Stock is purchased monthly with OCPs.
- Purchasing and selling fees are brokerage commission.

- Approximately 150 shareholders in plan.

Performance Rating: **

Carolina Power & Light Co.
(NYSE:CPL)
P.O. Box 1551
Raleigh, NC 27602
(800) 662-7232   (800) 334-4374

Business Profile: Electric utility serving North and South Carolinas.

Plan Specifics:
- Partial dividend reinvestment is available.
- No Discount.
- OCP: $25 to $2000 per month.
- Company purchases stock monthly with OCPs.
- Buying and selling costs are approximately 4 1/2 cents per share.
- Approximately 30,000 shareholders in the plan.
- Preferred dividends may be reinvested for common shares under the program.

Performance Rating: ***

Carpenter Technology Corp.
(NYSE:CRS)
c/o First Chicago Trust-NY
P.O. Box 3506, Church St. Sta.
New York, NY 10008-3506
(212) 791-6422   (215) 371-2165

Business Profile: Produces stainless steel, special alloys, and tool steel.

Plan Specifics:
- Partial dividend reinvestment is not available.
- No Discount.
- OCP: $10 to $3000 per quarter.
- Stock is purchased quarterly with OCPs.

- Selling costs may include brokerage fees.

Performance Rating: **

Cascade Natural Gas Corp.
(NYSE:CGC)
222 Fairview Ave. N
Seattle, WA 98109
(206) 624-3900

Business Profile: Distributes natural gas to Washington and Oregon communities.

Plan Specifics:
- Partial dividend reinvestment is not available.
- No Discount.
- OCP: $25 to $3000 per quarter.
- Agent does not sell shares for participants; must go through own broker.
- Stock is purchased quarterly with OCPs.

Performance Rating: **

Caterpillar, Inc. (NYSE:CAT)
100 NE Adams St.
Peoria, IL 61629-7310
(309) 675-4619

Business Profile: Major supplier of construction machinery and equipment. Produces diesel and natural gas engines.

Plan Specifics:
- Partial dividend reinvestment is not available.
- No Discount.
- OCP: $10 to $5000 per month.
- Purchasing fees include service charge of 5 percent on amounts invested (no more than $2.50) plus brokerage fees.

- Company purchases stock monthly with OCPs.
- Selling costs include brokerage fees.
- Approximately 104,000 shares in the plan.

Performance Rating: **

CBI Industries, Inc. (NYSE:CBH)
c/o Shareholder Services
800 Jorie Blvd.
Oak Brook, IL 60522
(708) 572-7366

Business Profile: Construction of metal plate structures and other contracting services; industrial gases including carbon dioxide; oil transport and storage.

Plan Specifics:
- Partial dividend reinvestment is not available.
- No Discount.
- OCP: $25 to $3000 per month.
- Company invests OCPs approximately every month.
- Selling fees are very nominal.
- Less than 2000 shareholders in the plan.

Performance Rating: **

CBS, Inc. (NYSE:CBS)
c/o First Chicago Trust-NY
P.O. Box 3506
New York, NY 10008-3506
(212) 791-6422   (212) 975-4321

Business Profile: Owns major national TV network.

Plan Specifics:
- Partial dividend reinvestment is not available.
- No Discount.
- OCP: $25 to $1000 per month.

- Stock is purchased around the 12th of the month with OCPs.
- Purchasing fees are proportionate share of brokerage commission and 5 percent of total amount invested ($2.50 maximum).
- Selling costs are brokerage commission and related costs.

Performance Rating: ***

CCB Financial Corp.
(NASDAQ:CCBF)
P.O. Box 931
Durham, NC 27702
(919) 683-7777

Business Profile: Bank holding company operating in central North Carolina.

Plan Specifics:
- Partial dividend reinvestment is not available.
- No Discount.
- OCP: $5 to $1500 per month.
- Company purchases stock monthly with OCPs.
- Individual must go through a broker when selling shares.
- Approximately 900 shareholders in the plan.

Performance Rating: ***

CCNB Corp. (NASDAQ:CCNC)
P.O. Box 8874
Camp Hill, PA 17001-8874
(717) 730-2262

Business Profile: South central Pennsylvania-based bank holding organization.

Plan Specifics:
- Partial dividend reinvestment is not available.

- 5 percent discount on reinvested dividends.
- OCP: $25 to $1500 per quarter.
- Stock is purchased quarterly with OCPs.
- Selling costs are broker fees.
- Firm will attempt to sell shares within 5 days of receipt of notice to sell.
- Approximately 1035 shareholders in plan.

Performance Rating: ***

Centel Corp. (NYSE:CNT)
8725 Higgins Rd.
Chicago, IL 60631
(800) 323-2174

Business Profile: Provides telephone and cellular mobile telephone service.

Plan Specifics:
- Partial dividend reinvestment is available.
- No Discount.
- OCP: $25 to $5000 per quarter.
- Nominal, if any, selling costs.
- Company purchases stock monthly with OCPs.
- Approximately 8000 shareholders in the plan.

Performance Rating: ***

Centerbank (NASDAQ:CTBX)
60 North Main St.
Waterbury, CT 06702
(800) 288-9541

Business Profile: Connecticut-based savings bank.

Plan Specifics:
- Partial dividend reinvestment is not available.
- No Discount.
- OCP: $25 to $1000 per quarter.

- $10 termination fee.
- Selling costs include brokerage commissions.
- Company purchases stock monthly with OCPs.

Performance Rating: NR

Centerior Energy Corp. (NYSE:CX)
P.O. Box 94661
Cleveland, OH 44101-4661
(800) 433-7794

Business Profile: Electric utility holding company serving residential, commercial, and industrial customers in Northern Ohio.

Plan Specifics:
- Partial dividend reinvestment is available.
- No Discount.
- OCP: $10 to $40,000 per year.
- Minimal fees for purchasing and selling shares.
- Company purchases stock monthly with OCPs.
- 80,000 shareholders in the plan.
- May reinvest preferred dividends for common shares under the plan.
- Customers may make initial purchase of stock through the company with a minimum payment of $10.

Performance Rating: **

Central & South West Corp.
(NYSE:CSR)
P.O. Box 660164
Dallas, TX 75266-0164
(800) 527-5797

Business Profile: Utility holding company supplying electric and gas services to Texas, Oklahoma, Louisiana, and Arkansas customers.

Plan Specifics:
- Partial dividend reinvestment is available.
- No Discount.
- OCP: $10 to $5000 per quarter.
- Company purchases stock monthly with OCPs.
- Selling fees are very nominal, approximately 5 cents per share.
- If purchases are done on open market, small brokerage charges will be assessed.

Performance Rating: ***

Central Fidelity Banks, Inc.
(NASDAQ:CFBS)
1021 East Cary St.
Richmond, VA 23219
(804) 697-6942

Business Profile: Virginia-based bank holding company.

Plan Specifics:
- Partial dividend reinvestment is not available.
- No Discount.
- OCP: $25 to $10,000 per month.
- Company purchases stock monthly with OCPs.
- Nominal, if any, selling fees.
- Approximately 3000 shareholders in the plan.

Performance Rating: ****

Central Holding Co.
(NASDAQ:CHOL)
c/o NBD, N.A.
P.O. Box 330751
Detroit, MI 48232
(800) 395-1770   (313) 792-7000

Business Profile: Banking concern based in Michigan.

Plan Specifics:
- Partial dividend reinvestment is available.
- No Discount.
- OCP: $25 to $2000 per month.
- Company is not currently paying a dividend.
- Selling costs include $3 termination fee and brokerage costs.
- Stock is purchased monthly with OCPs.

Performance Rating: *

Central Hudson Gas & Electric Corp. (NYSE:CNH)
284 South Ave.
Poughkeepsie, NY 12601-4879
(914) 486-5204   (914) 452-2000

Business Profile: Distributes electricity and gas to residential, commercial, and industrial customers in Hudson River Valley region of New York.

Plan Specifics:
- Partial dividend reinvestment is not available.
- No Discount.
- OCP: $25 to $5000 per quarter.
- Company purchases stock quarterly with OCPs.
- Selling fees are brokerage commissions.

Performance Rating: **

Central Jersey Bancorp (NASDAQ:CJER)
P.O. Box 30
Freehold, NJ 07728
(201) 462-0011

Business Profile: Bank holding company in New Jersey.

Plan Specifics:
- Partial dividend reinvestment is available.
- No Discount.
- OCP: $10 to $1500 per quarter.
- Company purchases stock quarterly with OCPs.
- Termination fee or withdrawal fee of $5.
- Liquidation fee of $15.
- Selling fees include brokerage commissions and transfer taxes.
- Approximately 1263 shareholders in plan.

Performance Rating: NR

Central Louisiana Electric Co., Inc. (NYSE:CNL)
P.O. Box 5000
Pineville, LA 71361-5000
(318) 484-7400

Business Profile: Supplies electricity to residential, commercial, and industrial customers in portions of Louisiana.

Plan Specifics:
- Partial dividend reinvestment is available.
- No Discount.
- OCP: $25 to $5000 per month.
- Company purchases stock monthly with OCPs.
- Selling fees include $5 service charge and brokerage fees.
- Preferred dividends may be reinvested for additional common shares under the plan.
- Approximately 4800 shareholders in the plan.

Performance Rating: ***

**Central Maine Power Co.
(NYSE:CTP)
Edison Dr.
Augusta, ME 04336
(800) 695-4267**

Business Profile: Distributes electric service to residential, industrial, and commercial customers in central and southern Maine.

Plan Specifics:
- Partial dividend reinvestment is available.
- OCP: $10 to $40,000 per year.
- Company purchases stock monthly with OCPs.
- Selling fees are approximately 5 1/2 cents per share.
- Nonshareholders who are customers of the utility may join the plan by making an initial cash investment of at least $25 and up to $40,000 per year.
- Approximately 20,559 shareholders in the plan.

Performance Rating: **

**Central Vermont Public Service
Corp. (NYSE:CV)
77 Grove St.
Rutland, VT 05701
(802) 773-2711**

Business Profile: Provides electric power to residential, commercial, and industrial customers in Vermont and New Hampshire.

Plan Specifics:
- Partial dividend reinvestment is not available.
- No Discount.
- OCP: $50 to $2000 per month.

- Company purchases stock monthly with OCPs.
- Selling fee is approximately 15 cents per share.
- Over 5000 shareholders in the plan.
- Nonshareholders in certain states are permitted to make initial cash investments from $50 to $2000 by going directly through the company.

Performance Rating: **

**Century Telephone Enterprises, Inc.
(NYSE:CTL)
P.O. Box 4065
Monroe, LA 71211-4065
(800) 527-7844   (318) 388-9500**

Business Profile: Telephone holding company with operations in cellular telephone service and nationwide paging systems.

Plan Specifics:
- Partial dividend reinvestment is available.
- No Discount.
- OCP: $25 to $5000 per quarter.
- No selling costs.
- Company purchases stock monthly with OCPs.
- Approximately 3500 shareholders in the plan.

Performance Rating: ***

**Champion International Corp.
(NYSE:CHA)
c/o Manufacturers Hanover
P.O. Box 24850, Church St. Sta.
New York, NY 10249
(203) 358-7000**

Business Profile: Leading paper producer with interests in pulp and newsprint.

Plan Specifics:
- Partial dividend reinvestment is not available.
- No Discount.
- OCP: $10 to $5000 per month.
- Company purchases stock monthly with OCPs.
- No selling costs.
- Holders of preference shares may reinvest their dividends in additional common shares under the plan.
- Approximately 4000 shareholders in the plan.

Performance Rating: **

Charter One Financial, Inc.
(NASDAQ:COFI)
1215 Superior Ave.
Cleveland, OH 44114
(216) 566-5300

Business Profile: Bank holding company serving business and consumers in Ohio areas.

Plan Specifics:
- Partial dividend reinvestment is not available.
- No Discount.
- OCP: $10 to $5000 per quarter.
- Company purchases stock eight times a year.
- Selling fees are 5 percent, $1 minimum, or a maximum $5 service charge plus brokerage commission.

Performance Rating: NR

Chase Manhattan Corp.
(NYSE:CMB)
1 Chase Manhattan Plaza, 9th Floor
New York, NY 10081
(212) 552-4237   (800) 526-0801

Business Profile: Major banking concern based in New York.

Plan Specifics:
- Partial dividend reinvestment is available.
- 5 percent discount on reinvested dividends.
- OCP: $100 to $1000 per month.
- Company purchases stock monthly with OCPs.
- Selling fees include brokerage fees.

Performance Rating: **

Chemed Corp. (NYSE:CHE)
2600 Chemed Center
255 E. Fifth St.
Cincinnati, OH 45202-4726
(513) 762-6900   (800) 426-5754

Business Profile: Manufactures specialty chemicals, including janitorial supply products. Also provides sewer, drain, and pipe-cleaning services; medical and dental supply distribution; and pharmacy management services.

Plan Specifics:
- Partial dividend reinvestment is not available.
- No Discount.
- OCP: $10 to $1000 per month.
- Stock is purchased monthly with OCPs.
- Selling costs may include brokerage commissions.

Performance Rating: **

Chemical Banking Corp.
(NYSE:CHL)
c/o Harris Trust of NY
55 Water St.
New York, NY 10041
(212) 701-7609

Business Profile: Major New York-based banking company.

Plan Specifics:
- Partial dividend reinvestment is not available.
- No Discount.
- OCP: not available.
- Selling fees are approximately 10 cents a share and $1 for complete termination.
- Approximately 10,000 to 15,000 shareholders in the plan.
- Preferred dividends may be reinvested for common shares under the plan.

Performance Rating: **

Chemical Financial Corp.
(NASDAQ:CHFC)
c/o Ameritrust Co.
P.O. Box 6477
Cleveland, OH 44101
(216) 737-5742   (517) 839-5350

Business Profile: Bank holding company headquartered in Michigan.

Plan Specifics:
- Partial dividend reinvestment is not available.
- No Discount.
- OCP: $10 to $3000 per quarter.
- Termination fee is $2.
- Company purchases stock within 30 days of receipt of an amount sufficient to purchase at least 100 shares.

Performance Rating: NR

Chemical Waste Management, Inc.
(NYSE:CHW)
3001 Butterfield Rd.
Oak Brook, IL 60521
(708) 218-1500

Business Profile: Largest supplier of hazardous waste management services. Operations include disposal, resource recovery, and treatment.

Plan Specifics:
- Partial dividend reinvestment is not available.
- No Discount.
- OCP: $25 to $2000 per month.
- Selling fees are approximately 5 1/2 cents per share.
- Company purchases stock monthly with OCPs.
- There are 8000 to 9000 shareholders in the plan.

Performance Rating: ***

Chesapeake Corp. (NYSE:CSK)
PO Box 2350
1021 East Cary St.
Richmond, VA 23218-2350
(804) 697-1166

Business Profile: Manufactures paper, pulp, tissue, and wood products and has operations in packaging.

Plan Specifics:
- Partial dividend reinvestment is not available.
- No Discount.
- OCP: $10 to $5000 per quarter.
- Stock is purchased monthly with OCPs.
- Termination fee is $1 plus brokerage commissions.
- Approximately 1900 shareholders in the plan.

Performance Rating: **

Chevron Corp. (NYSE:CHV)
225 Bush St.
San Francisco, CA 94104
(415) 894-7700

Business Profile: Worldwide crude oil and natural gas company with important involvements in petrochemicals and minerals.

Plan Specifics:
- Partial dividend reinvestment is not available.
- No Discount.
- OCP: $25 to $1000 per month.
- Purchasing and selling fees include maximum $2.50 service charge per transaction plus nominal brokerage charges.
- Company purchases stock monthly with OCPs.
- 15 percent of common shareholders are in the plan.

Performance Rating: ***

Chittenden Corp. (NASDAQ:CNDN)
2 Burlington Sq.
Burlington, VT 05402
(802) 658-4000   (617) 575-2900

Business Profile: Bank holding company for largest commercial bank in Vermont.

Plan Specifics:
- Partial dividend reinvestment is not available.
- 5 percent discount on reinvested dividends (company is not currently paying dividend).
- OCP: $25 to $5000 per quarter.
- Selling costs are 5 percent of transaction value ($5 maximum) plus commissions.
- Company purchases stock quarterly with OCPs.
- Approximately 1282 shareholders in the plan.

Performance Rating: NR

Chrysler Corp. (NYSE:C)
12000 Chrysler Dr.
Highland Park, MI 48288-1919
(313) 956-3007

Business Profile: Third largest United States motor vehicle manufacturer.

Plan Specifics:
- Partial dividend reinvestment is not available.
- No Discount.
- OCP: $25 to $24,000 per year.
- Selling costs are broker fees.
- Company purchases stock on the 15th of each month with OCPs.

Performance Rating: **

Chubb Corp. (NYSE:CB)
P.O. Box 1615
15 Mountain View Rd.
Warren, NJ 07061-1615
(201) 580-2365   (201) 580-3579

Business Profile: Interests in property-casualty insurance, life and health insurance, and real estate development.

Plan Specifics:
- Partial dividend reinvestment is not available.
- No Discount.
- OCP: $10 to $3000 per quarter.
- Purchasing fees are 5 percent of each investment (maximum $2.50) and nominal brokerage fees.
- Selling fees are brokerage commission plus a $5 handling fee.
- Company purchases stock at least quarterly with OCPs.
- Approximately 350 shareholders in the plan.

Performance Rating: ***

CIGNA Corp. (NYSE:CI)
First Chicago Trust-NY
P.O. Box 3506, Church St. Sta.
New York, NY 10008-3506
(215) 523-3106

Business Profile: Insurance organization providing property-casualty, group life/health, and annuity coverage.

Plan Specifics:
- Partial dividend reinvestment is available.
- No Discount.
- OCP: $10 to $5000 per month.
- Stock is purchased around the 10th business day of the month with OCPs.
- Selling costs are brokerage commission and any other cost of sale.
- Approximately 2300 shareholders in plan.

Performance Rating: ***

CILCORP, Inc. (NYSE:CER)
300 Liberty St.
Peoria, IL 61602
(800) 622-5514   (800) 322-3569

Business Profile: Public utility holding company providing electricity and gas to residential, commercial, and industrial customers in central Illinois. Other businesses provide environmental consulting and analytical services.

Plan Specifics:
- Partial dividend reinvestment is available.
- No Discount.
- OCP: $25 to $5000 per quarter.
- Selling costs are brokerage fees.
- Company agent purchases stock monthly with OCPs.
- Preferred dividends may be reinvested for additional common shares under the plan.

Performance Rating: ***

Cincinnati Bell, Inc. (NYSE:CSN)
P.O. Box 2301
201 East 4th St.
Cincinnati, OH 45201
(800) 321-1355   (513) 397-9900

Business Profile: Provides telephone service in Ohio, Kentucky, and Indi-

ana. Engages in nonregulated communications-related businesses.

Plan Specifics:
- Partial dividend reinvestment is not available.
- No Discount.
- OCP: no minimum to $10,000 per quarter.
- Selling costs include brokerage commissions.
- Company purchases stock quarterly with OCPs.

Performance Rating: ****

Cincinnati Financial Corp.
(NASDAQ:CINF)
P.O. Box 145496
Cincinnati, OH 45250-5496
(513) 870-2000   (513) 579-6248

Business Profile: Insurance holding company. Sells property and casualty coverage and life insurance.

Plan Specifics:
- Partial dividend reinvestment is not available.
- No Discount.
- OCP: $25 to $1000 per month.
- Purchasing fees include brokerage commissions and service fees of $3 per transaction for voluntary cash investments and $1 to $3 per automatic dividend reinvestment.
- Stock is purchased monthly with OCPs.

Performance Rating: ***

Cincinnati Gas & Electric Co.
(NYSE:CIN)
P.O. Box 900
Cincinnati, OH 45201-0900
(800) 325-2945

Business Profile: Distributes electric power and natural gas to residential, commercial, and industrial customers in Ohio, Indiana, and Kentucky areas.

Plan Specifics:
- Partial dividend reinvestment is available.
- No Discount.
- OCP: $25 to $40,000 per year.
- Selling costs include small brokerage commission.
- Company purchases stock eight times a year with OCPs.
- Approximately 16,429 shareholders in the plan.
- Preferred dividends may be reinvested for additional common shares under the plan.

Performance Rating: **

Cincinnati Milacron, Inc. (NYSE:CMZ)
4701 Marburg Ave.
Cincinnati, OH 45209
(412) 236-8000   (513) 841-8100

Business Profile: Leading manufacturer of machine tools and inspection equipment.

Plan Specifics:
- Partial dividend reinvestment is not available.
- No Discount.
- OCP: $25 to $1000 per month.
- Selling costs are 10 to 20 cents a share.
- Company purchases stock monthly with OCPs.
- Approximately 9000 shareholders in the plan.

Performance Rating: **

CIPSCO, Inc. (NYSE:CIP)
607 East Adams St.
Springfield, IL 62739
(217) 525-5317

Business Profile: CIPSCO's principal subsidiary provides electricity and gas to residential, commercial, and industrial customers in central and southern Illinois.

Plan Specifics:
- Partial dividend reinvestment is available.
- No Discount.
- OCP: $10 to $50,000 per month.
- Brokerage commission for purchasing and selling.
- Company purchases stock monthly in OCPs.
- Preferred dividends may be reinvested in common shares.
- Shareholders of less than 50 shares may join the plan for the limited purpose of selling their shares.
- Approximately 12,172 shareholders in the plan.

Performance Rating: ***

Citicorp (NYSE:CCI)
Citicorp Investor Relations
850 Third Ave., 13th Floor
New York, NY 10043
(800) 342-6690

Business Profile: Largest banking company in the nation.

Plan Specifics:
- Partial dividend reinvestment is available.
- 3 percent discount on reinvested dividends.
- OCP: $250 to $20,000 per month.
- Selling costs are broker fees.

- Company purchases stock monthly with OCPs.
- Approximately 30,000 shareholders in the plan.

Performance Rating: **

Citizens Bancorp (NASDAQ:CIBC)
14401 Sweitzer Lane
Laurel, MD 20707
(301) 206-6000

Business Profile: Holding institution for banks in Maryland and Washington, D.C.

Plan Specifics:
- Partial dividend reinvestment is not available.
- No Discount.
- OCP: $25 to $3750 per quarter.
- Purchasing costs may include nominal brokerage fees.
- Selling costs are brokerage commission and $1 liquidation.
- Company purchases stock quarterly with OCPs.
- Approximately 2300 shareholders in the plan.

Performance Rating: NR

Citizens First Bancorp, Inc.
(ASE:CFB)
208 Harristown Rd.
Glen Rock, NJ 07452
(201) 670-2454

Business Profile: New Jersey-based bank holding company operating in commercial banking.

Plan Specifics:
- Partial dividend reinvestment is not available.
- No Discount.
- OCP: $10 to no maximum per month.

- Initial stock purchases may be made directly through the company (minimum investment of $10).
- Selling costs are small brokerage fees.
- Company purchases stock monthly with OCPs.
- Approximately 2000 shareholders in the plan.

Performance Rating: *

Clarcor, Inc. (NASDAQ:CLRK)
c/o First Chicago Trust-NY
P.O. Box 3506, Church St. Sta.
New York, NY 10008-3506
(212) 791-6422

Business Profile: Manufactures air, fuel, and hydraulic filters, plastic lithographed containers, and mechanical springs.

Plan Specifics:
- Partial dividend reinvestment is not available.
- No Discount.
- OCP: $25 to $3000 per month.
- Stock is purchased monthly with OCPs.
- Participants may incur brokerage fees when selling costs.

Performance Rating: ***

Cleveland-Cliffs, Inc. (NYSE:CLF)
1100 Superior Ave., 18th Floor
Cleveland, OH 44114-2589
(216) 694-5459   (216) 694-5700

Business Profile: Produces and markets iron ore pellets.

Plan Specifics:
- Partial dividend reinvestment is not available.
- No Discount.
- OCP: $10 to $2000 per month.

- Selling costs may include brokerage fees.
- Company purchases stock monthly with OCPs.
- Approximately 1000 shareholders in the plan.

Performance Rating: **

Clorox Co. (NYSE:CLX)
c/o First Chicago Trust Co.-NY
P.O. Box 3506, Church St. Sta.
New York, NY 10008-3506
(415) 271-2927   (212) 791-6422

Business Profile: Manufactures household products, including bleach and cleaners.

Plan Specifics:
- Partial dividend reinvestment is available.
- No Discount.
- OCP: $10 to $60,000 per year.
- Selling costs include brokerage commissions and any other costs of sale.
- Company purchases stock monthly with OCPs.

Performance Rating: ****

CMS Energy Corp. (NYSE:CMS)
212 West Michigan Ave.
Jackson, MI 49201
(517) 788-1867   (517) 788-0550

Business Profile: Electric and gas utility holding company serving residential, commercial, and industrial customers in Michigan.

Plan Specifics:
- Partial dividend reinvestment is not available.
- No Discount.
- OCP: $25 to $60,000 per year.
- Must go through own broker to sell shares.

- Company purchases stock monthly with OCPs.
- Approximately 28,000 shareholders in the plan.

Performance Rating: **

CNB Bancshares, Inc.
(NASDAQ:CNBE)
P.O. Box 778
Evansville, IN 47739
(812) 464-3416   (812) 464-3400

Business Profile: Offers banking services in the Midwest.

Plan Specifics:
- Partial dividend reinvestment is available.
- No Discount.
- OCP: $25 to $5000 per quarter.
- Company purchases stock quarterly with OCPs.
- Must go through own broker to sell shares.
- Approximately 5000 shareholders in the plan.

Performance Rating: NR

Coca-Cola Bottling Co. Consolidated
(NASDAQ:COKE)
c/o First Union Nat'l Bank
CMG-5, Two First Union Center
Charlotte, NC 28288-1154
(704) 374-2697

Business Profile: Bottles, cans, and sells carbonated soft drinks and products of Coca-Cola Company.

Plan Specifics:
- Partial dividend reinvestment is not available.
- No Discount.
- OCP: $10 to $1000 per month.
- Purchasing fees include brokerage commissions and service charge of 4

percent of investment ($2.50 maximum).
- Selling cost is brokerage commission.
- Stock is purchased monthly with OCPs.
- Approximately 280 shareholders in the plan.

Performance Rating: **

The Coca-Cola Company
(NYSE:KO)
P.O. Box 1734
Atlanta, GA 30301
(404) 676-2777 (800) 446-2617

Business Profile: World's largest soft drink company.

Plan Specifics:
- Partial dividend reinvestment is available.
- No Discount.
- OCP: $10 to $60,000 per year.
- Selling costs are approximately 10 cents per share.
- Company purchases stock monthly with OCPs.

Performance Rating: ****

Coca-Cola Enterprises, Inc.
(NYSE:CCE)
P.O. Box 1778
Atlanta, GA 30301-1778
(404) 676-7997

Business Profile: World's largest bottler of Coca-Cola beverages.

Plan Specifics:
- Partial dividend reinvestment is available.
- No Discount.
- OCP: $10 to $60,000 per year.
- Selling costs are brokerage fees.

- Company purchases stock monthly with OCPs.
- Approximately 2000 shareholders in the plan.

Performance Rating: **

Colgate-Palmolive Co. (NYSE:CL)
c/o First Chicago Trust-NY
P.O. Box 3506
New York, NY 10008-3506
(212) 791-6422

Business Profile: Produces household goods including detergents, soap, bleaches, and personal care products.

Plan Specifics:
- Partial dividend reinvestment is available.
- No Discount.
- OCP: $20 to $60,000 per year.
- Stock is purchased around the 15th of the month with OCPs.
- Selling costs are brokerage commission and any other cost of sale.

Performance Rating: ****

Colonial BancGroup, Inc. (AL)
(NASDAQ:CLBGA)
P.O. Box 1108
Montgomery, AL 36192
(205) 834-5500 (205) 240-5050

Business Profile: Alabama-based commercial banking company.

Plan Specifics:
- Partial dividend reinvestment is available.
- No Discount.
- OCP: $10 to $3000 per quarter.
- Selling costs may include brokerage fees.
- Company purchases stock quarterly with OCPs.

• Approximately 973 shareholders in the plan.

Performance Rating: **

Colonial Gas Co. (NASDAQ:CGES)
P.O. Box 3064
Lowell, MA 01853
(508) 458-3171

Business Profile: Supplies natural gas to residential, commercial, and industrial customers in Massachusetts regions.

Plan Specifics:
• Partial dividend reinvestment is available.
• 5 percent discount on reinvested dividends.
• OCP: $10 to $5000 per calendar quarter.
• Company purchases stock monthly with OCPs.
• Selling costs may be brokerage commissions.

Performance Rating: ***

Colorado National Bankshares, Inc. (NASDAQ:COLC)
P.O. Box 5168
Denver, CO 80217
(303) 629-1968   (212) 587-6396

Business Profile: Multibank holding company in Colorado.

Plan Specifics:
• Partial dividend reinvestment is available.
• 5 percent discount on reinvested dividends.
• OCP: $50 to $1000 per month.
• Selling costs are brokerage commission.
• Company usually purchases stock on the first business day of the month with OCPs.

• Approximately 30 percent of the registered shareholders are in the plan.

Performance Rating: **

Columbia Gas System, Inc. (NYSE:CG)
Stockholder Services Dept.
P.O. Box 2318
Columbus, OH 43216-2318
(614) 481-1421   (302) 429-5000

Business Profile: Natural gas holding company serving mid-Atlantic and Midwestern states.

Plan Specifics:
• Partial dividend reinvestment is not available.
• No Discount.
• OCP: $10 to $10,000 per quarter.
• Purchasing and selling fees are very nominal brokerage fees.
• $1 termination fee.
• Company purchases stock eight times a year with OCPs.
• Approximately 21,000 shareholders in the plan.

Performance Rating: **

Columbia Real Estate Investments, Inc. (ASE:CIV)
c/o 1st Nat'l Bank of Maryland
25 S. Charles St., 16th floor
Baltimore, MD 21201
(301) 244-4622   (301) 964-8875

Business Profile: Real estate investment trust.

Plan Specifics:
• Partial dividend reinvestment is not available.
• No Discount.
• OCP: not available.
• Purchasing fee is pro rata portion of

brokerage commission plus 6.5 percent of amount invested (maximum $2.60).
- Selling costs are brokerage commissions and $3 charge for termination.

Performance Rating: **

Comerica, Inc. (NYSE:CMA)
Attn: Stock Transfer Dept.
211 West Fort St.
Detroit, MI 48275-1093
(313) 222-3583   (212) 791-6422

Business Profile: Multibank holding company with locations in Michigan, Ohio, and Texas.

Plan Specifics:
- Partial dividend reinvestment is not available.
- No Discount.
- OCP: $10 to $3000 per quarter.
- Selling costs are minimal commissions and $5 termination fee.
- Company purchases stock quarterly with OCPs.
- Approximately 1000 shareholders in the plan.

Performance Rating: ***

Commercial Intertech Corp.
(NYSE:TEC)
P.O. Box 239
Youngstown, OH 44501-0239
(216) 746-8011

Business Profile: Designs, produces, and sells hydraulic components, fluid purification products, and fabricated metal products.

Plan Specifics:
- Partial dividend reinvestment is not available.
- No Discount.
- OCP: $30 to $5000 per quarter.

- Purchasing costs may include nominal brokerage fees.
- Participant must go through own broker to sell shares.
- Company purchases stock quarterly with OCPs.
- Approximately 1200 shareholders in the plan.

Performance Rating: **

Commonwealth Edison Co.
(NYSE:CWE)
P.O. Box 767
Chicago, IL 60690-0767
(312) 294-4321

Business Profile: Provides electricity in Chicago and northern Illinois areas. Owns largest network of nuclear plants.

Plan Specifics:
- Partial dividend reinvestment is available.
- No Discount.
- OCP: $25 to $3000 per quarter.
- Purchasing and selling costs include brokerage commissions (buying fees are not expected to exceed 10 cents per share).
- Company purchases stock quarterly with OCPs.
- Approximately 75,000 shareholders in the plan.

Performance Rating: **

Commonwealth Energy System
(NYSE:CES)
P.O. Box 9150
Cambridge, MA 02142-9150
(800) 447-1183

Business Profile: Electric and gas utility holding company serving portions of Massachusetts.

Plan Specifics:

- Partial dividend reinvestment is not available.
- No Discount.
- OCP: $10 to $5000 per quarter.
- Must go through own broker to sell shares.
- Company purchases stock monthly with OCPs.
- Approximately 5137 shareholders in the plan.

Performance Rating: **

Communications Satellite Corp. (NYSE:CQ)
c/o American Transtech, Inc.
Shareholder Services Agent
P.O. Box 44037
Jacksonville, FL 32231-4037
(202) 863-6200   (904) 636-1331

Business Profile: Provides satellite communications service, consulting service, and video entertainment operations.

Plan Specifics:

- Partial dividend reinvestment is not available.
- No Discount.
- OCP: $25 to $1000 per quarter.
- Selling costs are $1 fee and approximately 18 cents a share commission.
- Purchasing fees are 5 percent on amount invested ($2.50 maximum) plus brokerage fees.
- Company purchases stock quarterly with OCPs.

Performance Rating: ***

Community Bank System, Inc. (NY) (NASDAQ:CBSI)
5790 Widewaters Parkway
DeWitt, NY 13214
(315) 445-2282

Business Profile: New York-based bank holding organization.

Plan Specifics:

- Partial dividend reinvestment is not available.
- No Discount.
- OCP: $25 to $2000 per quarter.
- Selling costs are brokerage fees and $5 termination fee.
- Company purchases stock quarterly with OCPs.
- Approximately 554 shareholders in the plan.

Performance Rating: NR

ConAgra, Inc. (NYSE:CAG)
One ConAgra Drive
Omaha, NE 68102-5001
(402) 978-4005   (402) 595-4000

Business Profile: Supplies frozen foods, red meats, poultry, and seafood. Distributes pesticides and fertilizers.

Plan Specifics:

- Partial dividend reinvestment is not available.
- No Discount.
- OCP: $10 to $3000 per quarter.
- Selling costs are discounted brokerage fees.
- Company purchases stock twice a month with OCPs.
- Approximately 5000 shareholders in the plan.

Performance Rating: ****

Connecticut Energy Corp.
(NYSE:CNE)
P.O. Box 1540
Bridgeport, CT 06601
(203) 579-1732

Business Profile: Gas utility holding company serving parts of Connecticut.

Plan Specifics:
- Partial dividend reinvestment is available.
- No Discount.
- OCP: $50 to $6000 per quarter.
- Company purchases stock monthly with OCPs.
- Approximately 2500 shareholders in the plan.
- Selling costs include a service charge, a small brokerage commission, and transfer taxes.
- $3 one-time safekeeping charge.

Performance Rating: ***

Connecticut Natural Gas Corp.
(NYSE:CTG)
P.O. Box 1500
100 Columbus Blvd.
Hartford, CT 06144-1500
(203) 727-3203   (212) 613-7143

Business Profile: Provides gas to customers in central Connecticut communities.

Plan Specifics:
- Partial dividend reinvestment is available.
- No Discount.
- OCP: $25 to $5000 per quarter.
- Selling costs include brokerage fees.
- Company purchases stock monthly with OCPs.
- Preferred dividends may be reinvested for additional common shares under the plan.

Performance Rating: ***

Connecticut Water Service, Inc.
(NASDAQ:CTWS)
93 West Main St.
Clinton, CT 06413
(203) 669-8636

Business Profile: Holding company for Connecticut Water Co., a supplier of water and fire protection services in parts of Connecticut.

Plan Specifics:
- Partial dividend reinvestment is available.
- 5 percent discount on reinvested dividends.
- OCP: $100 to $3000 per quarter.
- Company purchases stock quarterly with OCPs.
- Approximately 1600 shareholders in the plan.
- Selling costs include brokerage commissions and any other fees or charges.

Performance Rating: **

Consolidated Edison Co. of New York (NYSE:ED)
Attn: Investors Service
P.O. Box 149
New York, NY 10003
(800) 221-6664   (800) 522-5522

Business Profile: Supplies electric power and gas to residential and commercial customers throughout New York City.

Plan Specifics:
- Partial dividend reinvestment is available.
- No Discount.
- OCP: $20 to $3000 per quarter.
- Selling costs are approximately 3 1/2 cents per share.

- Company purchases stock every month.
- Approximately 30,000 shareholders in the plan.

Performance Rating: ****

Consolidated Natural Gas Co.
(NYSE:CNG)
625 Liberty Ave.
Pittsburgh, PA 15222-3199
(412) 227-1125   (412) 227-1485

Business Profile: Explores for, produces, stores, and distributes natural gas to parts of Ohio, Pennsylvania, New York, and West Virginia.

Plan Specifics:
- Partial dividend reinvestment is available.
- No Discount.
- OCP: $25 to $5000 per quarter.
- Selling costs are discounted brokerage commissions.
- Company purchases stock quarterly with OCPs.
- Approximately 4498 shareholders in the plan.

Performance Rating: ****

Consolidated Rail Corp.
(NYSE:CRR)
Room 1820
Six Penn Center Plaza
Philadelphia, PA 19103-2959
(215) 977-5099

Business Profile: Major railroad concern. Primary hauler of chemicals, coal, and autos.

Plan Specifics:
- Partial dividend reinvestment is available.
- No Discount.
- OCP: up to $4000 per year.

- Selling costs are minimal brokerage commissions.
- Approximately 9400 shareholders in the plan.
- Stock is purchased monthly with OCPs.

Performance Rating: ***

Constellation Bancorp
(NASDAQ:CSTL)
68 Broad St.
Elizabeth, NJ 07207
(201) 354-4080   (201) 592-4083

Business Profile: New Jersey-based multibank holding company.

Plan Specifics:
- Partial dividend reinvestment is available.
- 5 percent discount on reinvested dividends.
- OCP: $25 to $3000 per month.
- Minimal, if any, selling costs.
- Company purchases stock around the 15th of the month with OCPs.

Performance Rating: **

Consumers Water Co.
(NASDAQ:CONW)
P.O. Box 599
Three Canal Plaza
Portland, ME 04112
(800) 292-2925   (207) 773-6438

Business Profile: Water utility holding company for portions of several northeastern states.

Plan Specifics:
- Partial dividend reinvestment is available.
- No Discount.
- OCP: $10 to $3000 per quarter.
- Selling costs are brokerage commissions (maximum fee $2.25).

- Company purchases stock at least quarterly with OCPs.
- Preferred shares may be reinvested for additional common shares under the plan.
- Approximately 2000 shareholders in the plan.

Performance Rating: ***

Control Data Corp. (NYSE:CDA)
P.O. Box 0
Minneapolis, MN 55440-4700
(612) 853-6701   (212) 791-6422

Business Profile: Supplies computer systems and services.

Plan Specifics:
- Partial dividend reinvestment is available.
- No Discount.
- OCP: $10 to $60,000 per year.
- Selling costs are 8 to 10 cents per share.
- Company purchases stock monthly with OCPs.

Performance Rating: **

Cooper Industries, Inc. (NYSE:CBE)
First City Tower
Houston, TX 77002
(713) 739-5400

Business Profile: Manufactures electrical power equipment, tools, automotive parts, and machinery for oil and gas industries.

Plan Specifics:
- Partial dividend reinvestment is available.
- No Discount.
- OCP: $25 per month to $24,000 per year.
- Selling costs are brokerage commission.

- Company purchases or issues stock monthly with OCPs.
- Approximately 6600 shareholders in the plan.

Performance Rating: ***

Copley Properties, Inc. (ASE:COP)
399 Boylston St.
Boston, MA 02116
(617) 578-1200

Business Profile: Real estate investment trust.

Plan Specifics:
- Partial dividend reinvestment is not available.
- No Discount.
- OCP: $100 to no maximum per quarter.
- Purchasing fees include brokerage commission.
- Company purchases stock quarterly with OCP.

Performance Rating: **

CoreStates Financial Corp.
** (NASDAQ:CSFN)**
c/o First Chicago Trust-NY
P.O. Box 3506, Church St. Sta.
New York, NY 10008-3506
(212) 791-6422   (215) 629-3827

Business Profile: Multibank holding company with banks in Pennsylvania and New Jersey.

Plan Specifics:
- Partial dividend reinvestment is not available.
- No Discount.
- OCP: $25 to $1000 per month.
- Stock is purchased around the 1st of the month with OCPs.
- Purchasing fees are proportionate share of brokerage commission and

4 percent of total funds invested (maximum $2.50).
- Selling costs are brokerage commission and any other costs.

Performance Rating: ***

Corning, Inc. (NYSE:GLW)
c/o Harris Trust & Savings Bank
Stock Transfer
P.O. Box 755
Chicago, IL 60690
(312) 461-6832

Business Profile: Manufactures products made from specialty glasses.

Plan Specifics:
- Partial dividend reinvestment is not available.
- No Discount.
- OCP: $10 to $5000 per month.
- Selling costs are 5 to 6 cents per share.
- Company purchases stock on the last business day of the month with OCPs.
- Approximately 2500 shareholders in the plan.

Performance Rating: ****

Countrywide Mortgage Investments, Inc. (NYSE:CWM)
450 West 33d St.
New York, NY 10001
(800) 647-4273

Business Profile: Real estate investment trust.

Plan Specifics:
- Partial dividend reinvestment is available.
- No Discount.
- OCP: $10 to $10,000 per quarter.
- Purchasing fees include brokerage and service charges.

- Participants may have to go through broker to sell shares.
- $1 fee for liquidation and for issuing certificates, as well as termination fee.
- Company purchases stock monthly with OCPs.

Performance Rating: **

CPC International, Inc. (NYSE:CPC)
P.O. Box 8000
International Plaza
Englewood Cliffs, NJ 07632-9976
(201) 894-2460   (212) 791-6422

Business Profile: International supplier of branded grocery products, including Hellmann's mayonnaise and Skippy peanut butter.

Plan Specifics:
- Partial dividend reinvestment is available.
- No Discount.
- OCP: $10 to $12,000 per year.
- Company purchases stock around the 25th of each month with OCPs.
- Selling fees are broker commissions.
- Approximately 4000 shareholders in the plan.

Performance Rating: ****

Crane Co. (NYSE:CR)
757 Third Ave.
New York, NY 10017
(212) 415-7300

Business Profile: Provides engineered products for aerospace, construction, and defense markets.

Plan Specifics:
- Partial dividend reinvestment is available.
- No Discount.
- OCP: $10 to $5000 per month.

- Selling costs are brokerage commissions and any other costs of sale.
- Company purchases stock around the 14th of the month with OCPs.
- Approximately 1800 shareholders in the plan.

Performance Rating: ***

Crestar Financial Corp.
(NASDAQ:CRFC)
Attn.: Corporate Trust
P.O. Box 26665
Richmond, VA 23261-6665
(804) 782-5055   (804) 782-5769

Business Profile: Important multibank holding company for Virginia, Maryland, and Washington, D.C. communities.

Plan Specifics:
- Partial dividend reinvestment is not available.
- 5 percent discount on reinvested dividends.
- OCP: $10 to $10,000 per quarter.
- Selling cost is a $5 service charge.
- Company purchases stock monthly with OCPs.
- Approximately 3246 shareholders in the plan.

Performance Rating: **

Crompton & Knowles Corp.
(NYSE:CNK)
One Station Place-Metro Center
Stamford, CT 06902
(203) 353-5400

Business Profile: Manufactures dyes, fabrics, food ingredients, and extrusion equipment.

Plan Specifics:
- Partial dividend reinvestment is not available.

- No Discount.
- OCP: $30 to $3000 per quarter.
- Service charge for depositing stock certificates is $5.
- Selling costs are brokerage commissions and transfer taxes.
- Company purchases stock quarterly with OCPs.

Performance Rating: ***

Cross & Trecker Corp.
(NASDAQ:CTCO)
P.O. Box 925
505 North Woodward Ave.
Bloomfield Hills, MI 48304
(313) 644-4343

Business Profile: Leading producer of machine tools and factory automation equipment.

Plan Specifics:
- Partial dividend reinvestment is not available.
- No Discount.
- OCP: $25 to $1000 per quarter.
- No selling costs.
- Approximately 457 shareholders in the plan.
- Stock purchased eight times a year with OCPs.

Performance Rating: **

CRSS, Inc. (NYSE:CRX)
P.O. Box 22427
1177 West Loop South
Houston, TX 77027-2427
(713) 546-2417   (713) 552-2000

Business Profile: Provides comprehensive services to architecture, construction, engineering, and project management businesses.

Plan Specifics:
* Partial dividend reinvestment is available.
* No Discount.
* OCP: $10 to $10,000 per quarter.
* Company purchases stock at least quarterly with OCPs.
* Purchasing fees are 5 percent service charge (maximum $3) plus nominal brokerage fees.
* Selling fees are $5 termination fee and brokerage commission.
* Approximately 207 shareholders in plan.

Performance Rating: **

CSX Corp. (NYSE:CSX)
c/o Harris Trust & Savings Bk.
P.O. Box 755
Chicago, IL 60690
(800) 521-5571   (804) 782-1400

Business Profile: Manages major rail system. Operates largest United States flag containership transporter and barge carrier.

Plan Specifics:
* Partial dividend reinvestment is not available.
* No Discount.
* OCP: $25 to $1500 per month.
* Purchasing and selling fees are nominal brokerage commissions.
* Company purchases stock around the 15th of the month with OCPs.

Performance Rating: ***

Cummins Engine Co., Inc.
(NYSE:CUM)
c/o First Chicago Trust-NY
P.O. Box 3506, Church St. Sta.
New York, NY 10008-3506
(212) 791-6422

Business Profile: Leading supplier of diesel engines, engine parts, and power systems for heavy-duty vehicles and equipment.

Plan Specifics:
* Partial dividend reinvestment is not available.
* No Discount.
* OCP: $10 to $6000 per quarter.
* Stock is purchased around the 15th of each month with OCPs.
* Participants may incur brokerage fees when selling from the plan.

Performance Rating: **

Curtice Burns Foods, Inc.
(ASE:CBI)
90 Linden Place
Rochester, NY 14625
(716) 383-1850

Business Profile: Processes canned goods, frozen vegetables, and snack foods.

Plan Specifics:
* Partial dividend reinvestment is not available.
* No Discount.
* OCP: $10 to $5000 per month.
* Buying and selling costs include brokerage commissions.
* Company purchases stock monthly with OCPs.

Performance Rating: **

Cyprus Minerals Co. (NYSE:CYM)
P.O. Box 3299
9100 East Mineral Circle
Englewood, CO 80155
(303) 643-5000

Business Profile: Important supplier of copper, coal, and other natural resources.

Plan Specifics:
* Partial dividend reinvestment is not available.

- No Discount.
- OCP: $50 to $3000 per month.
- Purchasing fees include service fee of 5 percent of dollars reinvested and 5 percent of each OCP invested (maximum $3), plus brokerage fees.
- Selling costs are brokerage commissions and a $5 termination fee.
- Company purchases stock with OCPs within 30 days of receipt.

Performance Rating: **

Dana Corp. (NYSE:DCN)
Shareholder Relations
P.O. Box 1000
Toledo, OH 43697
(419) 535-4633

Business Profile: Manufactures automotive parts and industrial products for original equipment and aftermarket distribution.

Plan Specifics:
- Partial dividend reinvestment is not available.
- No Discount.
- OCP: $10 to $1000 per month.
- Selling costs are brokerage commission and service fees.
- Stock is purchased monthly with OCPs.

Performance Rating: ***

Dayton Hudson Corp. (NYSE:DH)
Attn: Investor Relations Dept.
777 Nicollet Mall
Minneapolis, MN 55402
(612) 370-6732   (212) 791-6422

Business Profile: Operates department stores and retail stores in United States.

Plan Specifics:
- Partial dividend reinvestment is available.

- No Discount.
- OCP: $10 to $1000 per month.
- Selling costs are brokerage commission.
- Company purchases stock monthly with OCPs.
- Approximately 2500 shareholders in the plan.

Performance Rating: ***

Dean Foods Co. (NYSE:DF)
c/o Harris Trust & Savings Bk.
P.O. Box A3309, 111 W. Monroe St.
Chicago, IL 60690
(312) 461-2121   (312) 625-6200

Business Profile: Produces milk, dairy goods, canned vegetables, and other grocery items.

Plan Specifics:
- Partial dividend reinvestment is not available.
- No Discount.
- OCP: $25 to $3000 per quarter.
- Selling costs are 5 to 6 cents per share.
- Company purchases stock quarterly with OCPs.

Performance Rating: ****

Deere & Co. (NYSE:DE)
John Deere Rd.
Moline, IL 61265
(309) 765-8000

Business Profile: Largest worldwide manufacturer of farm equipment with significant operations in construction and lawn equipment.

Plan Specifics:
- Partial dividend reinvestment is not available.
- No Discount.
- OCP: $10 to $5000 per month.
- Purchasing fees are 5 percent on

each investment ($2.50 maximum) plus commissions.
- Selling costs are a $5 service fee and brokerage commissions.
- Company agent purchases stock around the 1st of the month with OCPs.

Performance Rating: **

Del-Val Financial Corp.
(NYSE:DVL)
c/o Continental Stock Transfer
72 Reade Street
New York, NY 10007
(212) 406-2740

Business Profile: Real estate investment trust.

Plan Specifics:
- Partial dividend reinvestment is not available.
- No Discount.
- OCP: $25 to $1000 per month.
- Must go through own broker to sell shares.
- Company purchases stock monthly with OCPs.
- Approximately 725 shareholders in the plan.
- Company is not currently paying a dividend.

Performance Rating: *

Delmarva Power & Light Co.
(NYSE:DEW)
Attn.: Shareholder Services
P.O. Box 231, 800 King St.
Wilmington, DE 19899
(800) 365-6495   (302) 429-3355

Business Profile: Supplies electricity and gas to residential, commercial, and industrial customers in parts of Delaware, Maryland, and Virginia.

Plan Specifics:
- Partial dividend reinvestment is available.
- No Discount.
- OCP: up to $100,000 per year.
- Selling costs are approximately 3 cents per share.
- Company purchases stock monthly with OCPs.
- Company may charge brokerage fees for any shares purchased on open market for shareholders.

Performance Rating: ***

Delta Air Lines, Inc. (NYSE:DAL)
Hartsfield Atlanta Int'l Airport
Atlanta, GA 30320
(404) 765-2170   (404) 897-3464

Business Profile: Major air carrier with route systems covering most of the United States as well as several foreign countries.

Plan Specifics:
- Partial dividend reinvestment is not available.
- No Discount.
- OCP: $25 to $10,000 per year.
- Selling costs are brokerage commissions.
- Company purchases stock around the 1st business day of the month with OCPs.
- Approximately 8300 shareholders in the plan.

Performance Rating: ***

Delta Natural Gas Co., Inc.
(NASDAQ:DGAS)
3617 Lexington Rd.
Winchester, KY 40391
(606) 744-6171

Business Profile: Supplies natural gas to portions of Kentucky.

Plan Specifics:

- Partial dividend reinvestment is available.
- No Discount.
- OCP: $25 to $3000 per quarter.
- Company purchases stock around the 15th business day of the month with OCPs.
- Approximately 600 shareholders in the plan.
- Termination fee is $5.

Performance Rating: **

Detroit Edison Co. (NYSE:DTE)
P.O. Box 33380
Detroit, MI 48232
(313) 237-8666

Business Profile: Supplies electricity and steam to residential, commercial, and industrial customers in southeastern Michigan.

Plan Specifics:

- Partial dividend reinvestment is not available.
- No Discount.
- OCP: $20 to $5000 per quarter.
- Purchasing fees are 50 cents per quarter administrative charge plus brokerage commissions.
- Must go through own broker to sell shares.
- Company purchases stock quarterly with OCPs.
- Approximately 60,000 shareholders in the plan.
- Firm suggests having at least five shares to enroll.
- Preferred dividends may be reinvested for additional common shares under the plan.

Performance Rating: **

Dexter Corp. (NYSE:DEX)
1 Elm Street
Windsor Locks, CT 06096
(203) 282-3509   (203) 627-9051

Business Profile: Produces specialty coatings, plastics, and materials used in aerospace, automotive, electronic, and industrial markets.

Plan Specifics:

- Partial dividend reinvestment is not available.
- No Discount.
- OCP: $25 to $3000 per month.
- Selling costs are brokerage commissions.
- Company purchases stock monthly with OCPs.
- Approximately 2000 shareholders in the plan.

Performance Rating: ***

Dial Corp. (NYSE:DL)
Shareholder Services Dept.
418 Greyhound Dial Tower
Phoenix, AZ 85077
(800) 453-2235

Business Profile: Produces consumer products, including soap and canned meats, and operates in-flight catering service.

Plan Specifics:

- Partial dividend reinvestment is not available.
- No Discount.
- OCP: $10 to $3000 per month.
- No selling costs.
- Company purchases stock once a month with OCPs.
- Approximately 9269 shareholders in the plan.

Performance Rating: ***

**Diamond Shamrock Offshore
Partners LP (NYSE:DSP)
717 North Harwood St.
Dallas, TX 75201
(214) 953-2100   (214) 953-2000**

Business Profile: Explores for and supplies crude oil and natural gas.

Plan Specifics:
- Partial dividend reinvestment is not available.
- No Discount.
- OCP: $100 to no maximum per quarter.
- Purchasing fees are 5 percent on amount invested ($2.50 maximum) and brokerage fees.
- Selling costs include brokerage fees and termination fee of $5.
- Company purchases stock quarterly with OCPs.
- Approximately 11,000 shareholders in the plan.

Performance Rating: **

**Dime Savings Bank of New York,
FSB (NYSE:DME)
Investor Relations
589 5th Ave., 4th Floor
New York, NY 10017
(800) 548-3463**

Business Profile: Thrift institution serving New York and New Jersey states.

Plan Specifics:
- Partial dividend reinvestment is not available.
- No Discount.
- OCP: $25 to $5000 per quarter.
- Selling costs are a service fee of $1 plus brokerage commissions.
- Company purchases stock quarterly with OCPs.

- Firm is not currently paying a dividend.

Performance Rating: *

**Dominion Bankshares Corp.
(NASDAQ:DMBK)
Attn: Financial Management
P.O. Box 13327
Roanoke, VA 24040
(703) 563-6226**

Business Profile: Multibank holding company serving Virginia, Maryland, Washington D.C., and Tennessee.

Plan Specifics:
- Partial dividend reinvestment is not available.
- 5 percent discount on reinvested dividends.
- OCP: not available.
- Selling costs are brokerage fees.
- Approximately 4000 shareholders in the plan.

Performance Rating: **

**Dominion Resources, Inc. (NYSE:D)
P.O. Box 26092
Richmond, VA 23260-6092
(800) 552-4034**

Business Profile: Electric utility holding company serving Virginia and North Carolina.

Plan Specifics:
- Partial dividend reinvestment is available.
- No Discount.
- OCP: up to $50,000 per quarter.
- Selling costs are approximately 7 cents per share.
- Company purchases stock around the 20th of each month with OCPs received by the 15th.
- Participants' shares will be sold at

least once per week, except between the 4th business day prior to a dividend record date and the following dividend payment date.
- Approximately 100,000 shareholders in the plan.

Performance Rating: *******

Donaldson Co., Inc. (NYSE:DCI)
P.O. Box 1299
Minneapolis, MN 55440
(612) 887-3131

Business Profile: International producer of air cleaners and filters for internal combustion engines.

Plan Specifics:
- Partial dividend reinvestment is not available.
- No Discount.
- OCP: $10 to $1000 per month.
- Selling costs are brokerage commissions and other costs of sale.
- Company purchases stock monthly if enough funds accumulate to purchase at least 100 shares.

Performance Rating: *******

Donnelley, R. R., & Sons Co.
(NYSE:DNY)
c/o First Chicago Trust Co.-NY
P.O. Box 3506, Church St. Sta.
New York, NY 10008-3506
(312) 326-8000

Business Profile: Largest commercial printer in United States. Provides catalogs, magazines, books, and directories.

Plan Specifics:
- Partial dividend reinvestment is available.
- No Discount.
- OCP: $10 to $60,000 per year.

- Selling costs are brokerage fees and other sale costs.
- Company purchases stock monthly with OCPs.

Performance Rating: ********

Dow Chemical Co. (NYSE:DOW)
c/o Ameritrust Co.
P.O. Box 6477
Cleveland, OH 44101-1477
(517) 636-1463   (216) 737-5745

Business Profile: Major chemical manufacturer. Supplies organic and inorganic chemicals, plastics, hydrocarbons, and agricultural products.

Plan Specifics:
- Partial dividend reinvestment is not available.
- No Discount.
- OCP: $10 to $25,000 per quarter.
- Selling costs are brokerage fees and $5 termination fee.
- Stock is purchased approximately every 4 weeks with OCPs.

Performance Rating: *******

Dow Jones & Co., Inc. (NYSE:DJ)
c/o First Chicago Trust-NY
P.O. Box 3506, Church St. Sta.
New York, NY 10008-3506
(212) 791-6422

Business Profile: Publishes business newspapers (*The Wall Street Journal* and *Barron's*), provides information services, and circulates community newspapers.

Plan Specifics:
- Partial dividend reinvestment is available.
- No Discount.
- OCP: $25 to $1000 per month.
- Stock is purchased around the 1st

business day of the month with OCPs.
- Selling costs are brokerage commission.

Performance Rating: ****

DPL, Inc. (NYSE:DPL)
P.O. Box 1247
Dayton, OH 45401
(513) 259-7150   (513) 224-6000

Business Profile: Electric utility holding company serving portions of Ohio.

Plan Specifics:
- Partial dividend reinvestment is available.
- No Discount.
- OCP: $25 to $1000 per quarter.
- Company purchases stock quarterly with OCPs.
- Selling costs are approximately 15 cents per share.
- Approximately 18,000 shareholders in the plan.
- Preferred dividends may be reinvested for additional common shares under the plan.

Performance Rating: **

DQE, Inc. (NYSE:DQE)
Dividend Reinvestment
P.O. Box 68
Pittsburgh, PA 15230-0068
(800) 247-0400   (412) 393-6167

Business Profile: Electric utility supplying power to residential, commercial, and industrial customers in southwestern Pennsylvania communities.

Plan Specifics:
- Partial dividend reinvestment is available.
- No Discount.
- OCP: $10 to $15,000 per quarter.

- Purchasing fees are approximately 4 cents a share.
- Selling costs are roughly 5 cents per share.
- Company purchases stock monthly with OCPs.
- Preferred shares may be reinvested for additional common shares under the plan.

Performance Rating: **

Dresser Industries, Inc. (NYSE:DI)
Shareholder Services
1600 Pacific
Dallas, TX 75201
(214) 740-6708

Business Profile: Significant supplier of products used in energy processing and oilfield operations.

Plan Specifics:
- Partial dividend reinvestment is not available.
- No Discount.
- OCP: $25 to $1000 per month.
- Selling costs are brokerage fees.
- Company purchases stock around the 20th of the month with OCPs.
- Approximately 2900 shareholders in the plan.

Performance Rating: **

Du Pont, E. I., de Nemours & Co.
(NYSE:DD)
Attn: Shareholder Relations
P.O. Box 470, Washington Bridge Sta.
New York, NY 10033
(302) 774-9656   (800) 526-0801

Business Profile: Nation's largest chemical producer with major operations in petroleum via its Conoco unit.

Plan Specifics:
- Partial dividend reinvestment is not available.
- No Discount.
- OCP: $10 to $1000 per quarter.
- Purchasing fees may include maximum service charge of $3 and brokerage commissions, usually around 1 percent of each amount invested.
- Selling costs are brokerage commissions and $5 service charge.
- Service charge for depositing certificates is $3.50.
- Preferred dividends may be reinvested for additional common shares under the plan.
- Stock is purchased approximately eight times a year with OCPs.

Performance Rating: ★★★★

Duke Power Co. (NYSE:DUK)
Attn: Investor Relations Dept.
P.O. Box 1005
Charlotte, NC 28201-1005
(800) 488-3853

Business Profile: Provides electricity to Piedmont regions of North and South Carolinas.

Plan Specifics:
- Partial dividend reinvestment is available.
- No Discount.
- OCP: $25 to $6000 per month, not to exceed $6000 per quarter.
- Selling costs are brokerage commissions (less than 5 cents a share).
- Preferred dividends are eligible for reinvestment in additional common shares.
- Customers may make initial purchase of stock directly through the company (minimum initial investment of $25).

- Company purchases stock monthly with OCPs.
- Approximately 45,000 shareholders in the plan.

Performance Rating: ★★★★

Duriron Co., Inc. (NASDAQ:DURI)
c/o Bank One, Indianapolis, NA
Corporate Trust Department
Bank One Center/Tower
111 Monument Circle, Suite 1611
Indianapolis, IN 46277-0116
(317) 321-8110

Business Profile: Manufactures equipment for chemical process markets.

Plan Specifics:
- Partial dividend reinvestment is not available.
- No Discount.
- OCP: $25 to $3000 per quarter.
- Selling costs are service charge of $3 and brokerage commissions.
- Service charge for depositing certificates is $5 for each deposit.
- Company purchases stock at least quarterly with OCPs.
- Approximately 740 shareholders in the plan.

Performance Rating: ★★

E-Systems, Inc. (NYSE:ESY)
c/o Ameritrust Texas
P.O. Box 2320
Dallas, TX 75221-2320
(800) 527-7844

Business Profile: Provides electronic systems and products for governmental defense markets.

Plan Specifics:
- Partial dividend reinvestment is available.
- No Discount.

- OCP: $25 to $5000 per quarter.
- Stock is purchased on 1st business day of every month with OCPs.
- Selling cost is a brokerage fee of approximately 6 cents a share.

Performance Rating: ***

E'Town Corp. (NASDAQ:EWAT)
c/o Nat'l State Bank
1320 N. Broad St.
Hillside, NJ 07205
(201) 354-3400   (201) 654-1234

Business Profile: Holding company for water utility company serving New Jersey.

Plan Specifics:
- Partial dividend reinvestment is available.
- 5 percent discount on both OCPs and reinvested dividends.
- OCP: $25 to $3000 per quarter.
- Selling costs may include brokerage commissions.
- Company purchases stock once a month with OCPs.

Performance Rating: **

Eagle-Picher Industries, Inc.
(NYSE:EPI)
Attn: Shareholder Services
P.O. Box 779
Cincinnati, OH 45201
(513) 721-7010

Business Profile: Manufactures automotive, machinery, and industrial products.

Plan Specifics:
- Partial dividend reinvestment is available.
- No Discount.
- OCP: $10 to $1000 per month.

- Selling costs are termination fee of $5 and brokerage commissions.
- Company purchases stock monthly with OCPs.
- Approximately 1000 shareholders in the plan.

Performance Rating: **

Eastern Co. (ASE:EML)
112 Bridge St.
Naugatuck, CT 06770
(203) 729-2255

Business Profile: Manufactures security locks and industrial products.

Plan Specifics:
- Partial dividend reinvestment is available.
- No Discount.
- OCP: $25 to $3000 per quarter.
- Selling costs are brokerage commissions and maximum $5 service fee.
- Company purchases stock quarterly with OCPs.
- Approximately 110 shareholders in the plan.

Performance Rating: **

Eastern Enterprises (NYSE:EFU)
9 Riverside Rd.
Weston, MA 02193
(617) 647-2300

Business Profile: Has operations in natural gas utility services, barge lines, and water products and purification systems.

Plan Specifics:
- Partial dividend reinvestment is not available.
- No Discount.
- OCP: $10 to $3000 per quarter.
- Selling costs are brokerage commissions.

- Company purchases stock quarterly with OCPs.
- Approximately 1500 shareholders in the plan.

Performance Rating: **

Eastern Utilities Associates (NYSE:EUA)
P.O. Box 2333
Boston, MA 02107
(617) 357-9590

Business Profile: Distributes electric power to residential, commercial, and industrial customers in Massachusetts and Rhode Island.

Plan Specifics:
- Partial dividend reinvestment is available.
- 5 percent discount on reinvested dividends.
- OCP: no minimum to $5000 per quarter.
- Selling costs are approximately 15 cents per share.
- Company purchases stock monthly with OCPs.

Performance Rating: **

Eastland Financial Corp. (NASDAQ:EAFC)
25 Cummings Way
Woonsocket, RI 02895
(401) 767-3900

Business Profile: Rhode Island bank holding company.

Plan Specifics:
- Partial dividend reinvestment is not available.
- No Discount.
- OCP: $25 to $5000 per quarter.
- Selling costs are brokerage commission.

- Stock is purchased quarterly with OCPs.
- The company is not currently paying a dividend.

Performance Rating: *

Eastman Kodak Co. (NYSE:EK)
c/o Chase Lincoln First Bank
P.O. Box 1507
Rochester, NY 14603
(716) 258-5853   (716) 232-5000

Business Profile: Largest worldwide manufacturer of photographic products. Products include chemicals and prescription drugs.

Plan Specifics:
- Partial dividend reinvestment is not available.
- No Discount.
- OCP: $10 to $5000 per month.
- Selling costs are $5 service charge (except in unusual instances, the firm pays brokerage commissions on stock sold through the plan).
- Company purchases stock weekly with OCPs.

Performance Rating: ****

Eaton Corp. (NYSE:ETN)
c/o Ameritrust Co.
P.O. Box 6477
Cleveland, OH 44101-1477
(216) 523-4408   (216) 737-5745

Business Profile: Important producer of vehicle components and electrical controls for automotive, commercial, defense, and industrial industries.

Plan Specifics:
- Partial dividend reinvestment is available.
- No Discount.
- OCP: $10 to $60,000 per year.

- No selling costs.
- Initial OCP of $100 is required if participant is just in the OCP program.
- The company purchases stock monthly with OCPs.
- Approximately 4200 shareholders in the plan.

Performance Rating: ***

Ecolab, Inc. (NYSE:ECL)
Ecolab Center
St. Paul, MN 55102
(612) 293-2233

Business Profile: Worldwide developer and marketer of institutional and residential services, including cleaning and sanitizing products and lawn-care and pest-control services.

Plan Specifics:
- Partial dividend reinvestment is available.
- No Discount.
- OCP: $10 to $60,000 per year.
- Selling costs are brokerage fees.
- Company purchases stock monthly with OCPs.
- Approximately 1500 shareholders in the plan.

Performance Rating: **

EG&G, Inc. (NYSE:EGG)
45 William St.
Wellesley, MA 02181-4078
(617) 237-5100

Business Profile: International supplier of scientific and technological products and services for aerospace, industrial, and defense markets.

Plan Specifics:
- Partial dividend reinvestment is not available.
- No Discount.

- OCP: $10 to $1000 per month.
- Selling costs are brokerage commission and a service charge of 5 percent of sale price net of commission up to a maximum of $2.50.
- Company purchases stock monthly with OCPs if enough funds accumulate to purchase at least a 100-share lot.
- Owner-held safekeeping services available.

Performance Rating: ****

Elco Industries, Inc.
(NASDAQ:ELCN)
P.O. Box 7009
Rockford, IL 61125
(815) 397-5151

Business Profile: Leading producer of metal and plastic components for industrial and constructional use.

Plan Specifics:
- Partial dividend reinvestment is not available.
- No Discount.
- OCP: $25 to $1000 per month.
- Selling costs are brokerage fees.
- Company purchases stock monthly with OCPs.
- Approximately 175 shareholders in the plan.

Performance Rating: **

Emerson Electric Co. (NYSE:EMR)
c/o Boatmen's Trust Co.
510 Locust
St. Louis, MO 63101
(314) 553-2197   (314) 982-1700

Business Profile: Manufactures electrical and electronic products for commercial, consumer, and industrial markets.

Plan Specifics:
- Partial dividend reinvestment is not available.
- No Discount.
- OCP: $25 to $2500 per quarter.
- Purchasing fees are very nominal brokerage fees.
- Selling costs include brokerage commissions and any service charge.
- Company purchases stock quarterly with OCPs.
- Less than 5000 shareholders in the plan.

Performance Rating: ****

Empire District Electric Co. (NYSE:EDE)
Attn: Shareholder Relations
P.O. Box 127
Joplin, MO 64802
(417) 623-4700

Business Profile: Provides electricity to residential, commercial, and industrial customers in Ozark region of Missouri and portions of neighboring states.

Plan Specifics:
- Partial dividend reinvestment is not available.
- 5 percent discount on reinvested dividend (doesn't apply to shares purchased on open market).
- OCP: $50 to $3000 per quarter.
- Selling costs include brokerage commissions and $5 handling charge.
- Company purchases stock quarterly with OCPs.
- Approximately 28 percent of all shareholders are enrolled in the plan.
- Preferred dividends may be reinvested for additional common shares under the plan.

Performance Rating: ***

Energen Corp. (NYSE:EGN)
2101 Sixth Ave. North
Birmingham, AL 35203
(205) 326-8421   (800) 654-3206

Business Profile: Parent company for Alabama gas utility and oil and gas exploration company.

Plan Specifics:
- Partial dividend reinvestment is available.
- No Discount.
- OCP: $25 to $5000 per quarter.
- Selling costs are brokerage commission and transfer taxes.
- Company purchases stock monthly with OCPs.
- Approximately 1113 shareholders in the plan.

Performance Rating: ***

EnergyNorth, Inc. (NASDAQ:ENNI)
P.O. Box 329
1260 Elm St.
Manchester, NH 03105
(603) 625-4000

Business Profile: Public utility holding company supplying natural and propane gas to residential, commercial, and industrial customers in southern and central New Hampshire.

Plan Specifics:
- Partial dividend reinvestment is available.
- 5 percent discount on reinvested dividends.
- OCP: $50 to $2500 per quarter.
- Must sell through own broker.
- Company purchases stock monthly with OCPs.
- Approximately 1500 shareholders in the plan.

Performance Rating: ***

Engelhard Corp. (NYSE:EC)
c/o First Chicago Trust-NY
P.O. Box 3506, Church St. Sta.
New York, NY 10008-3506
(212) 791-6422

Business Profile: Manufactures pigments and additives used in the paper, paint, and plastics industries.

Plan Specifics:
- Partial dividend reinvestment is not available.
- No Discount.
- OCP: $10 to $3000 per month.
- Stock is purchased monthly with OCPs.
- Selling costs are a $5 handling charge, brokerage commission, and any related expenses of sale.

Performance Rating: **

Engraph, Inc. (NASDAQ:ENGH)
2635 Century Parkway NE
Atlanta, GA 30345
(404) 329-0332

Business Profile: Manufactures printed packaging and product identification for beverage, consumer electronic, health care, personal care, and snack food industries.

Plan Specifics:
- Partial dividend reinvestment is not available.
- No Discount.
- OCP: $25 to $5000 per quarter.
- Must go through own broker to sell shares.
- Company purchases stock quarterly with OCPs.
- Approximately 902 participants in the plan.

Performance Rating: ***

Enron Corp. (NYSE:ENE)
1400 Smith St.
Houston, TX 77002
(713) 853-6161

Business Profile: Operates largest natural gas pipeline facility and is involved in oil and gas production.

Plan Specifics:
- Partial dividend reinvestment is not available.
- No Discount.
- OCP: $10 to $2000 per month.
- Selling costs are brokerage fees and transfer taxes.
- Company purchases stock around the 20th of the month with OCPs.
- Approximately 5400 shareholders in the plan.

Performance Rating: **

Enserch Corp. (NYSE:ENS)
c/o First Chicago Trust-NY
P.O. Box 3506, Church St. Sta.
New York, NY 10008-3506
(800) 367-3724   (214) 670-2649

Business Profile: Distributes natural gas to portions of Texas and Oklahoma.

Plan Specifics:
- Partial dividend reinvestment is not available.
- No Discount.
- OCP: $10 to $15,000 per quarter.
- Selling costs are brokerage commissions and $5 fee.
- Company purchases stock at least quarterly with OCPs.
- Approximately 6000 shareholders in the plan.

Performance Rating: **

**Enserch Exploration Partners Ltd.
(NYSE:EP)
300 South St. Paul
Dallas, TX 75201-9990
(800) 367-3724**

Business Profile: Explores for, produces, and sells natural gas and crude oil throughout Texas.

Plan Specifics:
- Partial dividend reinvestment is not available.
- No Discount.
- OCP: $100 to no maximum per quarter.
- Selling costs are brokerage commissions and $1 administrative fee.
- Company purchases stock quarterly with OCPs.
- Approximately 1700 shareholders in the plan.

Performance Rating: **

**Equifax, Inc. (NYSE:EFX)
P.O. Box 4081
1600 Peachtree St.
Atlanta, GA 30302
(404) 885-8000**

Business Profile: Provides information services to businesses for insurance claims and credit evaluation purposes.

Plan Specifics:
- Partial dividend reinvestment is not available.
- No Discount.
- OCP: $10 to $5000 per quarter.
- Selling costs are brokerage commissions.
- Company purchases stock around the 15th of each month with OCPs.
- 2000 to 3000 shareholders in the plan.

Performance Rating: ****

**Equimark Corp. (NYSE:EQK)
2 Oliver Plaza
Pittsburgh, PA 15222
(412) 288-5359   (412) 288-5000**

Business Profile: Multibank holding company in southwestern Pennsylvania.

Plan Specifics:
- Partial dividend reinvestment is not available.
- No Discount.
- OCP: $25 to $5000 per quarter.
- Selling costs may include brokerage fees.
- Company purchases stock monthly with OCPs.
- Approximately 4500 shareholders in the plan.
- Preferred dividends are eligible for reinvestment under the plan.
- Company is not currently paying a cash dividend on common stock.

Performance Rating: *

**Equitable Resources, Inc.
(NYSE:EQT)
420 Boulevard of the Allies
Pittsburgh, PA 15219
(412) 553-5877**

Business Profile: Provides natural gas and transmission services to customers in Greater Pittsburgh area. Operations in production and marketing of natural gas and oil.

Plan Specifics:
- Partial dividend reinvestment is not available.
- No Discount.
- OCP: $10 to $3000 per quarter.
- Selling costs are approximately 10 cents per share plus a $2.50 service charge.

- Company purchases stock eight times per year with OCPs.
- Approximately 2600 shareholders in the plan.

Performance Rating: ***

Ethyl Corp. (NYSE:EY)
c/o C & S/Sovran Trust Co.
P.O. Box 105555
Atlanta, GA 30348-5555
(800) 772-5564

Business Profile: Manufactures chemicals and lubricants for industrial markets. Operations in life insurance.

Plan Specifics:
- Partial dividend reinvestment is available.
- No Discount.
- OCP: $25 to $1000 per quarter.
- Selling costs are brokerage fees.
- Company purchases stock monthly with OCPs.

Performance Rating: ****

Exxon Corp. (NYSE:XON)
225 E. John W. Carpenter Freeway
Irving, TX 75062-2298
(214) 444-1000   (212) 791-3409

Business Profile: Major factor in worldwide petroleum markets.

Plan Specifics:
- Partial dividend reinvestment is available.
- No Discount.
- OCP: $10 to $60,000 per year.
- Selling costs may include brokerage fees.
- Company purchases stock around 10th of each month with OCPs.

- 200,000 to 300,000 shareholders in the plan.

Performance Rating: ****

F & M Financial Services Corp.
(NASDAQ:FMFS)
P.O. Box 10
Menomonee Falls, WI 53052-0010
(414) 253-2313

Business Profile: Wisconsin-based multibank holding company.

Plan Specifics:
- Partial dividend reinvestment is available.
- No Discount.
- OCP: $30 to $3000 per quarter.
- Must go through own broker to sell shares.
- Company purchases stock quarterly with OCPs.
- Approximately 40 percent of shareholders are in the plan.

Performance Rating: **

F & M National Corp. (VA)
(NASDAQ:FMNT)
P.O. Box 2800
Winchester, VA 22601
(703) 665-4200

Business Profile: Virginia-based commercial banking firm.

Plan Specifics:
- Partial dividend reinvestment is available.
- 5 percent discount on reinvested dividends.
- OCP: $25 to $5000 per quarter.
- Selling costs are brokerage commissions.

- Company purchases stock monthly with OCPs.

Performance Rating: NR

Fay's, Inc. (NYSE:FAY)
7245 Henry Clay Blvd.
Liverpool, NY 13088
(315) 451-8000

Business Profile: Operates discount drugstores in upstate New York.

Plan Specifics:
- Partial dividend reinvestment is available.
- No Discount.
- OCP: $25 to $5000 per month.
- Selling costs are nominal service fee and brokerage commissions.
- Company purchases stock each month with OCPs.

Performance Rating: **

FB & T Corp. (NASDAQ:FBTC)
13 Baltimore St.
Hanover, PA 17331
(717) 637-2291

Business Profile: Pennsylvania-based bank holding firm.

Plan Specifics:
- Partial dividend reinvestment is available.
- 5 percent discount on reinvested dividends and OCPs.
- OCP: $100 to $1000 per quarter.
- Selling costs may include brokerage commissions and $5 service charge.
- Company purchases stock quarterly with OCPs.
- Approximately 718 shareholders in the plan.

Performance Rating: NR

Federal-Mogul Corp. (NYSE:FMO)
P.O. Box 1966
Detroit, MI 48235
(800) 521-8607

Business Profile: Manufactures precision parts for the transportation, farm and construction equipment, and general manufacturing and aerospace industries.

Plan Specifics:
- Partial dividend reinvestment is available.
- No Discount.
- OCP: $10 to $25,000 per year.
- Selling costs are brokerage commissions.
- Company purchases stock monthly with OCPs.
- Approximately 12,000 shareholders in the plan.

Performance Rating: **

Federal National Mortgage
** Association (NYSE:FNM)**
c/o Manufacturers Hanover
P.O. Box 24850, Church St. Sta.
New York, NY 10249
(212) 613-7147   (212) 613-7053

Business Profile: Nation's largest mortgage lender.

Plan Specifics:
- Partial dividend reinvestment is not available.
- No Discount.
- OCP: $10 to $1000 per month.
- Purchasing fees are $1.50 for each quarterly dividend reinvestment, $5 for each OCP, and brokerage fees.
- $5 termination fee.
- Selling costs include brokerage fees and $15 handling charge.

- Stock is purchased at least quarterly with OCPs.

Performance Rating: ***

**Federal Paper Board Co., Inc.
(NYSE:FBO)
75 Chestnut Ridge Rd.
Montvale, NJ 07645
(201) 391-1776**

Business Profile: Manufactures paper, paperboard, pulp, and wood products.

Plan Specifics:
- Partial dividend reinvestment is not available.
- No Discount.
- OCP: $10 to $3000 per quarter.
- Purchasing fees are brokerage commissions and a service charge of 5 percent of the total funds invested (maximum, $2.50) for each investment.
- Selling costs are brokerage commissions and any other costs of sale.
- Company purchases stock quarterly with OCPs.

Performance Rating: **

**Federal Realty Investment Trust
(NYSE:FRT)
Suite 500
4800 Hampden Lane
Bethesda, MD 20814
(301) 652-3360**

Business Profile: Real estate investment trust.

Plan Specifics:
- Partial dividend reinvestment is not available.
- No Discount.
- OCP: $50 to $15,000 per quarter.

- Selling costs may include brokerage fees plus $3 service charge.
- Company purchases stock at least quarterly with OCPs.

Performance Rating: **

**Federal Signal Corp. (NYSE:FSS)
c/o Harris Trust & Savings Bank
P.O. Box A3309
Chicago, IL 60690
(312) 461-3932   (708) 954-2000**

Business Profile: Manufactures fire trucks, street cleaning trucks, signaling equipment, signs, and electronic message displays. Operations in industrial tools.

Plan Specifics:
- Partial dividend reinvestment is available.
- No Discount.
- OCP: $25 to $3000 per quarter.
- Stock is purchased at least quarterly with OCPs.
- Selling cost is 5 to 6 cents per share.

Performance Rating: ***

**Fifth Third Bancorp
(NASDAQ:FITB)
c/o Fifth Third Bank
38 Fountain Square Plaza
Cincinnati, OH 45263
(513) 579-5300**

Business Profile: Multibank holding company for Ohio, Kentucky, and Indiana.

Plan Specifics:
- Partial dividend reinvestment is not available.
- No Discount.
- OCP: $25 to $1000 per month.
- Purchasing fees include 5 percent on amount invested (minimum of $1

and maximum of $3) plus brokerage costs.
- Selling costs may include brokerage commissions.
- Company purchases stock monthly with OCPs.

Performance Rating: ****

Figgie International, Inc.
(NASDAQ:FIGI)
c/o American Transtech
P.O. Box 44037
Jacksonville, FL 32231
(904) 636-2378

Business Profile: Manufactures fire extinguishers, security systems, maintenance equipment, and other industrial and technical equipment.

Plan Specifics:
- Partial dividend reinvestment is not available.
- No Discount.
- OCP: $10 to $5000 per quarter.
- Selling costs are approximately 18 cents per share and a $1 termination fee.
- Company purchases stock monthly with OCPs.

Performance Rating: **

Fina, Inc. (ASE:FI)
c/o First Chicago Trust Co-NY
P.O. Box 3506
New York, NY 10008-3506
(212) 791-6422

Business Profile: Integrated oil and petrochemical firm active in refining and marketing petroleum products and producing petrochemicals, crude oil, and natural gas.

Plan Specifics:
- Partial dividend reinvestment is not available.
- No Discount.
- OCP: $10 to $1000 per month.
- Fees for purchasing stock are nominal broker commissions plus a service charge of 5 percent on the investment not to exceed $2.50.
- Selling fee is approximately 10 cents per share.
- Stock is purchased on the 15th of each month with OCPs.
- Approximately 129 shareholders in the plan.

Performance Rating: **

First Alabama Bancshares, Inc.
(NASDAQ:FABC)
P.O. Box 1448
Montgomery, AL 36102-1448
(205) 832-8450   (205) 832-8011

Business Profile: Multibank holding company serving Alabama and northwestern Florida.

Plan Specifics:
- Partial dividend reinvestment is not available.
- No Discount.
- OCP: $20 to $3000 per month.
- Selling costs may include brokerage fees.
- Company purchases stock monthly with OCPs.
- Approximately 3200 shareholders in the plan.

Performance Rating: ***

First American Corp. (TN)
(NASDAQ:FATN)
First American Center
Shareholder Services
Nashville, TN 37237-0721
(615) 748-2100   (615) 748-2498

Business Profile: Tennessee-based multi-bank holding company.

Plan Specifics:
- Partial dividend reinvestment is available.
- 5 percent discount on reinvested dividends.
- OCP: $25 to $2000 per quarter.
- Must go through own broker to sell shares.
- Company purchases stock once a month with OCPs.
- Company is not currently paying a dividend.
- Approximately 3000 shareholders in the plan.

Performance Rating: *

First Bancorp. of Ohio
(NASDAQ:FBOH)
106 South Main St.
Akron, OH 44308-1444
(216) 384-7347

Business Profile: Ohio-based multibank holding company.

Plan Specifics:
- Partial dividend reinvestment is not available.
- No Discount.
- OCP: $30 to $1000 per quarter.
- Selling costs include service fees of $2.50 for partial sales and $5 for full liquidation, plus brokerage commissions.
- Company purchases stock quarterly with OCPs.

- Approximately 2500 shareholders in the plan.

Performance Rating: ***

First Bank System, Inc. (NYSE:FBS)
P.O. Box 522
1200 1st Bank Place
Minneapolis, MN 55480
(612) 370-3500   (612) 370-5100

Business Profile: Multistate bank holding company based in Minnesota.

Plan Specifics:
- Partial dividend reinvestment is available.
- 3 percent discount on reinvested dividends.
- OCP: $25 to $5000 per quarter.
- Selling costs are $5 service fee and brokerage fees.
- Company purchases stock once a month with OCPs.
- Approximately 5480 shareholders in the plan.

Performance Rating: **

First Chicago Corp. (NYSE:FNB)
Office of the Treasurer
P.O. Box 3506, Church St. Sta.
New York, NY 10008-3506
(212) 587-6737

Business Profile: Chicago-based multibank holding company.

Plan Specifics:
- Partial dividend reinvestment is available.
- 4 percent discount on reinvested dividends.
- OCP: $25 to $5000 per month.
- Stock is purchased around the 1st trading day of the month with OCPs.

- Selling costs are brokerage commission and any transfer taxes.

Performance Rating: **

First Colonial Bankshares Corp.
(NASDAQ:FCOLA)
c/o First Nat'l Bank of Chicago
Suite 0128
Chicago, IL 60670
(312) 419-9891

Business Profile: Chicago-based multibank holding organization.

Plan Specifics:

- Partial dividend reinvestment is not available.
- No Discount.
- OCP: $25 to $3000 per month.
- Stock is purchased around the 10th of the month with OCPs.
- Selling costs are brokerage commissions and $5 service fee.

Performance Rating: ***

First Commerce Corp.
(NASDAQ:FCOM)
c/o First Chicago Trust-NY
P.O. Box 3506, Church St. Sta.
New York, NY 10008-3506
(212) 791-6422

Business Profile: Multibank holding company serving mainly Louisiana and Mississippi.

Plan Specifics:

- Partial dividend reinvestment is available.
- 5 percent discount on reinvested dividends.
- OCP: $50 to $3000 per quarter.
- Stock is purchased quarterly with OCPs.
- Selling costs are brokerage commis-

sion, transfer taxes, and other expenses related to sale.
- Preferred dividends are eligible for reinvestment for additional common shares under the plan.

Performance Rating: **

First Eastern Corp.
(NASDAQ:FEBC)
11 West Market St.
Wilkes-Barre, PA 18768
(717) 826-4623

Business Profile: Multibank holding company based in Pennsylvania.

Plan Specifics:

- Partial dividend reinvestment is available.
- 5 percent discount on reinvested dividends.
- OCP: $35 to $5000 per quarter.
- Selling costs may include brokerage fees.
- Company purchases stock quarterly with OCPs.
- Approximately 3000 shareholders in the plan.

Performance Rating: NR

First Fidelity Bancorp. (NYSE:FFB)
P.O. Box 1309
Newark, NJ 07101
(800) 458-0924

Business Profile: Bank holding company in New Jersey.

Plan Specifics:

- Partial dividend reinvestment is available.
- 5 percent discount on reinvested dividends.
- OCP: $50 to $60,000 per year.
- Selling costs are brokerage commissions.

- Company purchases stock monthly with OCPs.

Performance Rating: **

First Financial Holdings, Inc. (NASDAQ:FFCH)
34 Broad St.
Charleston, SC 29401
(803) 724-0931

Business Profile: Savings and loan holding company in Charleston, South Carolina.

Plan Specifics:
- Partial dividend reinvestment is not available.
- No Discount.
- OCP: $25 to $2000 per month.
- Selling costs may include brokerage fees.
- Company purchases stock once a month with OCPs.
- Approximately 1056 shareholders in the plan.

Performance Rating: NR

First Harrisburg Bancor, Inc. (NASDAQ:FFHP)
P.O. Box 1111
234 North 2d St.
Harrisburg, PA 17108
(717) 232-6661

Business Profile: Holding company for savings and loan institution in Pennsylvania.

Plan Specifics:
- Partial dividend reinvestment is available.
- No Discount.
- OCP: $25 to $250 per quarter.
- Selling costs may include broker fees.

- Stock is purchased quarterly with OCPs.
- 60 to 70 percent of total shareholders in the plan.

Performance Rating: NR

First Illinois Corp. (NASDAQ:FTIL)
800 Davis St.
Evanston, IL 60204
(708) 866-6000   (708) 866-5520

Business Profile: Multibank holding company serving suburbs of Chicago.

Plan Specifics:
- Partial dividend reinvestment is not available.
- No Discount.
- OCP: not available.
- Selling costs include brokerage commissions and handling charge of $1.50.

Performance Rating: **

First Interstate Bancorp (NYSE:I)
c/o First Interstate Bank, Ltd.
P.O. Box 4207
Woodland Hills, CA 91365-9784
(800) 522-6645

Business Profile: Multibank holding company serving western states.

Plan Specifics:
- Partial dividend reinvestment is available.
- No Discount.
- OCP: not available.
- Selling costs include brokerage commission.

Performance Rating: **

First Michigan Bank Corp.
(NASDAQ:FMBC)
Shareholder Services Dept.
115 Clover Ave.
Holland, MI 49423
(616) 396-9000

Business Profile: Multibank holding company serving western Michigan.

Plan Specifics:
- Partial dividend reinvestment is available.
- 5 percent discount on reinvested dividends.
- OCP: $100 to $500 per quarter.
- Selling costs are $3 termination fee.
- Company purchases stock quarterly with OCPs.
- Approximately 1900 shareholders in the plan.

Performance Rating: ***

First Midwest Bancorp, Inc.
(NASDAQ:FMBI)
c/o First Midwest Trust
P.O. Box 6380
Chicago, IL 60680-6380
(815) 740-7742

Business Profile: Multibank holding company based in Illinois.

Plan Specifics:
- Partial dividend reinvestment is available.
- 3 percent discount on reinvested dividends.
- OCP: $100 to $5000 per quarter.
- Company purchases stock monthly with OCPs.
- May have to go through own broker to sell whole shares.

Performance Rating: **

First Mississippi Corp. (NYSE:FRM)
P.O. Box 1249
700 North St.
Jackson, MS 39215-1249
(601) 948-7550   (216) 737-4127

Business Profile: Operations in fertilizer, industrial chemicals, oil, gas, and coal.

Plan Specifics:
- Partial dividend reinvestment is not available.
- No Discount.
- OCP: $25 to $3000 per month.
- Service charge of $5 for depositing certificates.
- Selling costs are $5 termination charge and brokerage fees.
- Stock is purchased monthly with OCPs.

Performance Rating: **

First National Bank Corp. (MI)
(NASDAQ:MTCL)
49 Macomb Place
Mount Clemens, MI 48043
(313) 465-2400

Business Profile: Banking organization based in Michigan.

Plan Specifics:
- Partial dividend reinvestment is available.
- No Discount.
- OCP: $50 to $5000 per quarter.
- Termination fee of $3.
- Participants may incur brokerage costs when selling shares.
- Company purchases stock quarterly, and sometimes more often, with OCPs.

Performance Rating: NR

First of America Bank Corp.
(NYSE:FOA)
211 South Ross St.
Kalamazoo, MI 49007-9915
(616) 383-9389   (800) 782-4040

Business Profile: Multibank holding company serving parts of Michigan, Indiana, and Illinois.

Plan Specifics:

- Partial dividend reinvestment is not available.
- 5 percent discount on reinvested dividends.
- OCP: $25 to $25,000 per quarter.
- Selling costs are brokerage commissions.
- Company purchases stock monthly with OCPs.
- Preferred dividends are eligible for reinvestment in additional common under the plan.

Performance Rating: ***

First Security Corp.
(NASDAQ:FSCO)
Stock Transfer Svcs., 3rd Floor
P.O. Box 30007
Salt Lake City, UT 84130
(801) 350-5289

Business Profile: Multibank holding company serving customers in Utah, Idaho, Oregon, and Wyoming.

Plan Specifics:

- Partial dividend reinvestment is available.
- OCP: $50 to $5000 per month.
- Must go through own broker to sell shares.
- Company purchases stock monthly with OCPs.

- Approximately 1050 shareholders in the plan.

Performance Rating: ***

First Security Corp. of Kentucky
(NASDAQ:FSKY)
One First Security Plaza
Lexington, KY 40507
(606) 231-1000

Business Profile: Holding company for several banks in Kentucky.

Plan Specifics:

- Partial dividend reinvestment is available.
- No Discount.
- OCP: not available.
- Selling costs for fractional shares are brokerage commissions.
- Whole shares must be sold through own broker.

Performance Rating: **

First Tennessee National Corp.
(NASDAQ:FTEN)
Attn.: Investor Relations
P.O. Box 84
Memphis, TN 38101
(901) 523-5630

Business Profile: Holding company for banks in Tennessee.

Plan Specifics:

- Partial dividend reinvestment is available.
- No Discount.
- OCP: $25 to $5000 per quarter.
- Must go through own broker to sell shares.
- Company purchases stock monthly with OCPs.

Performance Rating: **

First Union Corp. (NYSE:FTU)
First Union Center
Charlotte, NC 28288-0206
(704) 374-6782

Business Profile: Interstate bank holding company headquartered in North Carolina.

Plan Specifics:
- Partial dividend reinvestment is not available.
- 5 percent discount on reinvested dividends and 3 percent on OCPs.
- OCP: $25 to $15,000 per quarter.
- Participants with less than 100 shares in the plan account may sell shares through the plan, and the company will pay commission costs; over 100 shares must go through own broker.
- Stock is purchased quarterly with OCPs.
- Approximately 14,000 shareholders in the plan.

Performance Rating: ***

First Union Real Estate Investments
(NYSE:FUR)
Suite 1900
55 Public Square
Cleveland, OH 44113
(216) 781-4030   (216) 575-2532

Business Profile: Real estate investment trust.

Plan Specifics:
- Partial dividend reinvestment is available.
- No Discount.
- OCP: $20 to $5000 per month.
- Purchasing fees include brokerage commissions and a bank fee of 5 percent of the dividend and OCP invested (maximum, $3).

- Selling costs are brokerage commissions.
- Company purchases stock monthly with OCPs.

Performance Rating: **

First Virginia Banks, Inc.
(NYSE:FVB)
6400 Arlington Blvd.
Falls Church, VA 22042-2336
(703) 241-3669   (703) 241-4000

Business Profile: Multibank holding company with a major presence in Virginia and Washington, D.C.

Plan Specifics:
- Partial dividend reinvestment is not available.
- No Discount.
- OCP: $25 to $5000 per quarter.
- Selling costs are service charge of $1 and brokerage commissions.
- Company purchases stock monthly with OCPs.

Performance Rating: ****

Firstar Corp. (NYSE:FSR)
777 East Wisconsin Ave.
Milwaukee, WI 53202
(414) 765-4321

Business Profile: Multibank holding company controlling banks in Wisconsin, Illinois, Iowa, Minnesota, and Arizona.

Plan Specifics:
- Partial dividend reinvestment is available.
- No Discount.
- OCP: $25 to $10,000 per month.
- Selling costs are brokerage and administrative fees.

* Stock is purchased monthly with OCPs.

Performance Rating: ***

Fleet/Norstar Financial Group, Inc.
(NYSE:FNG)
50 Kennedy Plaza
Providence, RI 02903
(401) 278-6242   (401) 278-5879

Business Profile: New England multibank holding company.

Plan Specifics:
* Partial dividend reinvestment is not available.
* 5 percent discount on reinvested dividends.
* OCP: $10 to $10,000 per quarter.
* May have to sell shares through own broker.
* Company purchases stock quarterly with OCPs.

Performance Rating: **

Fleming Companies, Inc.
(NYSE:FLM)
P.O. Box 26647
6301 Waterford Blvd.
Oklahoma City, OK 73126-0647
(405) 840-7200

Business Profile: Important distributor of wholesale food and related products.

Plan Specifics:
* Partial dividend reinvestment is available.
* 5 percent discount on reinvested dividends.
* OCP: $25 to $5000 per quarter.
* Stock is purchased around the 10th of each month with OCPs.
* Selling costs may include broker fees.

* Approximately 4560 shareholders in plan.

Performance Rating: ***

Florida Progress Corp. (NYSE:FPC)
P.O. Box 33042
St. Petersburg, FL 33733-8042
(813) 895-1736

Business Profile: Holding company for Florida electric utility. Operations in coal mining, real estate, and technology development.

Plan Specifics:
* Partial dividend reinvestment is available.
* No Discount.
* OCP: $10 to $2000 per month.
* Purchasing fees are approximately 5 cents per share.
* Selling costs are approximately 8 cents per share.
* Company purchases stock monthly with OCPs.
* Approximately 17,182 shareholders in the plan.

Performance Rating: ***

Florida Public Utilities Co.
(ASE:FPU)
P.O. Drawer C
West Palm Beach, FL 33402
(407) 832-2461

Business Profile: Supplies electricity, water, and gas services to communities in Florida.

Plan Specifics:
* Partial dividend reinvestment is available.
* No Discount.
* OCP: $25 to $2000 per quarter.
* If company sells shares, brokerage fees will be charged to participants.

- Stock is purchased quarterly with OCPs.
- Approximately 250 shareholders in the plan.

Performance Rating: NR

Flowers Industries, Inc.
(NYSE:FLO)
c/o C & S/Sovran Trust Co.
P.O. Box 105555
Atlanta, GA 30348-5555
(800) 772-5564

Business Profile: Produces bread and baked goods for grocery and food service industries.

Plan Specifics:
- Partial dividend reinvestment is available.
- No Discount.
- OCP: $25 to $3000 per month.
- Selling costs are brokerage fees of approximately 30 cents per share.
- Company purchases stock once a month with OCPs.
- Approximately 1200 shareholders in the plan.

Performance Rating: ***

Foote, Cone & Belding
Communications (NYSE:FCB)
101 East Erie
Chicago, IL 60611-2897
(312) 751-7000

Business Profile: Provides advertising, direct marketing, and sales promotion.

Plan Specifics:
- Partial dividend reinvestment is not available.
- No Discount.
- OCP: $25 to $1000 per month.
- Must go through own broker to sell.

- Approximately 740 shareholders in the plan.

Performance Rating: ***

Ford Motor Co. (NYSE:F)
c/o Manufacturers Nat'l Bank
P.O. Box 55106
Detroit, MI 48255-0106
(313) 222-4381   (800) 521-1190

Business Profile: World's second largest motor vehicle manufacturer.

Plan Specifics:
- Partial dividend reinvestment is not available.
- No Discount.
- OCP: $10 to $1000 per month.
- Purchasing costs are a very nominal brokerage fee plus service charge of 5 percent of funds invested up to a maximum of $3 per investment made.
- Selling costs are $1 handling fee and brokerage fees.
- Company purchases stock monthly with OCPs.

Performance Rating: **

Foster Wheeler Corp. (NYSE:FWC)
c/o Bank of New York
P.O. Box 11002, Church St. Sta.
New York, NY 10249
(800) 524-4458   (201) 730-4090

Business Profile: Provides design, engineering, and construction services to chemical and petroleum industries.

Plan Specifics:
- Partial dividend reinvestment is not available.
- No Discount.
- OCP: $10 to no maximum per month.

- Purchasing fees may include very nominal service charge.
- Selling fees include service charge and any applicable brokerage charges.
- Company purchases stock around the 1st business day of the month with OCPs.

Performance Rating: **

**Fourth Financial Corp.
(NASDAQ:FRTH)
P.O. Box 4
Wichita, KS 67201-0004
(316) 261-4256**

Business Profile: Kansas-based bank holding company.

Plan Specifics:
- Partial dividend reinvestment is available.
- No Discount.
- OCP: not available.
- Must go through own broker to sell shares.
- Approximately 1300 shareholders in the plan.

Performance Rating: ***

**FPL Group, Inc. (NYSE:FPL)
c/o The Bank of Boston
P.O. Box 1681
Boston, MA 02105
(407) 694-6304   (617) 929-5445**

Business Profile: Florida-based electric utility holding company.

Plan Specifics:
- Partial dividend reinvestment is available.
- No Discount.
- OCP: $25 to $5000 per quarter.
- Selling cost is approximately 15 cents per share.

- Company purchases stock quarterly with OCPs.
- Preferred dividends are eligible for dividend reinvestment under the plan.

Performance Rating: ***

**Freeport-McMoRan, Inc.
(NYSE:FTX)
c/o Chase Manhattan Bank
P.O. Box 283, Bowling Green Sta.
New York, NY 10274
(504) 582-4000**

Business Profile: Leading natural-resources concern with operations in fertilizer, copper and mining, and oil and gas industries.

Plan Specifics:
- Partial dividend reinvestment is not available.
- No Discount.
- OCP: $10 to $1000 per month.
- Stock is purchased monthly with OCPs.
- Selling costs are a $5 service charge plus brokerage commission.
- $5 service charge for each deposit of certificates.

Performance Rating: ***

**Fuller, H. B., Co. (NASDAQ:FULL)
c/o Norwest Bank
P.O. Box 738, 161 N. Concord Ex.
South St. Paul, MN 55075-0738
(612) 450-4064   (612) 450-4075**

Business Profile: Worldwide producer of adhesives, sealants, coatings, paints, and waxes.

Plan Specifics:
- Partial dividend reinvestment is not available.
- No Discount.

- OCP: $10 to $6000 per quarter.
- Selling costs include $3 sale fee and brokerage commission of approximately 20 cents per share.
- Company purchases stock around the 10th of each month provided there are enough funds to purchase at least 100 shares.

Performance Rating: ***

**Fulton Financial Corp.
(NASDAQ:FULT)
#1 Penn Square
Lancaster, PA 17602
(717) 291-2546**

Business Profile: Pennsylvania-based bank holding company.

Plan Specifics:
- Partial dividend reinvestment is available.
- No Discount.
- OCP: $25 to $1000 per month.
- Stock is purchased monthly with OCPs.
- Selling costs are $35 fee.
- Approximately 4000 shareholders in plan.

Performance Rating: NR

**Gannett Co., Inc. (NYSE:GCI)
1100 Wilson Blvd.
Arlington, VA 22234
(703) 284-6000**

Business Profile: Operations in newspaper publishing, broadcasting, and outdoor advertising.

Plan Specifics:
- Partial dividend reinvestment is available.
- No Discount.
- OCP: $10 to $5000 per month.

- Selling costs are brokerage fees and any service charge.
- Company purchases stock monthly with OCPs.

Performance Rating: ****

**GATX Corp. (NYSE:GMT)
c/o Manufacturers Hanover
P.O. Box 24850, Church St. Sta.
New York, NY 10242
(312) 621-6603**

Business Profile: Interests in railcar leasing, tank terminal operations, and shipping services.

Plan Specifics:
- Partial dividend reinvestment is not available.
- No Discount.
- OCP: $25 to $3000 per month.
- Stock is purchased quarterly, and most likely more frequently, with OCPs.
- Selling costs may include brokerage fees.

Performance Rating: **

**GenCorp, Inc. (NYSE:GY)
175 Ghent Rd.
Fairlawn, OH 44333-3300
(216) 869-4453   (216) 869-4200**

Business Profile: Manufactures products for governmental aerospace and defense markets. Activities in polymer products and automotive components.

Plan Specifics:
- Partial dividend reinvestment is not available.
- No Discount.
- OCP: $10 to $3000 per quarter.
- Selling cost is commission of approximately 7 to 15 cents per share.

- Company purchases stock every 45 days with OCPs.
- Approximately 3598 shareholders in the plan.

Performance Rating: **

General Cinema Corp. (NYSE:GCN)
P.O. Box 1000
27 Boylston St.
Chestnut Hill, MA 02167
(617) 232-8200

Business Profile: Operates motion picture theaters and has equity interest in Neiman Marcus Group.

Plan Specifics:
- Partial dividend reinvestment is not available.
- No Discount.
- OCP: $25 to $2500 per quarter.
- Selling costs are brokerage commission and bank charges of $10 per transaction.
- Stock is purchased approximately eight times a year with OCPs.

Performance Rating: ***

General Electric Co. (NYSE:GE)
Reinvestment Plan Services
P.O. Box 120068
Stamford, CT 06912
(203) 373-2816   (203) 326-4040

Business Profile: Operations in aerospace, aircraft engines, major appliances, power systems, broadcasting, and financial services.

Plan Specifics:
- Partial dividend reinvestment is available.
- No Discount.
- OCP: $10 to $10,000 per month.
- Stock is purchased monthly with OCPs.

- Selling cost is approximately 15 cents per share.

Performance Rating: ****

General Mills, Inc. (NYSE:GIS)
c/o Harris Trust & Savings Bank
P.O. Box 755, 111 West Monroe
Chicago, IL 60690
(612) 540-3888   (800) 445-4802

Business Profile: Produces consumer foods and owns and operates chain restaurants (The Olive Garden and Red Lobster).

Plan Specifics:
- Partial dividend reinvestment is available.
- No Discount.
- OCP: $10 to $3000 per quarter.
- Selling cost is approximately 7 cents per share.
- Company purchases stock monthly with OCPs.
- Approximately one-third of total shareholders in the plan.

Performance Rating: ****

General Motors Corp. (NYSE:GM)
3044 West Grand Blvd.
Detroit, MI 48202
(313) 556-2044   (212) 791-3909

Business Profile: World's largest automobile manufacturer.

Plan Specifics:
- Partial dividend reinvestment is available.
- No Discount.
- OCP: $25 to $5000 per quarter.
- Participants may have to pay nominal brokerage costs if stock is purchased on the open market.
- Selling costs are $5 liquidation fee

and approximately 10 cents per share.

- Company purchases stock monthly with OCPs.
- Approximately 138,620 shareholders in the plan.

Performance Rating: *******

General Public Utilities Corp.
(NYSE:GPU)
c/o Manufacturers Hanover
P.O. Box 24935, Church St. Sta.
New York, NY 10249
(201) 263-6500

Business Profile: Electric utility holding company serving New Jersey and Pennsylvania regions.

Plan Specifics:

- Partial dividend reinvestment is not available.
- No Discount.
- OCP: $50 to $6000 per quarter.
- Selling costs are brokerage commissions and $15 transaction fee.
- $5 fee for withdrawal of certificates.
- $3 service fee for safekeeping feature.
- Company purchases stock quarterly with OCPs.
- Approximately 5000 shareholders in the plan.

Performance Rating: ******

General Re Corp. (NYSE:GRN)
P.O. Box 10351
Financial Center
Stamford, CT 06904-2351
(203) 328-5000   (800) 524-4458

Business Profile: Holding company for largest property-casualty reinsurance firm in country.

Plan Specifics:·

- Partial dividend reinvestment is not available.
- No Discount.
- OCP: $10 to $10,000 per quarter.
- Selling costs are brokerage fees.
- Company purchases stock monthly with OCPs.

Performance Rating: ********

General Signal Corp. (NYSE:GSX)
P.O. Box 10010
High Ridge Park
Stamford, CT 06904
(203) 357-8800   (203) 329-4344

Business Profile: Produces equipment and systems for process controls, electrical equipment, semiconductor, and telecommunications industries.

Plan Specifics:

- Partial dividend reinvestment is not available.
- No Discount.
- OCP: $25 to $10,000 per quarter.
- Must go through own broker to sell shares.
- Company purchases stock around the 15th of each month with OCPs.

Performance Rating: *******

Genuine Parts Co. (NYSE:GPC)
2999 Circle 75 Parkway
Atlanta, GA 30339
(404) 588-7822   (404) 953-1700

Business Profile: Supplies automotive replacement parts and industrial equipment.

Plan Specifics:

- Partial dividend reinvestment is not available.
- No Discount.
- OCP: $10 to $3000 per quarter.

* Brokerage commission when purchasing and selling.
* OCP is invested roughly 30 days after receipt provided that total funds for investment are enough to purchase at least a 100-share lot.
* Approximately 900 shareholders in the plan.

Performance Rating: ****

Georgia-Pacific Corp. (NYSE:GP)
c/o First Chicago Trust-NY
P.O. Box 3506, Church St. Sta.
New York, NY 10008-3506
(212) 791-6422

Business Profile: Leading provider of plywood, lumber, paper, and pulp.

Plan Specifics:
* Partial dividend reinvestment is available.
* No Discount.
* OCP: $25 to $5000 per month.
* Stock is purchased around the 10th of the month with OCPs.
* Purchasing fee includes 5 percent of total amount invested with a $2.50 maximum.
* Selling costs are brokerage commission and any other cost of sale.

Performance Rating: ***

Gerber Products Co. (NYSE:GEB)
445 State St.
Fremont, MI 49413
(616) 928-2224   (312) 461-2549

Business Profile: Largest producer of baby foods with operations in children's apparel.

Plan Specifics:
* Partial dividend reinvestment is available.
* No Discount.

* OCP: $25 to $3000 per quarter.
* Selling cost is approximately 5 1/2 cents per share brokerage commission.
* Company purchases stock quarterly with OCPs.
* Approximately 6000 shareholders in the plan.

Performance Rating: ****

Giant Food, Inc. (ASE:GFS.A)
Office of the Sec. (Dept. 559)
P.O. Box 1804
Washington, DC 20013
(301) 341-8480

Business Profile: Operates chain of food and drug supermarkets in metropolitan Washington D.C., Baltimore, and nearby areas.

Plan Specifics:
* Partial dividend reinvestment is not available.
* No Discount.
* OCP: $10 to $1000 per quarter.
* Selling costs are $3 service charge and brokerage commissions.
* Company purchases stock bi-monthly if there are enough funds to buy at least 100 shares.

Performance Rating: ***

Gillette Co. (NYSE:GS)
Prudential Tower Building
Boston, MA 02199
(617) 421-7000

Business Profile: Manufactures razor blades, toiletries, cosmetics, and electric shavers.

Plan Specifics:
* Partial dividend reinvestment is not available.
* No Discount.

- OCP: $10 to $1000 per month.
- Selling costs are brokerage commissions.
- Company purchases stock monthly with OCPs.
- Approximately 4000 shareholders in the plan.

Performance Rating: ****

Goodrich, B. F., Co. (NYSE:GR)
3925 Embassy Parkway
Akron, OH 44313
(216) 374-2613

Business Profile: Produces resins and compounds, specialty chemicals, and aerospace products.

Plan Specifics:
- Partial dividend reinvestment is not available.
- No Discount.
- OCP: $25 to $1000 per month.
- Must go through own broker to sell shares.
- Company purchases stock around the last day of the month with OCPs.

Performance Rating: **

Goodyear Tire & Rubber Co.
(NYSE:GT)
1144 East Market St.
Akron, OH 44316
(216) 796-3751   (216) 796-2121

Business Profile: Supplies tires and rubber-related products to original equipment and replacement markets.

Plan Specifics:
- Partial dividend reinvestment is available.
- No Discount.
- OCP: $10 to $15,000 per quarter.
- Selling costs are $5 termination

charge, brokerage fees, and service charge.
- Company purchases stock every month with OCPs.
- 11,000 to 12,000 shareholders in the plan.

Performance Rating: **

Gorman-Rupp Co. (ASE:GRC)
P.O. Box 1217
Mansfield, OH 44901-1217
(419) 755-1011   (216) 575-2532

Business Profile: Develops pumps, sewage pumping stations, and powered pumps for liquid handling applications.

Plan Specifics:
- Partial dividend reinvestment is not available.
- No Discount.
- OCP: $20 to $1000 per month.
- Company purchases stock once a month with OCPs.
- Selling costs may include brokerage fees.

Performance Rating: NR

Goulds Pumps, Inc.
(NASDAQ:GULD)
c/o Chase Manhattan Bank
Dividend Reinvestment Services
P.O. Box 283, Bowling Green Sta.
New York, NY 10274
(716) 258-5621

Business Profile: Produces service pumps, motors, and accessories for industrial and agricultural use.

Plan Specifics:
- Partial dividend reinvestment is not available.
- No Discount.
- OCP: $10 to $5000 per month.

- Stock is purchased monthly with OCPs.
- Purchasing fees are proportionate share of brokerage commission and 5 percent of amount invested ($3 maximum).
- Selling costs are brokerage commission and a small service fee.

Performance Rating: ***

Grace, W. R., & Co. (NYSE:GRA)
1114 Ave. of the Americas
New York, NY 10036-7794
(800) 824-4022   (212) 819-5500

Business Profile: Produces wide range of specialty chemicals. Also involved in specialty businesses.

Plan Specifics:
- Partial dividend reinvestment is available.
- No Discount.
- OCP: $50 to $100,000 per year.
- Selling costs are approximately 10 cents per share and a $5 handling fee.
- Company purchases stock around the 10th and 24th of the month with OCPs.
- Approximately 13,000 shareholders in the plan.
- Preferred dividends are eligible for reinvestment for additional common shares under the plan.
- Investors may make initial purchases of stock directly through the company (minimum initial investment $50).

Performance Rating: **

Graco, Inc. (NYSE:GGG)
c/o Norwest Bank MN
161 N. Concord Exchange
P.O. Box 738
South St. Paul, MN 55075-0738
(612) 450-4075

Business Profile: Supplies specialized fluid-handling pumps and fluid-handling equipment.

Plan Specifics:
- Partial dividend reinvestment is not available.
- No Discount.
- OCP: $25 to $1000 per quarter.
- Stock purchased monthly with OCPs.
- Selling costs are $3 service fee and approximately 20 cents per share broker fee.
- Approximately 350 shareholders in plan.

Performance Rating: ***

Great American Bank (NYSE:GTA)
600 B St.
San Diego, CA 92183
(619) 231-6231

Business Profile: Savings institution serving clients in California, Arizona, Colorado, and Montana.

Plan Specifics:
- Partial dividend reinvestment is not available.
- No Discount.
- OCP: $25 to $5000 per month.
- Selling costs are brokerage fees and service and handling charges.
- Company purchases stock monthly with OCPs.
- Approximately 3000 shareholders in the plan.

• Firm is not currently paying a dividend.

Performance Rating: *

Great Lakes Bancorp, FSB
(NASDAQ:GLBC)
One Great Lakes Plaza
401 East Liberty St.
Ann Arbor, MI 48107-8600
(313) 769-8300

Business Profile: Leading savings institution in Michigan.

Plan Specifics:
• Partial dividend reinvestment is not available.
• No Discount.
• OCP: $100 to $5000 per quarter.
• Selling costs are brokerage commissions and service charges.
• Company purchases stock each month with OCPs.

Performance Rating: **

Great Western Financial Corp.
(NYSE:GWF)
8484 Wilshire Blvd.
Beverly Hills, CA 90211-3213
(213) 852-3411   (818) 992-7173

Business Profile: Holding company for thrift bank with operations primarily in Florida and California.

Plan Specifics:
• Partial dividend reinvestment is available.
• 3 percent discount on reinvested dividends.
• OCP: $100 to $10,000 per quarter.
• Selling costs include brokerage fees and transfer taxes.
• Company purchases stock quarterly with OCPs.

Performance Rating: **

Green Mountain Power Corp.
(NYSE:GMP)
P.O. Box 850
25 Green Mountain Dr.
South Burlington, VT 05402
(802) 864-5731

Business Profile: Vermont-based electric utility serving residential, commercial, and industrial customers.

Plan Specifics:
• Partial dividend reinvestment is available.
• 5 percent discount on reinvested dividends.
• OCP: $50 to $6000 per quarter.
• Selling costs are brokerage fees.
• Company purchases stock monthly with OCPs.
• Approximately 2400 shareholders in the plan.

Performance Rating: **

Grumman Corp. (NYSE:GQ)
c/o Bank of New York
101 Barclay St., 22nd Floor
New York, NY 10286
(516) 575-5287   (516) 575-3202

Business Profile: Manufactures military aircraft for the United States Navy.

Plan Specifics:
• Partial dividend reinvestment is not available.
• No Discount.
• OCP: $25 to $10,000 per quarter.
• May have to go through own broker to sell shares.
• Company purchases stock monthly with OCPs.

Performance Rating: **

GTE Corp. (NYSE:GTE)
1776 Heritage Dr.
North Quincy, MA 02171
(800) 225-5160

Business Profile: Operates large telephone system and engages in manufacture of telecommunication and electrical products.

Plan Specifics:
- Partial dividend reinvestment is available.
- No Discount.
- OCP: $25 to $5000 per quarter.
- Selling cost is approximately 44 cents per share.
- Company purchases stock once a quarter with OCPs.
- Corporate preferred dividends are eligible for reinvestment for additional common shares under the plan.

Performance Rating: ****

Guardsman Products, Inc.
(NYSE:GPI)
P.O. Box 1521
2960 Lucerne Dr. SE
Grand Rapids, MI 49501-1521
(616) 957-2600   (212) 613-7147

Business Profile: Manufactures industrial coatings and home-care products.

Plan Specifics:
- Partial dividend reinvestment is not available.
- No Discount.
- OCP: $200 to $3000 per quarter.
- Selling costs are $15 service charge and any brokerage commission.
- Company purchases stock quarterly with OCPs.

Performance Rating: **

Gulf States Utilities Co.
(NYSE:GSU)
P.O. Box 1671
Beaumont, TX 77704
(800) 231-9266

Business Profile: Provides electric power to portions of Louisiana and Texas.

Plan Specifics:
- Partial dividend reinvestment is available.
- No Discount.
- OCP: $25 to $9000 per quarter.
- Purchasing fees are approximately 10 cents per share.
- Must go through own broker to sell shares.
- Company purchases stock once a month with OCPs.
- Approximately 22,000 shareholders in the plan.
- Preferred dividends are eligible for reinvestment for additional shares

Performance Rating: **

Handleman Co. (NYSE:HDL)
c/o National Bank of Detroit
P.O. Box 751
Detroit, MI 48232
(313) 225-2993   (313) 362-4400

Business Profile: Leading supplier of prerecorded music and videocassettes, books, and computer software for home entertainment.

Plan Specifics:
- Partial dividend reinvestment is not available.
- No Discount.
- OCP: $10 to $3000 per month.

- Selling costs are handling charge of $1 and brokerage commission.
- Stock is purchased at least quarterly with OCPs and most likely more frequently throughout the year.

Performance Rating: ***

Handy & Harman (NYSE:HNH)
850 Third Ave.
New York, NY 10022
(212) 207-2690 (212) 752-3400

Business Profile: Produces and refines precious metals. Manufactures automotive components for original equipment and replacement industries.

Plan Specifics:
- Partial dividend reinvestment is not available.
- No Discount.
- OCP: $10 to $60,000 per year.
- Selling costs include brokerage commissions.
- Company purchases stock each month with OCPs.

Performance Rating: **

Hanna, M. A., Co. (NYSE:MAH)
Suite #3600
1301 East 9th St.
Cleveland, OH 44114-1860
(216) 589-4201 (216) 737-5745

Business Profile: Produces formulated polymers, plastics, and rubber compounds. Also has interests in natural resources.

Plan Specifics:
- Partial dividend reinvestment is available.
- No Discount.
- OCP: $25 to $3000 per month.
- Selling costs are brokerage fees.

- Company purchases stock every month with OCPs.

Performance Rating: **

Hannaford Brothers Co.
(NYSE:HRD)
145 Pleasant Hill Rd.
Scarborough, ME 04074
(207) 883-2911

Business Profile: Largest food retailer in northern New England states with operations in drugstores.

Plan Specifics:
- Partial dividend reinvestment is not available.
- No Discount.
- OCP: $25 to $2000 per month.
- Selling costs are brokerage commissions and a handling charge of 5 percent of the amount invested (maximum of $2.50).
- Company purchases stock monthly with OCPs.

Performance Rating: ***

Harris Corp. (NYSE:HRS)
1025 West NASA Blvd.
Melbourne, FL 32919
(305) 727-9283 (305) 727-9100

Business Profile: Manufactures electronic systems, semiconductors, and communication equipment.

Plan Specifics:
- Partial dividend reinvestment is not available.
- No Discount.
- OCP: $10 to $5000 per quarter.
- Stock is purchased monthly with OCPs.
- Selling costs may include brokerage commissions.

Performance Rating: ***

Harsco Corp. (NYSE:HSC)
P.O. Box 8888
350 Poplar Church Rd.
Camp Hill, PA 17001-8888
(717) 763-7064   (201) 296-4070

Business Profile: Produces military defense vehicles, building products, and fabricated metals.

Plan Specifics:
- Partial dividend reinvestment is not available.
- No Discount.
- OCP: $10 to no maximum per month.
- Selling costs are $5 service charge and brokerage commissions.
- Company purchases stock monthly with OCPs.
- Approximately 2800 shareholders in the plan.
- Service charge of $5 for deposit of certificates.

Performance Rating: ***

Hartford Steam Boiler Inspection &
  Insurance Co. (NYSE:HSB)
One State Street
Hartford, CT 06102
(203) 722-1866   (800) 442-2001

Business Profile: Underwriter of property insurance for boilers and machinery.

Plan Specifics:
- Partial dividend reinvestment is not available.
- No Discount.
- OCP: $10 to $1000 per month.
- Stock is purchased monthly with OCPs.
- Selling costs include nominal brokerage fees.

Performance Rating: ***

Hartmarx Corp. (NYSE:HMX)
101 North Wacker Dr.
Chicago, IL 60606-7389
(312) 372-6300

Business Profile: Manufactures and retails men's and women's apparel.

Plan Specifics:
- Partial dividend reinvestment is not available.
- No Discount.
- OCP: $25 to $1000 per month.
- Selling costs may include brokerage fees.
- Company purchases stock around the 15th of the month with OCPs.

Performance Rating: **

Haverfield Corp. (NASDAQ:HVFD)
14650 Detroit Ave.
Lakewood, OH 44107
(216) 575-2532

Business Profile: Multibank holding company based in Ohio.

Plan Specifics:
- Partial dividend reinvestment is not available.
- No Discount.
- OCP: $20 to $1000 per month.
- No fees for selling shares.
- Company purchases stock monthly with OCPs.
- Approximately 100 shareholders in the plan.

Performance Rating: NR

Hawaiian Electric Industries, Inc.
  (NYSE:HE)
P.O. Box 730
Honolulu, HI 96808-0730
(808) 543-4605

Business Profile: Hawaii-based electric utility holding company.

Plan Specifics:
- Partial dividend reinvestment is not available.
- No Discount.
- OCP: $25 to $5000 per quarter.
- Selling costs are brokerage fees and a $5 service charge.
- Company purchases stock once a month with OCPs.
- Approximately 15,200 shareholders in the plan.
- Residents of the state of Hawaii who are not shareholders may make initial purchases of stock directly through the company; minimum initial investment is $100.

Performance Rating: ****

Health & Rehabilitation Properties Trust (NYSE:HRP)
400 Centre St.
Newton, MA 02158-2076
(617) 332-3990   (617) 328-5000

Business Profile: Real estate investment trust investing in income-producing health care real estate.

Plan Specifics:
- Partial dividend reinvestment is not available.
- No Discount.
- OCP: up to $10,000 per quarter.
- Selling costs include brokerage fees and $2.50 service fee.

Performance Rating: **

Health Care REIT, Inc. (ASE:HCN)
P.O. Box 1475
Toledo, OH 43603-1475
(419) 247-2800

Business Profile: Real estate investment trust investing in nursing homes, retirement homes, and psychiatric hospitals.

Plan Specifics:
- Partial dividend reinvestment is available.
- 4 percent discount on both reinvested dividends and OCPs.
- OCP: $10 to $2500 per quarter.
- Selling costs may include brokerage fees and any applicable service charges.
- Company purchases stock each quarter with OCPs.
- Minimum of 10 shares in order to enroll in the plan.

Performance Rating: **

Health Equity Properties, Inc. (NYSE:EQP)
P.O. Box 48
915 West 4th St.
Winston-Salem, NC 27102
(919) 723-7580

Business Profile: Real estate investment trust investing in income-producing health care facilities.

Plan Specifics:
- Partial dividend reinvestment is not available.
- No Discount.
- OCP: $100 to $2500 per quarter.
- Purchasing fees are brokerage costs.
- Selling costs include brokerage commissions and other costs of the sale.
- Company purchases stock quarterly with OCPs.

Performance Rating: **

HealthVest (ASE:HVT)
P.O. Box 4008
Austin, TX 78765
(512) 343-5234   (704) 374-6531

Business Profile: Real estate investment trust investing in health-care-related facilities.

Plan Specifics:
- Partial dividend reinvestment is available.
- No Discount.
- OCP: $50 to $5000 per quarter.
- Selling cost is brokerage commission.
- Company purchases stock monthly with OCPs.

Performance Rating: *

Heinz, H. J., Co. (NYSE:HNZ)
c/o Mellon Bank
P.O. Box 444
Pittsburgh, PA 15230
(412) 236-8000   (412) 456-5700

Business Profile: Produces ketchup, tuna fish, frozen potatoes, and other consumer items.

Plan Specifics:
- Partial dividend reinvestment is not available.
- No Discount.
- OCP: $25 to $1000 per month.
- Stock is purchased around the 10th of each month with OCPs.
- Selling cost is approximately 10 cents per share.

Performance Rating: ****

Hercules, Inc. (NYSE:HPC)
c/o Manufacturers Hanover
P.O. Box 24850, Church St. Sta.
New York, NY 10249
(212) 613-7147

Business Profile: Operations in specialty chemicals, aerospace, and fiber products.

Plan Specifics:
- Partial dividend reinvestment is not available.

- No Discount.
- OCP: $10 to $2000 per month.
- Selling costs are brokerage fees and $5 handling charge.
- Stock is purchased monthly with OCPs.

Performance Rating: **

Heritage Financial Corp.
 (NASDAQ:HFHC)
500 Forest Ave.
Richmond, VA 23229
(804) 344-1351

Business Profile: Virginia-based bank holding institution.

Plan Specifics:
- Partial dividend reinvestment is available.
- 5 percent discount on both reinvested dividends and OCPs.
- OCP: no minimum to $3000 per quarter.
- Stock is purchased quarterly with OCPs.
- Must go through own broker to sell shares.

Performance Rating: NR

Hershey Foods Corp. (NYSE:HSY)
P.O. Box 814
14 East Chocolate Ave.
Hershey, PA 17033-0814
(717) 534-7527   (212) 613-7147

Business Profile: Leading producer of chocolate, confectionery, and pasta products.

Plan Specifics:
- Partial dividend reinvestment is available.
- No Discount.
- OCP: $50 to $20,000 per year.
- Purchasing fees are brokerage fee

(approximately 5 to 8 cents per share) for OCPs plus service fee of 5 percent of total contribution (maximum, $5).
- Selling costs are sales fee of $15 per transaction plus brokerage commissions.
- $5 charge for withdrawal of certificates.
- Stock is purchased monthly with OCPs.
- Approximately 9615 shareholders in the plan.

Performance Rating: ****

Hexcel Corp. (NYSE:HXL)
Attn.: Corporate Secretary
11555 Dublin Blvd.
Dublin, CA 94568-0705
(415) 828-4200

Business Profile: Produces aerospace materials, fiber composites, and resins.

Plan Specifics:
- Partial dividend reinvestment is available.
- 5 percent discount on reinvested dividends.
- OCP: not available.
- Selling costs are brokerage commission and any other cost of sale.
- Approximately 3000 shareholders in the plan.

Performance Rating: **

Hibernia Corp. (NYSE:HIB)
P.O. Box 61540
313 Carondelet
New Orleans, LA 70161
(404) 897-3135 (504) 586-5552

Business Profile: Holding company for banks in Louisiana and Texas.

Plan Specifics:
- Partial dividend reinvestment is not available.
- 5 percent discount on reinvested dividends.
- OCP: $100 to $3000 per quarter.
- Selling of whole shares must be done through own broker.
- Company purchases stock once a month with OCPs.
- Approximately 2776 shareholders in the plan.

Performance Rating: *

Homestake Mining Co. (NYSE:HM)
c/o Bank of America
P.O. Box 37002
San Francisco, CA 94137
(415) 624-4100

Business Profile: Major gold producer in the United States.

Plan Specifics:
- Partial dividend reinvestment is not available.
- No Discount.
- OCP: $25 to $5000 per quarter.
- Selling cost is approximately 6 cents per share.
- Company purchases stock quarterly with OCPs.

Performance Rating: **

Honeywell, Inc. (NYSE:HON)
P.O. Box 524
Honeywell Plaza
Minneapolis, MN 55440
(612) 870-6887   (800) 647-4273

Business Profile: Manufactures automation and control systems including thermostats, fire controls, and guidance systems for home, industrial, and aerospace markets.

Plan Specifics:
- Partial dividend reinvestment is not available.
- No Discount.
- OCP: $25 to $3000 per month.
- Selling costs are brokerage commissions and related expenses of sale.
- Company purchases stock on the 20th day of the month with OCPs.

Performance Rating: ***

Hormel, Geo A., & Co. (NYSE:HRL)
c/o Norwest Bank MN
161 N. Concord Exchange
South St. Paul, MN 55075-0738
(612) 450-4075

Business Profile: Processes pork, poultry, and fish food items.

Plan Specifics:
- Partial dividend reinvestment is not available.
- No Discount.
- OCP: $25 to $1000 per month.
- Stock is purchased around the 15th of each month with OCPs, provided there are enough funds to purchase at least 100 shares.
- Selling costs are a $3 sales fee and 20 cents per share broker fee.
- Approximately 3000 shareholders in plan.

Performance Rating: ***

Hotel Investors Trust/Corp.
(NYSE:HOT)
Suite 610
11726 San Vicente Blvd.
Los Angeles, CA 90049
(213) 207-2505

Business Profile: Invests in and manages hotels.

Plan Specifics:
- Partial dividend reinvestment is available.
- No Discount.
- OCP: $25 to $3000 per quarter.
- Selling costs are brokerage commissions.
- Company purchases stock quarterly with OCPs.
- Approximately 800 shareholders in the plan.

Performance Rating: **

Household International, Inc.
(NYSE:HI)
2700 Sanders Rd.
Prospect Heights, IL 60070
(708) 564-5000

Business Profile: Holding company for financial services concern.

Plan Specifics:
- Partial dividend reinvestment is not available.
- No Discount.
- OCP: $10 to $5000 per quarter.
- Selling costs are brokerage commissions and a handling charge of $1.
- Stock is purchased at least quarterly, and most likely more frequently, with OCPs.
- Preferred dividends are eligible for reinvestment for additional common shares under the plan.

Performance Rating: ***

Houston Industries, Inc.
(NYSE:HOU)
P.O. Box 4505
Houston, TX 77210
(713) 629-3060   (800) 231-6406

Business Profile: Electric utility holding company provides electricity and cable television to regions of the Texas Gulf Coast.

Plan Specifics:
- Partial dividend reinvestment is available.
- No Discount.
- OCP: $50 to $6000 per quarter.
- Purchasing fees are 5 to 10 cents per share.
- Must sell shares through own broker.
- Company purchases stock monthly with OCPs.

Performance Rating: **

HRE Properties (NYSE:HRE)
c/o First Nat'l Bank of Boston
P.O. Box 1681
Boston, MA 02105
(212) 642-4800

Business Profile: Real estate investment trust.

Plan Specifics:
- Partial dividend reinvestment is available.
- No Discount.
- OCP: not available.
- May incur brokerage costs when selling shares.
- Approximately 800 shareholders in the plan.

Performance Rating: **

Hubbell, Inc. (ASE:HUB.B)
c/o Manufacturers Hanover
P.O. Box 24850, Church St. Sta.
New York, NY 10249
(212) 613-7147

Business Profile: Manufactures a variety of electrical equipment and supplies.

Plan Specifics:
- Partial dividend reinvestment is available.
- No Discount.
- OCP: $100 to $1000 per quarter.
- Selling costs include brokerage commissions and service charges.
- $5 fee for issuance of certificates.
- Stock is purchased monthly with OCPs.

Performance Rating: ****

Huffy Corp. (NYSE:HUF)
P.O. Box 1204
Dayton, OH 45401
(317) 639-7627

Business Profile: Largest United States manufacturer of bicycles.

Plan Specifics:
- Partial dividend reinvestment is not available.
- No Discount.
- OCP: $10 to $1000 per month.
- Participants may have to go through broker to sell shares.
- $2.50 charge for liquidation.
- Company purchases stock monthly with OCPs.

Performance Rating: **

Humana, Inc. (NYSE:HUM)
P.O. Box 1438
Louisville, KY 40201-1438
(502) 580-3761   (502) 580-1000

Business Profile: Major hospital management chain. Offers group health insurance.

Plan Specifics:
- Partial dividend reinvestment is not available.
- No Discount.

• OCP: not available.
• There is a small administrative fee when selling shares (less than $5) plus brokerage commissions.

Performance Rating: ****

Huntington Bancshares, Inc. (NASDAQ:HBAN)
c/o Huntington National Bank
P.O. Box 5065
Cleveland, OH 44101
(216) 344-6822   (614) 463-4304

Business Profile: Multibank holding company headquartered in Ohio.

Plan Specifics:
• Partial dividend reinvestment is not available.
• 5 percent discount on reinvested dividends.
• OCP: $50 to $5000 per quarter.
• Selling costs are minimal.
• Company purchases stock monthly with OCPs.
• 4000 to 4500 shareholders in the plan.

Performance Rating: ***

IBP, Inc. (NYSE:IBP)
c/o Chase Manhattan
P.O. Box 283, Bowling Green Sta.
New York, NY 10274
(402) 494-2061   (201) 592-4115

Business Profile: Largest provider of fresh, boxed beef and pork goods.

Plan Specifics:
• Partial dividend reinvestment is not available.
• No Discount.
• OCP: $10 to $1000 per month.
• Stock is purchased around the 15th of the month with OCPs.
• Purchasing fees are 5 percent on

each investment ($3 maximum) plus brokerage fees.
• $5 service fee for depositing certificates.
• Selling costs are $1 service fee plus brokerage fees.

Performance Rating: **

ICM Property Investors, Inc. (NYSE:ICM)
c/o Chase Manhattan
P.O. Box 283, Bowling Green Sta.
New York, NY 10274
(201) 592-4000   (212) 986-5640

Business Profile: Real estate investment trust.

Plan Specifics:
• Partial dividend reinvestment is not available.
• No Discount.
• OCP: $25 to $5000 per quarter.
• Stock is purchased quarterly with OCPs.

Performance Rating: **

Idaho Power Co. (NYSE:IDA)
P.O. Box 70
Boise, ID 83707
(800) 635-5406

Business Profile: Electric utility serving Idaho and sections of Oregon and Nevada.

Plan Specifics:
• Partial dividend reinvestment is available.
• No Discount.
• OCP: $10 to $15,000 per quarter.
• Purchasing fees are approximately 5 cents per share.
• Must go through own broker to sell shares.

- Company purchases stock quarterly with OCPs.
- Approximately 12,000 shareholders in the plan.

Performance Rating: ***

IE Industries, Inc. (NYSE:IEL)
P.O. Box 351
Cedar Rapids, IA 52406
(800) 247-9785

Business Profile: Holding company for electric utility in Iowa.

Plan Specifics:
- Partial dividend reinvestment is not available.
- No Discount.
- OCP: $25 minimum per month.
- Selling costs include brokerage fees.
- Company purchases stock once a month with OCPs.
- Although there is no maximum OCP, company reserves right to refuse OCPs of more than $5000 per month.

Performance Rating: ***

Illinois Power Co. (NYSE:IPC)
Attn.: Shareholder Services
500 S. 27th St.
Decatur, IL 62525-1805
(800) 800-8220

Business Profile: Provides electric and gas services to residential, industrial, and commercial customers in Illinois.

Plan Specifics:
- Partial dividend reinvestment is available.
- No Discount.
- OCP: $25 to $5000 per quarter.
- Stock is purchased monthly with OCPs.

- Selling cost is around 10 cents per share.
- Preferred dividends are eligible for reinvestment for additional common shares under the plan.

Performance Rating: **

IMCERA Group, Inc. (NYSE:IMA)
2315 Sanders Rd.
Northbrook, IL 60062
(708) 564-8600

Business Profile: Manufactures medical products, specialty chemicals, and animal health products.

Plan Specifics:
- Partial dividend reinvestment is not available.
- No Discount.
- OCP: up to $1000 per month.
- Selling cost is approximately 10 cents per share.
- Company purchases stock once a month with OCPs.
- Approximately 2000 shareholders in the plan.

Performance Rating: **

Imperial Bancorp (NASDAQ:IBAN)
c/o Security Pacific Nat'l Bank
P.O. Box 3546, Terminal Annex
Los Angeles, CA 90051
(818) 507-2215

Business Profile: Holding company for major bank in California.

Plan Specifics:
- Partial dividend reinvestment is not available.
- No Discount.
- OCP: not available.
- Brokerage fees and other costs when purchasing and selling.

Performance Rating: **

Imperial Oil Ltd. (ASE:IMO)
111 St. Clair Ave. West
Toronto, Ont. M5W 1K3 Canada
(416) 968-5076

Business Profile: Produces crude oil, natural gas, and petroleum in Canada; 70 percent owned by Exxon.

Plan Specifics:
- Partial dividend reinvestment is available.
- OCP: $50 to $5000 (Canadian) per quarter.
- Must go through own broker to sell shares.
- Company purchases stock four times a year with OCPs.
- 30 to 35 percent of the total shareholders are enrolled in the plan.

Performance Rating: ***

INB Financial Corp.
(NASDAQ:INBF)
One Indiana Sq.
Indianapolis, IN 46266
(317) 266-6824

Business Profile: Offers banking services in Indiana.

Plan Specifics:
- Partial dividend reinvestment is not available.
- No Discount.
- OCP: $100 to $5000 per quarter.
- Selling costs are brokerage commissions.
- Company purchases stock monthly with OCPs.
- Approximately 1293 shareholders in the plan.

Performance Rating: **

Inco Ltd. (NYSE:N)
One New York Plaza
New York, NY 10004
(212) 612-5845   (212) 612-5500

Business Profile: Leading producer of nickel with operations in copper and other metals.

Plan Specifics:
- Partial dividend reinvestment is available.
- 5 percent discount on reinvested dividends.
- OCP: $30 to $10,000 per quarter.
- Participants may have to go through own broker to sell shares.
- Company purchases stock once each quarter with OCPs.

Performance Rating: **

Independence Bancorp (PA)
(NASDAQ:INBC)
One Hillendale Rd.
Perkasie, PA 18944
(215) 453-3005

Business Profile: Pennsylvania-based multibank holding company.

Plan Specifics:
- Partial dividend reinvestment is not available.
- 5 percent discount on reinvested dividends.
- OCP: $50 to $3000 per quarter.
- Selling costs are brokerage commissions and $3.50 service charge.
- Company purchases stock monthly with OCPs.
- Approximately 4500 shareholders in the plan.

Performance Rating: **

Independent Bank Corp. (MA)
(NASDAQ:INDB)
288 Union St.
Rockland, MA 02370
(617) 878-6100

Business Profile: Massachusetts-based bank holding company.

Plan Specifics:
- Partial dividend reinvestment is available.
- 5 percent discount on reinvested dividends.
- OCP: $25 up to the amount shareholder receives annually in dividends.
- Participants may have to go through own broker to sell shares.
- Company purchases stock every month with OCPs.
- Approximately 622 shareholders in the plan.
- Company is not currently paying a dividend.

Performance Rating: *

Independent Bank Corp. (MI)
(NASDAQ:IBCP)
c/o NBD Bank
900 Tower Dr.
Troy, MI 48098
(313) 828-6900

Business Profile: Michigan-based bank holding company.

Plan Specifics:
- Partial dividend reinvestment is available.
- 5 percent discount on reinvested dividends.
- OCP: $15 to $1000 per quarter.
- Stock is purchased quarterly with OCPs.
- Selling costs include $3 service fee.

Performance Rating: NR

Indiana Energy, Inc. (NYSE:IEI)
1630 North Meridian St.
Indianapolis, IN 46202-1496
(317) 921-0509   (317) 926-3351

Business Profile: Holding company for Indiana-based natural gas distributor.

Plan Specifics:
- Partial dividend reinvestment is available.
- No Discount.
- OCP: $25 to $3000 per quarter.
- Selling costs are brokerage fees.
- Company purchases stock each quarter with OCPs.
- Approximately 2200 shareholders in the plan.

Performance Rating: ****

Ingersoll-Rand Co. (NYSE:IR)
c/o Bank of New York
101 Barclay St.
New York, NY 10286
(201) 573-0123   (800) 524-4458

Business Profile: Designs and produces compressed air systems. Produces equipment for mining, construction, and automotive markets.

Plan Specifics:
- Partial dividend reinvestment is not available.
- No Discount.
- OCP: $10 to $3000 per quarter.
- Stock is purchased around the 1st of each month with OCPs.
- Selling cost is pro rata share of brokerage fees.

Performance Rating: ***

Inland Steel Industries, Inc.
(NYSE:IAD)
30 West Monroe St.
Chicago, IL 60603
(312) 346-0300   (312) 461-3932

Business Profile: Major integrated steel producer.

Plan Specifics:
* Partial dividend reinvestment is not available.
* No Discount.
* OCP: up to $10,000 per quarter.
* Selling costs include small brokerage fee.
* Company purchases stock once a month with OCPs.
* Approximately 3500 shareholders in the plan.

Performance Rating: **

Integra Financial Corp.
(NASDAQ:ITGR)
4th Ave. & Wood St.
Pittsburgh, PA 15278-2331
(412) 644-7515   (412) 644-8400

Business Profile: Multibank holding company serving Pennsylvania communities.

Plan Specifics:
* Partial dividend reinvestment is not available.
* No Discount.
* OCP: $100 to $3000 per quarter.
* Selling costs are brokerage fees and service charge.
* Company purchases stock quarterly with OCPs.

Performance Rating: NR

Intermark, Inc. (ASE:IMI)
1020 Prospect St.
La Jolla, CA 92037
(619) 459-3841

Business Profile: Has major holdings in several mid-sized companies.

Plan Specifics:
* Partial dividend reinvestment is not available.
* No Discount.
* OCP: $10 to $1000 per month.
* Selling cost is brokerage commission.
* Company purchases stock every month with OCPs.
* Approximately 1000 shareholders in the plan.
* Preferred dividends are eligible for reinvestment for additional common shares under the plan.
* Company is not currently paying a dividend.

Performance Rating: *

International Business Machines Corp. (NYSE:IBM)
590 Madison Ave.
New York, NY 10022
(212) 735-7000

Business Profile: Largest producer of mainframe, small business, and personal computers.

Plan Specifics:
* Partial dividend reinvestment is available.
* No Discount.
* OCP: $10 to $5000 per quarter.
* Stock is purchased around the 10th of the month with OCPs.
* Selling cost is approximately 10 cents per share.

Performance Rating: ****

International Multifoods Corp. (NYSE:IMC)
P.O. Box 2942
Multifoods Tower
Minneapolis, MN 55402-0942
(612) 340-3677 (212) 791-6422

Business Profile: International food company with operations in frozen foods and bakery items.

Plan Specifics:
- Partial dividend reinvestment is available.
- No Discount.
- OCP: $10 to $60,000 per year.
- Selling costs are small brokerage fees.
- Company purchases stock beginning on the 15th day of each month with OCPs.
- Approximately 1546 shareholders in the plan.

Performance Rating: ***

International Paper Co. (NYSE:IP)
2 Manhattanville Rd.
Purchase, NY 10577
(914) 397-1500 (212) 613-7147

Business Profile: Leading manufacturer of paper and related items.

Plan Specifics:
- Partial dividend reinvestment is available.
- No Discount.
- OCP: $25 to $20,000 per year.
- Stock is purchased monthly with OCPs.
- Selling costs include $15 liquidation fee and $5 fee for issuing certificates.

Performance Rating: ***

Interpublic Group of Companies, Inc. (NYSE:IPG)
c/o First Chicago Trust-NY
P.O. Box 3506, Church St. Sta.
New York, NY 10008-3506
(212) 791-6422

Business Profile: Leading advertising agency system.

Plan Specifics:
- Partial dividend reinvestment is not available.
- No Discount.
- OCP: $10 to $3000 per quarter.
- Stock is purchased quarterly with OCPs.
- Purchasing fees are 5 percent of total funds invested with a $2.50 maximum and small brokerage commission of about 1 percent of amount invested.
- Selling costs are brokerage commission and other costs of sale.

Performance Rating: ***

Interstate Power Co. (NYSE:IPW)
P.O. Box 769
1000 Main St.
Dubuque, IA 52004-0769
(319) 582-5421

Business Profile: Provides electric power and natural gas to Iowa, Minnesota, and Illinois.

Plan Specifics:
- Partial dividend reinvestment is available.
- No Discount.
- OCP: $25 to $3000 per quarter.
- Purchasing fees are very minimal, probably less than 10 cents per share.
- Selling costs are minimal brokerage fees.

- Company purchases stock once a quarter with OCPs.
- Approximately 5000 shareholders in the plan.

Performance Rating: **

Investors Financial Corp.
(NASDAQ:INVF)
9201 Forest Hill Ave.
Richmond, VA 23235
(804) 323-4604

Business Profile: Virginia-based savings and loan organization.

Plan Specifics:
- Partial dividend reinvestment is not available.
- No Discount.
- OCP: $25 to $10,000 per quarter.
- Brokerage costs will be incurred when selling shares.
- Company purchases stock once a month with OCPs.
- Approximately 1200 shareholders in the plan.
- Firm is not currently paying a dividend.

Performance Rating: *

Iowa-Illinois Gas & Electric Co.
(NYSE:IWG)
P.O. Box 4350
Davenport, IA 52808
(800) 373-4443

Business Profile: Markets gas and electricity to Illinois and Iowa cities.

Plan Specifics:
- Partial dividend reinvestment is available.
- No Discount.
- OCP: $25 to $5000 per quarter.
- Purchasing fees are approximately 4 to 8 cents per share.

- Must go through own broker to sell shares.
- Company purchases stock quarterly with OCPs.
- Approximately 8000 shareholders in the plan.

Performance Rating: ***

IPALCO Enterprises, Inc.
(NYSE:IPL)
P.O. Box 798
Indianapolis, IN 46206
(317) 261-8394 (317) 261-8261

Business Profile: Holding company for electric utility serving Indianapolis.

Plan Specifics:
- Partial dividend reinvestment is available.
- No Discount.
- OCP: $25 to $3000 per month.
- Purchasing and selling fees are approximately 6 cents per share.
- Company purchases stock once a month with OCPs.
- Approximately 25 percent of the shareholders are enrolled in the plan.

Performance Rating: ****

IRT Property Co. (NYSE:IRT)
Suite 1400
200 Galleria Pkwy.
Atlanta, GA 30339
(404) 955-4406

Business Profile: Real estate investment trust.

Plan Specifics:
- Partial dividend reinvestment is available.
- 5 percent discount on reinvested dividends.
- OCP: not available.

- Selling costs may include brokerage fees.
- Approximately 1000 shareholders in the plan.

Performance Rating: **

ITT Corp. (NYSE:ITT)
P.O. Box 1507
Secaucus, NJ 07096-1507
(201) 601-4202

Business Profile: Manufactures automotive, electrical, and industrial products. Provides services in finance and insurance.

Plan Specifics:
- Partial dividend reinvestment is not available.
- No Discount.
- OCP: $50 to $60,000 per year.
- Selling costs are brokerage commissions.
- Company purchases stock every month with OCPs.
- Approximately 22,078 shareholders in the plan.

Performance Rating: ***

IWC Resources Corp.
(NASDAQ:IWCR)
P.O. Box 1220
1220 Waterway Blvd.
Indianapolis, IN 46206
(317) 263-6358   (317) 639-1501

Business Profile: Holding company for public water utility serving Indianapolis-area communities.

Plan Specifics:
- Partial dividend reinvestment is available.
- No Discount.
- OCP: $25 to $5000 per quarter.

- Selling costs are brokerage commission and other charges incurred.
- Company agent purchases stock around the 1st business day of the month with OCPs.

Performance Rating: **

Jefferson Bankshares, Inc.
(NASDAQ:JBNK)
123 East Main St.
Charlottesville, VA 22901
(804) 972-1115   (804) 972-1100

Business Profile: Virginia-based bank holding company.

Plan Specifics:
- Partial dividend reinvestment is not available.
- 5 percent discount on reinvested dividends.
- OCP: $30 to $1500 per quarter.
- Participants may have to sell through own broker.
- Company purchases stock quarterly with OCPs.
- Approximately 2100 shareholders in the plan.

Performance Rating: NR

Jefferson-Pilot Corp. (NYSE:JP)
c/o First Union Nat'l Bank
Stock Transfer CMG-5
Charlotte, NC 28288-1154
(919) 691-3000   (919) 691-3375

Business Profile: Insurance holding company with operations in life insurance, television, and radio communications.

Plan Specifics:
- Partial dividend reinvestment is not available.
- No Discount.
- OCP: $20 to $1000 per month.

- Purchasing fees include investor's share of brokerage expenses plus 4 percent service fee (up to $2.50).
- Selling costs may include brokerage fees.
- Plan has about 1500 members.
- Shares will be purchased at least monthly if funds are available for round-lot purchase.

Performance Rating: ***

Johnson & Johnson (NYSE:JNJ)
One Johnson & Johnson Plaza
New Brunswick, NJ 08933
(201) 524-3376   (212) 791-6422

Business Profile: Leading supplier of health care products and consumer products.

Plan Specifics:
- Partial dividend reinvestment is available.
- No Discount.
- OCP: $25 to $3000 per quarter.
- Selling costs are brokerage commissions and any other costs of sale.
- Company purchases stock beginning on the 7th of the month with OCPs.

Performance Rating: ****

Johnson Controls, Inc. (NYSE:JCI)
Investor Relations
P.O. Box 591
Milwaukee, WI 53201-0591
(414) 287-3956   (414) 228-2363

Business Profile: Major producer of automated building controls, batteries, automotive seating, and plastics.

Plan Specifics:
- Partial dividend reinvestment is available.
- No Discount.
- OCP: $50 to $15,000 per quarter.

- Selling costs are brokerage fees and $5 fee when account is closed.
- Company purchases stock once a month with OCPs.
- Approximately 12,000 shareholders in the plan.
- Initial purchase of stock can be made through the company with a minimum payment of $50.

Performance Rating: ***

Jostens, Inc. (NYSE:JOS)
c/o Norwest Bank Minnesota
P.O. Box 738
South St. Paul, MN 55075
(612) 450-4064   (612) 830-3287

Business Profile: Leading provider of class rings, yearbooks, and diplomas for schools and universities.

Plan Specifics:
- Partial dividend reinvestment is not available.
- No Discount.
- OCP: $25 to $1000 per month.
- Selling costs are brokerage commissions and service fees.
- Company purchases stock around the 1st of each month with OCPs, provided there are enough funds to purchase at least 100 shares.

Performance Rating: ****

Justin Industries, Inc.
** (NASDAQ:JSTN)**
P.O. Box 425
2821 West Seventh St.
Fort Worth, TX 76101
(817) 390-2415   (817) 336-5125

Business Profile: Manufactures western-style footwear, building materials, and industrial equipment.

Plan Specifics:
- Partial dividend reinvestment is not available.
- No Discount.
- OCP: $25 to $1000 per month.
- Purchasing fees are service charge of 5 percent of the amount of the dividend or OCP submitted for investment (maximum $3 per investment) plus brokerage costs.
- Company suggests having a quarterly dividend of at least $20 to enroll.
- Selling costs are brokerage fees.
- Company purchases stock monthly with OCPs.

Performance Rating: **

K N Energy, Inc. (NYSE:KNE)
P.O. Box 15265
Lakewood, CO 80215-0265
(303) 989-1740

Business Profile: Natural gas company serving customers in Colorado, Kansas, Nebraska, and Wyoming.

Plan Specifics:
- Partial dividend reinvestment is available.
- No Discount.
- OCP: $5 to $3000 per quarter.
- Must go through own broker to sell.
- Purchasing fees are 6 to 7 cents per share.
- Company purchases stock once a month with OCPs.
- Preferred dividends are eligible for reinvestment for additional common shares under the plan.
- Approximately 2400 shareholders in the plan.

Performance Rating: **

Kaman Corp. (NASDAQ:KAMNA)
c/o Manufacturers Hanover
P.O. Box 24850, Church St. Sta.
New York, NY 10249
(212) 613-7147   (203) 243-6307

Business Profile: Provides scientific systems and services for government. Distributes industrial parts and musical instruments.

Plan Specifics:
- Partial dividend reinvestment is not available.
- No Discount.
- OCP: $25 to $5000 per quarter.
- Selling costs are brokerage fees.
- Company purchases stock at least once a quarter with OCPs.

Performance Rating: **

Kansas Gas & Electric Co.
(NYSE:KGE)
P.O. Box 208
Wichita, KS 67201-0208
(316) 261-6640   (800) 527-2495

Business Profile: Electric utility serving residential, commercial, and industrial customers in southeastern Kansas.

Plan Specifics:
- Partial dividend reinvestment is available.
- No Discount.
- OCP: $25 to $5000 per quarter.
- Purchasing and selling fees are approximately 5 cents per share.
- Company purchases stock every month with OCPs.
- Approximately 13,000 shareholders in the plan.

Performance Rating: **

**Kansas Power & Light Co.
(NYSE:KAN)
P.O. Box 889
818 Kansas
Topeka, KS 66601
(913) 296-1950 (800) 647-4273**

Business Profile: Supplies electricity to residential, commercial, and industrial customers in Kansas, Oklahoma, Nebraska, and Missouri.

Plan Specifics:
- Partial dividend reinvestment is not available.
- No Discount.
- OCP: $25 to $3000 per quarter.
- Purchasing costs include brokerage fees of 5 to 10 cents per share.
- Termination fee of $15.
- Company purchases stock once a quarter with OCPs.
- Approximately 7200 shareholders in the plan.

Performance Rating: ***

**Kelley Oil & Gas Partners, Ltd.
(ASE:KLY)
601 Jefferson
Suite 1100
Houston, TX 77002
(713) 652-5200**

Business Profile: Texas-based oil and gas publicly traded master limited partnership.

Plan Specifics:
- Partial dividend reinvestment is available.
- No Discount.
- OCP: $25 to no maximum per payment.
- Purchasing fees are brokerage costs plus 5 percent of the amount reinvested up to a maximum of $3.50 per investment.
- Participant may have to sell shares through own broker.
- $5 service charge for termination.
- OCPs will be used to purchase shares as soon as practicable within a 30-day period after receipt.

Performance Rating: **

**Kellogg Co. (NYSE:K)
One Kellogg Square
P.O. Box 3599
Battle Creek, MI 49016-3599
(616) 961-2765**

Business Profile: Leading supplier of cereals and other breakfast items.

Plan Specifics:
- Partial dividend reinvestment is available.
- No Discount.
- OCP: $25 to $25,000 per year.
- Selling costs are brokerage commission and other expenses.
- Company purchases stock around the 15th of the month with OCPs.

Performance Rating: ****

**Kemper Corp. (NYSE:KEM)
c/o Harris Trust & Savings Bank
P.O. Box A3309
Chicago, IL 60690
(800) 526-8762**

Business Profile: Financial services holding firm with operations in life and property-casualty insurance, reinsurance, and investment services.

Plan Specifics:
- Partial dividend reinvestment is not available.
- 5 percent discount on reinvested dividends.

- OCP: $10 to $5000 per quarter.
- Stock is purchased monthly with OCPs.
- Selling costs are 5 to 6 cents per share.

Performance Rating: **

Kennametal, Inc. (NYSE:KMT)
P.O. Box 231
Latrobe, PA 15650
(412) 539-5204 (412) 539-5000

Business Profile: Manufactures cemented carbide tools, ceramics, and metalworking supplies.

Plan Specifics:
- Partial dividend reinvestment is not available.
- 5 percent discount on reinvested dividends.
- OCP: $25 to $3000 per quarter.
- Selling costs may include brokerage fees.
- Company purchases stock four times a year with OCPs.
- Approximately 1000 shareholders in the plan.

Performance Rating: **

Kentucky Utilities Co. (NYSE:KU)
One Quality St.
Lexington, KY 40507
(606) 255-2100 (606) 288-1188

Business Profile: Provides electric power to residential, commercial, and industrial population in Kentucky and Virginia.

Plan Specifics:
- Partial dividend reinvestment is available.
- No Discount.
- OCP: $20 to $10,000 per quarter.
- Approximately 5 cents per share

commission when purchasing and selling.
- Company purchases stock quarterly with OCPs.
- Approximately 9094 shareholders in the plan.

Performance Rating: ***

Kerr-McGee Corp. (NYSE:KMG)
c/o Liberty National B & T
P.O. Box 25848
Oklahoma City, OK 73125
(405) 231-6711 (405) 270-1313

Business Profile: Produces natural gas and crude oil. Operations in chemicals and contract drilling.

Plan Specifics:
- Partial dividend reinvestment is not available.
- No Discount.
- OCP: $10 to $1000 per month.
- Selling costs may include brokerage fees.
- Stock is purchased at least quarterly with OCPs.

Performance Rating: ***

Key Centurion Bancshares, Inc.
(NASDAQ:KEYC)
c/o Pittsburgh National Bank
P.O. Box 548
Pittsburgh, PA 15230
(304) 345-2828 (800) 752-9678

Business Profile: Virginia-based commercial banking firm.

Plan Specifics:
- Partial dividend reinvestment is not available.
- No Discount.
- OCP: $25 to $1000 per quarter.
- Selling costs are service charge and any brokerage charges.

* Company purchases stock quarterly with OCPs.

Performance Rating: NR

KeyCorp (NYSE:KEY)
One KeyCorp Plaza
P.O. Box 88
Albany, NY 12201-0088
(800) 888-7412

Business Profile: Interstate bank holding company headquartered in Albany, New York.

Plan Specifics:
* Partial dividend reinvestment is not available.
* No Discount.
* OCP: $10 to $10,000 per month.
* Selling costs include a handling charge of $5 per transaction.
* Company purchases stock monthly with OCPs.

Performance Rating: ***

Keystone Financial, Inc.
(NASDAQ:KSTN)
P.O. Box 1653
225 Market Bldg.
Harrisburg, PA 17105-1653
(717) 233-1555

Business Profile: Pennsylvania multibank holding company.

Plan Specifics:
* Partial dividend reinvestment is not available.
* No Discount.
* OCP: $100 to $5000 per dividend payment date.
* Stock is purchased quarterly with OCPs.
* Participants may have to go through broker to sell shares.

* Approximately 1330 shareholders in the plan.

Performance Rating: NR

Keystone Heritage Group, Inc.
(NASDAQ:KHGI)
P.O. Box 1285
Lebanon, PA 17042-1285
(717) 274-6800

Business Profile: Bank holding company based in Pennsylvania.

Plan Specifics:
* Partial dividend reinvestment is not available.
* No Discount.
* OCP: $10 to $2000 per quarter.
* Participants may have to pay brokerage costs if shares are purchased on the open market.
* $3 termination fee.
* Participants may have to go through own broker to sell.
* Company purchases stock quarterly with OCPs.

Performance Rating: NR

Keystone International, Inc.
(NYSE:KII)
9600 W Gulf Bank Dr.
P.O. Box 40010
Houston, TX 77240
(713) 937-5301

Business Profile: Produces flow control equipment and systems.

Plan Specifics:
* Partial dividend reinvestment is available.
* No Discount.
* OCP: $50 to $5000 per quarter.
* Selling costs are nominal brokerage commission and $1 service fee.

- Company purchases stock quarterly with OCPs.

Performance Rating: ***

Kimberly-Clark Corp. (NYSE:KMB)
P.O. Box 619100
DFW Airport Station
Dallas, TX 75261-9100
(214) 830-1200   (800) 442-2001

Business Profile: Produces facial tissues, feminine napkins, disposable diapers, and paper towels.

Plan Specifics:
- Partial dividend reinvestment is available.
- No Discount.
- OCP: $25 to $3000 per quarter.
- Stock is purchased approximately eight times a year with OCPs.
- Purchasing fees are a 5 percent service charge on the amount invested (maximum of $2.50) plus brokerage commissions of approximately 1 percent of amount invested.
- Selling costs include brokerage fees plus service charge (maximum of $3.50).

Performance Rating: ****

Knight-Ridder, Inc. (NYSE:KRI)
One Herald Plaza
Miami, FL 33132
(305) 376-3938   (212) 613-7147

Business Profile: Leading newspaper publisher with operations in electronic information distribution.

Plan Specifics:
- Partial dividend reinvestment is not available.
- No Discount.
- OCP: $25 to $1000 per month.

- Selling costs may include brokerage fees.
- Company purchases stock monthly with OCPs.
- Approximately 3400 shareholders in the plan.

Performance Rating: ****

Koger Properties, Inc. (NYSE:KOG)
P.O. Box 4520
Jacksonville, FL 32201
(904) 396-4811   (800) 633-4236

Business Profile: Manages suburban office centers in the Sunbelt.

Plan Specifics:
- Partial dividend reinvestment is available.
- No Discount.
- OCP: $100 to $2500 per month.
- Selling costs are brokerage commissions.
- Company purchases stock monthly with OCPs.

Performance Rating: *

Kroger Co. (NYSE:KR)
1014 Vine St.
Cincinnati, OH 45201-1119
(513) 762-4808   (212) 791-6422

Business Profile: Manages supermarkets and convenience stores.

Plan Specifics:
- Partial dividend reinvestment is not available.
- No Discount.
- OCP: $20 to $60,000 per year.
- Selling cost is approximately 10 cents per share.
- Company purchases stock monthly with OCPs.
- Nonshareholders may make initial

purchase of stock directly through the plan (minimum of $20).
* Company is not currently paying a dividend.

Performance Rating: **

Kuhlman Corp. (NYSE:KUH)
P.O. Box 3021
Birmingham, MI 48012
(313) 222-4381   (313) 828-6900

Business Profile: Produces electric transformers and plastic and metal products.

Plan Specifics:
* Partial dividend reinvestment is not available.
* No Discount.
* OCP: $10 to $3000 per quarter.
* Selling costs include service fee of $3.
* Company purchases stock once a month with OCPs.

Performance Rating: **

La-Z-Boy Chair Co. (NYSE:LZB)
1284 N. Telegraph Rd.
Monroe, MI 48161-3390
(212) 936-5100

Business Profile: Manufactures reclining chairs and upholstered furniture.

Plan Specifics:
* Partial dividend reinvestment is not available.
* No Discount.
* OCP: $25 to $1000 per month.
* Selling costs are brokerage commission and charge of $5.
* Company purchases stock each month with OCPs.

Performance Rating: ***

Laclede Gas Co. (NYSE:LG)
720 Olive St.
St Louis, MO 63101
(314) 342-0506   (314) 466-1579

Business Profile: Retail supplier of natural gas in St. Louis communities.

Plan Specifics:
* Partial dividend reinvestment is available.
* No Discount.
* OCP: not available.
* No Selling costs.
* Approximately 2044 shareholders in the plan.

Performance Rating: ***

Lafarge Corp. (NYSE:LAF)
c/o NCNB Texas
901 Main St., P.O. Box 831402
Dallas, TX 75283-1402
(214) 508-1707   (703) 264-3600

Business Profile: Produces cement and other construction materials.

Plan Specifics:
* Partial dividend reinvestment is not available.
* 5 percent discount on reinvested dividends.
* OCP: not available.
* Must go through own broker to sell shares.

Performance Rating: **

Lakeland First Financial Group, Inc.
  (NASDAQ:LLSL)
P.O. Box 364
Succasunna, NJ 07876
(201) 584-6666

Business Profile: New Jersey-based financial institution.

Plan Specifics:
- Partial dividend reinvestment is not available.
- No Discount.
- OCP: $100 to $2000 per quarter.
- Participants may incur brokerage fees when selling shares.
- Company purchases stock once a quarter with OCPs.

Performance Rating: NR

Lance, Inc. (NASDAQ:LNCE)
P.O. Box 32368
Charlotte, NC 28232
(704) 554-1421

Business Profile: Produces snack foods and bakery items.

Plan Specifics:
- Partial dividend reinvestment is not available.
- No Discount.
- OCP: $10 to $1000 per month.
- DRIP fee is service charge of 4 percent of amount invested with OCPs up to a maximum of $2.50 for each investment period.
- Selling costs are brokerage fees.
- Company purchases stock monthly with OCPs.

Performance Rating: ***

Landmark Bancshares Corp.
(NYSE:LBC)
c/o Boatmen's Trust Co.
P.O. Box 14737
St. Louis, MO 63178
(314) 963-2500

Business Profile: Multibank holding company with offices in St. Louis area.

Plan Specifics:
- Partial dividend reinvestment is available.

- 5 percent discount on reinvested dividends.
- OCP: $25 to $2500 per quarter.
- Participant may have to go through own broker to sell shares, although fractional shares will be sold by company for no cost.
- Company purchases stock monthly with OCPs.

Performance Rating: *

LG&E Energy Corp. (NYSE:LGE)
P.O. Box 32010
Louisville, KY 40232
(502) 627-3445   (800) 235-9705

Business Profile: Provides electric power and gas to Louisville customers.

Plan Specifics:
- Partial dividend reinvestment is available.
- No Discount.
- OCP: $25 to $5000 per quarter.
- May sell reinvested shares through company if terminating account; brokers' fee of $0.05 per share sold.
- Company purchases stock around the 15th of the month with OCPs.

Performance Rating: ***

Liberty National Bancorp, Inc.
(NASDAQ:LNBC)
P.O. Box 32500
Louisville, KY 40232
(502) 566-2059

Business Profile: Offers banking services in Kentucky, primarily in the Louisville area.

Plan Specifics:
- Partial dividend reinvestment is available.
- No Discount.
- OCP: $25 to $5000 per quarter.

- Selling costs are $5 termination fee and $2.50 fee for each certificate withdrawn plus any brokerage fees.
- Company purchases stock quarterly with OCPs.
- At least 1300 shareholders in the plan.

Performance Rating: NR

Lilly, Eli, & Co. (NYSE:LLY)
Lilly Corporate Center
Indianapolis, IN 46285
(800) 833-8699

Business Profile: Leading supplier of prescription drugs including antibiotics.

Plan Specifics:
- Partial dividend reinvestment is not available.
- No Discount.
- OCP: $25 to $25,000 per year.
- No selling costs.
- Company purchases stock monthly with OCPs.
- Approximately 15,000 shareholders in the plan.

Performance Rating: ****

Limited, The, Inc. (NYSE:LTD)
c/o First Chicago Trust-NY
P.O. Box 3506, Church St. Sta.
New York, NY 10008-3506
(212) 791-6422   (614) 479-7000

Business Profile: Leading retailer of women's apparel.

Plan Specifics:
- Partial dividend reinvestment is not available.
- No Discount.
- OCP: $30 to $6000 per quarter.
- Selling costs are brokerage commissions and related expenses of sale.

- Company purchases stock approximately eight times a year with OCPs.

Performance Rating: ***

Lincoln National Corp. (NYSE:LNC)
c/o First Nat'l Bank of Boston
P.O. Box 644
Boston, MA 02102
(800) 442-2001   (617) 575-2900

Business Profile: Insurance-based holding company offering life, health, and property-casualty coverage.

Plan Specifics:
- Partial dividend reinvestment is available.
- No Discount.
- OCP: $25 to $1700 per month.
- Stock is purchased monthly with OCPs.
- Selling costs are $1 fee plus brokerage fees.
- Preferred dividends are eligible for reinvestment for additional common shares under the plan.

Performance Rating: ***

Lincoln NC Realty Fund, Inc.
(ASE:LRF)
c/o First Interstate Bank of CA
P.O. Box 30609 Terminal Annex
Los Angeles, CA 90030
(818) 992-7385   (415) 329-8867

Business Profile: Real estate investment trust investing in California income-producing properties.

Plan Specifics:
- Partial dividend reinvestment is available.
- No Discount.
- OCP: not available.
- Purchasing fees are brokerage commissions.

- Administrative fees are bank's service charge and costs of administration of the plan ($1.50 per quarter), $1.50 for each common stock certificate issued under the plan, and $10 for each withdrawal or redemption under the plan.
- Selling costs include brokerage fees and other expenses.

Performance Rating: *

Lincoln Telecommunications Co. (NASDAQ:LTEC)
P.O. Box 81309
Lincoln, NE 68501
(402) 476-5277

Business Profile: Provides telephone service to Nebraska counties.

Plan Specifics:
- Partial dividend reinvestment is not available.
- No Discount.
- OCP: $100 to $3000 per quarter.
- Must go through own broker to sell shares.
- Company purchases stock quarterly with OCPs.
- Approximately 1100 shareholders in the plan.

Performance Rating: ***

Liz Claiborne, Inc. (NASDAQ:LIZC)
c/o Chase Manhattan Bank
P.O. Box 283, Bowling Green Sta.
New York, NY 10274
(212) 676-3822   (212) 354-4900

Business Profile: Markets men's and women's apparel, cosmetics, and accessories.

Plan Specifics:
- Partial dividend reinvestment is not available.

- No Discount.
- OCP: $25 to $1000 per month.
- Selling costs are $1 service charge and brokerage commissions.
- $1 service charge for sending certificates to participants.
- Company purchases stock each month with OCPs.

Performance Rating: ***

Loctite Corp. (NYSE:LOC)
c/o First Nat'l Bank of Boston
P.O. Box 1681
Boston, MA 02105
(617) 575-2900

Business Profile: Manufactures chemical adhesives and sealants.

Plan Specifics:
- Partial dividend reinvestment is available.
- No Discount.
- OCP: $25 to $1000 per month.
- Selling costs are brokerage fees.
- Company purchases stock each month with OCPs if there are enough funds to purchase at least a 100-share lot.

Performance Rating: ***

Louisiana-Pacific Corp. (NYSE:LPX)
111 S.W. 5th Ave.
Portland, OR 97204
(503) 221-0800

Business Profile: Leading manufacturer of lumber, particleboard, plywood, and pulp.

Plan Specifics:
- Partial dividend reinvestment is not available.
- No Discount.
- OCP: $25 to $12,000 per year.
- Selling costs are brokerage commis-

sions and $5 service fee when termi-
nating the account.
* Stock is purchased monthly with
OCPs.

Performance Rating: ***

Lowe's Companies, Inc.
(NYSE:LOW)
P.O. Box 1111
N. Wilkesboro, NC 28656-0001
(919) 651-4000

Business Profile: Sells lumber, building
materials, home decorations, and hardware through retail outlets.

Plan Specifics:
* Partial dividend reinvestment is
available.
* No Discount.
* OCP: $10 to $1000 per month.
* Selling costs are $1 service fee and
brokerage fees.
* Stock is purchased approximately
eight times a year with OCPs.

Performance Rating: ***

Luby's Cafeterias, Inc. (NYSE:LUB)
P.O. Box 33069
San Antonio, TX 78265-3069
(512) 654-9000

Business Profile: Operates a cafeteria-
style chain of restaurants primarily in
Texas.

Plan Specifics:
* Partial dividend reinvestment is
available.
* No Discount.
* OCP: $20 to $5000 per quarter.
* Selling costs are nominal.
* Company purchases stock once a
month with OCPs.
* Approximately 1000 shareholders in
the plan.

Performance Rating: ***

Lukens, Inc. (NYSE:LUC)
c/o Mellon Bank
P.O. Box 444
Pittsburgh, PA 15230
(215) 383-2601

Business Profile: Provides steel plates
for construction and transportation
markets, safety products, and corrosion protection.

Plan Specifics:
* Partial dividend reinvestment is not
available.
* No Discount.
* OCP: $50 to $6000 per month.
* Stock is purchased around the 15th
of the month with OCPs.
* Selling costs are brokerage commis-
sion and other expenses of sale.

Performance Rating: ***

Lyondell Petrochemical Co.
(NYSE:LYO)
c/o Bank of New York
P.O. Box 11260, Church St. Sta.
New York, NY 10277-0760
(713) 652-7367   (713) 652-7200

Business Profile: Produces petrochemicals and refines petroleum products.

Plan Specifics:
* Partial dividend reinvestment is not
available.
* No Discount.
* OCP: $25 to $10,000 per quarter.
* Selling costs are brokerage commis-
sions and $5 handling fee.
* Company purchases stock quarterly
with OCPs.
* 300 to 400 shareholders in the plan.

Performance Rating: **

MacDermid, Inc. (NASDAQ:MACD)
P.O. Box 671
Waterbury, CT 06720
(203) 575-5813   (203) 575-5700

Business Profile: Manufactures specialty chemicals, equipment, and supplies for electronic and metal markets.

Plan Specifics:
- Partial dividend reinvestment is available.
- No Discount.
- OCP: minimum of $50 and no maximum.
- For partial dividend reinvestment, need at least 25 shares.
- Selling costs may include brokerage fees and $1 service charge.
- Stock is purchased at least quarterly, and probably between dividend-payment dates if demand is sufficient, with OCPs.
- Approximately 150 shareholders in the plan.

Performance Rating: **

Madison Gas & Electric Co.
(NASDAQ:MDSN)
P.O. Box 1231
133 S. Blair St.
Madison, WI 53701-1231
(800) 356-6423

Business Profile: Wisconsin-based electric utility.

Plan Specifics:
- Partial dividend reinvestment is available.
- No Discount.
- OCP: $10 to $3000 per quarter.
- Minimal, if any, selling costs.
- Company purchases stock around the 15th of every month with OCPs.
- Approximately 5700 shareholders in the plan.
- Initial investments may be made di-

rectly through the plan (minimum initial investment $10).
- Participants may have to pay brokerage costs of $0.125 if shares are purchased on the open market.

Performance Rating: ***

Magna Group, Inc.
(NASDAQ:MAGI)
P.O. Box 523
222 E. Main St
Belleville, IL 62222
(618) 233-2120

Business Profile: Illinois multibank holding company.

Plan Specifics:
- Partial dividend reinvestment is not available.
- No Discount.
- OCP: $25 to $5000 per month.
- Selling cost is brokerage commission.
- Company purchases stock once a month with OCPs.
- Approximately 1400 to 1500 shareholders in the plan.

Performance Rating: **

Manufacturers Hanover Corp.
(NYSE:MHC)
Dividend Reinvestment
P.O. Box 24850, Church St. Sta.
New York, NY 10242-4850
(212) 613-7147   (212) 613-7142

Business Profile: Major bank holding institution.

Plan Specifics:
- Partial dividend reinvestment is available.
- 3 percent discount on reinvested dividends.
- OCP: $1000 to $100,000 per year.
- Selling costs include $15 service fee

and brokerage costs (approximately 8 to 12 cents per share).
- Company purchases stock around the 25th of the month with OCPs.
- Approximately 9000 shareholders in the plan.
- 50 shares are needed to be in the plan if participant goes through a broker, although initial investments may be made directly through the plan (minimum investment of $1000).

Performance Rating: **

Manufacturers National Corp.
  (NASDAQ:MNTL)
P.O. Box 55106
Detroit, MI 48255-0106
(800) 521-1190   (313) 222-4380

Business Profile: Holding company for banks located in Michigan and Chicago and surrounding areas.

Plan Specifics:
- Partial dividend reinvestment is available.
- 5 percent discount on reinvested dividends.
- OCP: $10 to $1000 per month.
- Selling cost is brokerage commission, which may run from 10 to 70 cents a share.
- Company purchases stock once a month with OCPs.
- Approximately 1990 shareholders in the plan.

Performance Rating: ***

MAPCO, Inc. (NYSE:MDA)
P.O. Box 645
Tulsa, OK 74101-0645
(918) 599-6045   (212) 701-7607

Business Profile: Operations in retail gas transportation, refining, gas transmission, and coal production.

Plan Specifics:
- Partial dividend reinvestment is not available.
- No Discount.
- OCP: $10 to $3000 per quarter.
- Selling costs may include brokerage fees.
- Company purchases stock monthly with OCPs.

Performance Rating: **

Marion Merrell Dow, Inc.
  (NYSE:MKC)
c/o First Chicago Trust-NY
P.O. Box 3506, Church St. Sta.
New York, NY 10008-3506
(212) 791-6422

Business Profile: Manufactures pharmaceutical products, including Cardizem, a calcium channel blocker.

Plan Specifics:
- Partial dividend reinvestment is not available.
- No Discount.
- OCP: up to $3000 per quarter.
- Stock is purchased quarterly with OCPs.
- Selling costs are brokerage commission and related expenses of sale.

Performance Rating: ***

Mark Twain Bancshares, Inc.
  (NASDAQ:MTWN)
8820 Ladue Rd.
St. Louis, MO 63124
(314) 727-1000   (216) 687-5745

Business Profile: Multibank holding company serving St. Louis metropolitan areas. Operations in brokerage services.

Plan Specifics:
- Partial dividend reinvestment is not available.

- No Discount.
- OCP: $10 to $2000 per month.
- Selling costs are handling charge and brokerage commissions.
- Stock is purchased at least quarterly with OCPs.

Performance Rating: ***

Marsh & McLennan Companies, Inc. (NYSE:MMC)
c/o First Chicago Trust-NY
P.O. Box 3506, Church St. Sta.
New York, NY 10008-3506
(212) 791-6422

Business Profile: Insurance and reinsurance brokerage holding company with operations in investment services and consulting.

Plan Specifics:
- Partial dividend reinvestment is not available.
- No Discount.
- OCP: $10 to $3000 per quarter.
- Stock is purchased quarterly with OCPs.
- Purchasing fees are 5 percent of amount invested ($2.50 maximum) and proportionate share of brokerage commission.
- Selling costs are brokerage commission and any other cost of sale.

Performance Rating: ****

Marsh Supermarkets, Inc.
(NASDAQ:MARS)
501 Depot St.
Yorktown, IN 47396-1599
(317) 759-8101

Business Profile: Manages Midwestern supermarkets and convenience stores.

Plan Specifics:
- Partial dividend reinvestment is available.

- No Discount.
- OCP: $10 to $5000 per quarter.
- Company purchases stock approximately eight times a year with OCPs.
- Selling costs may include brokerage fees.

Performance Rating: ***

Marshall & Ilsley Corp.
(NASDAQ:MRIS)
770 N. Water St.
P.O. Box 2035
Milwaukee, WI 53201
(414) 765-7801

Business Profile: Holding company for banks throughout Wisconsin.

Plan Specifics:
- Partial dividend reinvestment is not available.
- No Discount.
- OCP: $25 to $3000 per quarter.
- Selling costs are service fee of $2.50 and brokerage fees.
- Company purchases stock around the first of the month with OCPs.

Performance Rating: ***

Martin Marietta Corp. (NYSE:ML)
6801 Rockledge Dr.
Bethesda, MD 20817
(301) 897-6309   (301) 897-6000

Business Profile: Produces spacecraft, missile launching systems, and defense programs for United States government.

Plan Specifics:
- Partial dividend reinvestment is available.
- No Discount.
- OCP: $50 to $100,000 per year.
- Selling costs are brokerage commission.

- Company purchases stock monthly with OCPs.

Performance Rating: ***

MASSBANK Corp.
(NASDAQ:MASB)
159 Haven St.
Reading, MA 01867
(617) 662-0100

Business Profile: Massachusetts-based bank holding company.

Plan Specifics:
- Partial dividend reinvestment is available.
- No Discount.
- OCP: $50 to $1500 per quarter.
- Selling costs are minimal.
- Company purchases stock quarterly with OCPs.
- Approximately 825 shareholders in the plan.

Performance Rating: NR

Maytag Corp. (NYSE:MYG)
403 W. 4th St. North
Newton, IA 50208
(515) 792-7000   (515) 792-8000

Business Profile: Important supplier of laundry equipment and kitchen appliances.

Plan Specifics:
- Partial dividend reinvestment is not available.
- No Discount.
- OCP: $25 to $5000 per month.
- No brokerage fees for selling shares.
- Company purchases stock around the 15th of the month with OCPs.

Performance Rating: **

McCormick & Co., Inc.
(NASDAQ:MCCRK)
11350 McCormick Rd.
Hunt Valley, MD 21031-1066
(301) 771-7244   (301) 771-7786

Business Profile: Manufactures spices, flavorings, seasonings, and specialty foods.

Plan Specifics:
- Partial dividend reinvestment is available.
- No Discount.
- OCP: $100 to $3000 per quarter.
- Selling costs may include brokerage commissions.
- Company purchases stock quarterly with OCPs.
- Approximately 2000 shareholders in the plan.

Performance Rating: ***

McDermott International, Inc.
(NYSE:MDR)
P.O. Box 61961
1010 Common St.
New Orleans, LA 70161
(504) 587-5682   (212) 679-3960

Business Profile: Constructs power generation systems and installs oil and gas pipelines.

Plan Specifics:
- Partial dividend reinvestment is available.
- No Discount.
- OCP: $25 to $15,000 per quarter.
- Selling costs may include brokerage fees.
- Company purchases stock every quarter with OCPs.
- Preferred dividends and interest on 10 percent subordinated debentures

are eligible for reinvestment in common shares under the plan.
- Approximately 2275 shareholders in the plan.

Performance Rating: **

McDonald's Corp. (NYSE:MCD)
c/o First Chicago Trust-NY
P.O. Box 3506, Church St. Station
New York, NY 10008-3591
(212) 791-6422   (800) 621-7825

Business Profile: Worldwide leader in the fast-food industry.

Plan Specifics:
- Partial dividend reinvestment is not available.
- No Discount.
- OCP: $50 to $75,000 per year.
- Selling costs are brokerage commission and a $5 service fee.
- Firm will sell shares for participants at least once a week.
- Company purchases stock twice a month with OCPs.

Performance Rating: ****

McGraw-Hill, Inc. (NYSE:MHP)
1221 Ave. of the Americas
New York, NY 10020
(212) 512-4150   (212) 512-2000

Business Profile: Publishes educational and professional books and magazines (*Business Week*) and offers financial informational services.

Plan Specifics:
- Partial dividend reinvestment is not available.
- No Discount.
- OCP: $10 to $1000 per quarter.
- Stock is purchased quarterly with OCPs.

- Selling costs are brokerage commission and $1 termination fee.
- $5 service fee for withdrawal of certificates.

Performance Rating: ***

McKesson Corp. (NYSE:MCK)
One Post St.
San Francisco, CA 94104
(415) 983-8367

Business Profile: Distributes drugs, toiletry products, beauty aids, and household items.

Plan Specifics:
- Partial dividend reinvestment is available.
- No Discount.
- OCP: $10 to $60,000 per year.
- Selling costs may include brokerage fees.
- Company purchases stock monthly with OCPs.
- Series A preferred dividends are eligible for reinvestment in additional common shares under the plan.

Performance Rating: ***

MCN Corp. (NYSE:MCN)
500 Griswold St.
Detroit, MI 48226
(313) 256-6324   (313) 256-5500

Business Profile: Natural gas holding company serving portions of Michigan.

Plan Specifics:
- Partial dividend reinvestment is available.
- No Discount.
- OCP: $10 to $25,000 per year.
- Selling costs include brokerage commission and $3 handling charge.

- Company purchases stock monthly with OCPs.
- Approximately 7600 shareholders in the plan.

Performance Rating: *******

MDU Resources Group, Inc.
(NYSE:MDU)
400 N. 4th St.
Bismarck, ND 58501
(701) 222-7621

Business Profile: Supplies electricity and gas to customers in North and South Dakotas, Montana, and Wyoming.

Plan Specifics:
- Partial dividend reinvestment is available.
- No Discount.
- OCP: $50 to $5000 per quarter.
- Selling costs may include brokerage fees.
- Company purchases stock quarterly with OCPs.
- Approximately 6000 shareholders in the plan.

Performance Rating: *******

Mead Corp. (NYSE:MEA)
Courthouse Plaza N.E.
Dayton, OH 45463
(513) 222-6323

Business Profile: Manufactures paper, paperboard, packaging systems, and building materials.

Plan Specifics:
- Partial dividend reinvestment is not available.
- No Discount.
- OCP: $25 to $2000 per month.
- Selling costs may include brokerage fees.

- Company purchases stock every month with OCPs.
- Approximately 5000 shareholders in the plan.

Performance Rating: ******

Medalist Industries, Inc.
(NASDAQ:MDIN)
10850 W. Park Place
Milwaukee, WI 53224
(414) 359-3000

Business Profile: Operations in specialty fasteners, insulated apparel, and machine tools.

Plan Specifics:
- Partial dividend reinvestment is not available.
- No Discount.
- OCP: $10 to $1000 per month.
- Selling costs may include brokerage fees.
- Stock is purchased at least quarterly with OCPs.
- Company is not currently paying a dividend.

Performance Rating: ******

Media General, Inc. (ASE:MEG.A)
P.O. Box C-32333
Richmond, VA 23293-0001
(804) 649-6000

Business Profile: Operations in newspaper publishing, newsprint, and broadcasting.

Plan Specifics:
- Partial dividend reinvestment is available.
- No Discount.
- OCP: $25 to $5000 per month.
- Selling costs may include brokerage fees.

- Company purchases stock monthly with OCPs.
- Approximately 600 shareholders in the plan.

Performance Rating: ***

Mellon Bank Corp. (NYSE:MEL)
P.O. Box 444
Pittsburgh, PA 15230
(412) 236-8000

Business Profile: Pittsburgh-based holding company for banks in Pennsylvania, Maryland, and Delaware.

Plan Specifics:
- Partial dividend reinvestment is not available.
- No Discount.
- OCP: $50 to $5000 per quarter.
- Selling costs are service charge of $2.50 and brokerage commissions of 10 to 20 cents per share.
- Company purchases stock each month with OCPs.

Performance Rating: **

Mellon Participating Mortgage Trust
(NASDAQ:MPMTS)
c/o Mellon Bank
P.O. Box 444
Pittsburgh, PA 15230
(412) 236-8000   (412) 236-8064

Business Profile: Finite-life real estate investment trust.

Plan Specifics:
- Partial dividend reinvestment is not available.
- No Discount.
- OCP: not available.
- Purchasing fees are 5 percent charge on each amount ($3 maximum) and proportionate share of brokerage commission.

- Selling costs are $2.50 service charge, brokerage commission, and any other cost of sale.

Performance Rating: NR

Mercantile Bancorp., Inc.
(NASDAQ:MTRC)
c/o Ameritrust Co N.A.
P.O. Box 6477
Cleveland, OH 44101-9990
(314) 241-4002   (314) 425-2525

Business Profile: Holding company for Missouri and Illinois banks.

Plan Specifics:
- Partial dividend reinvestment is not available.
- No Discount.
- OCP: $10 to $3000 per month.
- Minimal, if any, selling costs.
- Company purchases stock at least quarterly and most likely monthly if enough funds accumulate to purchase at least 100 shares.

Performance Rating: **

Mercantile Bankshares Corp.
(NASDAQ:MRBK)
P.O. Box 2438
Baltimore, MD 21203
(301) 237-5698

Business Profile: Maryland-based bank holding company.

Plan Specifics:
- Partial dividend reinvestment is not available.
- 5 percent discount on reinvested dividends.
- OCP: $25 to $5000 per quarter.
- Must go through own broker to sell shares.
- Fee of $3 when withdrawing certificates.

* Company purchases stock quarterly with OCPs.

Performance Rating: ***

Merck & Co., Inc. (NYSE:MRK)
P.O. Box 2000
Rahway, NJ 07065-0909
(908) 594-6627

Business Profile: Leading producer of human and animal pharmaceuticals and specialty chemicals.

Plan Specifics:
* Partial dividend reinvestment is not available.
* No Discount.
* OCP: $25 to $5000 per quarter.
* Minimal, if any, selling costs.
* Company purchases stock monthly with OCPs.
* Approximately 30,000 shareholders in the plan.

Performance Rating: ****

Meridian Bancorp, Inc.
(NASDAQ:MRDN)
P.O. Box 1102
35 N. 6th St.
Reading, PA 19603
(215) 320-2437

Business Profile: Multibank holding company in Pennsylvania.

Plan Specifics:
* Partial dividend reinvestment is available.
* 5 percent discount on reinvested dividends.
* OCP: $10 to $4000 per quarter.
* Selling costs are brokerage fees.
* Company purchases stock quarterly with OCPs.

* Approximately 7000 shareholders in the plan.

Performance Rating: **

Merrill Lynch & Co., Inc.
(NYSE:MER)
World Financial Center
New York, NY 10281-1332
(212) 510-6834   (212) 449-1000

Business Profile: Major financial services holding organization.

Plan Specifics:
* Partial dividend reinvestment is not available.
* No Discount.
* OCP: not available.
* Selling costs are brokerage fees and transfer taxes.

Performance Rating: **

Merrimack Bancorp, Inc.
(NASDAQ:MRMK)
18 Shattuck St.
Lowell, MA 01852
(508) 459-5752

Business Profile: Bank holding company.

Plan Specifics:
* Partial dividend reinvestment is available.
* No Discount.
* OCP: $50 to $1500 per quarter.
* Stock is purchased quarterly with OCPs.
* Selling costs are brokerage commissions.
* Company has suspended its dividend, but the DRIP is still open for OCPs.

Performance Rating: *

Merry Land & Investment Co., Inc.
(NASDAQ:MERY)
c/o C & S/Sovran Trust Co.
P.O. Box 105555
Atlanta, GA 30348-5555
(800) 772-5564

Business Profile: Acquires, develops, and manages real estate properties primarily in Georgia and South Carolina.

Plan Specifics:
- Partial dividend reinvestment is available.
- 5 percent discount on reinvested dividends.
- OCP: not available.
- Must go through own broker to sell shares.

Performance Rating: *

Metropolitan Financial Corp.
(NYSE:MFC)
c/o American Stock Transfer
99 Wall St.
New York, NY 10005
(701) 293-2600

Business Profile: Operates savings and loan operations in North and South Dakotas, Minnesota, Iowa, Wisconsin, and Arizona.

Plan Specifics:
- Partial dividend reinvestment is available.
- No Discount.
- OCP: $50 to $2500 per quarter; $10,000 maximum per year.
- Stock is purchased quarterly with OCPs.
- Selling costs are brokerage commissions.

Performance Rating: **

Michigan National Corp.
(NASDAQ:MNCO)
P.O. Box 9065
Farmington Hills, MI 48333-9065
(313) 473-8600   (313) 473-3076

Business Profile: Michigan-based bank holding company.

Plan Specifics:
- Partial dividend reinvestment is not available.
- No Discount.
- OCP: $25 to $5000 per month.
- Selling costs may include brokerage fees.
- Company purchases stock around the 15th of the month with OCPs.

Performance Rating: **

Middlesex Water Co.
(NASDAQ:MSEX)
P.O. Box 1500
Iselin, NJ 08830-0452
(908) 634-1500

Business Profile: Supplies water service to customers throughout New Jersey communities.

Plan Specifics:
- Partial dividend reinvestment is available.
- No Discount.
- OCP: $25 to $3000 per quarter.
- Selling costs are brokerage commissions.
- Company purchases stock each month with OCPs.

Performance Rating: ***

Midlantic Corp. (NASDAQ:MIDL)
c/o First Chicago Trust-NY
P.O. Box 3506, Church St. Sta.
New York, NY 10008-3506
(212) 791-6422   (201) 321-8127

Business Profile: Multibank holding firm serving areas in New Jersey, Pennsylvania, and New York.

Plan Specifics:
- Partial dividend reinvestment is not available.
- No Discount.
- OCP: $10 to $3000 per quarter.
- Stock is purchased quarterly with OCPs.
- Selling cost is a nominal brokerage fee.
- Approximately 7235 shareholders in plan.

Performance Rating: **

Millipore Corp. (NYSE:MIL)
80 Ashby Rd.
Bedford, MA 01730
(617) 275-9200   (617) 575-2900

Business Profile: Manufactures products used in analysis and purification of liquids.

Plan Specifics:
- Partial dividend reinvestment is not available.
- No Discount.
- OCP: $25 to $3000 per quarter.
- Selling costs are brokerage commissions and a termination fee of 5 percent (maximum of $3).
- Company purchases stock quarterly with OCPs.

Performance Rating: ***

Minnesota Mining & Manufacturing Co. (NYSE:MMM)
3M Center
St. Paul, MN 55144-1000
(612) 450-4064   (612) 733-1110

Business Profile: Manufactures industrial, electronic, medical, and consumer products.

Plan Specifics:
- Partial dividend reinvestment is not available.
- No Discount.
- OCP: $10 to $10,000 per quarter.
- Selling costs are $3 sales fee and 20 cents per share.
- Company purchases stock once a month with OCPs.
- Approximately 20,000 shareholders in the plan.

Performance Rating: ****

Minnesota Power & Light Co. (NYSE:MPL)
30 W. Superior St.
Duluth, MN 55802-2093
(218) 723-3974   (218) 722-2641

Business Profile: Provides electric services in a 26,000-square mile area of upper Minnesota and northwestern Wisconsin.

Plan Specifics:
- Partial dividend reinvestment is available.
- No Discount.
- OCP: $10 to $10,000 per quarter.
- Company will sell up to 25 shares for a participant and charge brokerage fees; otherwise must go through own broker to sell shares.
- Company purchases stock monthly with OCPs.
- Preferred dividends are eligible for

reinvestment for additional common shares under the plan.

- Customers of the utility may make initial purchases directly through the plan (minimum $10).

Performance Rating: ****

MNC Financial Corp. (NYSE:MNC)
P.O. Box 995
Baltimore, MD 21203
(301) 244-6168   (301) 244-6230

Business Profile: Maryland-based bank holding company.

Plan Specifics:
- Partial dividend reinvestment is not available.
- 5 percent discount on reinvested dividends.
- OCP: $50 to $5000 per quarter.
- Selling costs are brokerage commissions.
- Company purchases stock quarterly with OCPs.

Performance Rating: *

Mobil Corp. (NYSE:MOB)
3225 Gallows Rd.
Fairfax, VA 22037-0001
(800) 648-9291   (703) 849-3000

Business Profile: Leading worldwide integrated oil company.

Plan Specifics:
- Partial dividend reinvestment is available.
- No Discount.
- OCP: $10 to $5000 per month.
- Initial purchases may be made directly through the company (minimum initial investment $10).
- Selling costs are brokerage commission plus $5 service charge.

- Company purchases stock around the 10th of the month with OCPs.
- Approximately 38,030 shareholders in the plan.
- $5 charge for depositing a participant's certificates.

Performance Rating: ***

Mobile Gas Service Corp.
(NASDAQ:MBLE)
P.O. Box 2248
Mobile, AL 36652
(205) 476-2720

Business Profile: Distributes natural gas to utilities and unregulated customers in Mobile, Alabama.

Plan Specifics:
- Partial dividend reinvestment is available.
- No Discount.
- OCP: not available.
- Selling costs are brokerage commissions.

Performance Rating: ***

Modine Manufacturing Co.
(NASDAQ:MODI)
1500 DeKoven Ave.
Racine, WI 53403
(414) 636-1200

Business Profile: Produces heat-transfer equipment for cooling engines, transmissions, and air compressors.

Plan Specifics:
- Partial dividend reinvestment is not available.
- No Discount.
- OCP: $10 to $5000 per month.
- Selling costs may include brokerage fees.

• Company purchases stock each month with OCPs.

Performance Rating: **

Monsanto Co. (NYSE:MTC)
800 N. Lindbergh Blvd.
St. Louis, MO 63167
(314) 694-5353   (314) 694-1000

Business Profile: Manufactures herbicides, industrial chemicals, plastics, pharmaceuticals, and low calorie sweeteners.

Plan Specifics:
• Partial dividend reinvestment is not available.
• No Discount.
• OCP: $10 to $3000 per quarter.
• Selling costs include brokerage fees.
• Purchasing costs are 3 percent service charge (maximum of $2) plus brokerage fees.
• Company purchases stock monthly with OCPs.
• Approximately 8100 shareholders in the plan.

Performance Rating: ***

Montana Power Co. (NYSE:MTP)
40 E. Broadway
Butte, MT 59701-9989
(800) 245-6767   (406) 723-5421

Business Profile: Supplies electric power and natural gas to Montana customers. Operations in coal mining, oil production, and telecommunications.

Plan Specifics:
• Partial dividend reinvestment is available.
• No Discount.
• OCP: $10 to $2000 per month.
• Selling cost is approximately 18 cents per share.

• Company purchases stock monthly with OCPs.
• Over 11,000 shareholders in the plan.
• Preferred dividends are eligible for reinvestment for additional common shares under the plan.

Performance Rating: **

Moore Corp. Ltd. (NYSE:MCL)
P.O. Box 78
1 First Canadian Place
Toronto, Ontario M5X 1G5 Canada
(416) 364-2600

Business Profile: International manufacturer of business forms and related items.

Plan Specifics:
• Partial dividend reinvestment is not available.
• 5 percent discount on reinvested dividends.
• OCP: not available.
• 35 to 40 percent of total shareholders are in the plan.
• Participant must go through own broker to sell shares.

Performance Rating: ***

Morgan, J. P., & Co., Inc.
(NYSE:JPM)
c/o First Chicago Trust-NY
P.O. Box 3506, Church St. Sta.
New York, NY 10008-3506
(212) 791-6422

Business Profile: Leading bank holding company emphasizing services for corporations.

Plan Specifics:
• Partial dividend reinvestment is available.

- 3 percent discount on reinvested dividends.
- OCP: $50 to $5000 per month.
- Stock is purchased around the 15th of the month with OCPs.
- Selling cost is brokerage commission.

Performance Rating: ****

Morrison Knudsen Corp.
(NYSE:MRN)
P.O. Box 73
Boise, ID 83707
(208) 345-5000

Business Profile: Operations in construction, engineering, and rail systems.

Plan Specifics:
- Partial dividend reinvestment is not available.
- No Discount.
- OCP: $25 to $1000 per quarter.
- Any fees associated with buying or selling should be minimal.
- Company purchases stock every quarter with OCPs.
- Approximately 1100 shareholders in the plan.

Performance Rating: **

Motorola, Inc. (NYSE:MOT)
c/o Harris Trust
P.O. Box A3309
Chicago, IL 60690
(312) 461-5535

Business Profile: Provides radio communication systems, semiconductors, and cellular telephone systems.

Plan Specifics:
- Partial dividend reinvestment is available.
- No Discount.

- OCP: $25 to $5000 per quarter.
- Selling costs are brokerage commissions and other expenses.
- Company purchases stock monthly if there is enough money to buy at least a 100-share lot.

Performance Rating: ***

Multibank Financial Corp.
(NASDAQ:MLTF)
100 Rustcraft Rd.
Dedham, MA 02026
(617) 929-5445 (617) 461-1820

Business Profile: Holding company for banks throughout Massachusetts.

Plan Specifics:
- Partial dividend reinvestment is available.
- 5 percent discount on reinvested dividends.
- OCP: $25 to $5000 per quarter.
- Stock is purchased monthly with OCPs.
- Agent will sell up to 500 shares for participants and charge brokerage commission and transfer taxes.

Performance Rating: *

Nalco Chemical Co. (NYSE:NLC)
One Nalco Center
Naperville, IL 60563-1198
(708) 305-1000

Business Profile: Manufactures specialty chemicals, including water and waste treatment, process chemicals, and petroleum chemicals.

Plan Specifics:
- Partial dividend reinvestment is available.
- No Discount.
- OCP: $50 to $15,000 per quarter.
- Selling costs include brokerage fees.

- Stock is purchased quarterly with OCPs.

Performance Rating: ****

Napa Valley Bancorp (ASE:NVB)
P.O. Box 2848
Napa, CA 94558-0848
(707) 255-8300

Business Profile: California multibank holding firm.

Plan Specifics:
- Partial dividend reinvestment is available.
- 5 percent discount on reinvested dividends.
- OCP: $100 to $1000 per month.
- Stock is purchased around the 20th of the month with OCPs.
- Minimal, if any, selling costs.
- Approximately 1500 shareholders in plan.

Performance Rating: NR

Nash-Finch Co. (NASDAQ:NAFC)
3381 Gorham Ave.
Minneapolis, MN 55426
(612) 929-0371

Business Profile: Manages food stores and engages in wholesale distribution.

Plan Specifics:
- Partial dividend reinvestment is available.
- No Discount.
- OCP: $10 to $1000 per month.
- Selling cost is brokerage commission.
- Company purchases stock monthly if enough funds accumulate to purchase at least a 100-share lot.

Performance Rating: ***

Nashua Corp. (NYSE:NSH)
44 Franklin St.
Nashua, NH 03061
(603) 880-2323

Business Profile: Provides office supplies, such as facsimile papers, coated papers, and adhesive labels, and mail-order film processing services. Manufactures computer memory disks.

Plan Specifics:
- Partial dividend reinvestment is not available.
- No Discount.
- OCP: $100 to $5000 per quarter.
- Company purchases stock approximately eight times a year.
- Minimal, if any, brokerage fees when selling.
- Approximately 289 shareholders in the plan.

Performance Rating: **

National City Corp. (NYSE:NCC)
P.O. Box 92301
Cleveland, OH 44193-0900
(216) 575-2640

Business Profile: Multibank holding company serving Ohio, Kentucky, and Indiana.

Plan Specifics:
- Partial dividend reinvestment is not available.
- No Discount.
- OCP: $20 to $2500 per month.
- Selling costs may include brokerage fees.
- Company purchases stock monthly with OCPs.

Performance Rating: ***

National Commerce Bancorp (TN)
(NASDAQ:NCBC)
One Commerce Square
Memphis, TN 38150
(404) 588-7822   (901) 523-3245

Business Profile: Tennessee-based commercial banking institution.

Plan Specifics:
▪ Partial dividend reinvestment is available.
▪ No Discount.
▪ OCP: $100 to $10,000 per quarter.
▪ Selling costs include brokerage fees and service charges.
▪ Company purchases stock at least quarterly with OCPs.
▪ Approximately 550 shareholders in the plan.

Performance Rating: NR

National Community Banks, Inc.
(NJ) (NASDAQ:NCBR)
113 W. Essex St.
Maywood, NJ 07607
(201) 845-1000

Business Profile: New Jersey-based bank holding company.

Plan Specifics:
▪ Partial dividend reinvestment is not available.
▪ No Discount.
▪ OCP: $40 to $100,000 per year.
▪ Company purchases stock monthly with OCPs.
▪ Customers of the bank who reside in New Jersey and New York may make initial investments in the company directly through the plan (minimum investment of $100).

Performance Rating: **

National Data Corp.
(NASDAQ:NDTA)
c/o Trust Co. Bank-Atlanta
P.O. Box 4625
Atlanta, GA 30302
(404) 588-7822   (404) 728-2000

Business Profile: Provides data processing services, including credit card processing, bank deposit reporting, money transfer functions, and health care data services.

Plan Specifics:
▪ No Discount.
▪ OCP: $25 to $1000 per quarter.
▪ Stock is purchased quarterly with OCPs.
▪ Purchasing costs may include brokerage fees.
▪ Selling costs may include brokerage fees.
▪ Approximately 590 shareholders in the plan.

Performance Rating: **

National Fuel Gas Co. (NYSE:NFG)
30 Rockefeller Plaza
New York, NY 10112
(212) 541-7533

Business Profile: The company and its subsidiaries constitute an integrated natural gas operation represented by three major business segments: Utility Operation; Supply, Transmission, and Storage; and Exploration and Production.

Plan Specifics:
▪ Partial dividend reinvestment is not available.
▪ No Discount.
▪ OCP: $25 to $5000 per month.
▪ Stock is purchased monthly with OCPs.

- Selling costs include brokerage commissions, transfer taxes, and $15 bank service charge.

Performance Rating: ***

National Medical Enterprises, Inc. (NYSE:NME)
c/o Manufacturers Hanover
P.O. Box 24850, Church St. Sta.
New York, NY 10242
(212) 613-7147   (213) 315-8000

Business Profile: Major hospital management company with general and specialty hospitals.

Plan Specifics:
- Partial dividend reinvestment is not available.
- No Discount.
- OCP: $10 to $1000 per month.
- Selling costs are brokerage fees and $1 handling charge.
- Stock is purchased around the 15th of the month with OCPs.

Performance Rating: ***

National Service Industries, Inc. (NYSE:NSI)
c/o Wachovia Bank and Trust
P.O. Box 3001
Winston-Salem, NC 27102
(404) 770-6000

Business Profile: Produces lighting equipment and has operations in textiles and chemicals.

Plan Specifics:
- Partial dividend reinvestment is not available.
- No Discount.
- OCP: $10 to $4000 per month.
- Purchasing fees are service charge of 5 percent of the amount invested (maximum of $2.50) per investment

transaction plus brokerage commissions.
- Selling costs are brokerage commissions and other costs of sale.

Performance Rating: ****

National-Standard Co. (NYSE:NSD)
1618 Terminal Rd.
Niles, MI 49120
(616) 683-8100   (800) 777-1618

Business Profile: Manufactures carbon and steel wires and related products for reinforcement of rubber products.

Plan Specifics:
- Partial dividend reinvestment is not available.
- No Discount.
- OCP: $10 to $3000 per month.
- Must go through own broker to sell shares.
- Stock is purchased monthly with OCPs.

Performance Rating: *

NBD Bancorp, Inc. (NYSE:NBD)
611 Woodward Ave.
Detroit, MI 48226
(313) 225-1000   (313) 828-6916

Business Profile: Holding company for banks in Michigan, Illinois, Indiana, Ohio, and Florida.

Plan Specifics:
- Partial dividend reinvestment is not available.
- No Discount.
- OCP: $10 to $10,000 per quarter.
- Selling costs include brokerage fees and $3 service charge.
- Company purchases stock at least quarterly with OCPs.

Performance Rating: ****

NBSC Corp. (NASDAQ:NSCB)
13 E. Canal St.
Sumter, SC 29150
(803) 775-1211

Business Profile: Bank holding company headquartered in South Carolina.

Plan Specifics:
- Partial dividend reinvestment is not available.
- No Discount.
- OCP: $25 to $3000 per quarter.
- Selling fees may include nominal brokerage costs.
- Company purchases stock once a quarter with OCPs.
- Approximately 467 shareholders in the plan.

Performance Rating: NR

NCNB Corp. (NYSE:NCB)
One NCNB Plaza
Charlotte, NC 28255
(704) 374-5000

Business Profile: Multibank holding company for Southeast states.

Plan Specifics:
- Partial dividend reinvestment is available.
- 5 percent discount on reinvested dividends.
- OCP: $20 to $3000 per quarter.
- Stock is purchased monthly with OCPs.
- Selling costs are brokerage fees and any transfer taxes.

Performance Rating: ***

Neiman-Marcus Group, Inc.
(NYSE:NMG)
27 Boylston St.
Chestnut Hill, MA 02167
(617) 232-0760   (617) 575-2900

Business Profile: Owns and operates fashion apparel stores.

Plan Specifics:
- Partial dividend reinvestment is not available.
- No Discount.
- OCP: $25 to $2500 per quarter.
- Stock is purchased monthly with OCPs.
- Selling costs are brokerage fees and any transfer taxes.

Performance Rating: **

Nevada Power Co. (NYSE:NVP)
P.O. Box 230
Las Vegas, NV 89151
(702) 367-5000   (800) 344-9239

Business Profile: Provides electric service to Las Vegas areas.

Plan Specifics:
- Partial dividend reinvestment is available.
- No Discount.
- OCP: $25 to $5000 per quarter.
- Selling costs include brokerage fees.
- Company purchases stock monthly with OCPs.
- Preferred dividends are eligible for reinvestment for additional common under the plan.
- Approximately 15,000 shareholders in the plan.
- Customers may make initial investments directly through the plan (minimum investment, $25).

Performance Rating: ***

New England Electric System
(NYSE:NES)
P.O. Box 770
Westborough, MA 01581-0770
(508) 366-9011

Business Profile: Supplies electric power to communities in Massachusetts, Rhode Island, and New Hampshire.

Plan Specifics:
- Partial dividend reinvestment is available.
- No Discount.
- OCP: $25 to $5000 per month.
- Selling cost is approximately 15 cents per share.
- Company purchases stock monthly with OCPs.
- Approximately 19,402 shareholders in the plan.

Performance Rating: ***

New Hampshire Savings Bank Corp.
(NASDAQ:NHSB)
P.O. Box 40
27 North State Street
Concord, NH 03301-0040
(603) 224-7711

Business Profile: Multibank holding company headquartered in New Hampshire.

Plan Specifics:
- Partial dividend reinvestment is not available.
- No Discount.
- OCP: $100 to $5000 per quarter.
- Selling costs are applicable commissions and termination fees.
- Company purchases stock quarterly with OCPs.
- Company is not currently paying a dividend.

Performance Rating: *

New Jersey Resources Corp.
(NYSE:NJR)
P.O. Box 1468
1350 Campus Pkwy.
Wall, NJ 07719
(201) 938-1230

Business Profile: Holding company with the principal subsidiary a natural gas utility serving New Jersey communities.

Plan Specifics:
- Partial dividend reinvestment is not available.
- No Discount.
- OCP: $25 to $30,000 per year.
- Selling costs are approximately 10 cents per share brokerage fees.
- Company purchases stock monthly with OCPs.
- Approximately 10,000 shareholders in the plan.

Performance Rating: **

New Plan Realty Trust (NYSE:NPR)
1120 Ave. of the Americas
New York, NY 10036
(212) 869-3000

Business Profile: Real estate investment trust.

Plan Specifics:
- Partial dividend reinvestment is available.
- 5 percent discount on reinvested dividends.
- OCP: $100 to $5000 per quarter.
- May have to go through own broker to sell shares.
- Company purchases stock at least quarterly with OCPs.

Performance Rating: **

New York State Electric & Gas Corp. (NYSE:NGE)
P.O. Box 200
Ithaca, NY 14851
(800) 225-5643

Business Profile: Supplies electricity and gas to portions within New York State.

Plan Specifics:
- Partial dividend reinvestment is not available.
- No Discount.
- OCP: $10 to $5000 per quarter.
- Selling cost is 7 to 8 cents per share.
- Company purchases stock around the 1st of the month with OCPs.

Performance Rating: **

New York Times Co. (ASE:NYT.A)
c/o First Chicago Trust-NY
P.O. Box 3506, Church St. Sta.
New York, NY 10008-3506
(212) 791-6422

Business Profile: Publishes newspaper and magazines, operates radio and television stations, and provides broadcasting and information services.

Plan Specifics:
- Partial dividend reinvestment is not available.
- No Discount.
- OCP: $10 to $3000 per quarter.
- Stock is purchased quarterly with OCPs.
- Purchasing fees are proportionate share of brokerage commission and 5 percent of total funds ($2.50 maximum).
- Selling costs are brokerage commission and any other cost of sale.

Performance Rating: ***

Niagara Mohawk Power Corp. (NYSE:NMK)
P.O. Box 7058
Syracuse, NY 13261
(800) 448-5450   (800) 962-3236

Business Profile: Electric and gas utility serving portions of New York.

Plan Specifics:
- Partial dividend reinvestment is not available.
- No Discount.
- OCP: $25 to $5000 per quarter.
- Selling costs are approximately 4 cents a share.
- Company purchases stock monthly with OCPs.

Performance Rating: **

NICOR, Inc. (NYSE:GAS)
P.O. Box 3014
1700 West Ferry Rd.
Naperville, IL 60566-7014
(708) 305-9500

Business Profile: Operations in gas distribution, oil and gas exploration, and containerized shipping.

Plan Specifics:
- Partial dividend reinvestment is available.
- No Discount.
- OCP: $25 to $5000 per month.
- Must go through own broker to sell shares.
- Company purchases stock around the 1st day of each month with OCPs.
- Approximately 12,600 shareholders in the plan.
- Preferred dividends are eligible for reinvestment for additional common shares under the plan.

Performance Rating: ***

NIPSCO Industries, Inc. (NYSE:NI)
5265 Hohman Ave.
Hammond, IN 46320
(219) 853-5200

Business Profile: Indiana-based electric and gas utility holding company.

Plan Specifics:

- Partial dividend reinvestment is not available.
- No Discount.
- OCP: $25 to $5000 per quarter.
- Selling cost is approximately 8 cents per share.
- Company purchases stock monthly with OCPs.
- Approximately 11,990 shareholders in the plan.

Performance Rating: **

Nooney Realty Trust, Inc.
(NASDAQ:NRTI)
7701 Forsyth Blvd.
St. Louis, MO 63105-1877
(314) 863-7700

Business Profile: Real estate investment trust.

Plan Specifics:

- Partial dividend reinvestment is not available.
- No Discount.
- OCP: minimum of $50 per payment.
- Stock is purchased quarterly with OCPs.
- Purchasing fees are 5 percent of amount invested ($2.50 maximum) and brokerage commissions.
- Selling costs are brokerage commission and termination fee of $1.

Performance Rating: NR

Nordson Corp. (NASDAQ:NDSN)
28601 Clemens Rd.
Westlake, OH 44145-1148
(216) 892-1580

Business Profile: Engineers, manufactures, and markets sophisticated equipment and systems used to apply advanced technology adhesives, sealants, and coatings during manufacturing processes.

Plan Specifics:

- Partial dividend reinvestment is not available.
- No Discount.
- OCP: $10 to $4000 per quarter.
- Selling costs include brokerage fees and $5 termination fee.
- Company purchases stock at least quarterly with OCPs.
- Approximately 426 shareholders in the plan.

Performance Rating: ***

Norfolk Southern Corp.
(NYSE:NSC)
c/o First Chicago Trust-NY
P.O. Box 3506, Church St. Sta.
New York, NY 10008-3506
(212) 791-6422   (804) 533-4811

Business Profile: Major railroad concern with operations in coal.

Plan Specifics:

- Partial dividend reinvestment is not available.
- No Discount.
- OCP: $10 to $3000 per quarter.
- Stock is purchased quarterly with OCPs.
- Purchasing fees are pro rata portion of brokerage commission and 5 percent on each investment ($2.50 maximum).

- Selling costs are a pro rata portion of brokerage commission and a termination fee of $5.
- Approximately 5000 shareholders in the plan.

Performance Rating: ****

North Carolina Natural Gas Corp. (NASDAQ:NCNG)
P.O. Box 909
Fayetteville, NC 28302-0909
(919) 483-0315

Business Profile: Provides natural gas to customers in central and eastern North Carolina.

Plan Specifics:
- Partial dividend reinvestment is available.
- 5 percent discount on reinvested dividends.
- OCP: $25 to $3000 per quarter.
- Selling costs may include brokerage fees.
- Company purchases stock quarterly with OCPs.
- Approximately 1100 shareholders in the plan.

Performance Rating: ***

North Fork Bancorporation, Inc. (NYSE:NFB)
9025 Main Rd.
Mattituck, NY 11952-9339
(516) 298-5000

Business Profile: Bank holding company for parts of New York.

Plan Specifics:
- Partial dividend reinvestment is available.
- 5 percent discount on reinvested dividends.
- OCP: $500 to $10,000 per quarter.

- Selling costs include small brokerage fee.
- Company purchases stock quarterly with OCPs.

Performance Rating: **

Northeast Bancorp, Inc. (CT) (NASDAQ:NBIC)
Attn: Dividend Reinvestment
c/o Bank of New York
P.O. Box 11260, Church St. Sta.
New York, NY 10277-0760
(212) 815-2434   (800) 524-4458

Business Profile: Connecticut-based bank bank holding company.

Plan Specifics:
- Partial dividend reinvestment is not available.
- No Discount.
- OCP: $25 to $5000 per quarter.
- Selling costs are bank service fee and brokerage fees.
- Company purchases stock each month with OCPs.

Performance Rating: *

Northeast Utilities Service Co. (NYSE:NU)
P.O. Box 5006
Berlin, CT 06102-5006
(203) 665-5154   (800) 999-7269

Business Profile: Electric utility serving parts of Connecticut and Massachusetts.

Plan Specifics:
- Partial dividend reinvestment is available.
- No Discount.
- OCP: $100 to $25,000 per month.
- Selling cost is approximately 5 cents per share.

- Company purchases stock once a month with OCPs.
- Approximately 50,000 shareholders in the plan.

Performance Rating: **

Northern States Power Co.
 (NYSE:NSP)
414 Nicollet Mall
Minneapolis, MN 55401
(800) 527-4677

Business Profile: Distributes electric power and gas to upper Midwest customers.

Plan Specifics:
- Partial dividend reinvestment is not available.
- No Discount.
- OCP: $10 to $5000 per quarter.
- Must go through own broker to sell shares.
- Company purchases stock once a month with OCPs.
- 20,000 to 24,000 shareholders in the plan.
- Preferred dividends are eligible for reinvestment for additional shares of common stock under the plan.

Performance Rating: ****

Northern Telecom Ltd. (NYSE:NT)
c/o Montreal Trust
151 Front St. W.
Toronto, Ont. M5J 2N1 Canada
(416) 981-9636   (416) 897-9000

Business Profile: Leading producer of telecommunications equipment in Canada.

Plan Specifics:
- Partial dividend reinvestment is not available.

- 5 percent discount on reinvested dividends.
- OCP: $40 to $4000 per quarter (United States funds).
- Selling costs may include brokerage fees.
- Company purchases stock quarterly with OCPs.

Performance Rating: ***

Northrop Corp. (NYSE:NOC)
c/o Manufacturers Hanover
P.O. Box 24850, Church St. Sta.
New York, NY 10249
(212) 613-7147

Business Profile: Manufacturer of military aircraft and other defense products.

Plan Specifics:
- Partial dividend reinvestment is not available.
- No Discount.
- OCP: $100 to $1000 per month.
- Selling costs may include brokerage fees.
- Stock is purchased around the 15th of the month with OCPs.

Performance Rating: **

Northwest Illinois Bancorp, Inc.
 (NASDAQ:NWIB)
c/o Continental Bank
231 S. LaSalle Street
Chicago, IL 60697
(312) 828-4181   (815) 235-8459

Business Profile: Multibank holding company serving Illinois clients.

Plan Specifics:
- Partial dividend reinvestment is not available.
- No Discount.
- OCP: $100 to $10,000 per quarter.

- Selling costs are brokerage commissions.
- Company purchases stock quarterly with OCPs.

Performance Rating: ***

Northwest Natural Gas Co.
(NASDAQ:NWNG)
220 N.W. 2d Ave.
Portland, OR 97209
(503) 220-2591

Business Profile: Distributes natural gas to residential, commercial, and industrial customers in Oregon and Washington.

Plan Specifics:
- Partial dividend reinvestment is available.
- No Discount.
- OCP: $25 to $5000 per quarter.
- Selling costs include service fee of $4.50.
- Firm will sell shares from a participant's account within 5 days after receiving notice to sell, except between record date and dividend payment date.
- Company purchases stock once a month with OCPs.
- Approximately 5500 shareholders in the plan.

Performance Rating: ***

Northwestern Public Service Co.
(NYSE:NPS)
3d St. and Dakota Ave. S.
Huron, SD 57350
(605) 352-8411

Business Profile: Provides electric service to communities in South Dakota. Supplies natural gas to Nebraska and South Dakota cities.

Plan Specifics:
- Partial dividend reinvestment is available.
- No Discount.
- OCP: $10 to $5000 per quarter.
- Selling cost is approximately 6 cents per share.
- Company purchases stock once a quarter with OCPs.
- Approximately 2600 shareholders in the plan.

Performance Rating: ***

Norwest Corp. (NYSE:NOB)
6th & Marquette
Minneapolis, MN 55479
(612) 450-4180

Business Profile: Bank holding institution with outlets in the upper Midwest and Arizona.

Plan Specifics:
- Partial dividend reinvestment is available.
- No Discount.
- OCP: $25 to $30,000 per quarter.
- Selling costs are brokerage commission and service charges.
- Company purchases stock monthly with OCPs.

Performance Rating: **

NOVA Corp. of Alberta
(NYSE:NVA)
P.O. Box 2535
Station "M"
Calgary, Alberta T2P 2N6 Canada
(800) 661-8686   (403) 263-1460

Business Profile: Operations in petrochemicals, petroleum, gas transmission, and pipeline development.

Plan Specifics:
- Partial dividend reinvestment is not available.
- No Discount.
- OCP: $50 to $5000 (Canadian) per quarter.
- Must go through own broker to sell.
- Company purchases stock quarterly with OCPs.

Performance Rating: **

Novo-Nordisk A/S (NYSE:NVO)
c/o First Chicago Trust-NY
P.O. Box 3506, Church St. Sta.
New York, NY 10008-3506
(212) 791-6422

Business Profile: Denmark-based company that manufactures insulin and industrial enzymes.

Plan Specifics:
- Partial dividend reinvestment is not available.
- No Discount.
- OCP: not available.
- Purchasing fees are proportionate share of brokerage commission and 5 percent of total funds invested ($2.50 maximum).
- Selling costs are $5 handling charge, brokerage commission, and any other cost of sale.

Performance Rating: ***

Nucor Corp. (NYSE:NUE)
4425 Randolph Rd.
Charlotte, NC 28211
(704) 366-7000   (704) 374-6531

Business Profile: Leading manufacturer of steel joists and steel products.

Plan Specifics:
- Partial dividend reinvestment is not available.

- No Discount.
- OCP: $10 to $1000 per month.
- Selling costs include brokerage fees.
- Company purchases stock approximately eight times a year.

Performance Rating: ***

NUI Corp. (NYSE:NUI)
P.O. Box 760
550 Route 202-206
Bedminster, NJ 07921-0760
(201) 781-0500   (201) 592-4128

Business Profile: Transports, distributes, and markets natural gas in parts of New Jersey and Florida.

Plan Specifics:
- Partial dividend reinvestment is available.
- 5 percent discount on reinvested dividends.
- OCP: $25 to $3000 per quarter.
- Selling costs are brokerage commission.
- Company purchases stock once a month with OCPs.

Performance Rating: **

Numerica Financial Corp.
** (NASDAQ:NUME)**
P.O. Box 60
Manchester, NH 03105
(603) 624-2424

Business Profile: New Hampshire savings and loan holding organization.

Plan Specifics:
- Partial dividend reinvestment is available.
- No Discount.
- OCP: $25 to $5000 per quarter.
- Company is not currently paying a dividend.

- Selling costs may include brokerage fees.
- Company purchases stock quarterly with OCPs.
- Approximately 565 shareholders in the plan.

Performance Rating: *

NYNEX Corp. (NYSE:NYN)
c/o American Transtech
P.O. Box 45024
Jacksonville, FL 32232
(800) 358-1133

Business Profile: Major telephone holding company in New York and New England. Firm also has activities in data base management, mobile communications, and directory publishing.

Plan Specifics:

- Partial dividend reinvestment is available.
- No Discount.
- OCP: up to $5000 per quarter.
- Selling cost is approximately 10 cents per share.
- Company purchases stock each month with OCPs.

Performance Rating: ****

Occidental Petroleum Corp.
(NYSE:OXY)
10889 Wilshire Blvd.
Los Angeles, CA 90024
(213) 879-1700

Business Profile: Refines, produces, and markets natural gas and oil. Also has operations in chemicals.

Plan Specifics:

- Partial dividend reinvestment is not available.
- No Discount.

- OCP: $10 to $1000 per month.
- Stock is purchased monthly with OCPs.
- Purchasing fees are never more than 1 percent on each amount invested plus service charges.
- Selling costs are never more than 1 percent on amount sold plus service fee.
- Preferred dividends are eligible for reinvestment for additional common shares under the plan.
- Approximately 40,000 shareholders in the plan.

Performance Rating: **

Ohio Casualty Corp.
(NASDAQ:OCAS)
136 N. Third St.
Hamilton, OH 45025-0001
(513) 867-3903

Business Profile: Insurance holding company with emphasis in property-casualty insurance.

Plan Specifics:

- Partial dividend reinvestment is available.
- No Discount.
- OCP: $10 to $5000 per month.
- Purchasing fees are a maximum $3 charge per purchase plus brokerage fees.
- Selling costs are brokerage fees plus $1 service charge.

Performance Rating: ***

Ohio Edison Co. (NYSE:OEC)
76 S. Main St.
Akron, OH 44308-1890
(800) 633-4766

Business Profile: Electric utility serving residential, commercial, and industrial population in Ohio and Pennsylvania.

Plan Specifics:
- Partial dividend reinvestment is available.
- No Discount.
- OCP: $10 to $40,000 per year.
- Selling costs include brokerage fees.
- Company purchases stock every month with OCPs.
- Preferred dividends are eligible for reinvestment for additional common shares under the plan.
- Approximately 62,000 shareholders in the plan.

Performance Rating: **

Oklahoma Gas & Electric Co.
(NYSE:OGE)
P.O. Box 321
Oklahoma City, OK 73101
(800) 633-5115

Business Profile: Provides electricity to residential, commercial, and industrial customers in Oklahoma and portions of Arkansas.

Plan Specifics:
- Partial dividend reinvestment is available.
- No Discount.
- OCP: $25 to $1000 per quarter.
- Selling costs are brokerage commissions.
- Company purchases stock each month with OCPs.
- Preferred dividends are eligible for reinvestment in additional common shares under the plan.

Performance Rating: ****

Old National Bancorp (IN)
(NASDAQ:OLDB)
P.O. Box 718
Evansville, IN 47705
(812) 464-1296   (812) 464-1504

Business Profile: Indiana-based holding company for banks in Indiana, Kentucky, and Illinois.

Plan Specifics:
- Partial dividend reinvestment is available.
- No Discount.
- OCP: $25 to $2500 per quarter.
- Must go through own broker to sell shares.
- Company purchases stock once each quarter with OCPs.
- Approximately 3000 shareholders in the plan.

Performance Rating: NR

Old Republic International Corp.
(NYSE:ORI)
c/o First Chicago Trust-NY
P.O. Box 3506, Church St. Sta.
New York, NY 10008-3506
(212) 791-6422   (312) 346-8100

Business Profile: Chicago-based insurance holding firm. Writes and sells property and liability, life and disability, and mortgage guaranty insurance.

Plan Specifics:
- Partial dividend reinvestment is available.
- No Discount.
- OCP: $100 to $5000 per quarter.
- Stock is purchased quarterly with OCPs.
- Selling costs are brokerage commissions and any transfer taxes incurred.

Performance Rating: NR

Old Stone Corp. (NASDAQ:OSTN)
P.O. Box 1536
Providence, RI 02901
(401) 825-3564

Business Profile: Rhode Island-based financial services holding company.

Plan Specifics:
- Partial dividend reinvestment is not available.
- No Discount.
- OCP: $25 to $3000 per quarter.
- Purchasing fees are a maximum $2.50 service charge plus brokerage fees.
- Selling costs are small brokerage fees and $3 termination fee.
- Company purchases stock once a month with OCPs.

Performance Rating: **

Olin Corp. (NYSE:OLN)
c/o Manufacturers Hanover
P.O. Box 24850, Church St. Sta.
New York, NY 10249
(212) 613-7147   (203) 356-2000

Business Profile: Producer of industrial and specialty chemicals, metals, and defense products.

Plan Specifics:
- Partial dividend reinvestment is not available.
- No Discount.
- OCP: $50 to $5000 per month.
- Purchasing fees are brokerage commissions and 5 percent service charge (maximum, $2.50) plus $5 fee for each investment of OCPs.
- $5 fee for issuance of certificates.
- Selling costs are brokerage commissions and $15 handling charge.
- Stock is purchased monthly with OCPs.

Performance Rating: ***

Omnicare, Inc. (NYSE:OCR)
1300 Fountain Square South
Cincinnati, OH 45202
(513) 762-6967

Business Profile: Produces medical and dental products and provides pharmacy management services.

Plan Specifics:
- Partial dividend reinvestment is not available.
- No Discount.
- OCP: $10 to $1000 per month.
- Selling costs are brokerage commissions.
- Stock is purchased monthly with OCPs.

Performance Rating: **

Oneida Ltd. (NYSE:OCQ)
Executive Offices
Oneida, NY 13421
(315) 361-3636

Business Profile: Produces stainless steel and silverplated flatware. Operations in industrial wire products.

Plan Specifics:
- Partial dividend reinvestment is available.
- 5 percent discount on reinvested dividends.
- OCP: not available.
- Selling costs are brokerage fees and service charges.

Performance Rating: **

Oneok, Inc. (NYSE:OKE)
P.O. Box 871
Tulsa, OK 74102-0871
(800) 395-2662   (405) 231-6711

Business Profile: Natural gas utility in Oklahoma with interests in gas and oil exploration and production.

Plan Specifics:
* Partial dividend reinvestment is available.
* No Discount.
* OCP: $25 to $5000 per quarter.
* Selling costs are brokerage commissions.
* Company purchases stock each month with OCPs.

Performance Rating: **

Orange & Rockland Utilities, Inc.
(NYSE:ORU)
c/o Manufacturers Hanover
P.O. Box 24850, Church St. Sta.
New York, NY 10249
(212) 613-7147 (914) 577-2512

Business Profile: Provides electric and gas services to portions of New York, New Jersey, and Pennsylvania.

Plan Specifics:
* Partial dividend reinvestment is available.
* No Discount.
* OCP: $25 to $5000 per quarter.
* Stock is purchased monthly with OCPs.
* Selling cost is small brokerage commission.
* Approximately 7851 shareholders in the plan.

Performance Rating: ****

Otter Tail Power Co.
(NASDAQ:OTTR)
215 S. Cascade St.
Fergus Falls, MN 56537
(218) 739-8479

Business Profile: Supplies electric power to customers in Minnesota and the Dakotas.

Plan Specifics:
* Partial dividend reinvestment is not available.
* No Discount.
* OCP: $10 to $2000 per month.
* Selling costs may include brokerage fees.
* Company purchases stock monthly with OCPs.
* 5000 to 5100 shareholders in the plan.
* Preferred dividends are eligible for reinvestment for additional common shares under the plan.

Performance Rating: ***

Pacific Enterprises (NYSE:PET)
633 W. Fifth St., Suite 5400
Los Angeles, CA 90071-2006
(800) 722-5483

Business Profile: California-based natural gas holding company.

Plan Specifics:
* Partial dividend reinvestment is available.
* No Discount.
* OCP: $25 to $25,000 per quarter.
* Must go through own broker to sell shares.
* Company purchases stock monthly with OCPs.

Performance Rating: **

Pacific Gas & Electric Co.
(NYSE:PCG)
Room 2600
77 Beale St.
San Francisco, CA 94106
(800) 367-7731

Business Profile: Natural gas and electric utility serving regions of California.

Plan Specifics:
- Partial dividend reinvestment is not available.
- No Discount.
- OCP: not available.
- Company will sell less than 100 shares for participants for no charge; otherwise must go through own broker to sell shares.
- Preferred dividends are eligible for reinvestment for additional common shares under the plan.

Performance Rating: **

Pacific Telesis Group (NYSE:PAC)
c/o American Transtech
P.O. Box 44444
Jacksonville, FL 32231-4444
(800) 637-6373

Business Profile: Important telephone holding company serving portions of California and Nevada.

Plan Specifics:
- Partial dividend reinvestment is available.
- No Discount.
- OCP: $250 to $50,000 per year.
- DRIP fees are $1 per quarter.
- Selling cost is approximately 10 cents per share.
- Company purchases stock monthly with OCPs.
- Need a minimum of two shares to purchase additional shares and need five shares for full reinvestment.
- Company permits automatic supplemental contributions of a minimum $50 per month via direct electronic funds transfer from a participant's bank account.

Performance Rating: ****

Pacific Western Bancshares, Inc.
(ASE:PWB)
333 W. Santa Clara St.
San Jose, CA 95113
(800) 522-6645

Business Profile: California bank holding firm.

Plan Specifics:
- Partial dividend reinvestment is available.
- 5 percent discount on reinvested dividends and OCP on shares purchased from the company; no discount on shares purchased on the open market.
- OCP: $25 to $3000 semiannually.
- Termination fee of $5.
- The company purchases stock semiannually with OCPs.
- Must go through own broker to sell shares.

Performance Rating: **

PacifiCorp (NYSE:PPW)
700 N.E. Multnomah St.
Portland, OR 97232-4107
(800) 233-5453

Business Profile: Electric and telephone holding company with operations in resource development.

Plan Specifics:
- Partial dividend reinvestment is available.
- No Discount.
- OCP: $25 to $25,000 per quarter.
- Purchasing and selling fees are approximately 5 to 10 cents per share, with no fee charged on original issue investments.
- Company purchases stock every month with OCPs.

• Approximately 55,000 shareholders in the plan.
• Preferred dividends are eligible for reinvestment for additional common shares under the plan.

Performance Rating: ***

PaineWebber Group, Inc.
(NYSE:PWJ)
c/o Chase Manhattan
P.O. Box 283, Bowling Green Sta.
New York, NY 10274
(212) 713-2722   (212) 713-2000

Business Profile: Holding company for large investment services firm.

Plan Specifics:
• Partial dividend reinvestment is not available.
• No Discount.
• OCP: $10 to $3000 per quarter.
• Stock is purchased at least quarterly with OCPs.
• Selling costs are brokerage commission and any taxes.
• Approximately 650 shareholders in the plan.

Performance Rating: **

Pall Corp. (ASE:PLL)
30 Sea Cliff Ave.
Glen Cove, NY 11542
(516) 484-5400

Business Profile: Manufacturer of filtration products used in the health care, aerospace, and fluid processing markets.

Plan Specifics:
• Partial dividend reinvestment is not available.
• No discount.
• OCP: $25 to $5000 per month.

• Stock is purchased once a month with OCPs.
• Selling costs may include brokerage fees.

Performance Rating: ***

Panhandle Eastern Corp.
(NYSE:PEL)
Shareholder Services
P.O. Box 1642
Houston, TX 77251
(713) 627-4681   (800) 225-5838

Business Profile: Transports and markets natural gas in midwestern and eastern states.

Plan Specifics:
• Partial dividend reinvestment is available.
• 5 percent discount on reinvested dividends.
• OCP: $25 to $60,000 per year.
• Must sell shares through own broker, although the company will buy back holdings of less than 10 shares.
• Company purchases stock monthly with OCPs.
• Approximately 9030 shareholders in the plan.

Performance Rating: **

Paramount Communications, Inc.
(NYSE:PCI)
15 Columbus Circle
New York, NY 10023-7780
(212) 373-8100

Business Profile: Produces filmed entertainment and publishes books.

Plan Specifics:
• Partial dividend reinvestment is not available.
• No Discount.
• OCP: $10 to $1000 per month.

- Selling costs are $15 bank charge and brokerage fees.
- Company purchases stock monthly with OCPs.

Performance Rating: ***

Parker Hannifin Corp. (NYSE:PH)
17325 Euclid Ave.
Cleveland, OH 44112-1290
(216) 531-3000

Business Profile: Creates devices for fluid power systems used in industrial, aerospace, and automotive markets.

Plan Specifics:
- Partial dividend reinvestment is not available.
- No Discount.
- OCP: $10 to $1000 per month.
- Stock is purchased with OCPs within 30 days of receipt of any amount sufficient to purchase at least 100 shares.
- Selling costs are brokerage commissions.

Performance Rating: ***

Peerless Tube Co. (ASE:PLS)
58-76 Locust Ave.
Bloomfield, NJ 07003
(201) 743-5100

Business Profile: Manufacturer of metal and plastic products for pharmaceutical and consumer-product firms.

Plan Specifics:
- Partial dividend reinvestment is not available.
- No Discount.
- OCP: $10 to $1000 per quarter.
- Company is not currently paying a dividend.
- Participants may have to go through own broker to sell shares.

- Stock is purchased quarterly with OCPs.

Performance Rating: *

Penney, J. C., Co., Inc. (NYSE:JCP)
P.O. Box 407
Pittsburgh, PA 15230
(412) 854-1000

Business Profile: Major retailing operation with outlets in all 50 states.

Plan Specifics:
- Partial dividend reinvestment is not available.
- No Discount.
- OCP: $10 to $1000 per month.
- Purchasing and selling costs are brokerage fees plus service charge ($2 maximum).
- Company purchases stock each month with OCPs.
- Approximately 4500 shareholders in the plan.

Performance Rating: ****

Pennsylvania Power & Light Co.
(NYSE:PPL)
Two North Ninth St.
Allentown, PA 18101-1179
(800) 345-3085

Business Profile: Provides residential, commercial, and industrial customers in central-eastern Pennsylvania with electric power.

Plan Specifics:
- Partial dividend reinvestment is not available.
- No Discount.
- OCP: up to $15,000 per quarter.
- Selling cost is approximately 12 cents per share.
- Company purchases stock once a month with OCPs.

- Preferred dividends are eligible for reinvestment for additional common shares under the plan.
- Approximately 50,000 shareholders in the plan.

Performance Rating: ***

Pennzoil Co. (NYSE:PZL)
P.O. Box 2967
Houston, TX 77252-2967
(713) 546-4000

Business Profile: Explores, produces, and refines natural gas and crude oil. Operations in sulfur, motor oil, and auto parts.

Plan Specifics:

- Partial dividend reinvestment is not available.
- No Discount.
- OCP: $40 to $6000 per quarter.
- Must go through own broker to sell shares.
- Company purchases stock quarterly with OCPs.
- Approximately 4500 shareholders in the plan.

Performance Rating: **

Pentair, Inc. (NASDAQ:PNTA)
c/o Norwest Bank MN
P.O. Box 738, 161 N. Concord Exch.
South St. Paul, MN 55075-0738
(612) 450-4075

Business Profile: Manufactures paper products, sporting ammunition, power tools, and industrial equipment.

Plan Specifics:

- Partial dividend reinvestment is not available.
- No Discount.
- OCP: $10 to $3000 per quarter.

- Selling costs are brokerage commissions and service charges.
- Company purchases stock around the 12th of each month with OCPs if enough funds accumulate to purchase at least 100 shares.
- Preferred dividends are eligible for reinvestment for additional common shares under the plan.

Performance Rating: **

Peoples Energy Corp. (NYSE:PGL)
122 S. Michigan Ave.
Chicago, IL 60603
(312) 431-4292   (800) 228-6888

Business Profile: A holding company for two natural gas utilities which serve nearly one million customers in Chicago and communities in northeastern Illinois.

Plan Specifics:

- Partial dividend reinvestment is not available.
- No Discount.
- OCP: $25 to $3000 per month.
- Selling costs include brokerage fees.
- Company purchases stock every month with OCPs.

Performance Rating: ***

PepsiCo, Inc. (NYSE:PEP)
700 Anderson Hill Rd.
Purchase, NY 10577
(914) 253-3055

Business Profile: Produces soft drinks and snack foods and owns several fast-food restaurants (Pizza Hut, Kentucky Fried Chicken, and Taco Bell).

Plan Specifics:

- Partial dividend reinvestment is available.
- No Discount.

- OCP: $10 to $60,000 per year.
- Minimal, if any, selling costs.
- Stock is purchased monthly with OCPs.

Performance Rating: ****

Perkin-Elmer Corp. (NYSE:PKN)
761 Main Ave.
Norwalk, CT 06859-0001
(203) 762-1000   (617) 575-2900

Business Profile: Manufactures scientific analytical instruments and combustion, electric arc, and plasma thermal spray equipment.

Plan Specifics:
- Partial dividend reinvestment is not available.
- No Discount.
- OCP: not available.
- Selling costs may include brokerage and service fees.

Performance Rating: ***

Pfizer, Inc. (NYSE:PFE)
Shareholders Services
235 E. 42nd St.
New York, NY 10017-5755
(212) 573-3704

Business Profile: Produces health care products, consumer products, pharmaceuticals, and animal health care items.

Plan Specifics:
- Partial dividend reinvestment is not available.
- No Discount.
- OCP: $10 to $10,000 per month.
- Selling costs include brokerage commissions and applicable taxes.
- Company purchases stock monthly with OCPs.

Performance Rating: ****

Phelps Dodge Corp. (NYSE:PD)
2600 N. Central Ave.
Phoenix, AZ 85004-3014
(602) 234-8199   (602) 234-8100

Business Profile: Leading United States copper provider with interests in carbon black and truck wheels and rims.

Plan Specifics:
- Partial dividend reinvestment is not available.
- No Discount.
- OCP: $10 to $2000 per quarter.
- Selling costs are $5 termination fee, $15 service charge, and brokerage commission.
- Company purchases stock quarterly with OCPs.

Performance Rating: ***

Philadelphia Electric Co. (NYSE:PE)
Shareholder Relations
P.O. Box 8487
Philadelphia, PA 19101
(800) 626-8729

Business Profile: Supplies electricity and natural gas to residential, commercial, and industrial customers in southeastern Pennsylvania.

Plan Specifics:
- Partial dividend reinvestment is available.
- No Discount.
- OCP: $25 to $50,000 per year.
- Selling costs are brokerage fees.
- Stock is purchased quarterly with OCPs.
- Preferred dividends are eligible for reinvestment for additional common shares under the plan.
- Customers of the utility may make initial investments directly through

the company (minimum initial investment of $25).

Performance Rating: **

Philadelphia Suburban Corp.
(NYSE:PSC)
762 Lancaster Ave.
Bryn Mawr, PA 19010-3489
(215) 527-8000

Business Profile: Philadelphia-based water utility holding company.

Plan Specifics:
- Partial dividend reinvestment is available.
- 5 percent discount on reinvested dividends.
- OCP: $25 to $10,000, up to three times per year.
- Selling costs are brokerage commission and any applicable taxes.

Performance Rating: **

Philip Morris Companies, Inc.
(NYSE:MO)
c/o First Chicago Trust-NY
P.O. Box 3506, Church St. Sta.
New York, NY 10008-3506
(212) 791-6422   (212) 880-5000

Business Profile: Major supplier of cigarettes (Marlboro), beer (Miller), and consumer foods (Oscar Mayer, Maxwell House, Jell-O).

Plan Specifics:
- Partial dividend reinvestment is not available.
- No Discount.
- OCP: $10 to $60,000 per year.
- Stock is purchased around the 10th day of the month with OCPs.
- Selling costs are brokerage commission and other costs of sale.

Performance Rating: ****

Phillips Petroleum Co. (NYSE:P)
Stockholder Records
Section 6C1 Phillips Building
Bartlesville, OK 74004
(800) 356-0066

Business Profile: Major integrated crude oil and natural gas concern with operations in chemicals.

Plan Specifics:
- Partial dividend reinvestment is not available.
- No Discount.
- OCP: $10 to $10,000 per month.
- Selling costs include $5 liquidation fee.
- Stock purchased monthly with OCPs.

Performance Rating: **

Piccadilly Cafeterias, Inc.
(NASDAQ:PICC)
P.O. Box 2467
Baton Rouge, LA 70821-2467
(504) 293-9440

Business Profile: Manages chain of cafeterias in southern and southwestern states.

Plan Specifics:
- Partial dividend reinvestment is available.
- 5 percent discount on reinvested dividends.
- OCP: $100 to $5000 per quarter.
- Selling costs are brokerage commission and any service fees and transfer taxes.
- Company purchases stock quarterly with OCPs.

Performance Rating: **

**Piedmont Natural Gas Co.
(NYSE:PNY)
P.O. Box 33068
Charlotte, NC 28233
(800) 438-8410**

Business Profile: Provides natural gas to Piedmont region of North and South Carolina and metropolitan Nashville, Tennessee.

Plan Specifics:
- Partial dividend reinvestment is available.
- 5 percent discount on reinvested dividends.
- OCP: $25 to $3000 per month.
- Selling costs are brokerage commission and any transfer tax.
- Stock is purchased monthly with OCPs.

Performance Rating: ***

**Pinnacle West Capital Corp.
(NYSE:PNW)
P.O. Box 52133
Phoenix, AZ 85072-2133
(800) 457-2983**

Business Profile: Electric utility holding company providing services to portions of Arizona.

Plan Specifics:
- Partial dividend reinvestment is available.
- No Discount.
- OCP: $10 to $5000 per quarter.
- Selling cost is approximately 10 cents a share.
- Purchasing fee is approximately 6 cents per share if firm buys stock on the open market.
- Company purchases stock monthly with OCPs.

Performance Rating: **

**Pittston Co. (NYSE:PCO)
c/o First Chicago Trust-NY
P.O. Box 3508, Church St. Sta.
New York, NY 10008
(212) 791-6422 (203) 622-0918**

Business Profile: Operations in coal, armored car security services, and airfreight forwarding.

Plan Specifics:
- Partial dividend reinvestment is not available.
- No Discount.
- OCP: $10 to $3000 per quarter.
- Stock is purchased quarterly with OCPs.
- No selling costs.

Performance Rating: **

**PNC Financial Corp. (NYSE:PNC)
Stock Transfer Dept.
P.O. Box 548
Pittsburgh, PA 15230
(412) 762-2666**

Business Profile: Multibank holding company offering services through subsidiaries in Pennsylvania, Indiana, Kentucky, Ohio, New Jersey, and Delaware.

Plan Specifics:
- Partial dividend reinvestment is available.
- No Discount.
- OCP: $50 to $1000 per month.
- Must go through own broker to sell shares.
- Company purchases stock monthly with OCPs.
- Preferred dividends are eligible for reinvestment for additional common shares under the plan.

Performance Rating: **

Polaroid Corp. (NYSE:PRD)
549 Technology Square
Cambridge, MA 02139
(617) 577-2000

Business Profile: Leading manufacturer of cameras, photographic equipment, and film.

Plan Specifics:
* Partial dividend reinvestment is not available.
* No Discount.
* OCP: $10 to $3000 per quarter.
* Stock is purchased every quarter with OCPs.
* Selling costs are brokerage commissions.

Performance Rating: **

Portland General Corp.
 (NYSE:PGN)
c/o First Chicago Trust Co. of NY
P.O. Box 3506, Church St. Sta.
New York, NY 10008-3506
(212) 791-6422

Business Profile: Electric utility holding company serving residential, commercial, and industrial customers in Oregon.

Plan Specifics:
* Partial dividend reinvestment is available.
* No Discount.
* OCP: $25 to $6000 per quarter.
* Selling and buying costs are brokerage commissions.
* Company purchases stock quarterly with OCPs.

Performance Rating: **

Portsmouth Bank Shares, Inc.
 (NASDAQ:POBS)
333 State St.
Portsmouth, NH 03801
(603) 436-6630

Business Profile: New Hampshire-based bank holding company.

Plan Specifics:
* Partial dividend reinvestment is not available.
* No Discount.
* OCP: not available.
* Purchasing costs are low brokerage fees.
* Selling costs are brokerage commission and handling fee of 5 percent of amount invested (maximum of $5).
* 400 to 500 shareholders in the plan.
* Minimum of 25 shares needed to be in the plan.

Performance Rating: NR

Potlatch Corp. (NYSE:PCH)
P.O. Box 193591
San Francisco, CA 94119-3591
(415) 576-8803   (415) 576-8800

Business Profile: Manufactures lumber, plywood, paper, paperboard, and pulp products.

Plan Specifics:
* Partial dividend reinvestment is not available.
* No Discount.
* OCP: $25 to $1000 per month.
* Selling costs are brokerage commissions.
* Company purchases stock monthly with OCPs.

Performance Rating: ***

Potomac Electric Power Co. (NYSE:POM)
Shareholder Service Dept.
P.O. Box 1936
Washington, DC 20013
(800) 527-3726

Business Profile: Provides electric service for residential, commercial, and governmental use in Washington, D.C., and Maryland areas.

Plan Specifics:

- Partial dividend reinvestment is available.
- No Discount.
- OCP: $25 to $5000 per month.
- Stock is purchased monthly with OCPs.
- Selling costs are $3 service fee and brokerage fees.
- Approximately 23,400 shareholders in plan.

Performance Rating: ****

PPG Industries, Inc. (NYSE:PPG)
One PPG Place
Pittsburgh, PA 15272
(412) 434-2120   (412) 434-3131

Business Profile: Produces glass, protective and decorative coatings for automotive and industrial markets, and specialty chemicals.

Plan Specifics:

- Partial dividend reinvestment is not available.
- No Discount.
- OCP: $10 to $3000 per quarter.
- Selling costs are brokerage commissions, any other costs, and administrator's charge of $1.
- Company purchases stock monthly with OCPs.

- Approximately 8000 shareholders in the plan.

Performance Rating: ****

Premier Bancorp, Inc. (NASDAQ:PRBC)
P.O. Box 1511
Baton Rouge, LA 70821-1511
(504) 334-7277

Business Profile: Louisiana-based bank holding institution.

Plan Specifics:

- Partial dividend reinvestment is available.
- No Discount.
- OCP: $25 to $7500 per quarter.
- Selling costs are brokerage commission and other reasonable costs of sale.
- Company purchases stock at least quarterly with OCPs.
- Approximately 1748 shareholders in the plan.
- Company is not currently paying a dividend.

Performance Rating: *

Premier Industrial Corp. (NYSE:PRE)
4500 Euclid Ave.
Cleveland, OH 44103-3780
(216) 391-8300

Business Profile: Distributes electronic and electrical products used in the production and maintenance of equipment.

Plan Specifics:

- Partial dividend reinvestment is available.
- No Discount.
- OCP: $10 to $5000 per quarter.
- Bank charges an administration fee.

• Selling costs include service fees.
• Stock is purchased monthly with OCPs.

Performance Rating: ***

Presidential Realty Corp.
(ASE:PDL.B)
c/o American Stock Transfer
99 Wall Street
New York, NY 10005
(212) 936-5100   (914) 948-1300

Business Profile: Real estate investment trust.

Plan Specifics:
• Partial dividend reinvestment is available.
• 5 percent discount on reinvested dividends.
• OCP: $100 to $10,000 per quarter.
• Stock is purchased monthly with OCPs.
• Selling costs are brokerage commission and any transfer taxes incurred.

Performance Rating: *

Preston Corp. (NASDAQ:PTRK)
151 Easton Blvd.
Preston, MD 21655
(301) 673-7151

Business Profile: Transportation-based trucking firm with a major position in nonunion regional motor carriage.

Plan Specifics:
• Partial dividend reinvestment is not available.
• No Discount.
• OCP: $25 to $2500 per quarter.
• Company purchases stock monthly with OCPs.
• May have to go through own broker to sell shares.

Performance Rating: **

Procter & Gamble Co. (NYSE:PG)
P.O. Box 599
Cincinnati, OH 45201-0599
(800) 742-6253

Business Profile: Markets household items, personal care products, and consumer foods.

Plan Specifics:
• Partial dividend reinvestment is available.
• No Discount.
• OCP: $2 to $120,000 per year.
• Purchasing fees are brokerage commissions and other costs of purchase.
• Selling costs may include brokerage fees.
• Company purchases stock monthly with OCPs.
• Initial investments in the company may be made directly through the plan (minimum purchase of one share, with brokerage fee of approximately 8 cents per share).

Performance Rating: ****

Providence Energy Corp.
(ASE:PVY)
100 Weybosset St.
Providence, RI 02903
(401) 272-9191   (800) 426-5523

Business Profile: Rhode Island natural gas holding company.

Plan Specifics:
• Partial dividend reinvestment is available.
• No Discount.
• OCP: $25 to $5000 per quarter.
• Selling costs are service charge of 5 percent of amount invested (maximum of $2.50) and brokerage fee of approximately 15 cents a share; if

amount is over 1000 shares, it is 10 cents a share.
- Company purchases stock around the 15th of the month with OCPs.

Performance Rating: **

PSI Resources, Inc. (NYSE:PIN)
1000 E. Main St.
Plainfield, IN 46168
(317) 838-1157

Business Profile: Indiana-based electric utility holding firm.

Plan Specifics:
- Partial dividend reinvestment is available.
- No Discount.
- OCP: $25 to $7000 per month.
- Selling costs are small commission fees.
- Company purchases stock monthly with OCPs.
- Preferred dividends are eligible for reinvestment for additional common shares under the plan.

Performance Rating: **

Public Service Co. of Colorado
(NYSE:PSR)
Room 160B
P.O. Box 840
Denver, CO 80201-0840
(303) 571-7514   (800) 635-0566

Business Profile: Provides electricity and and natural gas service to Colorado regions.

Plan Specifics:
- Partial dividend reinvestment is available.
- 3 percent discount on reinvested dividends.
- OCP: $25 to $100,000 per year.
- Participants may incur small broker-

age fees if company purchases stock in open market.
- Selling cost is approximately 5 cents per share.
- Company purchases stock monthly with OCPs.
- Approximately 27,000 shareholders in the plan.

Performance Rating: **

Public Service Co. of North Carolina
(NASDAQ:PSNC)
Dividend Reinvestment Service
P.O. Box 1398
Gastonia, NC 28053-1398
(704) 864-6731

Business Profile: Provides natural gas to residential, commercial, and industrial clients throughout North Carolina.

Plan Specifics:
- Partial dividend reinvestment is available.
- 5 percent discount on reinvested dividends.
- OCP: $25 to $3000 per quarter.
- Must go through own broker to sell shares.
- Company purchases stock around the 1st of each month with OCPs.
- Preferred dividends are eligible for reinvestment for additional common shares under the plan.

Performance Rating: ***

Public Service Enterprise Group, Inc. (NYSE:PEG)
P.O. Box 1171
Newark, NJ 07101-1171
(800) 526-8050

Business Profile: New Jersey-based public utility holding company.

Plan Specifics:
- Partial dividend reinvestment is available.
- No Discount.
- OCP: $25 to $100,000 per year.
- Selling cost is approximately 3 cents per share.
- Company purchases stock around the 21st of the month with OCPs.

Performance Rating: ***

**Puget Sound Bancorp
(NASDAQ:PSNB)
P.O. Box 11500
Tacoma, WA 98411-5052
(206) 383-2871**

Business Profile: Washington-based commercial banking firm.

Plan Specifics:
- Partial dividend reinvestment is available.
- 5 percent discount on reinvested dividends.
- OCP: not available.
- Selling costs are liquidation and brokerage fees.
- Approximately 2300 shareholders in the plan.

Performance Rating: NR

**Puget Sound Power & Light Co.
(NYSE:PSD)
P.O. Box 96010
Bellevue, WA 98009-9610
(206) 462-3719**

Business Profile: Provides electric service to nearly 1.7 million people in the state of Washington.

Plan Specifics:
- Partial dividend reinvestment is not available.

- No Discount.
- OCP: $25 to $20,000 per year.
- Purchasing and selling fees are brokerage commission.
- Company purchases stock around the 15th of each month with OCPs.
- Preferred dividends may be reinvested for additional common shares.
- Customers may make initial purchase of stock directly through the company (minimum initial investment of $25).

Performance Rating: **

**Quaker Oats Co. (NYSE:OAT)
P.O. Box 9001
321 N. Clark
Chicago, IL 60604-9001
(800) 344-1198**

Business Profile: Important producer of cereals, pancake mixes, frozen breakfast items, and pet foods.

Plan Specifics:
- Partial dividend reinvestment is available.
- No Discount.
- OCP: $10 to $30,000 per year.
- Selling cost is approximately 5 1/2 cents per share.
- Company purchases stock every month with OCPs.
- Approximately 14,000 shareholders in the plan.

Performance Rating: ****

**Quaker State Corp. (NYSE:KSF)
P.O. Box 989
255 Elm Street
Oil City, PA 16301
(814) 676-7676   (212) 676-5754**

Business Profile: Produces and markets motor oil and provides vehicle maintenance services.

Plan Specifics:
- Partial dividend reinvestment is not available.
- No Discount.
- OCP: $10 to $3000 per quarter.
- Selling costs are brokerage commissions.
- Company purchases stock at least quarterly with OCPs.

Performance Rating: **

Quanex Corp. (NYSE:NX)
Suite 1500
1900 West Loop South
Houston, TX 77027
(800) 231-8176

Business Profile: Manufactures carbon and alloy steel bars, steel tubing, aluminum building materials, and titanium.

Plan Specifics:
- Partial dividend reinvestment is not available.
- No Discount.
- OCP: $10 to $1000 per month.
- Selling costs are minimal.
- Company purchases stock the 1st business day of the month with OCPs.
- Approximately 1000 shareholders in the plan.

Performance Rating: **

Quantum Chemical Corp.
(NYSE:CUE)
99 Park Ave.
New York, NY 10016
(212) 949-5000

Business Profile: Supplier of petrochemicals and propane.

Plan Specifics:
- Partial dividend reinvestment is not available.

- No Discount.
- OCP: $25 to $3000 per month.
- Company charges a $5 transaction charge for each investment with OCPs.
- Selling costs are a $15 handling charge, brokerage commission, and any transfer tax.
- $5 charge for issuance of certificates.
- Company purchases stock around the 1st of the month with OCPs.

Performance Rating: **

Questar Corp. (NYSE:STR)
P.O. Box 11150
Salt Lake City, UT 84147
(801) 534-5885   (801) 534-5000

Business Profile: Energy-based holding company engaged in retail distribution, interstate transmission, and exploration of natural gas. The firm is also involved in the telecommunications business.

Plan Specifics:
- Partial dividend reinvestment is available.
- No Discount.
- OCP: $50 to $15,000 per quarter.
- Participants may incur brokerage fees if company purchases stock in the open market.
- Initial purchases may be made directly through the company (minimum initial investment of $50).
- Company purchases stock each month with OCPs.
- Approximately 2000 shareholders in the plan.

Performance Rating: ***

RAC Mortgage Investment Corp.
(NYSE:RMR)
P.O. Box 4000
10221 Wincopin Circle
Columbia, MD 21044
(301) 730-6851   (301) 347-9126

Business Profile: Real estate investment trust.

Plan Specifics:
* Partial dividend reinvestment is available.
* No Discount.
* OCP: $50 to $1000 per quarter.
* Selling costs are brokerage commissions, $2.50 service fee, and $3 to terminate.
* Company purchases stock quarterly with OCPs.
* Approximately 279 shareholders in the plan.

Performance Rating: *

Ralston Purina Co. (NYSE:RAL)
Attn.: Investors Relations
Checkerboard Square
St. Louis, MO 63164
(314) 982-3002

Business Profile: Leading producer of cat and dog food, dry cell batteries, and bakery items.

Plan Specifics:
* Partial dividend reinvestment is available.
* No Discount.
* OCP: $10 to $25,000 per year.
* Stock is purchased monthly with OCPs.
* Selling costs may include brokerage fees.
* Approximately 10,000 shareholders in plan.

Performance Rating: ****

Raymond Corp. (NASDAQ:RAYM)
Corporate Headquarters
Greene, NY 13778
(607) 656-2311

Business Profile: Provides equipment and systems used in warehouse distribution and manufacturing industries.

Plan Specifics:
* Partial dividend reinvestment is not available.
* No Discount.
* OCP: $10 to $3000 per month.
* Selling costs are brokerage commissions.
* Company purchases stock monthly with OCPs.

Performance Rating: **

Raytheon Co. (NYSE:RTN)
141 Spring St.
Lexington, MA 02173
(617) 862-6600   (617) 575-2900

Business Profile: Supplies government with defense electronics. Also has operations in commercial aircraft, appliances, and engineering.

Plan Specifics:
* Partial dividend reinvestment is not available.
* No Discount.
* OCP: $10 to $5000 per quarter.
* Purchasing and selling fees are service charge of 5 percent (maximum of $2.50) plus brokerage commissions.
* Stock is purchased approximately eight times a year with OCPs.

Performance Rating: ****

Real Estate Investment Trust of CA
(NYSE:RCT)
Suite 700
12011 San Vicente Blvd.
Los Angeles, CA 90049
(213) 476-7793

Business Profile: Real estate investment trust.

Plan Specifics:
• Partial dividend reinvestment is available.
• No Discount.
• OCP: $500 to $5000 per quarter.
• Must go through own broker to sell shares.
• Company purchases stock once a quarter with OCPs.
• Approximately 900 shareholders in the plan.

Performance Rating: **

Realty South Investors, Inc.
(ASE:RSI)
1395 S. Marietta Pkwy #500-200
Marietta, GA 30067
(404) 423-5295   (404) 897-3394

Business Profile: Real estate investment trust with operations in the Southeast.

Plan Specifics:
• Partial dividend reinvestment is available.
• No Discount.
• OCP: $25 to $3000 per month.
• Purchasing fees include brokerage commissions and administrative fees of 4 percent of amount invested (maximum of $2.50).
• Selling costs are brokerage commission.
• Company purchases stock monthly with OCPs.

Performance Rating: *

Regional Bancorp, Inc.
(NASDAQ:REGB)
Attn.: Shareholder Relations
29 High St.
Medford, MA 02155
(617) 395-7700

Business Profile: Holding firm for Massachusetts bank.

Plan Specifics:
• Partial dividend reinvestment is available.
• No Discount.
• OCP: $100 to $1000 each quarter.
• Selling costs are brokerage fees, service charges, and any transfer taxes.
• Company purchases stock quarterly with OCPs.

Performance Rating: NR

Resort Income Investors, Inc.
(ASE:RII)
c/o Midlantic Bank
499 Thornall St.
Edison, NJ 08810
(312) 444-1400

Business Profile: Real estate investment trust.

Plan Specifics:
• Partial dividend reinvestment is available.
• No Discount.
• OCP: not available.
• Purchasing fees are approximately $1 per transaction and any brokerage fees.
• Selling cost is brokerage commission.

Performance Rating: *

Reynolds & Reynolds Co.
(NYSE:REY)
P.O. Box 2608
Dayton, OH 45401
(513) 443-2000

Business Profile: Supplies automotive, business, and medical markets with business forms and computer systems.

Plan Specifics:
- Partial dividend reinvestment is not available.
- No Discount.
- OCP: $100 to $1000 per quarter.
- Selling costs are $1 bank service charge and brokerage fees.
- Company purchases stock quarterly with OCPs.
- Approximately 255 shareholders in the plan.

Performance Rating: ***

Reynolds Metals Co. (NYSE:RLM)
P.O. Box 27003
Richmond, VA 23261-7703
(804) 281-4765   (804) 281-2000

Business Profile: Leading aluminum producer. Supplies aluminum cans, aluminum foil, and other food wraps.

Plan Specifics:
- Partial dividend reinvestment is not available.
- No Discount.
- OCP: $25 to $3000 per quarter.
- Selling costs are brokerage commission and a $5 service charge.
- Company purchases stock monthly with OCPs.
- Approximately 2500 shareholders in the plan.

Performance Rating: **

Rhone-Poulenc Rorer, Inc.
(NYSE:RPR)
500 Virginia Drive
Fort Washington, PA 19034
(215) 628-6007   (800) 524-4458

Business Profile: Manufactures pharmaceuticals and chemicals.

Plan Specifics:
- Partial dividend reinvestment is not available.
- No Discount.
- OCP: $25 to $3000 per quarter.
- Selling costs include a $2.50 charge.
- Company purchases stock quarterly with OCPs.

Performance Rating: ***

Roadway Services, Inc.
(NASDAQ:ROAD)
c/o Ameritrust Co.
P.O. Box 6477
Cleveland, OH 44101
(216) 384-8184

Business Profile: Transportation holding company offering long-haul, regional, small package, and express services.

Plan Specifics:
- Partial dividend reinvestment is not available.
- No Discount.
- OCP: $10 to $3000 per month.
- Purchasing fees are brokerage commission.
- Selling costs include $5 service charge and brokerage commissions.
- Company purchases stock monthly with OCPs.

Performance Rating: ***

Rochester Gas & Electric Corp.
(NYSE:RGS)
89 East Ave.
Rochester, NY 14649-0001
(716) 546-2700   (716) 232-5000

Business Profile: Supplies electric and gas service to city of Rochester, New York.

Plan Specifics:
- Partial dividend reinvestment is available.
- No Discount.
- OCP: $10 to $5000 per month.
- Selling costs are approximately 7 cents per share brokerage fee and service charge.
- Company purchases stock monthly with OCPs.
- Approximately 16,000 shareholders in the plan.

Performance Rating: **

Rochester Telephone Corp.
(NYSE:RTC)
c/o First Chicago Trust Co.-NY
P.O. Box 3506, Church St. Sta.
New York, NY 10008
(800) 446-2617

Business Profile: Provides telephone service to Rochester, New York, and neighboring areas.

Plan Specifics:
- Partial dividend reinvestment is not available.
- No Discount.
- OCP: $25 to $5000 per month.
- Stock is purchased monthly with OCPs.
- Selling costs are brokerage fees and a nominal service fee.
- Approximately 4500 shareholders in the plan.

Performance Rating: ***

Rockefeller Center Properties, Inc.
(NYSE:RCP)
c/o Manufacturers Hanover
P.O. Box 24850, Church St. Sta.
New York, NY 10249
(212) 613-7147

Business Profile: Real estate investment trust.

Plan Specifics:
- Partial dividend reinvestment is not available.
- No Discount.
- OCP: $100 to $5000 per month.
- Selling costs include brokerage and handling fees.
- Stock is purchased monthly with OCPs.

Performance Rating: **

Rockwell International Corp.
(NYSE:ROK)
625 Liberty Ave.
Pittsburgh, PA 15222-3123
(412) 565-7120   (412) 236-8000

Business Profile: Operations in space systems, defense systems, military equipment, and automotive components.

Plan Specifics:
- Partial dividend reinvestment is not available.
- No Discount.
- OCP: $10 to $1000 per month.
- Selling costs may include brokerage fees.
- Stock is purchased at least quarterly with OCPs.

Performance Rating: ****

Rollins, Inc. (NYSE:ROL)
2170 Piedmont Rd., N.E.
Atlanta, GA 30324
(404) 888-2000

Business Profile: Operations in pest control, protective services, and lawn care.

Plan Specifics:
- Partial dividend reinvestment is not available.
- No Discount.
- OCP: not available.
- Selling costs are brokerage commission.
- Must have a minimum of 50 shares to enroll in the plan.

Performance Rating: ***

Rollins Truck Leasing Corp.
(NYSE:RLC)
P.O. Box 1791
Wilmington, DE 19899
(302) 479-2700   (800) 637-2441

Business Profile: A major provider of truck leasing and rental services.

Plan Specifics:
- Partial dividend reinvestment is not available.
- No Discount.
- OCP: no maximum or minimum.
- Participants will incur brokerage fees when buying and selling through the plan.

Performance Rating: **

Rose's Stores, Inc.
(NASDAQ:RSTO)
c/o Wachovia Bank & Trust
P.O. Box 3001
Winston-Salem, NC 27102
(919) 770-6000   (919) 430-2100

Business Profile: Owns and operates general merchandise discount stores in southeastern states.

Plan Specifics:
- Partial dividend reinvestment is available.
- No Discount.
- OCP: $10 to $3000 per quarter.
- Stock is purchased monthly with OCPs.
- Selling costs are brokerage commission and termination fee.

Performance Rating: *

Rouse Co. (NASDAQ:ROUS)
10275 Little Patuxent Parkway
Columbia, MD 21044-3456
(301) 992-6000

Business Profile: Engages in possession, development, and management of income-producing real estate.

Plan Specifics:
- Partial dividend reinvestment is not available.
- No Discount.
- OCP: minimum of $50 per payment per quarter.
- May have to go through own broker to sell shares.
- Company purchases stock quarterly with OCPs.
- Approximately 587 shareholders in the plan.

Performance Rating: **

RPM, Inc. (NASDAQ:RPOW)
P.O. Box 777
Medina, OH 44258
(216) 225-3192   (216) 737-5745

Business Profile: Manufactures protective coatings, wallcoverings, and fabrics for industrial and hobby markets.

Plan Specifics:
- Partial dividend reinvestment is not available.
- No Discount.

- OCP: $10 to $2000 per month.
- Selling costs include applicable taxes.
- Company purchases stock on the 10th and last business days of month with OCPs.
- Approximately 7000 shareholders in the plan.

Performance Rating: *******

Rubbermaid, Inc. (NYSE:RBD)
1147 Akron Rd.
Wooster, OH 44691-0800
(216) 264-6464

Business Profile: Manufactures rubber and plastic houseware products and children's toys.

Plan Specifics:
- Partial dividend reinvestment is not available.
- No Discount.
- OCP: $10 to $3000 per quarter, in multiples of $10.
- Selling costs may include brokerage fees plus $5 terminating fee.
- Stock is purchased monthly with OCPs if enough funds accumulate to purchase a 100-share round lot (or lesser number if bank deems practical).

Performance Rating: ********

Russell Corp. (NYSE:RML)
P.O. Box 272
Alexander City, AL 35010
(205) 329-4832

Business Profile: Manufactures and sells leisure apparel, athletic uniforms, knit shirts, and woven fabrics.

Plan Specifics:
- Partial dividend reinvestment is not available.
- No Discount.

- OCP: $10 to $3000 per quarter.
- Selling costs are $1 service charge, brokerage commission, and any applicable taxes.
- Company purchases stock quarterly with OCPs.

Performance Rating: *******

Ryder System, Inc. (NYSE:R)
3600 N.W. 82d Ave.
Miami, FL 33166
(305) 593-3726

Business Profile: Provides truck leasing, truck rental, automobile hauling, and school bus transportation services.

Plan Specifics:
- Partial dividend reinvestment is available.
- No Discount.
- OCP: $10 to $12,000 per year.
- Selling costs are minimal brokerage commission and related expenses of sale.
- Company purchases stock monthly with OCPs.

Performance Rating: ******

St. Joseph Light & Power Co. (NYSE:SAJ)
520 Francis St.
St. Joseph, MO 64502
(816) 233-8888

Business Profile: Provides electric power and natural gas to regions of northwestern Missouri.

Plan Specifics:
- Partial dividend reinvestment is not available.
- No Discount.
- OCP: $100 to $7500 per quarter.
- Selling costs are brokerage commission and any other expenses.
- Company purchases stock quarterly with OCPs.

- Approximately 2100 shareholders in the plan.

Performance Rating: ***

St. Paul Bancorp, Inc.
(NASDAQ:SPBC)
c/o Bank of Boston
P.O. Box 1681
Boston, MA 02105
(617) 575-2900   (312) 622-5000

Business Profile: Chicago savings bank holding company.

Plan Specifics:
- Partial dividend reinvestment is not available.
- No Discount.
- OCP: $50 to $1500 per quarter.
- Selling costs are brokerage commissions, transfer tax, and administrative charges of 5 percent of the amount of the sale (maximum $3).
- Company purchases stock quarterly, and more frequently if enough funds accumulate, with OCPs.

Performance Rating: **

St. Paul Companies, Inc.
(NASDAQ:STPL)
385 Washington St.
St. Paul, MN 55102
(612) 221-7911

Business Profile: Insurance and investment banking concern with major operations in property-liability markets.

Plan Specifics:
- Partial dividend reinvestment is available.
- No Discount.
- OCP: $10 to $60,000 per year.
- Selling costs are brokerage fees.
- Company purchases stock monthly with OCPs.

- Approximately 2091 shareholders in the plan.

Performance Rating: ***

Salomon, Inc. (NYSE:SB)
1 New York Plaza
New York, NY 10004
(800) 772-7865   (212) 791-6422

Business Profile: Investment banking and market-making holding firm.

Plan Specifics:
- Partial dividend reinvestment is not available.
- No Discount.
- OCP: $10 to $3000 per quarter.
- Selling costs are brokerage commissions.
- Company purchases stock quarterly with OCPs.

Performance Rating: ***

Samson Energy Co., L.P. (ASE:SAM)
Two West 2d St.
Tulsa, OK 74103
(918) 583-1791

Business Profile: Consolidates business and property of oil and gas drilling partnerships as well as produces property partnerships.

Plan Specifics:
- Partial dividend reinvestment is available.
- No Discount.
- OCP: $150 to $5000 per quarter.
- Selling costs are brokerage fee and any other applicable transfer tax.
- Company purchases stock quarterly with OCPs.
- Approximately 220 shareholders in the plan.

Performance Rating: **

Santa Anita Companies (NYSE:SAR)
285 W. Huntington Drive
Arcadia, CA 91007-3439
(818) 574-6371

Business Profile: Real estate investment trust.

Plan Specifics:
- Partial dividend reinvestment is available.
- 5 percent discount on reinvested dividends.
- OCP: $50 to $2000 per month.
- Participants may have to go through own broker to sell shares.
- Company purchases stock monthly with OCPs.

Performance Rating: **

Sara Lee Corp. (NYSE:SLE)
3 First National Plaza
Chicago, IL 60602-4260
(312) 558-8450

Business Profile: Produces packaged meats, bakery, and coffee products and has operations in food service and personal items.

Plan Specifics:
- Partial dividend reinvestment is not available.
- No Discount.
- OCP: $10 to $5000 per quarter.
- Selling costs are approximately 10 cents per share brokerage commission, transfer taxes, and service charge of 5 percent of the value ($10 maximum).
- Stock is purchased approximately eight times a year with OCPs.

Performance Rating: ****

Savannah Foods & Industries, Inc.
(NASDAQ:SVAN)
P.O. Box 339
Savannah, GA 31402-0339
(912) 234-1261

Business Profile: Refines and markets beet and cane sugar.

Plan Specifics:
- Partial dividend reinvestment is not available.
- No Discount.
- OCP: $10 to $3000 per quarter.
- Selling costs are brokerage commissions.
- Company purchases stock quarterly with OCPs.

Performance Rating: ***

SCANA Corp. (NYSE:SCG)
Shareholder Services 054
Columbia, SC 29218
(803) 748-3669   (800) 763-5891

Business Profile: Public utility holding company supplying electric power and gas service to South Carolina residents.

Plan Specifics:
- Partial dividend reinvestment is available.
- No Discount.
- OCP: $25 to $3000 per month.
- Purchasing fees are approximately 4 cents per share.
- Selling costs are brokerage commission and any transfer tax.
- Company purchases stock monthly with OCPs.
- Approximately 15,782 shareholders in the plan.

Performance Rating: ***

SCEcorp (NYSE:SCE)
P.O. Box 400-Secretary's Dept.
Rosemead, CA 91770
(800) 347-8625

Business Profile: Electric utility holding company serving commercial, residential, and industrial customers.

Plan Specifics:
* Partial dividend reinvestment is available.
* No Discount.
* OCP: up to $10,000 per month.
* Purchasing fees are approximately 4 cents per share.
* Must go through own broker to sell shares.
* Company purchases stock monthly with OCPs.
* Approximately 40,000 shareholders in the plan.

Performance Rating: ****

Schering-Plough Corp. (NYSE:SGP)
1 Giralda Farms
Madison, NJ 07940-1000
(201) 822-7000

Business Profile: Major supplier of pharmaceuticals and consumer products.

Plan Specifics:
* Partial dividend reinvestment is available.
* No Discount.
* OCP: $25 to $36,000 per year.
* Selling costs are a $2.50 termination fee and brokerage fees for liquidation.
* Company purchases stock around the 10th and the 25th of each month with OCPs.
* Approximately 6984 shareholders in the plan.

Performance Rating: ****

Scott Paper Co. (NYSE:SPP)
Scott Plaza
Philadelphia, PA 19113
(215) 522-5942   (212) 791-6422

Business Profile: Largest manufacturer of paper tissues, napkins, and towels with interests in printing and publishing.

Plan Specifics:
* Partial dividend reinvestment is not available.
* No Discount.
* OCP: $10 to $3000 per quarter.
* Purchasing fees are proportionate share of the brokerage commissions and a 5 percent service charge ($2.50 maximum) for each investment of a dividend and any voluntary cash payments.
* Stock is purchased quarterly with OCPs.
* Approximately 6500 shareholders in the plan.

Performance Rating: ***

Seafield Capital Corp.
  (NASDAQ:SFLD)
c/o First Chicago Trust-NY
P.O. Box 3506
New York, NY 10008-3506
(212) 791-6422   (816) 753-8000

Business Profile: Insurance-based holding company.

Plan Specifics:
* Partial dividend reinvestment is available.
* No Discount.
* OCP: $25 to $5000 per quarter.
* Stock is purchased quarterly with OCPs.
* Selling costs are brokerage commission and any other cost of sale.

Performance Rating: NR

Sears, Roebuck & Co. (NYSE:S)
c/o First Chicago Trust-NY
P.O. Box 3506, Church St. Sta.
New York, NY 10008-3506
(212) 791-6422

Business Profile: Manages general merchandise stores nationwide and engages in insurance and financial services operations.

Plan Specifics:
- Partial dividend reinvestment is not available.
- No Discount.
- OCP: $25 to $3000 per month.
- Stock is purchased monthly with OCPs.
- Purchasing fees are brokerage commission and 5 percent of total amount invested ($2.50 maximum).
- Selling costs are a $5 charge and brokerage commission.

Performance Rating: ***

Security Bancorp, Inc. (MI)
(NASDAQ:SECB)
16333 Trenton Rd.
Southgate, MI 48195
(313) 281-5433

Business Profile: Multibank holding company serving Michigan clients.

Plan Specifics:
- Partial dividend reinvestment is available.
- No Discount.
- OCP: $10 to $5000 per month.
- Selling costs are brokerage commission, service charges, any transfer taxes, and a $3 termination fee.
- Company purchases stock monthly with OCPs.

- Preferred dividends are eligible for reinvestment for additional common shares under the plan.

Performance Rating: ***

Security Pacific Corp. (NYSE:SPC)
P.O. Box 3546
Los Angeles, CA 90051
(818) 507-2215

Business Profile: Major multibank holding company headquartered in California.

Plan Specifics:
- Partial dividend reinvestment is available.
- 3 percent discount on reinvested dividends, 2 1/2 percent discount on OCP
- OCP: not more than $0.50 multiplied by the number of shares held ($100 if less than 200 shares held).
- Must go through own broker to sell shares.
- Company purchases stock monthly with OCPs.
- Approximately 12,000 shareholders in the plan.

Performance Rating: **

Seibels Bruce Group, Inc.
(NASDAQ:SBIG)
P.O. Box 1
Columbia, SC 29202
(803) 765-3447

Business Profile: Insurance-based holding organization with emphasis on property-casualty insurance.

Plan Specifics:
- Partial dividend reinvestment is available.
- 5 percent discount on reinvested dividends.

- OCP: $20 to $3000 per quarter.
- Must go through own broker to sell shares.
- Company purchases stock quarterly with OCPs.
- Approximately 280 shareholders in the plan.

Performance Rating: *

Selective Insurance Group, Inc.
(NASDAQ:SIGI)
40 Wantage Ave.
Branchville, NJ 07890
(201) 948-3000

Business Profile: Insurance holding company offering property-casualty coverage.

Plan Specifics:
- Partial dividend reinvestment is available.
- No Discount.
- OCP: $100 to $1000 per quarter.
- Selling costs may be brokerage commission and any transfer tax.
- Company purchases stock quarterly with OCPs.
- Approximately 1773 shareholders in the plan.

Performance Rating: **

Shawmut National Corp.
(NYSE:SNC)
777 Main St.
Hartford, CT 06115
(203) 728-2028   (203) 728-2000

Business Profile: Holding firm for banks in Massachusetts, Connecticut, and Rhode Island. Interests in cash management and trust services.

Plan Specifics:
- Partial dividend reinvestment is available.

- No Discount.
- OCP: $25 to $5000 per quarter.
- Selling costs include brokerage fees.
- Company purchases stock monthly with OCPs.

Performance Rating: *

The Sherwin-Williams Company
(NYSE:SHW)
101 Prospect Ave., N.W.
Cleveland, OH 44115-1075
(216) 566-2000

Business Profile: Leading manufacturer and retailer of paints, varnishes, and wallcoverings.

Plan Specifics:
- Partial dividend reinvestment is not available.
- No Discount.
- OCP: $10 to $2000 per month.
- No selling costs.
- Stock is purchased at least quarterly with OCPs.

Performance Rating: ***

Sierra Pacific Resources
(NYSE:SRP)
P.O. Box 30150
6100 Neil Rd.
Reno, NV 89520-3150
(800) 662-7575   (702) 689-3610

Business Profile: Public utility holding company supplying electric, gas, and water service to customers in portions of Nevada and California.

Plan Specifics:
- Partial dividend reinvestment is not available.
- No Discount.
- OCP: $25 to $5000 per quarter.
- Selling costs are approximately 6

cents per share brokerage commission and any transfer tax.
- Company purchases stock quarterly with OCPs.
- 39 percent of the shareholders are in the plan.

Performance Rating: **

SIFCO Industries, Inc. (ASE:SIF)
970 E. 64th St.
Cleveland, OH 44103-1694
(216) 881-8600   (216) 575-2532

Business Profile: Provides metalworking products and services to aerospace, shipbuilding, and defense industries.

Plan Specifics:
- Partial dividend reinvestment is not available.
- No Discount.
- OCP: $20 to $3000 per quarter.
- Selling costs are approximately 8 to 20 cents per share brokerage charges.
- Company purchases stock monthly with OCPs.

Performance Rating: **

Signet Banking Corp. (NYSE:SBK)
c/o Signet Trust Co.
P.O. Box 444
Pittsburgh, PA 15230
(800) 451-7392   (804) 747-2000

Business Profile: Multibank holding company serving Virginia, Maryland, and Washington, D.C., areas.

Plan Specifics:
- Partial dividend reinvestment is not available.
- 5 percent discount on reinvested dividends.
- OCP: $10 to $10,000 per month.

- Selling costs are $5 service charge and approximately 10 cents per share commission.
- Company purchases stock on the 1st and 15th of every month with OCPs.

Performance Rating: **

Simpson Industries, Inc. (NASDAQ:SMPS)
32100 Telegraph Rd.
Birmingham, MI 48010
(313) 540-6200

Business Profile: Manufactures machined components and assemblies for vehicle original equipment makers.

Plan Specifics:
- Partial dividend reinvestment is not available.
- No Discount.
- OCP: $10 to $1000 per month.
- Selling costs may include brokerage fees and handling charges.
- Stock is purchased monthly with OCPs.
- Approximately 550 shareholders in the plan.

Performance Rating: **

Smith, A. O., Corp. (ASE:SMC.A)
11270 West Park Place
Milwaukee, WI 53223-0972
(414) 359-4000   (414) 359-4060

Business Profile: Manufactures truck frames and components, electric motors, and fiberglass piping systems.

Plan Specifics:
- Partial dividend reinvestment is not available.
- No Discount.
- OCP: up to $5000 per quarter.
- Selling costs are brokerage fees.

- Company purchases stock at least quarterly with OCPs.

Performance Rating: **

Smucker, J. M., Co. (NYSE:SJM)
Strawberry Lane
Orrville, OH 44667-0280
(216) 682-3000

Business Profile: Leading producer of jellies, preserves, syrups, peanut butter, and fruit-related items.

Plan Specifics:
- Partial dividend reinvestment is available.
- No Discount.
- OCP: $20 to $1500 per month.
- Selling costs are brokerage charges.
- Company purchases stock around the 1st business day of the month with OCPs.

Performance Rating: ****

Society Corp. (NASDAQ:SOCI)
800 Superior Ave.
Cleveland, OH 44114
(216) 689-8179

Business Profile: Interstate bank holding company headquartered in Ohio.

Plan Specifics:
- Partial dividend reinvestment is available.
- No Discount.
- OCP: $25 to $5000 per quarter.
- Selling cost is approximately 10 cents per share.
- Company purchases stock every month with OCPs.
- Approximately 8100 shareholders in the plan.
- Preferred dividends are eligible for reinvestment for additional common shares under the plan.

Performance Rating: ***

Sonat, Inc. (NYSE:SNT)
c/o Manufacturers Hanover
P.O. Box 24850, Church St. Sta.
New York, NY 10249
(212) 613-7147   (800) 633-8570

Business Profile: Natural gas pipeline concern with operations in oil-field services.

Plan Specifics:
- Partial dividend reinvestment is not available.
- No Discount.
- OCP: $25 to $6000 per quarter.
- Selling costs include $15 handling charge and brokerage commissions.
- Stock is purchased monthly with OCPs.

Performance Rating: **

Sonoco Products Co.
(NASDAQ:SONO)
North Second St.
Hartsville, SC 29550-0160
(803) 383-7277   (803) 383-7000

Business Profile: International supplier of paper and plastic packaging items.

Plan Specifics:
- Partial dividend reinvestment is not available.
- No Discount.
- OCP: $10 to $500 per month.
- Selling and purchasing costs may include brokerage fees of approximately 9 cents a share.
- Company purchases stock monthly with OCPs.

Performance Rating: ***

South Carolina National Corp.
(NASDAQ:SCNC)
c/o Securities Transfer Svcs.
101 Greystone Blvd.
Columbia, SC 29226
(803) 765-3447   (803) 765-3000

Business Profile: South Carolina-based bank holding company.

Plan Specifics:
- Partial dividend reinvestment is available.
- No Discount.
- OCP: $25 to $3000 per quarter.
- Purchasing fees are brokerage commissions.
- Must sell whole shares through own broker.
- Company purchases stock around the 1st business day of the month with OCPs.

Performance Rating: **

South Jersey Industries, Inc.
(NYSE:SJI)
One S. Jersey Plaza, Route 54
Folsom, NJ 08037
(609) 561-9000

Business Profile: New Jersey gas utility holding company with operations in sand mining.

Plan Specifics:
- Partial dividend reinvestment is available.
- 3 percent discount on both reinvested dividends and OCPs.
- OCP: $25 to $1000 per quarter.
- Selling cost is approximately 7 cents per share.
- Company purchases stock quarterly with OCPs.

Performance Rating: ***

Southeast Banking Corp. (FL)
(NYSE:STB)
One Southeast Financial Center
Miami, FL 33131
(305) 375-7984

Business Profile: Florida-based bank holding company stressing commercial lending and retail banking.

Plan Specifics:
- Partial dividend reinvestment is available.
- 5 percent discount on reinvested dividends.
- OCP: $25 to $10,000 per month.
- Selling costs are minimal brokerage and service charges.
- Company purchases stock around the 1st business day of the month with OCPs.
- Company is not currently paying a dividend.

Performance Rating: *

Southeastern Michigan Gas
Enterprises (NASDAQ:SMGS)
405 Water St.
Port Huron, MI 48060
(313) 987-2200

Business Profile: Supplier of natural gas to parts of Michigan.

Plan Specifics:
- Partial dividend reinvestment is not available.
- No Discount.
- OCP: $25 to $5000 per quarter.
- Must go through own broker to sell shares.
- Company purchases stock quarterly with OCPs.
- Approximately 65 percent of the shareholders are in the plan.

Performance Rating: ***

Southern California Water Co. (NASDAQ:SWTR)
630 E. Foothill Blvd.
San Dimas, CA 91773
(714) 394-3600

Business Profile: Provides water and, to a lesser extent, electric services to customers in regions of northern and southern California.

Plan Specifics:
- Partial dividend reinvestment is available.
- No Discount.
- OCP: not available.
- Must go through own broker to sell shares.

Performance Rating: ***

Southern Co. (NYSE:SO)
P.O. Box 88300
Atlanta, GA 30356
(404) 393-4498   (404) 668-2774

Business Profile: Electric utility holding company serving much of the Southeast.

Plan Specifics:
- Partial dividend reinvestment is available.
- No Discount.
- OCP: $25 to $6000 per quarter.
- Selling cost is approximately 6 cents per share.
- Company purchases stock quarterly with OCPs.
- Approximately 136,410 shareholders in the plan.

Performance Rating: **

Southern Indiana Gas & Electric Co. (NYSE:SIG)
20 N.W. 4th St.
Evansville, IN 47741-0001
(812) 464-4553   (812) 424-6411

Business Profile: Distributes electricity and natural gas in southwestern Indiana.

Plan Specifics:
- Partial dividend reinvestment is available.
- No Discount.
- OCP: $25 to $5000 per month.
- Must go through own broker to sell whole shares; selling costs for fractional shares sold by the company include brokerage commissions.
- Company purchases stock monthly with OCPs.
- Approximately 3000 shareholders in the plan.

Performance Rating: ****

Southern New England Telecommunications (NYSE:SNG)
P.O. Box 1562
New Haven, CT 06506
(800) 243-1110

Business Profile: Telecommunications holding company providing service throughout Connecticut.

Plan Specifics:
- Partial dividend reinvestment is not available.
- No Discount.
- OCP: up to $3000 per quarter.
- Selling costs are brokerage fees and any transfer tax.
- Company purchases stock quarterly with OCPs.
- Approximately 17,000 shareholders in the plan.

Performance Rating: ***

SouthTrust Corp. (NASDAQ:SOTR)
P.O. Box 2554
Birmingham, AL 35290
(205) 254-5509

Business Profile: Alabama-based multi-bank holding company serving clients in Alabama, Florida, Georgia, South Carolina, and Tennessee.

Plan Specifics:
- Partial dividend reinvestment is available.
- No Discount.
- OCP: $25 to $5000 per month.
- May have to pay brokerage fees on any shares purchased in the open market.
- Selling costs are brokerage commissions.
- Stock is purchased at least quarterly with OCPs.

Performance Rating: ***

Southwest Gas Corp. (NYSE:SWX)
Attn.: Shareholder Relations Dept.
P.O. Box 98510
Las Vegas, NV 89193-8510
(702) 876-7280

Business Profile: Supplies natural gas to areas of Arizona, Nevada, and California. Activities in savings and loan.

Plan Specifics:
- Partial dividend reinvestment is not available.
- No Discount.
- OCP: $10 to $25,000 per year.
- Selling cost is approximately 5 cents a share.
- Company purchases stock once a month with OCPs.
- Customers of the company may make initial investments directly

through the company (minimum investment $10).

Performance Rating: **

Southwest Water Co.
(NASDAQ:SWWC)
16340 E. Maplegrove St.
La Puente, CA 91744-1399
(818) 918-1231

Business Profile: Holding company providing sewage disposal, wastewater treatment, and water services in regions of California, New Mexico, Texas, and Mississippi.

Plan Specifics:
- Partial dividend reinvestment is available.
- 5 percent discount on reinvested dividends.
- OCP: $25 to $3000 per quarter.
- Must go through own broker to sell shares.
- Company purchases stock quarterly with OCPs.
- Approximately 500 shareholders in the plan.

Performance Rating: ***

Southwestern Bell Corp.
(NYSE:SBC)
c/o American Transtech
P.O. Box 45029
Jacksonville, FL 32232
(800) 351-7221

Business Profile: Important telecommunications holding company providing local exchange service in Arkansas, Kansas, Missouri, Oklahoma, and Texas.

Plan Specifics:
- Partial dividend reinvestment is available.

- No Discount.
- OCP: $50 to $50,000 per year.
- Selling costs (the company will sell a maximum 99 shares for participants) are approximately 8 cents per share and any transfer tax.
- Company purchases stock on the 1st business day of every month with OCPs.

Performance Rating: ****

Southwestern Electric Service Co.
(NASDAQ:SWEL)
Suite 3300
1717 Main St.
Dallas, TX 75201
(214) 741-3125   (214) 586-9851

Business Profile: Provides electric service for customers in Texas.

Plan Specifics:
- Partial dividend reinvestment is available.
- 5 percent discount on reinvested dividends.
- OCP: $25 to $3000 per quarter.
- Selling costs (company will sell up to 99 shares for participants) are brokerage commissions and transfer tax.
- Company purchases stock monthly with OCPs.
- Approximately 200 shareholders in the plan.

Performance Rating: ***

Southwestern Energy Co.
(NYSE:SWN)
c/o First Chicago Trust-NY
P.O. Box 3506, Church St. Sta.
New York, NY 10008-3506
(800) 446-2617   (501) 521-1141

Business Profile: Natural gas holding company. Utility operation serves parts of Arkansas and Missouri.

Plan Specifics:
- Partial dividend reinvestment is not available.
- No Discount.
- OCP: $25 to $1000 per month.
- Selling costs are 10 cents per share brokerage commissions and any applicable taxes.
- Purchasing fees are proportionate share of broker commissions, service charge of 5 percent per dividend investment (maximum, $3), and $3 charge per OCP.
- Company purchases stock monthly with OCPs.
- Approximately 280 shareholders in the plan.

Performance Rating: **

Southwestern Public Service Co.
(NYSE:SPS)
P.O. Box 1261
Amarillo, TX 79170
(806) 378-2841

Business Profile: Electric utility serving portions of Kansas, New Mexico, Oklahoma, and Texas.

Plan Specifics:
- Partial dividend reinvestment is available.
- No Discount.
- OCP: $25 to $3000 per quarter.
- Purchasing and selling fees are minimal brokerage commissions.
- Company purchases stock monthly with OCPs.
- Approximately 13,018 shareholders in the plan.

Performance Rating: ***

SPX Corp. (NYSE:SPW)
700 Terrace Point Dr.
Muskegon, MI 49443
(616) 724-5564   (800) 524-4458

Business Profile: Produces precision engineered tools for maintenance and repair of vehicles.

Plan Specifics:
▪ Partial dividend reinvestment is not available.
▪ No Discount.
▪ OCP: $25 to $10,000 per quarter.
▪ Selling costs are brokerage commission, transfer taxes, and bank's fee of $2.50.
▪ Company purchases stock around the 1st of each month with OCPs.

Performance Rating: **

Standard Commercial Corp.
(NYSE:STW)
P.O. Box 450
Wilson, NC 27894-0450
(919) 291-5507

Business Profile: Buys, processes, and markets tobacco and wool.

Plan Specifics:
▪ Partial dividend reinvestment is available.
▪ No Discount.
▪ OCP: not available.
▪ Selling costs are brokerage fees and transfer tax.
▪ Approximately 185 shareholders in the plan.

Performance Rating: **

Standard Products Co. (NYSE:SPD)
2130 W. 110th St.
Cleveland, OH 44102-3590
(216) 281-8300   (216) 575-2532

Business Profile: Manufactures rubber and plastic components for automotive, marine, and construction industries.

Plan Specifics:
▪ Partial dividend reinvestment is not available.
▪ No Discount.
▪ OCP: $50 to $3000 per quarter.
▪ Stock is purchased monthly with OCPs.
▪ Selling costs may include brokerage fees.
▪ Approximately 70 shareholders in plan.

Performance Rating: **

Standex International Corp.
(NYSE:SXI)
6 Manor Parkway
Salem, NH 03079
(603) 893-9701

Business Profile: Conglomerate with operations in industrial, institutional, graphic, and electronic products.

Plan Specifics:
▪ Partial dividend reinvestment is not available.
▪ No Discount.
▪ OCP: $50 to $2500 per quarter.
▪ Selling costs are brokerage commission and a bank charge of 5 percent up to a maximum of $2.50.
▪ Company purchases stock quarterly with OCPs.

Performance Rating: ***

Stanhome, Inc. (NYSE:STH)
333 Western Ave.
Westfield, MA 01085
(800) 628-1918   (413) 562-3631

Business Profile: Produces and markets household items and distributes giftware.

Plan Specifics:
- Partial dividend reinvestment is not available.
- No Discount.
- OCP: $10 to $5000 per quarter.
- Selling costs are minimal brokerage commissions.
- Company purchases stock quarterly with OCPs.
- Approximately 422 shareholders in the plan.

Performance Rating: ***

Stanley Works (NYSE:SWK)
P.O. Box 7000
New Britain, CT 06050
(203) 225-5111

Business Profile: Manufactures home-improvement items such as hand tools and hardware. Operations in industrial tools, fasteners, and power-operated doors.

Plan Specifics:
- Partial dividend reinvestment is not available.
- No Discount.
- OCP: $10 to $5000 per month.
- Stock is purchased monthly with OCPs.
- Selling costs include brokerage fees.

Performance Rating: ***

Star Banc Corp. (NASDAQ:STRZ)
P.O. Box 1038
Cincinnati, OH 45201
(513) 632-4000

Business Profile: Ohio-based multibank holding company with offices in Ohio, Indiana, and Kentucky.

Plan Specifics:
- Partial dividend reinvestment is not available.
- No Discount.
- OCP: $50 to $5000 per quarter.
- Selling costs are minimal.
- Company purchases stock quarterly with OCPs.
- Approximately 1300 shareholders in the plan.

Performance Rating: ***

State Street Boston Corp.
(NASDAQ:STBK)
P.O. Box 1681
Boston, MA 02105
(617) 575-2900

Business Profile: Massachusetts bank holding company and a leading mutual fund custodian.

Plan Specifics:
- Partial dividend reinvestment is not available.
- No Discount.
- OCP: $10 to $1000 per month.
- Selling cost is approximately 15 cents per share.
- Purchasing fees are brokerage and service charges.
- Company purchases stock once a month with OCPs.

Performance Rating: ***

Stone & Webster, Inc. (NYSE:SW)
c/o Chase Manhattan
P.O. Box 283, Bowling Green Sta.
New York, NY 10004
(212) 676-3822   (201) 592-4074

Business Profile: Provides engineering, construction, and management services to companies in the industrial, chemical, and energy-based industries.

Plan Specifics:
- Partial dividend reinvestment is not available.
- No Discount.
- OCP: $10 to $3000 per quarter.
- Selling costs are $5 service charge and any commission.
- Company purchases stock quarterly with OCPs.

Performance Rating: **

Stride Rite Corp. (NYSE:SRR)
5 Cambridge Center
Cambridge, MA 02142
(617) 491-8800

Business Profile: Major supplier of athletic and casual footwear for children and adults.

Plan Specifics:
- Partial dividend reinvestment is available.
- No Discount.
- OCP: $10 to $1000 per month.
- Buying cost is 5 percent of the sales price (maximum of $2.50).
- Must go through own broker to sell shares.
- Company purchases stock monthly with OCPs.

Performance Rating: ***

Suffolk Bancorp (NASDAQ:SUBK)
6 West 2d St.
Riverhead, NY 11901
(516) 727-2700   (212) 613-7147

Business Profile: Bank holding company in New York.

Plan Specifics:
- Partial dividend reinvestment is available.
- 3 percent discount on reinvested dividends and OCPs.

- OCP: $300 to $3500 per quarter.
- Selling fees are $15 termination fee, brokerage fees, and any other costs of sale.
- Stock is purchased at least quarterly with OCPs.

Performance Rating: NR

Sumitomo Bank of California
(NASDAQ:SUMI)
Attn.: Corporate Secretary
320 California Street
San Francisco, CA 94104
(415) 445-8000

Business Profile: Conducts commercial banking and trust services throughout California.

Plan Specifics:
- Partial dividend reinvestment is available.
- No Discount.
- OCP: not available.
- Must go through own broker to sell shares.
- Approximately 400 shareholders in plan.

Performance Rating: NR

Summit Bancorporation (NJ)
(NASDAQ:SUBN)
367 Springfield Ave.
Summit, NJ 07901-2702
(201) 522-8402

Business Profile: Multibank holding company headquartered in New Jersey.

Plan Specifics:
- Partial dividend reinvestment is not available.
- No Discount.
- OCP: $50 to $5000 per month.
- Selling costs are brokerage commis-

sions, transfer taxes, and a sales fee of $15.
- $5 charge for withdrawing shares.
- Stock is purchased on the 15th of each month with OCPs.

Performance Rating: **

Summit Holding Corp. (WV)
 (NASDAQ:SUHC)
P.O. Box 1269
Beckley, WV 25802-1269
(304) 256-7298

Business Profile: West Virginia-based bank holding company.

Plan Specifics:
- Partial dividend reinvestment is not available.
- No Discount.
- OCP: $25 to $1000 per quarter.
- Selling costs are service charge and brokerage fees.
- Company purchases stock quarterly with OCPs.
- Approximately 165 shareholders in the plan.

Performance Rating: NR

Summit Tax Exempt Bond Fund,
 L.P. (ASE:SUA)
c/o Bank of New York
P.O. Box 11002, Church St. Sta.
New York, NY 10277-0702
(800) 524-4458

Business Profile: Invests in tax-exempt first mortgage bonds.

Plan Specifics:
- Partial dividend reinvestment is not available.
- No Discount.
- OCP: $25 minimum per payment.
- Stock is purchased monthly with OCPs.

- Purchasing fees are $1 per transaction and brokerage commission.
- Selling costs are $1 issuance charge for certificates, $2.50 termination fee, and brokerage costs.

Performance Rating: *

Sun Co., Inc. (NYSE:SUN)
Ten Penn Center
1801 Market St.
Philadelphia, PA 19103-1699
(800) 323-3025

Business Profile: Refines, produces, and markets petroleum serving portions of the Northeast and Midwest.

Plan Specifics:
- Partial dividend reinvestment is not available.
- No Discount.
- OCP: up to $10,000 per quarter.
- Selling cost is approximately 10 cents per share.
- Commission to purchase shares is approximately 5 cents a share.
- Company purchases stock twice per quarter with OCPs.

Performance Rating: **

Sundstrand Corp. (NYSE:SNS)
P.O. Box 7003
4949 Harrison Ave.
Rockford, IL 61125-7003
(815) 226-2136

Business Profile: Produces aircraft components and systems and industrial equipment.

Plan Specifics:
- Partial dividend reinvestment is not available.
- No Discount.
- OCP: $25 to $3000 per month.
- Selling costs, if any, are minimal.

- Company purchases stock monthly with OCPs.

Performance Rating: **

SunTrust Banks, Inc. (NYSE:STI)
P.O. Box 4625
Atlanta, GA 30302
(404) 588-7822

Business Profile: Holding company for banks in Florida, Georgia, and Tennessee.

Plan Specifics:
- Partial dividend reinvestment is not available.
- No Discount.
- OCP: $10 to $60,000 per year.
- Selling costs are approximately 9 cents per share brokerage fee.
- Company purchases stock monthly with OCPs.
- Approximately 11,000 shareholders in the plan.

Performance Rating: ***

Sunwest Financial Services, Inc.
(NASDAQ:SFSI)
Corporate Trust
P.O. Box 26900
Albuquerque, NM 87125-6900
(505) 765-2403

Business Profile: New Mexico-based multibank holding company.

Plan Specifics:
- Partial dividend reinvestment is available.
- 5 percent discount on reinvested dividends.
- OCP: not available.
- Must go through own broker to sell shares.

- Approximately 1000 shareholders in plan.

Performance Rating: NR

Super Valu Stores, Inc. (NYSE:SVU)
c/o Norwest Bank Minnesota
P.O. Box 738
South St. Paul, MN 55075-0738
(612) 450-4075

Business Profile: Leading food wholesaler and manager of retail supermarkets and general merchandise stores.

Plan Specifics:
- Partial dividend reinvestment is not available.
- No Discount.
- OCP: $10 to $3000 per quarter.
- Selling costs are brokerage commissions and any other fees.
- Company purchases stock around the 15th of each month if there are enough funds to purchase at least 100 shares.

Performance Rating: ***

Susquehanna Bancshares, Inc.
(NASDAQ:SUSQ)
26 N. Cedar St.
Lititz, PA 17543-7000
(717) 626-4721

Business Profile: Offers banking services in Pennsylvania.

Plan Specifics:
- Partial dividend reinvestment is not available.
- No Discount.
- OCP: $100 to $1000 per quarter.
- Purchasing fees for OCPs are $5 per investment.
- Selling costs are brokerage fees and a service charge.
- Company purchases stock around

the 20th day of the month with OCPs.

Performance Rating: NR

Synovus Financial Corp. (NYSE:SNV)
Corporate Trust Dept.
P.O. Box 120
Columbus, GA 31902
(404) 649-2387

Business Profile: Southeast interstate bank holding company. Nonbanking operations in credit card processing.

Plan Specifics:
- Partial dividend reinvestment is not available.
- No Discount.
- OCP: up to $6000 per quarter.
- Must go through own broker to sell shares.
- Company purchases stock quarterly with OCPs.
- Over 1850 shareholders in the plan.

Performance Rating: ***

Talley Industries, Inc. (NYSE:TAL)
2800 N. 44th St.
Phoenix, AZ 85008
(602) 957-7711

Business Profile: Supplies solid propellant products for government use and manufactures industrial products.

Plan Specifics:
- Partial dividend reinvestment is not available.
- No Discount.
- OCP: $10 to $1000 per month.
- Selling costs are service charge of $1 and brokerage commissions.
- Company purchases stock monthly with OCPs.
- Preferred dividends are eligible for

reinvestment for additional common shares under the plan.

Performance Rating: **

TCF Financial Corp. (NYSE:TCB)
801 Marquette Ave.
Minneapolis, MN 55402
(612) 370-7390   (800) 647-4273

Business Profile: Minnesota-based bank holding company.

Plan Specifics:
- Partial dividend reinvestment is not available.
- No Discount.
- OCP: $25 to $5000 per quarter.
- Selling costs are $15 service fee and commissions.
- $5 withdrawal fee for certificates.
- $3 fee for depositing certificates with the firm.
- Company purchases stock quarterly with OCPs.
- Approximately 2500 shareholders in the plan.

Performance Rating: **

Telephone & Data Systems, Inc. (ASE:TDS)
c/o Harris Trust and Savings
P.O. Box 755
Chicago, IL 60690
(312) 461-2339   (312) 630-1900

Business Profile: Telephone holding company with operations in local telephone service, cellular telephones, and radio paging.

Plan Specifics:
- Partial dividend reinvestment is not available.
- 5 percent discount on reinvested dividends.
- OCP: $10 to $5000 per quarter.

- Must go through own broker to sell shares.
- Company purchases stock monthly with OCPs.
- Preferred dividends are eligible for reinvestment for additional common shares under the plan.
- At least 10 shares needed in order to enroll in the plan.

Performance Rating: *******

Temple-Inland, Inc. (NYSE:TIN)
c/o NCNB Texas National Bank
P.O. Box 830345
Dallas, TX 75283-0345
(214) 508-1782

Business Profile: Manufactures containers, paperboard, containerboard, market pulp, and building materials.

Plan Specifics:
- Partial dividend reinvestment is available.
- No Discount.
- OCP: $25 to $1000 per quarter.
- Stock is purchased at least quarterly with OCPs.
- Selling costs are $1 service fee plus pro rata share of brokerage commissions.

Performance Rating: ******

Tenneco, Inc. (NYSE:TGT)
c/o First Chicago Trust-NY
P.O. Box 3506, Church St. Sta.
New York, NY 10008-3506
(212) 791-6422

Business Profile: Holding company with interests in natural gas pipelines, construction, and farm equipment.

Plan Specifics:
- Partial dividend reinvestment is available.

- No Discount.
- OCP: $10 to $3000 per quarter.
- Stock is purchased quarterly with OCPs.
- Selling cost is broker commission.
- Preferred dividends are eligible for reinvestment in additional common shares under the plan.

Performance Rating: ******

Texaco, Inc. (NYSE:TX)
2000 Westchester Ave.
White Plains, NY 10650
(914) 253-6084

Business Profile: Refines, produces, and markets crude oil, natural gas, and petrochemicals.

Plan Specifics:
- Partial dividend reinvestment is available.
- No Discount.
- OCP: $50 to $10,000 per month.
- Commission of 7 to 15 cents per share for both purchasing and selling.
- $5 service charge when selling.
- Company purchases stock every month with OCPs.
- Initial purchases of stock may be made directly through the company (minimum investment, $250).
- Participants may purchase shares of common stock for family members and others by making an initial cash investment in that person's name.

Performance Rating: *******

Texas Utilities Co. (NYSE:TXU)
2001 Bryan Tower
Dallas, TX 75201
(214) 742-4000   (800) 828-0812

Business Profile: Texas electric utility holding company.

Plan Specifics:
- Partial dividend reinvestment is not available.
- 5 percent discount on reinvested dividends.
- OCP: $25 to $3000 per quarter.
- Selling cost is brokerage commission.
- Company purchases stock quarterly with OCPs.
- Approximately 44,500 shareholders in the plan.

Performance Rating: **

Textron, Inc. (NYSE:TXT)
c/o First Chicago Trust-NY
P.O. Box 3506, Church St. Sta.
New York, NY 10008-3506
(212) 791-6422

Business Profile: Manufactures aerospace equipment for government defense market. Also has operations in automotive parts, outdoor products, and financial services.

Plan Specifics:
- Partial dividend reinvestment is available.
- No Discount.
- OCP: $25 to $1000 per month.
- Stock is purchased around the 1st business day of the month with OCPs.
- Selling costs are brokerage commission and any related expenses of sale.

Performance Rating: **

Thomas & Betts Corp. (NYSE:TNB)
1001 Frontier Rd.
Bridgewater, NJ 08807-0993
(201) 685-1600   (212) 791-6422

Business Profile: Leading supplier of electronic connectors, accessories, and systems.

Plan Specifics:
- Partial dividend reinvestment is not available.
- No Discount.
- OCP: $10 to $3000 per quarter.
- Stock is purchased monthly with OCPs.
- Selling costs are $5 handling fee and small brokerage commission.
- Approximately 24 percent of all shareholders in the plan.

Performance Rating: ***

Tidewater, Inc. (NYSE:TDW)
1440 Canal St.
New Orleans, LA 70112
(504) 568-1010

Business Profile: Energy services concern providing support services for offshore drilling activities.

Plan Specifics:
- Partial dividend reinvestment is not available.
- No Discount.
- OCP: $25 to $5000 per quarter.
- Purchasing fees are brokerage costs and 5 percent service charge (maximum, $2.50).
- Selling costs include brokerage and handling costs and $1 termination fee.
- Stock is purchased quarterly, and more often if enough funds accumulate, with OCPs.

Performance Rating: *

Time Warner, Inc. (NYSE:TWX)
c/o First Chicago Trust-NY
P.O. Box 3506, Church St. Sta.
New York, NY 10008-3506
(212) 791-6422   (212) 522-1212

Business Profile: Operations in magazines, filmed entertainment, cable television, music recording, and book publishing.

Plan Specifics:
- Partial dividend reinvestment is available.
- No Discount.
- OCP: $25 to $1000 per month.
- Stock is purchased monthly with OCPs.
- Selling costs are brokerage commission and any transfer taxes.

Performance Rating: ***

Timken Co. (NYSE:TKR)
1835 Dueber Ave. S.W.
Canton, OH 44706-2798
(216) 438-3376

Business Profile: World's largest manufacturer of tapered roller bearings. Also has operations in steel.

Plan Specifics:
- Partial dividend reinvestment is available.
- 5 percent discount on reinvested dividends.
- OCP: not available.
- Must go through own broker to sell shares.
- Approximately 3305 shareholders in the plan.

Performance Rating: **

TNP Enterprises, Inc. (NYSE:TNP)
P.O. Box 2943
Fort Worth, TX 76113
(817) 731-0099

Business Profile: Texas-based electric utility holding firm serving residential, industrial, and commercial clients in Texas and New Mexico.

Plan Specifics:
- Partial dividend reinvestment is available.
- No Discount.
- OCP: $25 to $5000 per quarter.
- Must go through own broker to sell shares.
- Company purchases stock monthly with OCPs.

Performance Rating: ***

Toro Co. (NYSE:TTC)
c/o Norwest Bank Minnesota
P.O. Box 738
South St. Paul, MN 55075-0738
(612) 887-8526   (612) 888-8801

Business Profile: Important supplier of commercial and consumer lawn equipment, snow throwers, and irrigation systems.

Plan Specifics:
- Partial dividend reinvestment is not available.
- No Discount.
- OCP: $10 to $1000 per month.
- Selling costs are brokerage commissions and other costs of sale.
- Company purchases stock around the 12th of each month if enough funds accumulate to purchase at least 100 shares.

Performance Rating: **

Total Petroleum (North America)
  Ltd. (ASE:TPN)
P.O. Box 500
Denver, CO 80202
(303) 291-2000

Business Profile: Refines, transports, and sells petroleum and petroleum products.

Plan Specifics:
- Partial dividend reinvestment is available.
- 5 percent discount on reinvested dividends.
- OCP: not available.
- Must go through own broker to sell shares.
- Preferred dividends are eligible for reinvestment for additional common shares under the plan.
- Approximately 61 percent of common stockholders and 62 percent of preferred stockholders in the plan.

Performance Rating: **

Total System Services, Inc.
(NYSE:TSS)
P.O. Box 120
Columbus, GA 31902
(404) 649-2204   (404) 649-2387

Business Profile: Provides credit-card data processing services for financial institutions. Synovus Financial Corp. owns 82 percent.

Plan Specifics:
- Partial dividend reinvestment is not available.
- No Discount.
- OCP: up to $6000 per quarter.
- Must go through own broker to sell shares.
- Purchasing costs include brokerage fees.
- Stock is purchased quarterly with OCPs.
- Approximately 550 shareholders in the plan.

Performance Rating: ***

Trammell Crow Real Estate
 Investors (NYSE:TCR)
c/o Ameritrust Texas
1900 Pacific Ave.
Dallas, TX 75201
(800) 527-7844   (214) 979-5100

Business Profile: Real estate investment trust.

Plan Specifics:
- Partial dividend reinvestment is available.
- No Discount.
- OCP: not available.
- Selling costs are approximately 3 to 5 cents per share.
- Small service fees may be charged for purchases.

Performance Rating: *

Transamerica Corp. (NYSE:TA)
c/o First Interstate Bank-CA
P.O. Box 60975
Los Angeles, CA 90060
(800) 522-6645   (213) 742-4969

Business Profile: Financial service institution engaging in lending, leasing, and real estate finance and property-casualty insurance.

Plan Specifics:
- Partial dividend reinvestment is available.
- No Discount.
- OCP: $10 to $5000 per month.
- Selling costs are brokerage commissions and a small handling fee.
- Company purchases stock monthly with OCPs.

Performance Rating: ***

**TransCanada Pipelines Ltd.
(NYSE:TRP)**
c/o Montreal Trust
66 Temperance St.
Toronto, Ont. M5H 1Y7 Canada
(416) 981-9637   (416) 869-2111

Business Profile: Owns Canada's major pipeline system used to transport natural gas from western to eastern markets.

Plan Specifics:
- Partial dividend reinvestment is not available.
- 5 percent discount on reinvested dividends.
- OCP: $50 to $5000 per quarter (Canadian).
- Must go through own broker to sell shares.
- Company purchases stock quarterly with OCPs.
- Preferred dividends are eligible for reinvestment for additional common shares under the plan.

Performance Rating: **

Travelers Corp. (NYSE:TIC)
One Tower Square
Hartford, CT 06183
(203) 277-2819   (203) 277-0111

Business Profile: Insurance and financial services company.

Plan Specifics:
- Partial dividend reinvestment is available.
- No Discount.
- OCP: $5 to $5000 per month.
- Participants may incur brokerage fees when selling shares.
- Company purchases stock around the 10th day of the month with OCPs.

- Approximately 12,000 shareholders in the plan.

Performance Rating: **

Trinova Corp. (NYSE:TNV)
c/o NBD Bank
P.O. Box 330751
Detroit, MI 48232-6751
(313) 828-6900   (419) 867-2294

Business Profile: Worldwide supplier of engineered components for original equipment and replacement manufacturers.

Plan Specifics:
- Partial dividend reinvestment is not available.
- No Discount.
- OCP: $10 to $5000 per quarter.
- Stock is purchased at least quarterly with OCPs.
- Selling cost is approximately 8 cents per share or pro rata portion of $25, whichever is greater.
- Approximately 3300 shareholders in the plan.

Performance Rating: **

TRW, Inc. (NYSE:TRW)
1900 Richmond Rd.
Cleveland, OH 44124
(800) 442-2001

Business Profile: Leading provider of space and defense products, car and truck components, and information systems.

Plan Specifics:
- Partial dividend reinvestment is not available.
- No Discount.
- OCP: $10 to $1000 per month.
- Stock is purchased monthly with OCPs.

• Selling cost is approximately 15 cents per share.

Performance Rating: ***

Twin Disc, Inc. (NYSE:TDI)
1328 Racine St.
Racine, WI 53403
(414) 634-1981

Business Profile: Manufactures heavy-duty transmission equipment.

Plan Specifics:

• Partial dividend reinvestment is not available.
• No Discount.
• OCP: $10 to $2000 per month.
• Selling cost is 8 to 12 cents per share.
• Stock is purchased quarterly, and possibly more frequently, with OCPs.

Performance Rating: **

Tyco Laboratories, Inc. (NYSE:TYC)
One Tyco Park
Exeter, NH 03833
(603) 778-9700

Business Profile: Leading worldwide provider of fire protection systems, flow control products, electronic components, and packaging materials.

Plan Specifics:

• Partial dividend reinvestment is not available.
• No Discount.
• OCP: $25 to $1000 per month.
• Selling costs are service charge of $2.50 and brokerage commission.
• Company purchases stock monthly with OCPs.

Performance Rating: ***

UGI Corp. (NYSE:UGI)
P.O. Box 858
Valley Forge, PA 19482
(215) 337-1000

Business Profile: Supplies natural gas and electric service to customers in Pennsylvania. Operations in propane and related products.

Plan Specifics:

• Partial dividend reinvestment is available.
• 5 percent discount on reinvested dividends.
• OCP: $25 to $3000 per quarter.
• Selling costs are brokerage fees.
• Company purchases stock monthly with OCPs.
• Preferred dividends are eligible for reinvestment for additional common shares under the plan.

Performance Rating: **

UJB Financial Corp. (NYSE:UJB)
301 Carnegie Center
P.O. Box 2066
Princeton, NJ 08543-2066
(609) 987-3442   (212) 791-6422

Business Profile: New Jersey-based bank holding firm.

Plan Specifics:

• Partial dividend reinvestment is not available.
• No Discount.
• OCP: $10 to $10,000 per quarter.
• Selling costs are service fee and any brokerage commissions.
• Company purchases stock around the 1st trading day of each month with OCPs.

Performance Rating: **

Union Bank (NASDAQ:UBNK)
Attn.: Manager, Corporate Trust
P.O. Box 2529
San Diego, CA 92112-4200
(619) 230-4660

Business Profile: Banking institution in California.

Plan Specifics:
- Partial dividend reinvestment is available.
- 5 percent discount on reinvested dividends.
- OCP: $25 to $3000 per quarter.
- Stock is purchased quarterly with OCPs.
- Costs include $2.50 charge for each withdrawal of full-share certificates from plan and $2.50 charge for transfer of shares to plan account.
- Must go through own broker to sell shares.

Performance Rating: ***

Union Camp Corp. (NYSE:UCC)
c/o Bank of New York
P.O. Box 11002, Church St. Sta.
New York, NY 10277-0702
(201) 628-2000

Business Profile: Manufactures paper, paperboard, and wood-based chemicals.

Plan Specifics:
- Partial dividend reinvestment is not available.
- No Discount.
- OCP: $25 to $15,000 per year.
- Must go through own broker to sell shares.
- Company purchases stock around the 1st business day of the month with OCPs.

Performance Rating: ***

Union Carbide Corp. (NYSE:UK)
Shareholder Services
39 Old Ridgebury Rd.
Danbury, CT 06817-0001
(203) 794-2212

Business Profile: Supplies petrochemicals, specialty chemicals, and industrial gases.

Plan Specifics:
- Partial dividend reinvestment is not available.
- No Discount.
- OCP: $25 to $1000 per month.
- Selling costs are nominal brokerage commissions.
- Company purchases stock monthly with OCPs.
- Approximately 25,000 shareholders in the plan.

Performance Rating: **

Union Electric Co. (NYSE:UEP)
P.O. Box 149
St. Louis, MO 63166
(800) 255-2237

Business Profile: Electric utility serving residential, commercial, and industrial customers in Missouri, Illinois, and Iowa.

Plan Specifics:
- Partial dividend reinvestment is available.
- No Discount.
- OCP: up to $60,000 per year.
- Selling cost is approximately 5 cents per share.
- Company purchases stock monthly with OCPs.
- Approximately 43,000 shareholders in the plan.
- Preferred dividends are eligible for reinvestment for additional shares under the plan.

• Customers may make initial purchase of stock directly through the company (no minimum initial investment).

Performance Rating: **

Union Pacific Corp. (NYSE:UNP)
c/o First Chicago Trust-NY
P.O. Box 3506, Church St. Sta.
New York, NY 10008
(212) 791-6422   (215) 861-3200

Business Profile: Owns major railroad and motor carrier operations. Also has oil and gas interests.

Plan Specifics:
• Partial dividend reinvestment is available.
• No Discount.
• OCP: $10 to $60,000 per year.
• Stock is purchased monthly with OCPs.
• Selling costs are small broker commissions.
• Approximately 16,600 shareholders in the plan.

Performance Rating: ****

Union Planters Corp. (NYSE:UPC)
P.O. Box 387
Memphis, TN 38147
(901) 523-6656

Business Profile: Interstate bank holding company with operations in Tennessee, Alabama, Arkansas, and Mississippi.

Plan Specifics:
• Partial dividend reinvestment is available.
• 5 percent discount on reinvested dividends.
• OCP: $10 to $2000 per quarter.
• Must go through broker to sell shares.

• Company purchases stock monthly with OCPs.
• Approximately 3500 shareholders in the plan.

Performance Rating: **

United Carolina Bancshares Corp.
(NASDAQ:UCAR)
P.O. Box 632
127 West Webster St.
Whiteville, NC 28472
(919) 642-5131

Business Profile: North Carolina-based bank holding organization.

Plan Specifics:
• Partial dividend reinvestment is not available.
• No Discount.
• OCP: $25 to $5000 per month.
• Purchasing costs may include brokerage fees.
• Must go through own broker to sell shares.
• Company purchases stock monthly with OCPs.
• Approximately 3000 shareholders in the plan.

Performance Rating: NR

United Cities Gas Co.
(NASDAQ:UCIT)
5300 Maryland Way
Brentwood, TN 37027
(615) 373-0104

Business Profile: Provides residents in 11 states with natural gas.

Plan Specifics:
• Partial dividend reinvestment is available.
• 5 percent discount on reinvested dividends.
• OCP: $25 to $3000 per quarter.

- Must go through own broker to sell shares.
- Company purchases stock monthly with OCPs.
- Preferred dividends are eligible for reinvestment for additional common shares under the plan.

Performance Rating: ***

United Illuminating Co.
(NYSE:UIL)
P.O. Box 1948
New Haven, CT 06509-1948
(203) 787-7200

Business Profile: Electric utility servicing Connecticut communities.

Plan Specifics:
- Partial dividend reinvestment is available.
- No Discount.
- OCP: $10 to $10,000 per quarter.
- Selling fees are brokerage fees and any handling charges.
- Company purchases stock quarterly with OCPs.

Performance Rating: **

United States Bancorp
(NASDAQ:USBC)
P.O. Box 3850
Portland, OR 97208
(503) 275-6472

Business Profile: Holding company for major banks in Oregon and Washington.

Plan Specifics:
- Partial dividend reinvestment is available.
- No Discount.

- OCP: $25 to $6000 per quarter.
- Must go through own broker to sell shares.
- Company purchases stock monthly with OCPs.

Performance Rating: ***

United States Shoe Corp.
(NYSE:USR)
c/o First Chicago Trust-NY
P.O. Box 3506, Church St. Sta.
New York, NY 10008
(212) 791-6422

Business Profile: Retails brand name footwear, women's apparel, and eyewear.

Plan Specifics:
- Partial dividend reinvestment is not available.
- No Discount.
- OCP: $25 to $1000 per month.
- Purchasing fees are brokerage commissions and 5 percent of amount invested (maximum, $2.50).
- Selling costs include brokerage fees.
- Company purchases stock monthly with OCPs.

Performance Rating: **

United States Trust Corp.
(NASDAQ:USTC)
P.O. Box 843, Cooper Sta.
New York, NY 10276-0843
(800) 548-6565

Business Profile: Operations in corporate trust, private banking, and fiduciary services.

Plan Specifics:
- Partial dividend reinvestment is not available.
- No Discount.

- OCP: $30 to $1000 per month.
- Participants may incur brokerage costs and service charge (maximum, $2.50) on shares purchased with OCPs.
- Stock is purchased monthly with OCPs.
- Selling cost is fee or commission.

Performance Rating: ***

United Telecommunications, Inc. (NYSE:UT)
2330 Shawnee Mission Pkwy.
Westwood, KS 66205
(913) 676-3000

Business Profile: Provides local and long distance telephone service throughout the country.

Plan Specifics:
- Partial dividend reinvestment is available.
- No Discount.
- OCP: $10 to $3000 per quarter.
- Selling costs are $2 processing fee and approximately 5 to 25 cents per share commission.
- Company purchases stock monthly with OCPs.
- Approximately 20,623 shareholders in the plan.

Performance Rating: ***

United Water Resources, Inc. (NYSE:UWR)
200 Old Hook Rd.
Harrington Park, NJ 07640
(201) 767-2811

Business Profile: Public utility holding company supplying water to portions of New Jersey and New York.

Plan Specifics:
- Partial dividend reinvestment is available.
- 5 percent discount on reinvested dividends.
- OCP: $25 to $3000 per quarter.
- Selling costs are brokerage commissions.
- Company purchases stock monthly with OCPs.
- 5000 to 6000 shareholders in the plan.

Performance Rating: ***

UNITIL Corp. (ASE:UTL)
216 Epping Rd.
Exeter, NH 03833-1115
(603) 772-0775

Business Profile: New Hampshire-based electric utility holding company.

Plan Specifics:
- Partial divided reinvestment is available.
- 5 percent discount on reinvested dividends.
- OCP: $25 to $5000 per quarter.
- Stock is purchased quarterly with OCPs.
- Selling cost is brokerage commission.
- Approximately 250 shareholders in the plan.

Performance Rating: ***

Universal Corp. (NYSE:UVV)
P.O. Box 25099
Richmond, VA 23260
(804) 359-9311   (804) 254-1303

Business Profile: Major factor in leaf tobacco market with operations in agri-products.

Plan Specifics:
- Partial dividend reinvestment is available.
- No Discount.
- OCP: $10 to $1000 per month.
- No selling costs.
- Company purchases stock monthly with OCPs.

Performance Rating: ***

Universal Foods Corp. (NYSE:UFC)
433 E. Michigan St.
Milwaukee, WI 53202
(414) 271-6755

Business Profile: Produces frozen potato goods, yeast products, and food flavorings and colors.

Plan Specifics:
- Partial dividend reinvestment is available.
- 5 percent discount on reinvested dividends.
- OCP: $25 to $1000 per month.
- Selling costs may include fees, commissions, and other expenses.
- Company purchases stock around the 1st business day of the month with OCPs in months when a dividend is not payable.
- 57 percent of the shareholders in the plan.

Performance Rating: ***

Universal Health Realty Income
Trust (NYSE:UHT)
367 S. Gulph Rd.
King of Prussia, PA 19406
(215) 768-3300   (215) 265-0688

Business Profile: Real estate investment trust investing in income-producing health-care facilities.

Plan Specifics:
- Partial dividend reinvestment is available.
- No Discount.
- OCP: $25 to $5000 per month.
- Purchasing fees may include brokerage commissions and 5 percent charge on each investment (maximum, $3).
- Stock is purchased monthly with OCPs.
- Must go through own broker to sell shares.

Performance Rating: **

Unocal Corp. (NYSE:UCL)
c/o Manufacturers Hanover
P.O. Box 24850, Church St. Sta.
New York, NY 10242
(212) 613-7147   (800) 252-2233

Business Profile: Integrated crude oil and natural gas producer.

Plan Specifics:
- Partial dividend reinvestment is not available.
- No Discount.
- OCP: $25 to $1000 per payment.
- Purchasing costs are brokerage fees, service charge of 5 percent for reinvested dividends (maximum, $2), and 5 percent service charge on OCPs (maximum, $3).
- Selling costs are brokerage fees.
- Stock is purchased monthly with OCPs.

Performance Rating: **

Upjohn Co. (NYSE:UPJ)
7000 Portage Rd.
Kalamazoo, MI 49001
(800) 253-8600

Business Profile: Major provider of prescription pharmaceuticals, including steroids and antibiotics.

Plan Specifics:
- Partial dividend reinvestment is available.
- No Discount.
- OCP: $25 to $6000 per quarter.
- Selling costs are brokerage fees.
- Company purchases stock monthly with OCPs.
- Approximately 11,796 shareholders in the plan.

Performance Rating: ****

Upper Peninsula Energy Corp.
(NASDAQ:UPEN)
616 Shelden Ave.
Houghton, MI 49931
(906) 482-0220   (313) 828-6900

Business Profile: Holding company whose main subsidiary provides electric service to northern Michigan (Upper Peninsula) customers.

Plan Specifics:
- Partial dividend reinvestment is not available.
- No Discount.
- OCP: $50 to $5000 per quarter.
- Selling costs are brokerage fees and a handling charge of $3.
- Company purchases stock quarterly with OCPs.

Performance Rating: ***

USF&G Corp. (NYSE:FG)
c/o First Chicago Trust-NY
P.O. Box 3506, Church St. Sta.
New York, NY 10008-3506
(212) 791-6422

Business Profile: Leading property-casualty insurance company.

Plan Specifics:
- Partial dividend reinvestment is available.
- No Discount.

- OCP: $50 to $5000 per quarter.
- Selling costs are minimal brokerage fees.
- Company purchases stock monthly with OCPs.

Performance Rating: **

USLICO Corp. (NYSE:USC)
4601 Fairfax Dr.
Arlington, VA 22203
(703) 875-3400

Business Profile: Insurance-based holding company.

Plan Specifics:
- Partial dividend reinvestment is not available.
- No Discount.
- OCP: $100 to $2500 per quarter.
- Selling costs are brokerage commissions and $5 termination fee.
- Company purchases stock monthly with OCPs.
- Need 100 shares in order to make OCPs.

Performance Rating: **

USLIFE Corporation (NYSE:USH)
c/o Manufacturers Hanover Trust
Dividend Reinvestment Dept.
P.O. Box 24850, Church St. Sta.
New York, NY 10249
(212) 613-7147   (212) 709-6000

Business Profile: Holding company with major operations in life insurance.

Plan Specifics:
- Partial dividend reinvestment is available.
- No Discount.
- OCP: $10 to $4000 per quarter.
- Selling costs include brokerage and handling charges.
- Stock is purchased monthly with OCPs.

Performance Rating: ***

USP Real Estate Investment Trust (NASDAQ:USPT)
c/o Bank of America
P.O. Box 37002
San Francisco, CA 94137
(415) 624-4100

Business Profile: Real estate investment trust.

Plan Specifics:
- Partial dividend reinvestment is not available.
- No Discount.
- OCP: no limit on OCPs but only one investment during quarter.
- Purchasing costs are brokerage fees.
- Must go through own broker to sell shares.
- Company purchases stock quarterly with OCPs.

Performance Rating: NR

UST Corp. (NASDAQ:USTB)
P.O. Box 131
Boston, MA 02101
(617) 726-7000

Business Profile: Boston multibank holding company.

Plan Specifics:
- Partial dividend reinvestment is available.
- 10 percent discount on reinvested dividends.
- OCP: As voted by Board of Directors.
- Selling costs may include brokerage fees.
- 58 percent of shareholders are enrolled in the plan.

Performance Rating: **

UST, Inc. (NYSE:UST)
100 W. Putnam Ave.
Greenwich, CT 06830
(203) 622-3656

Business Profile: Leading producer of smokeless tobacco, cigars, pipes, and wine.

Plan Specifics:
- Partial dividend reinvestment is available.
- No Discount.
- OCP: $10 to $10,000 per month.
- Selling costs are brokerage fees and a $2.50 maximum handling charge.
- Company purchases stock around the 15th of each month with OCPs.
- Approximately 2000 shareholders in the plan.

Performance Rating: ****

U S West, Inc. (NYSE:USW)
c/o American Transtech
P.O. Box 45031
Jacksonville, FL 32232-5031
(800) 537-0222

Business Profile: Telecommunications holding company serving the Great Plains, Rocky Mountain, and Pacific Northwest states.

Plan Specifics:
- Partial dividend reinvestment is available.
- No Discount.
- OCP: up to $50,000 per year.
- DRIP fees are approximately $4 per year.
- Selling cost is approximately 10 cents per share.
- Company purchases stock once a month with OCPs.
- Need four shares to enroll in the plan.

Performance Rating: ****

USX-Marathon (NYSE:MRO)
Room 611
600 Grant St.
Pittsburgh, PA 15219-4776
(412) 433-4801   (412) 433-1121

Business Profile: Operations in steel, gas, and oil production.

Plan Specifics:
* Partial dividend reinvestment is not available.
* No Discount.
* OCP: $50 to $3000 per quarter.
* Selling costs are brokerage commissions.
* Company purchases stock quarterly with OCPs.

Performance Rating: **

UtiliCorp United, Inc. (NYSE:UCU)
Dividend Reinvestment
P.O. Box 13287
Kansas City, MO 64199-3287
(816) 421-6600

Business Profile: Provides electric power and natural gas to eight states and a Canadian province.

Plan Specifics:
* Partial dividend reinvestment is not available.
* 5 percent discount on reinvested dividends.
* OCP: up to $10,000 per quarter.
* Selling cost is approximately 8 cents per share.
* Company purchases stock monthly with OCPs.
* Approximately 8000 shareholders in the plan.

Performance Rating: ***

Valley Bancorporation (WI)
(NASDAQ:VYBN)
P.O. Box 1061
Appleton, WI 54912-1061
(414) 738-3829

Business Profile: Wisconsin-based multibank holding company.

Plan Specifics:
* Partial dividend reinvestment is available.
* No Discount.
* OCP: $10 to $25,000 per quarter.
* Selling costs are brokerage commissions.
* Company purchases stock every month with OCPs.
* Approximately 3400 shareholders in the plan.

Performance Rating: ***

Valley National Bancorp (NJ)
(NASDAQ:VNBP)
1445 Valley Rd.
Wayne, NJ 07470
(201) 777-1800

Business Profile: New Jersey bank holding company.

Plan Specifics:
* Partial dividend reinvestment is available.
* No Discount.
* OCP: $50 to $2000 per month.
* No selling costs.
* Company purchases stock at least monthly with OCPs or more frequently if enough funds accumulate to purchase 100 shares.
* Approximately 1100 shareholders in the plan.
* Company prefers that a minimum of 25 shares are held to enroll.

Performance Rating: NR

Valley Resources, Inc. (ASE:VR)
P.O. Box 1000
Cumberland, RI 02864-0701
(401) 333-1595   (800) 426-5523

Business Profile: Diversified energy company providing natural gas utility service in northern Rhode Island, with subsidiaries providing retail propane service, sales, and rental of gas-fired appliances.

Plan Specifics:
- Partial dividend reinvestment is available.
- 5 percent discount on reinvested dividends.
- OCP: $25 to $5000 per month.
- Participants may incur brokerage fees when selling.
- Company purchases stock monthly with OCPs.

Performance Rating: ***

Van Dorn Co. (NYSE:VDC)
c/o Ameritrust Co.
P.O. Box 6477
Cleveland, OH 44101
(216) 687-5744   (216) 361-5234

Business Profile: Important supplier of plastic and metal containers and plastic injection molding machinery.

Plan Specifics:
- Partial dividend reinvestment is not available.
- No Discount.
- OCP: $10 to $3000 per month.
- Selling costs are brokerage charges.
- Company purchases stock monthly if enough funds accumulate to purchase at least 100 shares.
- Must have at least 50 common shares to enroll in the plan.

Performance Rating: **

Varian Associates, Inc. (NYSE:VAR)
P.O. Box 10800
Palo Alto, CA 94303-0883
(415) 424-5314   (415) 424-5369

Business Profile: Manufactures electron devices, semiconductor equipment, and analytical instruments.

Plan Specifics:
- Partial dividend reinvestment is not available.
- No Discount.
- OCP: $10 to $1000 per month.
- Purchasing fees are brokerage commission and a service charge of 5 percent (maximum of $2.50) for each dividend and/or cash investment.
- Company purchases stock every month with OCPs.
- Selling costs include brokerage fees and service charges ($2.50 maximum).

Performance Rating: **

Vermont Financial Services Corp.
(NASDAQ:VFSC)
100 Main St.
Brattleboro, VT 05301
(802) 257-7151

Business Profile: Commercial banking organization in Vermont.

Plan Specifics:
- Partial dividend reinvestment is not available.
- No Discount.
- OCP: up to $3000 per quarter.
- Must go through own broker to sell shares.
- Company purchases stock quarterly with OCPs.

Performance Rating: NR

VF Corp. (NYSE:VFC)
c/o First Chicago Trust-NY
P.O. Box 3506, Church St. Sta.
New York, NY 10008-3506
(212) 791-6422   (215) 378-1151

Business Profile: Manufactures jeans, sportswear, intimate apparel, and occupational clothing.

Plan Specifics:
- Partial dividend reinvestment is not available.
- No Discount.
- OCP: $10 to $3000 per quarter.
- Purchasing fees are brokerage commissions and a service charge of 5 percent of the amount invested (maximum, $2.50).
- Company purchases stock quarterly with OCPs.
- Selling costs are brokerage fees.

Performance Rating: ***

VMS Hotel Investment Fund
(ASE:VHT)
c/o Mellon Bank Transfer Services
P.O. Box 444
Pittsburgh, PA 15230
(412) 236-8000   (800) 637-3820

Business Profile: Real estate investment trust investing in mortgage loans secured by hotels and resort properties.

Plan Specifics:
- Partial dividend reinvestment is not available.
- No Discount.
- OCP: not available.
- Company is not currently paying a dividend.
- Must go through own broker to sell shares.
- Purchasing fees are approximately

10 cents per share and service charges.

Performance Rating: *

VMS Short Term Income Trust
(ASE:VST)
c/0 Mellon Bank Transfer Services
P.O. Box 444
Pittsburgh, PA 15230
(412) 236-8000 (800) 637-3820

Business Profile: Real estate investment trust.

Plan Specifics:
- Partial dividend reinvestment is not available.
- No Discount.
- OCP: not available.
- Company is not currently paying a dividend.
- Purchasing fees are approximately 10 cents per share.
- Approximately 4233 shareholders in plan.
- $1 issuance fee for certificates.
- Participants must sell shares through broker.

Performance Rating: *

Volunteer Bancshares, Inc.
(NASDAQ:VOLB)
301 E. Main St.
P.O. Box 549
Jackson, TN 38302
(901) 422-9200

Business Profile: Tennessee-based bank holding company.

Plan Specifics:
- Partial dividend reinvestment is available.
- 5 percent discount on reinvested dividends.
- OCP: $25 to $3000 per quarter.

- Must go through own broker to sell shares.
- Company purchases stock on the day the cash is received.
- Over 600 shareholders in the plan.

Performance Rating: NR

Voplex Corp. (ASE:VOT)
c/o Chase Lincoln First Bank
P.O. Box 1507
Rochester, NY 14603
(716) 258-5833   (716) 258-5621

Business Profile: Manufactures interior and exterior plastic trim for automobiles and other plastic products for industrial use.

Plan Specifics:

- Partial dividend reinvestment is not available.
- No Discount.
- OCP: $10 to $3000 per quarter.
- Stock is purchased quarterly with OCPs.
- Selling costs are brokerage commission and $1 per transaction.
- Approximately 123 shareholders in plan.

Performance Rating: *

Vulcan Materials Co. (NYSE:VMC)
c/o First Chicago Trust-NY
P.O. Box 3506, Church St. Sta.
New York, NY 10008
(212) 791-6422   (205) 877-3202

Business Profile: Major supplier of construction material and industrial chemicals.

Plan Specifics:

- Partial dividend reinvestment is not available.
- No Discount.
- OCP: $10 to $3000 per quarter.

- Purchasing fees are brokerage commissions and a service charge of 5 percent (maximum, $2.50) for each investment of a dividend or OCP.
- Selling costs are brokerage commissions and other costs of sale.
- Company purchases stock quarterly with OCPs.

Performance Rating: ***

Wachovia Corp. (NYSE:WB)
301 North Main St.
Winston-Salem, NC 27150
(919) 770-5787

Business Profile: Holding bank for banks in North Carolina and Georgia.

Plan Specifics:

- Partial dividend reinvestment is available.
- No Discount.
- OCP: $20 to $2000 per month.
- Selling costs are brokerage fees.
- Company purchases stock once a month with OCPs.
- Over 7000 shareholders in the plan.

Performance Rating: ****

Walgreen Co. (NYSE:WAG)
200 Wilmot Rd.
Deerfield, IL 60015
(312) 461-5535

Business Profile: Largest United States retail drugstore chain.

Plan Specifics:

- Partial dividend reinvestment is not available.
- No Discount.
- OCP: $10 to $1000 eight times a year.
- Selling costs are brokerage commissions.

- Stock is purchased approximately eight times a year with OCPs.

Performance Rating: ****

Warner-Lambert Co. (NYSE:WLA)
201 Tabor Rd.
Morris Plains, NJ 07950
(201) 540-2000   (212) 791-6422

Business Profile: Leading provider of pharmaceuticals, over-the-counter drugs, and gum.

Plan Specifics:
- Partial dividend reinvestment is not available.
- No Discount.
- OCP: $10 to $1000 per month.
- Selling costs are brokerage commissions and related expenses of sale.
- Stock is purchased approximately eight times a year with OCPs.

Performance Rating: ****

Washington Energy Co.
(NASDAQ:WECO)
Attn.: Financial Services
P.O. Box 1869
Seattle, WA 98111
(206) 622-6767   (312) 461-4076

Business Profile: Washington-based gas utility holding company.

Plan Specifics:
- Partial dividend reinvestment is available.
- 5 percent discount on reinvested dividends.
- OCP: $25 to $3000 per quarter.
- Company issues stock to the plan quarterly with OCPs.
- Approximately one-third of the shareholders in the plan.

Performance Rating: ***

Washington Gas Light Co.
(NYSE:WGL)
1100 H St. N.W.
Washington, DC 20080
(800) 221-9427   (703) 750-4440

Business Profile: Supplies natural gas to areas of Washington, D.C., Virginia, and Maryland.

Plan Specifics:
- Partial dividend reinvestment is available.
- No Discount.
- OCP: $25 to $10,000 per quarter.
- Selling cost is approximately 10 cents per share.
- Company purchases stock on the 1st trading day of the month with OCPs.
- Approximately 8500 shareholders in the plan.
- Preferred dividends are eligible for reinvestment for additional common shares under the plan.

Performance Rating: ***

Washington Mutual Savings Bank
(NASDAQ:WAMU)
c/o First Interstate Bank
P.O. Box 60975, Terminal Annex
Los Angeles, CA 90060-9990
(206) 461-3184

Business Profile: Washington-based financial institution.

Plan Specifics:
- Partial dividend reinvestment is not available.
- No Discount.
- OCP: $100 to $5000 per quarter.
- Must go through own broker to sell shares.
- Company purchases stock monthly with OCPs.

Performance Rating: NR

Washington National Corp.
(NYSE:WNT)
1630 Chicago Ave.
Evanston, IL 60201
(708) 570-5500

Business Profile: Financial services holding organization. Writes and sells life, annuity, and health insurance.

Plan Specifics:
- Partial dividend reinvestment is available.
- 5 percent discount on reinvested dividends.
- OCP: $25 to $5000 per quarter.
- Selling costs may include brokerage fees.
- Company purchases stock quarterly with OCPs.
- Preferred dividends are eligible for reinvestment for additional common shares.
- Approximately 800 shareholders in the plan.

Performance Rating: **

Washington Real Estate Investment Trust (ASE:WRE)
c/o Riggs National Bank
P.O. Box 96213
Washington, DC 20077-7571
(301) 652-4300

Business Profile: Real estate investment trust investing in income-producing properties in metropolitan Washington, D.C.

Plan Specifics:
- Partial dividend reinvestment is not available.
- No Discount.
- OCP: $100 to $3000 per quarter.
- Selling costs are brokerage expenses.

- Company purchases stock quarterly with OCPs.

Performance Rating: ***

Washington Water Power Co.
(NYSE:WWP)
P.O. Box 3647
Spokane, WA 99220
(800) 727-9170   (509) 489-0500

Business Profile: Supplies electricity and gas service to customers in Washington and Idaho.

Plan Specifics:
- Partial dividend reinvestment is not available.
- No Discount.
- OCP: up to $100,000 per year.
- Selling costs are approximately 4 cents per share.
- Company purchases stock monthly with OCPs.

Performance Rating: **

Waste Management, Inc.
(NYSE:WMX)
3003 Butterfield Rd.
Oak Brook, IL 60521
(708) 572-8800

Business Profile: Largest operator of waste collection and disposal services.

Plan Specifics:
- Partial dividend reinvestment is not available.
- No Discount.
- OCP: $25 to $2000 per month.
- Company purchases stock monthly with OCPs.
- When selling shares, investors have choice of taking possession of stock free of charge and selling it themselves or allowing company to do it

at cost of approximately 5 cents per share.

Performance Rating: ****

**Weingarten Realty Investors
(NYSE:WRI)**
c/o Ameritrust Co.
P.O. Box 6477
Cleveland, OH 44101
(216) 737-5745

Business Profile: Real estate investment trust developing shopping centers primarily in southern states.

Plan Specifics:
- Partial dividend reinvestment is available.
- No Discount.
- OCP: $10 to $15,000 per quarter.
- Selling costs are brokerage commission and $5 service charge.
- $5 termination fee.
- Purchasing fees are 5 percent of amount invested (maximum, $3) and broker's fee.
- Company purchases stock at least quarterly and most likely monthly with OCPs.

Performance Rating: **

Weis Markets, Inc. (NYSE:WMK)
1000 S. Second St.
Sunbury, PA 17801
(717) 286-4571

Business Profile: Manages retail food stores located in Pennsylvania.

Plan Specifics:
- Partial dividend reinvestment is not available.
- No Discount.
- OCP: $10 to $3000 per quarter.

- Selling costs are brokerage commission.
- Company purchases stock quarterly with OCPs.

Performance Rating: ****

Wells Fargo & Co. (NYSE:WFC)
c/o Manufacturers Hanover
P.O. Box 24850, Church St. Sta.
New York, NY 10249
(212) 613-7147   (415) 396-0560

Business Profile: Major bank holding company based in California.

Plan Specifics:
- Partial dividend reinvestment is available.
- No Discount.
- OCP: $25 to $5000 per quarter.
- Selling fees include $15 handling charge and brokerage fees.
- Stock is purchased monthly with OCPs.

Performance Rating: ***

**Wendy's International, Inc.
(NYSE:WEN)**
4288 W. Dublin-Granville Rd.
Dublin, OH 43017
(614) 764-3100   (212) 936-5100

Business Profile: Owns and operates Wendy's fast food restaurants.

Plan Specifics:
- Partial dividend reinvestment is available.
- No Discount.
- OCP: minimum $20 per month to maximum $20,000 annually.
- Selling costs are brokerage charges.
- Company purchases stock monthly with OCPs.

Performance Rating: **

**West One Bancorp
(NASDAQ:WEST)
P.O. Box 8247
West One Plaza
Boise, ID 83733
(208) 383-7451   (208) 383-7177**

Business Profile: Multibank holding company serving western states.

Plan Specifics:
- Partial dividend reinvestment is not available.
- No Discount.
- OCP: $25 to $2500 per quarter.
- Must go through own broker to sell shares.
- Company purchases stock quarterly with OCPs.

Performance Rating: NR

**Westamerica Bancorp (ASE:WAB)
c/o Bank of America
P.O. Box 37002
San Francisco, CA 94137
(415) 624-4100**

Business Profile: California-based bank holding company.

Plan Specifics:
- Partial dividend reinvestment is not available.
- No Discount.
- OCP: $25 to $400 per month.
- Selling costs are brokerage fees.
- Company purchases stock monthly with OCPs.

Performance Rating: NR

**Westcoast Energy, Inc. (NYSE:WE)
c/o Montreal Trust
510 Burrard St.
Vancouver, BC V6C 3B9 Canada
(604) 691-5500**

Business Profile: Transports natural gas from Canada to United States Pa-

cific Northwest and British Columbia through major pipeline system.

Plan Specifics:
- Partial dividend reinvestment is available.
- 5 percent discount on reinvested dividends.
- OCP: $50 to $5000 (Canadian) per quarter.
- Stock is purchased quarterly with OCPs.
- Must go through own broker to sell shares.

Performance Rating: **

**Westvaco Corp. (NYSE:W)
299 Park Ave.
New York, NY 10171
(212) 688-5000**

Business Profile: Manufactures bleached board and converting and printing paper.

Plan Specifics:
- Partial dividend reinvestment is available.
- No Discount.
- OCP: up to $5000 per quarter.
- Selling costs are brokerage charges.
- Company purchases stock monthly with OCPs.
- Approximately 8000 shareholders in the plan.

Performance Rating: ***

**Wetterau, Inc. (NASDAQ:WETT)
8920 Pershall Rd.
Hazelwood, MO 63042
(314) 595-4173   (314) 524-5000**

Business Profile: Large distributor of wholesale food. Owns retail outlet stores.

Plan Specifics:
- Partial dividend reinvestment is not available.

- No Discount.
- OCP: $10 to $1000 per month.
- Selling costs are minimal brokerage and handling charges.
- Company purchases stock twice a quarter with OCPs.
- Almost 25 percent of shareholders in the plan.

Performance Rating: ***

Weyerhaeuser Co. (NYSE:WY)
c/o Manufacturers Hanover
P.O. Box 24850, Church St. Sta.
New York, NY 10242
(212) 613-7147   (800) 647-4273

Business Profile: Major producer of pulp, plywood, and building products.

Plan Specifics:
- Partial dividend reinvestment is available.
- No Discount.
- OCP: $100 to $5000 per quarter.
- Purchasing fees are brokerage commissions and 4 percent service charge (maximum, $1.50) on reinvested dividends and $5 charge for investments of OCPs.
- Selling costs are brokerage fees.
- $3 charge for safekeeping of certificates.
- $5 fee for issuance of certificates.
- Stock is purchased monthly with OCPs.

Performance Rating: ***

Whirlpool Corp. (NYSE:WHR)
c/o Harris Trust & Savings Bank
P.O. Box A3309
Chicago, IL 60690
(800) 526-8762

Business Profile: Leading supplier of household appliances, including re-

frigerators, freezers, air conditioners, and automatic washers.

Plan Specifics:
- Partial dividend reinvestment is not available.
- No Discount.
- OCP: $10 to $3000 per quarter.
- Stock is purchased quarterly with OCPs.
- Selling cost is 5 to 6 cents per share.

Performance Rating: ***

Whitman Corp. (NYSE:WH)
111 E. Wacker Drive
Chicago, IL 60601
(312) 565-3000   (800) 446-2617

Business Profile: Produces consumer foods and packages and distributes soft drinks.

Plan Specifics:
- Partial dividend reinvestment is available.
- No Discount.
- OCP: $10 to $60,000 per year.
- Selling costs include brokerage fees.
- Company purchases stock monthly with OCPs.
- Approximately 6000 shareholders in the plan.

Performance Rating: **

WICOR, Inc. (NYSE:WIC)
P.O. Box 334
Milwaukee, WI 53201
(414) 291-6550   (414) 291-6568

Business Profile: Natural gas utility holding company serving customers in Wisconsin.

Plan Specifics:
- Partial dividend reinvestment is not available.

- No Discount.
- OCP: $25 to $3000 per quarter.
- Selling costs are brokerage fees.
- Company purchases stock at least quarterly with OCPs.
- Approximately 5000 shareholders in the plan.

Performance Rating: *******

Wilmington Trust Co.
(NASDAQ:WILM)
Rodney Square North
Wilmington, DE 19890
(302) 651-1000   (302) 651-1448

Business Profile: Conducts commercial banking, savings, investment management, and savings operations.

Plan Specifics:
- Partial dividend reinvestment is available.
- No Discount.
- OCP: $10 to $5000 a quarter.
- Selling costs may include brokerage fees.
- Company purchases stock quarterly with OCPs.
- Approximately 1400 shareholders in the plan.

Performance Rating: *******

Winn-Dixie Stores, Inc.
(NYSE:WIN)
P.O. Box B
5050 Edgewood Ct.
Jacksonville, FL 32203-0297
(904) 783-5000

Business Profile: Owns and manages supermarkets in southern states.

Plan Specifics:
- Partial dividend reinvestment is not available.
- No Discount.

- OCP: $10 to $1000 per month.
- Must go through own broker to sell shares.
- Company purchases stock monthly with OCPs.
- Approximately 17,000 shareholders in the plan.

Performance Rating: ********

Wisconsin Energy Corp.
(NYSE:WEC)
P.O. Box 2949
231 W. Michigan
Milwaukee, WI 53201
(800) 558-9663

Business Profile: Provides electric power, gas, and steam to portions of Wisconsin and Michigan.

Plan Specifics:
- Partial dividend reinvestment is not available.
- No Discount.
- OCP: $25 to $3000 per month.
- Preferred dividends are eligible for reinvestment for additional common shares under the plan.
- Selling cost is approximately 3 cents per share.
- Company purchases stock monthly with OCPs.
- Approximately 22,000 shareholders in the plan.

Performance Rating: ********

Wisconsin Southern Gas Co., Inc.
(NASDAQ:WISC)
120 E. Sheridan Springs Rd.
Lake Geneva, WI 53147
(414) 248-8861

Business Profile: Wisconsin natural gas utility.

Plan Specifics:
- Partial dividend reinvestment is not available.
- No Discount.
- OCP: $50 to $2000 per quarter.
- Must go through own broker to sell shares.
- Company purchases stock quarterly with OCPs.
- Approximately 1255 shareholders in the plan.

Performance Rating: ***

Witco Corp. (NYSE:WIT)
520 Madison Ave.
New York, NY 10022-4236
(212) 605-3800

Business Profile: Manufactures specialty chemicals and petroleum products.

Plan Specifics:
- Partial dividend reinvestment is not available.
- No Discount.
- OCP: $10 to $3000 per quarter.
- Selling costs may include brokerage fees.
- Company purchases stock quarterly with OCPs.

Performance Rating: ***

Woolworth Corp. (NYSE:Z)
233 Broadway
Woolworth Bldg.
New York, NY 10279
(212) 553-2000

Business Profile: Owns and operates variety, discount, and shoe stores.

Plan Specifics:
- Partial dividend reinvestment is available.
- No Discount.

- OCP: $20 to $60,000 per year.
- Selling costs are brokerage commissions and other costs of sale.
- Company purchases stock monthly with OCPs.

Performance Rating: ****

Worthington Industries, Inc.
(NASDAQ:WTHG)
1205 Dearborn Drive
Columbus, OH 43085
(614) 438-3210   (800) 442-2001

Business Profile: Manufactures processed steel products, injection-molded plastic parts and steel castings.

Plan Specifics:
- Partial dividend reinvestment is available.
- No Discount.
- OCP: $50 to $5000 per quarter.
- Selling costs are brokerage fees.
- Company purchases stock quarterly with OCPs.

Performance Rating: ***

WPL Holdings, Inc. (NYSE:WPH)
P.O. Box 2568
Madison, WI 53701-2568
(800) 356-5343   (800) 622-2258

Business Profile: Public utility holding company providing electric, gas, and water service in south-central Wisconsin.

Plan Specifics:
- Partial dividend reinvestment is available.
- No Discount.
- OCP: $20 to $3000 per month.
- Preferred dividends are eligible for reinvestment for additional common shares under the plan.
- Selling costs include brokerage fees.

- Company purchases stock around the 15th of the month with OCPs.
- Approximately 12,000 shareholders in the plan.

Performance Rating: ****

Wrigley, William, Jr. Co.
(NYSE:WWY)
410 N. Michigan Ave.
Chicago, IL 60611-4287
(312) 644-2121

Business Profile: World's largest producer of chewing gum.

Plan Specifics:
- Partial dividend reinvestment is not available.
- No Discount.
- OCP: $50 to $5000 per month.
- No selling costs.
- Company purchases stock monthly with OCPs.
- Safekeeping services are available.

Performance Rating: ****

Xerox Corp. (NYSE:XRX)
Dividend Reinvestment Services
P.O. Box 23228
Rochester, NY 14603
(800) 828-6396

Business Profile: Leading producer of copiers and duplicators with operations in financial services.

Plan Specifics:
- Partial dividend reinvestment is available.
- No Discount.
- OCP: $10 to $5000 per month.
- Stock is purchased monthly with OCPs.

- Preferred dividends are eligible for reinvestment for additional common shares under the plan.
- Selling costs include broker fees.

Performance Rating: **

York Financial Corp.
(NASDAQ:YFED)
P.O. Box M-68
101 S. George St.
York, PA 17405-7068
(717) 846-8777

Business Profile: Pennsylvania-based bank holding company.

Plan Specifics:
- Partial dividend reinvestment is available.
- 10 percent discount on reinvested dividends.
- OCP: $25 to $2500 per quarter.
- Selling costs may include brokerage fees and $1.50 termination fee.
- Company purchases stock quarterly with OCPs.

Performance Rating: NR

Zero Corp. (NYSE:ZRO)
Suite 2100
444 S. Flower St.
Los Angeles, CA 90071-2922
(213) 629-7000

Business Profile: Manufactures enclosures and cooling equipment and provides packaging services for electronics industry. Produces enclosures for airline industry.

Plan Specifics:
- Partial dividend reinvestment is not available.
- No Discount.
- OCP: $25 to $8000 per month.
- Selling costs are brokerage fees.

• Purchasing fees are commissions.
• Company purchases stock monthly with OCPs.
• Approximately 1650 shareholders in the plan.

Performance Rating: ***

Zions Bancorporation (NASDAQ:ZION)
1380 Kennecott Bldg.
Salt Lake City, UT 84133
(801) 524-4787 (801) 524-4849

Business Profile: Bank holding company with operations in Utah, Nevada, and Arizona.

Plan Specifics:
• Partial dividend reinvestment is available.
• No Discount.
• OCP: $10 to $5000 per quarter.
• Preferred dividends are eligible for reinvestment for additional common shares under the plan.
• Stock is purchased quarterly with OCPs.

• Must go through own broker to sell shares.

Performance Rating: **

Zurn Industries, Inc. (NYSE:ZRN)
One Zurn Place
Erie, PA 16514-2000
(814) 452-2111

Business Profile: Supplies services and products for waste-to-energy plants and water quality control systems.

Plan Specifics:
• Partial dividend reinvestment is available.
• No Discount.
• OCP: $10 to $3000 per quarter.
• Selling costs are $5 termination charge and brokerage fees.
• Company purchases stock quarterly with OCPs.
• Approximately 956 shareholders in the plan.

Performance Rating: ***

DRIPs by Performance Ratings

Four Stars (****)

Abbott Laboratories

Air Products & Chemicals, Inc.

American Brands, Inc.

American Cyanamid Co.

American Home Products Corp.

American Telephone & Telegraph Co.

Ameritech

Amoco Corp.

AMP, Inc.

Anheuser-Busch Companies, Inc.

Atlantic Richfield Co.

Baltimore Gas and Electric Co.

Banc One Corp.

Bancorp Hawaii, Inc.

Bard, C. R., Inc.

Bausch & Lomb, Inc.

Baxter International, Inc.

BCE, Inc.

Becton, Dickinson & Co.

Bell Atlantic Corp.

BellSouth Corp.

Borden, Inc.

Bristol-Myers Squibb Co.

British Petroleum Co. Plc

Brooklyn Union Gas Co.

Browning-Ferris Industries, Inc.

Campbell Soup Co.

Central Fidelity Banks, Inc.

Cincinnati Bell, Inc.

Clorox Co.

Coca-Cola Co., The

Colgate-Palmolive Co.

ConAgra, Inc.

Consolidated Edison Co. of New York

Consolidated Natural Gas Co.

Corning, Inc.

CPC International, Inc.

Dean Foods Co.

Donnelley, R. R., & Sons Co.

Dow Jones & Co., Inc.

Du Pont, E. I., de Nemours & Co.

Duke Power Co.

Eastman Kodak Co.

EG&G, Inc.

Emerson Electric Co.

Equifax, Inc.

Ethyl Corp.

Exxon Corp.

Fifth Third Bancorp

First Virginia Banks, Inc.

Gannett Co., Inc.

General Electric Co.

General Mills, Inc.

General Re Corp.

Genuine Parts Co.

Gerber Products Co.

Gillette Co.

GTE Corp.

Hawaiian Electric Industries, Inc.

Heinz, H. J., Co.

Hershey Foods Corp.

Hubbell, Inc.

Humana, Inc.

Indiana Energy, Inc.

International Business Machines Corp.

IPALCO Enterprises, Inc.

Johnson & Johnson

Jostens, Inc.

Kellogg Co.

Kimberly-Clark Corp.

Knight-Ridder, Inc.

Lilly, Eli, & Co.

Marsh & McLennan Companies, Inc.

McDonald's Corp.

Merck & Co., Inc.

Minnesota Mining & Manufacturing
   Co.

Minnesota Power & Light Co.

Morgan, J. P., & Co., Inc.

Nalco Chemical Co.

National Service Industries, Inc.

NBD Bancorp, Inc.

Norfolk Southern Corp.

Northern States Power Co.

NYNEX Corp.

Oklahoma Gas & Electric Co.

Orange & Rockland Utilities, Inc.

Pacific Telesis Group

Penney, J. C., Co., Inc.

PepsiCo, Inc.

Pfizer, Inc.

Philip Morris Companies, Inc.

Potomac Electric Power Co.

PPG Industries, Inc.

Procter & Gamble Co.

Quaker Oats Co.

Ralston Purina Co.

Raytheon Co.

Rockwell International Corp.

Rubbermaid, Inc.

Sara Lee Corp.

SCEcorp

Schering-Plough Corp.

Smucker, J. M., Co.

Southern Indiana Gas & Electric Co.

Southwestern Bell Corp.

U S West, Inc.

Union Pacific Corp.

Upjohn Co.

UST, Inc.

Wachovia Corp.

Walgreen Co.

Warner-Lambert Co.

Waste Management, Inc.

Weis Markets, Inc.

Winn-Dixie Stores, Inc.

Wisconsin Energy Corp.

Woolworth Corp.

WPL Holdings, Inc.

Wrigley, William, Jr. Co.

Three Stars (***)

AAR Corp.

Aetna Life and Casualty Co.

Alcan Aluminium Ltd.

Alco Standard Corp.

Allegheny Power System, Inc.

Allied-Signal, Inc.

Aluminum Company of America

American Business Products, Inc.

American Express Co.

American Family Corp.

American General Corp.

American Greetings Corp.

American Heritage Life Investment Corp.

American Water Works Co., Inc.

AmSouth Bancorp.

Aon Corp.

ARCO Chemical Co.

Armstrong World Industries, Inc.

Associated Banc-Corp.

Atlanta Gas Light Co.

Atlantic Energy, Inc.

Atmos Energy Corp.

Avnet, Inc.

Ball Corp.

Bankers Trust New York Corp.

Banta Corp.

Barnes Group, Inc.

Barnett Banks, Inc.

Bay State Gas Co.

BB&T Financial Corp.

Bemis Co., Inc.

Beneficial Corp.

Black Hills Corp.

Block, H & R, Inc.

Boatmen's Bancshares, Inc.

Bob Evans Farms, Inc.

Boise Cascade Corp.

British Airways Plc

Brown-Forman Corp.

Brush Wellman, Inc.

California Water Service Co.

Capital Holding Corp.

Carlisle Companies, Inc.

Carolina Power & Light Co.

CBS, Inc.

CCB Financial Corp.

CCNB Corp.

Centel Corp.

Central & South West Corp.

Central Louisiana Electric Co., Inc.

Century Telephone Enterprises, Inc.

Chemical Waste Management, Inc.

Chevron Corp.

Chubb Corp.

CIGNA Corp.

CILCORP, Inc.

Cincinnati Financial Corp.

CIPSCO, Inc.

Clarcor, Inc.

Colonial Gas Co.

Comerica, Inc.

Communications Satellite Corp.

Connecticut Energy Corp.

Connecticut Natural Gas Corp.

Consolidated Rail Corp.

Consumers Water Co.

Cooper Industries, Inc.

CoreStates Financial Corp.

Crane Co.

Crompton & Knowles Corp.

CSX Corp.

Dana Corp.

Dayton Hudson Corp.

Delmarva Power & Light Co.

Delta Air Lines, Inc.

Dexter Corp.

Dial Corp.

Dominion Resources, Inc.

Donaldson Co., Inc.

Dow Chemical Co.

E-Systems, Inc.

Eaton Corp.

Empire District Electric Co.

Energen Corp.

EnergyNorth, Inc.

Engraph, Inc.

Equitable Resources, Inc.

Federal National Mortgage Association

Federal Signal Corp.

First Alabama Bancshares, Inc.

First Bancorp. of Ohio

First Colonial Bankshares Corp.

First Michigan Bank Corp.

First of America Bank Corp.

First Security Corp.

First Union Corp.

Firstar Corp.

Fleming Companies, Inc.

Florida Progress Corp.

Flowers Industries, Inc.

Foote, Cone & Belding Communications

Fourth Financial Corp.

FPL Group, Inc.

Freeport-McMoRan, Inc.

Fuller, H. B., Co.

General Cinema Corp.

General Motors Corp.

General Signal Corp.

Georgia-Pacific Corp.

Giant Food, Inc.

Goulds Pumps, Inc.

Graco, Inc.

Handleman Co.

Hannaford Brothers Co.

Harris Corp.

Harsco Corp.

Hartford Steam Boiler Inspection & Insurance Co.

Honeywell, Inc.

Hormel, Geo. A., & Co.

Household International, Inc.

Huntington Bancshares, Inc.

Idaho Power Co.

IE Industries, Inc.

Imperial Oil Ltd.

Ingersoll-Rand Co.

International Multifoods Corp.

International Paper Co.

Interpublic Group of Companies, Inc.

Iowa-Illinois Gas & Electric Co.

ITT Corp.

Jefferson-Pilot Corp.

Johnson Controls, Inc.

Kansas Power & Light Co.

Kentucky Utilities Co.

Kerr-McGee Corp.

KeyCorp

Keystone International, Inc.

La-Z-Boy Chair Co.

Laclede Gas Co.

Lance, Inc.

LG&E Energy Corp.

Limited, The, Inc.

Lincoln National Corp.

Lincoln Telecommunications Co.

Liz Claiborne, Inc.

Loctite Corp.

Louisiana-Pacific Corp.

Lowe's Companies, Inc.

Luby's Cafeterias, Inc.

Lukens, Inc.

Madison Gas & Electric Co.

Manufacturers National Corp.

Marion Merrell Dow, Inc.

Mark Twain Bancshares, Inc.

Marsh Supermarkets, Inc.

Marshall & Ilsley Corp.

Martin Marietta Corp.

McCormick & Co., Inc.

McGraw-Hill, Inc.

McKesson Corp.

MCN Corp.

MDU Resources Group, Inc.

Media General, Inc.

Mercantile Bankshares Corp.

Middlesex Water Co.

Millipore Corp.

Mobil Corp.

Mobile Gas Service Corp.

Monsanto Co.

Moore Corp. Ltd.

Motorola, Inc.

Nash-Finch Co.

National City Corp.

National Fuel Gas Co.

National Medical Enterprises, Inc.

NCNB Corp.

Nevada Power Co.

New England Electric System

New York Times Co.

NICOR, Inc.

Nordson Corp.

North Carolina Natural Gas Corp.

Northern Telecom Ltd.

Northwest Illinois Bancorp, Inc.

Northwest Natural Gas Co.

Northwestern Public Service Co.

Novo-Nordisk A/S

Nucor Corp.

Ohio Casualty Corp.

Olin Corp.

Otter Tail Power Co.

PacifiCorp

Pall Corp.

Paramount Communications, Inc.

Parker Hannifin Corp.

Pennsylvania Power & Light Co.

Peoples Energy Corp.

Perkin-Elmer Corp.

Phelps Dodge Corp.

Piedmont Natural Gas Co.

Potlatch Corp.

Premier Industrial Corp.

Public Service Co. of North Carolina

Public Service Enterprise Group, Inc.

Questar Corp.

Reynolds & Reynolds Co.

Rhone-Poulenc Rorer, Inc.

Roadway Services, Inc.

Rochester Telephone Corp.

Rollins, Inc.

RPM, Inc.

Russell Corp.

St. Joseph Light & Power Co.

St. Paul Companies, Inc.

Salomon, Inc.

Savannah Foods & Industries, Inc.

SCANA Corp.

Scott Paper Co.

Sears, Roebuck & Co.

Security Bancorp, Inc. (MI)

Sherwin-Williams Co., The

Society Corp.

Sonoco Products Co.

South Jersey Industries, Inc.

Southeastern Michigan Gas Enterprises

Southern California Water Co.

Southern New England Telecommunications

SouthTrust Corp.

Southwest Water Co.

Southwestern Electric Service Co.

Southwestern Public Service Co.

Standex International Corp.

Stanhome, Inc.

Stanley Works

Star Banc Corp.

State Street Boston Corp.

Stride Rite Corp.

SunTrust Banks, Inc.

Super Valu Stores, Inc.

Synovus Financial Corp.

Telephone & Data Systems, Inc.

Texaco, Inc.

Thomas & Betts Corp.

Time Warner, Inc.

TNP Enterprises, Inc.

Total System Services, Inc.

Transamerica Corp.

TRW, Inc.

Tyco Laboratories, Inc.

Union Bank

Union Camp Corp.

United Cities Gas Co.

United States Bancorp

United States Trust Corp.

United Telecommunications, Inc.

United Water Resources, Inc.

UNITIL Corp.

Universal Corp.

Universal Foods Corp.

Upper Peninsula Energy Corp.

USLIFE Corp.

Utilicorp United, Inc.

Valley Bancorporation (WI)

Valley Resources, Inc.

VF Corp.

Vulcan Materials Co.

Washington Energy Co.

Washington Gas Light Co.

Washington Real Estate Investment Trust

Wells Fargo & Co.

Westvaco Corp.

Wetterau, Inc.

Weyerhaeuser Co.

Whirlpool Corp.

WICOR, Inc.

Wilmington Trust Co.

Wisconsin Southern Gas Co., Inc.

Witco Corp.

Worthington Industries, Inc.

Zero Corp.

Zurn Industries, Inc.

Two Stars (**)

Acme Electric Corp.

Acme-Cleveland Corp.

Albany International Corp.

Allegheny Ludlum Corp.

Allied Group, Inc.

AMAX, Inc.

Amcast Industrial Corp.

AMCORE Financial, Inc.

Amerada Hess Corp.

Ameribanc, Inc.

American Colloid Co.

American Electric Power Co., Inc.

American Filtrona Corp.

American Health Properties, Inc.

American Real Estate Partners, LP

American Recreation Centers, Inc.

American Southwest Mortgage Investments

Ameritrust Corp.

AmVestors Financial Corp.

Angeles Mortgage Investment Trust

Angeles Participating Mortgage Trust

Apache Corp.

Aquarion Co.

Arkla, Inc.

Arrow Financial Corp.

Arvin Industries, Inc.

ASARCO, Inc.

Ashland Oil, Inc.

Asset Investors Corp.

Avery Dennison Corp.

Avon Products, Inc.

Baker Hughes, Inc.

Baltimore Bancorp

Bangor Hydro-Electric Co.

Bank of Boston Corp.

Bank of New York Co., Inc.

Bank South Corp.

BankAmerica Corp.

Banks of Mid-America, Inc.

BayBanks, Inc.

Berkshire Gas Co.

Bethlehem Steel Corp.

Beverly Enterprises

Black & Decker Corp.

Blount, Inc.

BMJ Financial Corp.

Boddie-Noell Restaurant Properties

Boston Bancorp

Boston Edison Co.

Bow Valley Industries Ltd.

Bowater, Inc.

Braintree Savings Bank, The

Briggs & Stratton Corp.

Brown Group, Inc.

Brunswick Corp.

Burnham Pacific Properties, Inc.

C & S/Sovran Corp.

Cabot Corp.

Canadian Pacific Ltd.

Carolina Freight Corp.

Carpenter Technology Corp.

Cascade Natural Gas Corp.

Caterpillar, Inc.

CBI Industries, Inc.

Centerior Energy Corp.

Central Hudson Gas & Electric Corp.

Central Maine Power Co.

Central Vermont Public Service Corp.

Champion International Corp.

Chase Manhattan Corp.

Chemed Corp.

Chemical Banking Corp.

Chesapeake Corp.

Chrysler Corp.

Cincinnati Gas & Electric Co.

Cincinnati Milacron, Inc.

Citicorp

Cleveland-Cliffs, Inc.

CMS Energy Corp.

Coca-Cola Bottling Co. Consolidated

Coca-Cola Enterprises, Inc.

Colonial BancGroup, Inc. (AL)

Colorado National Bankshares, Inc.

Columbia Gas System, Inc.

Columbia Real Estate Investments, Inc.

Commercial Intertech Corp.

Commonwealth Edison Co.

Commonwealth Energy System

Connecticut Water Service, Inc.

Constellation Bancorp

Control Data Corp.

Copley Properties, Inc.

Countrywide Mortgage Investments, Inc.

Crestar Financial Corp.

Cross & Trecker Corp.

CRSS, Inc.

Cummins Engine Co., Inc.

Curtice Burns Foods, Inc.

Cyprus Minerals Co.

Deere & Co.

Delta Natural Gas Co., Inc.

Detroit Edison Co.

Diamond Shamrock Offshore Partners LP

Dominion Bankshares Corp.

DPL, Inc.

DQE, Inc.

Dresser Industries, Inc.

Duriron Co., Inc.

E'Town Corp.

Eagle-Picher Industries, Inc.

Eastern Co.

Eastern Enterprises

Eastern Utilities Associates

Ecolab, Inc.

Elco Industries, Inc.

Engelhard Corp.

Enron Corp.

Enserch Corp.

Enserch Exploration Partners Ltd.

F & M Financial Services Corp.

Fay's, Inc.

Federal-Mogul Corp.

Federal Paper Board Co., Inc.

Federal Realty Investment Trust

Figgie International, Inc.

Fina, Inc.

First Bank System, Inc.

First Chicago Corp.

First Commerce Corp.

First Fidelity Bancorp.

First Illinois Corp.

First Interstate Bancorp

First Midwest Bancorp, Inc.

First Mississippi Corp.

First Security Corp. of Kentucky

First Tennessee National Corp.

First Union Real Estate Investments

Fleet/Norstar Financial Group, Inc.

Ford Motor Co.

Foster Wheeler Corp.

GATX Corp.

GenCorp, Inc.

General Public Utilities Corp.

Goodrich, B. F., Co.

Goodyear Tire & Rubber Co.

Grace, W. R., & Co.

Great Lakes Bancorp, FSB

Great Western Financial Corp.

Green Mountain Power Corp.

Grumman Corp.

Guardsman Products, Inc.

Gulf States Utilities Co.

Handy & Harman

Hanna, M. A., Co.

Hartmarx Corp.

Health & Rehabilitation Properties Trust

Health Care REIT, Inc.

Health Equity Properties, Inc.

Hercules, Inc.

Hexcel Corp.

Homestake Mining Co.

Hotel Investors Trust/Corp.

Houston Industries, Inc.

HRE Properties

Huffy Corp.

IBP, Inc.

ICM Property Investors, Inc.
Illinois Power Co.
IMCERA Group, Inc.
Imperial Bancorp
INB Financial Corp.
Inco Ltd.
Independence Bancorp (PA)
Inland Steel Industries, Inc.
Interstate Power Co.
IRT Property Co.
IWC Resources Corp.
Justin Industries, Inc.
K N Energy, Inc.
Kaman Corp.
Kansas Gas & Electric Co.
Kelley Oil & Gas Partners, Ltd.
Kemper Corp.
Kennametal, Inc.
Kroger Co.
Kuhlman Corp.
Lafarge Corp.
Lyondell Petrochemical Co.
MacDermid, Inc.
Magna Group, Inc.
Manufacturers Hanover Corp.
MAPCO, Inc.
Maytag Corp.
McDermott International, Inc.
Mead Corp.
Medalist Industries, Inc.
Mellon Bank Corp.
Mercantile Bancorp., Inc.
Meridian Bancorp, Inc.
Merrill Lynch & Co., Inc.
Metropolitan Financial Corp.
Michigan National Corp.
Midlantic Corp.
Modine Manufacturing Co.

Montana Power Co.
Morrison Knudsen Corp.
Nashua Corp.
National Community Banks, Inc. (NJ)
National Data Corp.
Neiman-Marcus Group, Inc.
New Jersey Resources Corp.
New Plan Realty Trust
New York State Electric & Gas Corp.
Niagara Mohawk Power Corp.
NIPSCO Industries, Inc.
North Fork Bancorporation, Inc.
Northeast Utilities Service Co.
Northrop Corp.
Norwest Corp.
NOVA Corp. of Alberta
NUI Corp.
Occidental Petroleum Corp.
Ohio Edison Co.
Old Stone Corp.
Omnicare, Inc.
Oneida Ltd.
Oneok, Inc.
Pacific Enterprises
Pacific Gas & Electric Co.
Pacific Western Bancshares, Inc.
PaineWebber Group, Inc.
Panhandle Eastern Corp.
Pennzoil Co.
Pentair, Inc.
Philadelphia Electric Co.
Philadelphia Suburban Corp.
Phillips Petroleum Co.
Piccadilly Cafeterias, Inc.
Pinnacle West Capital Corp.
Pittston Co.
PNC Financial Corp.
Polaroid Corp.

Portland General Corp.

Preston Corp.

Providence Energy Corp.

PSI Resources, Inc.

Public Service Co. of Colorado

Puget Sound Power & Light Co.

Quaker State Corp.

Quanex Corp.

Quantum Chemical Corp.

Raymond Corp.

Real Estate Investment Trust of
California

Reynolds Metals Co.

Rochester Gas & Electric Corp.

Rockefeller Center Properties, Inc.

Rollins Truck Leasing Corp.

Rouse Co.

Ryder System, Inc.

St. Paul Bancorp, Inc.

Samson Energy Co., L.P.

Santa Anita Companies

Security Pacific Corp.

Selective Insurance Group, Inc.

Sierra Pacific Resources

SIFCO Industries, Inc.

Signet Banking Corp.

Simpson Industries, Inc.

Smith, A. O., Corp.

Sonat, Inc.

South Carolina National Corp.

Southern Co.

Southwest Gas Corp.

Southwestern Energy Co.

SPX Corp.

Standard Commercial Corp.

Standard Products Co.

Stone & Webster, Inc.

Summit Bancorporation (NJ)

Sun Co., Inc.

Sundstrand Corp.

Talley Industries, Inc.

TCF Financial Corp.

Temple-Inland, Inc.

Tenneco, Inc.

Texas Utilities Co.

Textron, Inc.

Timken Co.

Toro Co.

Total Petroleum (North America)
Ltd.

TransCanada Pipelines Ltd.

Travelers Corp.

Trinova Corp.

Twin Disc, Inc.

UGI Corp.

UJB Financial Corp.

Union Carbide Corp.

Union Electric Co.

Union Planters Corp.

United Illuminating Co.

United States Shoe Corp.

Universal Health Realty Income
Trust

Unocal Corp.

USF&G Corp.

USLICO Corp.

UST Corp.

USX-Marathon

Van Dorn Co.

Varian Associates, Inc.

Washington National Corp.

Washington Water Power Co.

Weingarten Realty Investors

Wendy's International, Inc.

Westcoast Energy, Inc.

Whitman Corp.

Xerox Corp.

Zions Bancorporation

One Star (*)

Bank of New England Corp.

Banyan Short Term Income Trust

California Real Estate Investment
Trust

Central Holding Co.

Citizens First Bancorp, Inc.

Del-Val Financial Corp.

Dime Savings Bank of New York

Eastland Financial Corp.

Equimark Corp.

First American Corp. (TN)

Great American Bank

HealthVest

Hibernia Corp.

Independent Bank Corp. (MA)

Intermark, Inc.

Investors Financial Corp.

Koger Properties, Inc.

Landmark Bancshares Corp.

Lincoln NC Realty Fund, Inc.

Merrimack Bancorp, Inc.

Merry Land & Investment Co., Inc.

MNC Financial Corp.

Multibank Financial Corp.

National-Standard Co.

New Hampshire Savings Bank Corp.

Northeast Bancorp, Inc. (CT)

Numerica Financial Corp.

Peerless Tube Co.

Premier Bancorp, Inc.

Presidential Realty Corp.

RAC Mortgage Investment Corp.

Realty South Investors, Inc.

Resort Income Investors, Inc.

Rose's Stores, Inc.

Seibels Bruce Group, Inc.

Shawmut National Corp.

Southeast Banking Corp. (FL)

Summit Tax Exempt Bond Fund,
L.P.

Tidewater, Inc.

Trammell Crow Real Estate Investors

VMS Hotel Investment Fund

VMS Short Term Income Trust

Voplex Corp.

Top-Rated DRIPs by Industry Groups

The following three- and four-star rated DRIPs are broken down by industry groups:

Advertising

Foote, Cone & Belding Communications
Interpublic Group of Companies, Inc.

Aerospace and Defense

AAR Corp.
E-Systems, Inc.
Martin Marietta Corp.
Raytheon Co.
Rockwell International Corp.
TRW, Inc.

Agribusiness

ConAgra, Inc.
Freeport-McMoRan, Inc.
Ralston Purina Co.

Airlines

British Airways Plc
Delta Air Lines, Inc.

Aluminum

Alcan Aluminium Ltd.
Aluminum Company of America

Apparel Manufacturers

Liz Claiborne, Inc.
Russell Corp.
Stride Rite Corp.
VF Corp.

Appliances

Whirlpool Corp.

Automobiles

General Motors Corp.

Auto Equipment

Dana Corp.

Eaton Corp.

Genuine Parts Co.

Banking

AmSouth Bancorp

Associated Banc-Corp.

Banc One Corp.

Bancorp Hawaii, Inc.

Bankers Trust New York Corp.

Barnett Banks

BB&T Financial Corp.

Boatmen's Bancshares, Inc.

CCB Financial Corp.

CCNB Corp.

Central Fidelity Banks, Inc.

Comerica, Inc.

CoreStates Financial Corp.

Fifth Third Bancorp

First Alabama Bancshares, Inc.

First Bancorp. of Ohio

First Colonial Bankshares Corp.

First Michigan Bank Corp.

First of America Bank Corp.

First Security Corp.

First Union Corp.

First Virginia Banks, Inc.

Firstar Corp.

Fourth Financial Corp.

Huntington Bancshares, Inc.

KeyCorp

Manufacturers National Corp.

Mark Twain Bancshares, Inc.

Marshall & Ilsley Corp.

Mercantile Bankshares Corp.

Morgan, J. P., & Co., Inc.

National City Corp.

NBD Bancorp, Inc.

NCNB Corp.

Northwest Illinois Bancorp, Inc.

Security Bancorp, Inc. (MI)

Society Corp.

SouthTrust Corp.

Star Banc Corp.

State Street Boston Corp.

SunTrust Banks, Inc.

Synovus Financial Corp.

U.S. Bancorp

U.S. Trust Corp.

Union Bank

Valley Bancorporation (WI)

Wachovia Corp.

Wells-Fargo & Co.

Wilmington Trust Co.

Brewing

Anheuser-Busch Companies, Inc.

Broadcasting

CBS, Inc.

Building Supplies

Armstrong World Industries, Inc.

Boise Cascade Corp.

Georgia-Pacific Corp.

Johnson Controls, Inc.

Louisiana-Pacific Corp.

PPG Industries, Inc.

RPM, Inc.

Sherwin-Williams Co., The

Stanley Works

Weyerhaeuser Co.

Chemicals

Air Products & Chemicals, Inc.

American Cyanamid Co.

ARCO Chemical Co.

Crompton & Knowles Corp.

Dexter Corp.
Dow Chemical Co.
Du Pont, E. I., de Nemours & Co.
Ethyl Corp.
Loctite Corp.
Monsanto Co.
Nalco Chemical Co.
Witco Corp.

Communications

American Telephone & Telegraph Co.
Ameritech
BCE, Inc.
Bell Atlantic Corp.
BellSouth Corp.
Centel Corp.
Century Telephone Enterprises, Inc.
Cincinnati Bell, Inc.
Communications Satellite Corp.
GTE Corp.
Lincoln Telecommunications Co.
Northern Telecom Ltd.
NYNEX Corp.
Pacific Telesis Group
Rochester Telephone Corp.
Southern New England Telecommunications
Southwestern Bell Corp.
Telephone & Data Systems, Inc.
U S West, Inc.
United Telecommunications, Inc.

Computer Manufacturers

Honeywell, Inc.
International Business Machines Corp.

Containers and Packaging

Ball Corp.

Bemis Co., Inc.
Clarcor, Inc.
Engraph, Inc.
Fuller, H. B., Co.
Sonoco Products Co.

Cosmetics and Toiletries

Gillette Co.

Discount and Variety

Handleman Co.
Lowe's Companies, Inc.
Woolworth Corp.

Drug

Abbott Laboratories
American Home Products Corp.
Bristol-Myers Squibb Co.
Lilly, Eli, & Co.
Marion Merrell Dow, Inc.
Merck & Co., Inc.
Novo-Nordisk A/S
Pfizer, Inc.
Rhone-Poulenc Rorer, Inc.
Schering-Plough Corp.
Upjohn Co.
Warner-Lambert Co.

Drug Chains

Walgreen Co.

Electric Utilities

Allegheny Power System, Inc.
Atlantic Energy, Inc.
Baltimore Gas & Electric Co.
Black Hills Corp.
Carolina Power & Light Co.
Central & South West Corp.
Central Louisiana Electric Co., Inc.

CILCORP, Inc.
CIPSCO, Inc.
Consolidated Edison Co. of New York
Delmarva Power & Light Co.
Dominion Resources, Inc.
Duke Power Co.
Empire District Electric Co.
Florida Progress Corp.
FPL Group, Inc.
Hawaiian Electric Industries, Inc.
Idaho Power Co.
IE Industries, Inc.
Iowa-Illinois Gas & Electric Co.
IPALCO Enterprises, Inc.
Kansas Power & Light Co.
Kentucky Utilities Co.
LG&E Energy Corp.
Madison Gas & Electric Co.
MDU Resources Group, Inc.
Minnesota Power & Light Co.
Nevada Power Co.
New England Electric System
Northern States Power Co.
Northwestern Public Service Co.
Oklahoma Gas & Electric Co.
Orange & Rockland Utilities, Inc.
Otter Tail Power Co.
PacifiCorp
Pennsylvania Power & Light Co.
Potomac Electric Power Co.
Public Service Co. of North Carolina
Public Service Enterprise Group, Inc.
St. Joseph Light & Power Co.
SCANA Corp.
SCEcorp
Southern Indiana Gas & Electric Co.
Southwestern Electric Service Co.
Southwestern Public Service Co.

TNP Enterprises, Inc.
UNITIL Corp.
Upper Peninsula Energy Corp.
UtiliCorp United, Inc.
Wisconsin Energy Corp.
WPL Holdings, Inc.

Electrical Equipment

Emerson Electric Co.
Federal Signal Corp.
General Electric Co.
General Signal Corp.
Hubbell, Inc.
Motorola, Inc.
Thomas & Betts Corp.

Electronics, Components

AMP, Inc.
Avnet, Inc.
EG&G, Inc.
Harris Corp.
Zero Corp.

Electronics, Instruments

Perkin-Elmer Corp.

Filter Products

Millipore Corp.
Pall Corp.

Financial Services/Broker

American Express Co.
Beneficial Corp.
Federal National Mortgage Association
Household International, Inc.
Salomon, Inc.

Food

Borden, Inc.
Campbell Soup Co.
CPC International, Inc.

Dean Foods Co.

Fleming Companies, Inc.

Flowers Industries, Inc.

General Mills, Inc.

Gerber Products Co.

Heinz, H. J., Co.

Hershey Foods Corp.

Hormel, Geo. A., & Co.

International Multifoods Corp.

Kellogg Co.

Lance, Inc.

McCormick & Co., Inc.

Quaker Oats Co.

Sara Lee Corp.

Savannah Foods & Industries, Inc.

Smucker, J.M., Co.

Wrigley, William, Jr. Co.

Food Chain

Giant Food, Inc.

Hannaford Brothers Co.

Marsh Supermarkets, Inc.

Nash-Finch Co.

Super Valu Stores, Inc.

Universal Foods Corp.

Weis Markets, Inc.

Wetterau, Inc.

Winn-Dixie Stores, Inc.

Health Care

Bard, C. R., Inc.

Bausch & Lomb, Inc.

Baxter International, Inc.

Becton, Dickinson & Co.

Humana, Inc.

Johnson & Johnson

McKesson Corp.

National Medical Enterprises, Inc.

Household Furnishings

La-Z-Boy Chair Co.

Rubbermaid, Inc.

Stanhome, Inc.

Industrial Components

Barnes Group, Inc.

Harsco Corp.

Keystone International, Inc.

Premier Industrial Corp.

Industrial Machinery

Cooper Industries, Inc.

Crane Co.

Donaldson Co., Inc.

Goulds Pumps, Inc.

Graco, Inc.

Ingersoll-Rand Co.

Life Insurance

Aetna Life and Casualty Co.

American Family Corp.

American General Corp.

American Heritage Life Investment Corp.

Aon Corp.

Capital Holding Corp.

CIGNA Corp.

Jefferson-Pilot Corp.

Lincoln National Corp.

Transamerica Corp.

USLIFE Corp.

Liquor

Brown-Forman Corp.

Metal and Mining

Brush Wellman, Inc.

Phelps Dodge Corp.

Multi-industry

Allied-Signal, Inc.

Carlisle Companies, Inc.

Corning, Inc.

Dial Corp.

General Cinema Corp.

ITT Corp.

Minnesota Mining & Manufacturing Co.

National Services Industries, Inc.

Nordson Corp.

Olin Corp.

Paramount Communications, Inc.

Parker Hannifin Corp.

Standex International Corp.

Tyco Laboratories, Inc.

Vulcan Materials Co.

Natural Gas

Atlanta Gas Light Co.

Atmos Energy Corp.

Bay State Gas Co.

Brooklyn Union Gas Co.

Colonial Gas Co.

Connecticut Energy Corp.

Connecticut Natural Gas Corp.

Consolidated Natural Gas Co.

Energen Corp.

EnergyNorth, Inc.

Equitable Resources, Inc.

Indiana Energy, Inc.

Laclede Gas Co.

MCN Corp.

Mobile Gas Service Corp.

National Fuel Gas Co.

NICOR, Inc.

North Carolina Natural Gas

Northwest Natural Gas Co.

Peoples Energy Corp.

Piedmont Natural Gas Co.

Questar Corp.

South Jersey Industries, Inc.

Southeastern Michigan Gas Enterprises

United Cities Gas Co.

Valley Resources, Inc.

Washington Energy Co.

Washington Gas Light Co.

WICOR, Inc.

Wisconsin Southern Gas Co., Inc.

Office Supplies

American Business Products, Inc.

Moore Corp. Ltd.

Reynolds & Reynolds Co.

Oil

Amoco Corp.

Atlantic Richfield Co.

British Petroleum Plc

Chevron Corp.

Exxon Corp.

Imperial Oil Ltd.

Kerr-McGee Corp.

Mobil Corp.

Texaco, Inc.

Paper

Alco Standard Corp.

International Paper Co.

Kimberly-Clark Corp.

Potlatch Corp.

Scott Paper Co.

Union Camp Corp.

Westvaco Corp.

Photo Equipment

Eastman Kodak Co.

Pollution Control

Browning-Ferris Industries, Inc.
Chemical Waste Management, Inc.
Waste Management, Inc.
Zurn Industries, Inc.

Printing

American Greetings Corp.
Banta Corp.
Donnelley, R. R., & Sons Co.

Property Liability

Chubb Corp.
Cincinnati Financial Corp.
General RE Corp.
Hartford Steam Boiler Inspection &
     Insurance Co.
Marsh & McLennan Companies, Inc.
Ohio Casualty Corp.
St. Paul Companies, Inc.

Publishing

Dow Jones & Co., Inc.
Gannett Co., Inc.
Knight-Ridder, Inc.
McGraw-Hill, Inc.
Media General, Inc.
New York Times Co.
Time Warner, Inc.

Rails

Consolidated Rail Corp.
CSX Corp.

Norfolk Southern Corp.
Union Pacific Corp.

Real Estate Investment Trust

Washington Real Estate Investment
     Trust

Restaurants

Bob Evans Farms, Inc.
Luby's Cafeterias, Inc.
McDonald's Corp.

Retail Department Stores

Dayton-Hudson Corp.
Limited, The, Inc.
Penney, J. C., Co., Inc.
Sears, Roebuck & Co.

School Supplies

Jostens, Inc.

Services

Block, H & R, Inc.
Equifax, Inc.
Rollins, Inc.
Total System Services, Inc.

Soap Companies

Clorox Co.
Colgate-Palmolive Co.
Procter & Gamble Co.

Soft Drink

Coca-Cola Co.
PepsiCo, Inc.

Steel

Lukens, Inc.

Nucor Corp.

Worthington Industries, Inc.

Tobacco

American Brands, Inc.

Philip Morris Companies, Inc.

Universal Corp.

UST, Inc.

Trucking

Roadway Services, Inc.

Water Utilities

American Water Works Co., Inc.

California Water Service Co.

Consumers Water Co.

Middlesex Water Co.

Southern California Water Co.

Southwest Water Co.

United Water Resources, Inc.

Appendix C

Over-the-Counter Companies Offering DRIPs

Although most investors think of DRIPs as being the domain of large, New York Stock Exchange issues, that isn't necessarily the case. Many firms whose stocks trade on the over-the-counter markets offer DRIPs. Since commissions can be especially large on NASDAQ stocks, in part because of limited liquidity and wide bid and ask spreads in some cases, the commission savings can be even more dramatic. The issues here are all listed on the NASDAQ market. Investors should pay attention to the performance ratings (in parentheses) when making investment decisions among these stocks.

Allied Group, Inc. (**)

AMCORE Financial, Inc. (**)

Ameribanc, Inc. (**)

American Colloid Company (**)

American Filtrona Corp. (**)

American Greetings Corp. (***)

American Recreation Centers, Inc. (**)

Ameritrust Corp. (**)

AmVestors Financial Corp. (**)

Arrow Financial Corp. (**)

Associated Banc-Corp. (***)

Bangor Hydro-Electric Co. (**)

Bank of Granite Corp. (NR)

Bank South Corp. (**)

Bankers First Corp. (NR)

Banks of Mid-America, Inc. (**)

Banta Corp. (***)

BayBanks, Inc. (**)

BB&T Financial Corp. (***)

Berkshire Gas Co. (**)

BMJ Financial Corp. (**)

Boatmen's Bancshares, Inc. (***)

Bob Evans Farms, Inc. (***)

Boston Bancorp (**)

Braintree Savings Bank, The (**)

BSB Bancorp, Inc. (NR)

California Water Service Co. (***)

CCB Financial Corp. (***)

CCNB Corp. (***)

Centerbank (NR)

Central Fidelity Banks, Inc. (****)

Central Holding Co. (*)

Central Jersey Bancorp (NR)

Charter One Financial, Inc. (NR)

Chemical Financial Corp. (NR)

Chittenden Corp. (NR)

Cincinnati Financial Corp. (***)

Citizens Bancorp (NR)

Clarcor, Inc. (***)

CNB Bancshares, Inc. (NR)

Coca-Cola Bottling Co. Consolidated (**)

Colonial BancGroup, Inc. (AL) (**)

Colonial Gas Co. (***)

Colorado National Bankshares, Inc. (**)

Community Bank System, Inc. (NY) (NR)

Connecticut Water Service, Inc. (**)

Constellation Bancorp (**)

Consumers Water Co. (***)

CoreStates Financial Corp. (***)

Crestar Financial Corp. (**)

Cross & Trecker Corp. (**)

Delta Natural Gas Co., Inc. (**)

Dominion Bankshares Corp. (**)

Duriron Co., Inc. (**)

E'Town Corp. (**)

Eastland Financial Corp. (*)

Elco Industries, Inc. (**)

EnergyNorth, Inc. (***)

Engraph, Inc. (***)

F & M Financial Services Corp. (**)

F & M National Corp. (VA) (NR)

FB & T Corp. (NR)

Fifth Third Bancorp (****)

Figgie International, Inc. (**)

First Alabama Bancshares, Inc. (***)

First American Corp. (TN) (*)

First Bancorp. of Ohio (***)

First Colonial Bankshares Corp. (***)

First Commerce Corp. (**)

First Eastern Corp. (NR)

First Financial Holdings, Inc. (NR)

First Harrisburg Bancor, Inc. (NR)

First Illinois Corp. (**)

First Michigan Bank Corp. (***)

First Midwest Bancorp, Inc. (**)

First National Bank Corp. (MI) (NR)

First Security Corp. (***)

First Security Corp. of Kentucky (**)

First Tennessee National Corp. (**)

Fourth Financial Corp. (***)

Fuller, H. B., Co. (***)

Fulton Financial Corp. (NR)

Goulds Pumps, Inc. (***)

Great Lakes Bancorp, FSB (**)

Haverfield Corp. (NR)

Heritage Financial Corp. (NR)

Huntington Bancshares, Inc. (***)

Imperial Bancorp (**)

INB Financial Corp. (**)

Independence Bancorp (PA) (**)

Independent Bank Corp. (MA) (*)

Independent Bank Corp. (MI) (NR)

Integra Financial Corp. (NR)

Investors Financial Corp. (*)

IWC Resources Corp. (**)

Jefferson Bankshares, Inc. (NR)

Justin Industries, Inc. (**)

Kaman Corp. (**)

Key Centurion Bancshares, Inc. (NR)

Keystone Financial, Inc. (NR)

Keystone Heritage Group, Inc. (NR)

Lakeland First Financial Group, Inc. (NR)

Lance, Inc. (***)

Liberty National Bancorp, Inc. (NR)

Lincoln Telecommunications Co. (***)

Liz Claiborne, Inc. (***)

MacDermid, Inc. (**)

Madison Gas & Electric Co. (***)

Magna Group, Inc. (**)

Manufacturers National Corp. (***)

Mark Twain Bancshares, Inc. (***)

Marsh Supermarkets, Inc. (***)

Marshall & Ilsley Corp. (***)

MASSBANK Corp. (NR)

McCormick & Co., Inc. (***)

Medalist Industries, Inc. (**)

Mellon Participating Mortgage Trust (NR)

Mercantile Bancorp, Inc. (**)

Mercantile Bankshares Corp. (***)

Meridian Bancorp, Inc. (**)

Merrimack Bancorp, Inc. (*)

Merry Land & Investment Co., Inc. (*)

Michigan National Corp. (**)

Middlesex Water Co. (***)

Midlantic Corp. (**)

Mobile Gas Service Corp. (***)

Modine Manufacturing Co. (**)

Multibank Financial Corp. (*)

Nash-Finch Co. (***)

National Commerce Bancorp (TN) (NR)

National Community Banks, Inc. (NJ) (**)

National Data Corp. (**)

NBSC Corp. (NR)

New Hampshire Savings Bank Corp. (*)

Nooney Realty Trust, Inc. (NR)

Nordson Corp. (***)

North Carolina Natural Gas Corp. (***)

Northeast Bancorp, Inc. (CT) (*)

Northwest Illinois Bancorp, Inc. (***)

Northwest Natural Gas Co. (***)

Numerica Financial Corp. (*)

Ohio Casualty Corp. (***)

Old National Bancorp (IN) (NR)

Old Stone Corp. (**)

Otter Tail Power Co. (***)

Pentair, Inc. (**)

Piccadilly Cafeterias, Inc. (**)

Portsmouth Bank Shares, Inc. (NR)

Premier Bancorp, Inc. (*)

Preston Corp. (**)

Public Service Co. of North Carolina (***)

Puget Sound Bancorp (NR)

Raymond Corp. (**)

Regional Bancorp, Inc. (NR)

Roadway Services, Inc. (***)

Rose's Stores, Inc. (*)

Rouse Co. (**)

RPM, Inc. (***)

St. Paul Bancorp, Inc. (**)

St. Paul Companies, Inc. (**)

Savannah Foods & Industries, Inc. (***)

Seafield Capital Corp. (NR)

Security Bancorp, Inc. (MI) (***)

Seibels Bruce Group, Inc. (*)

Selective Insurance Group, Inc. (**)

Simpson Industries, Inc. (**)

Society Corp. (***)

Sonoco Products Co. (***)

South Carolina National Corp. (**)

Southeastern Michigan Gas Enterprises (***)

Southern California Water Co. (***)

SouthTrust Corp. (***)

Southwest Water Co. (***)

Southwestern Electric Service Co. (***)

Star Banc Corp. (***)

State Street Boston Corp. (***)

Suffolk Bancorp (NR)

Sumitomo Bank of California (NR)

Summit Bancorporation (NJ) (**)

Summit Holding Corp. (WV) (NR)

Sunwest Financial Services, Inc. (NR)

Susquehanna Bancshares, Inc. (NR)

Union Bank (***)

United Carolina Bancshares Corp. (NR)

United Cities Gas Co. (***)

United States Bancorp (***)

United States Trust Corp. (***)

Upper Peninsula Energy Corp. (***)

USP Real Estate Investment Trust (NR)

UST Corp. (**)

Valley Bancorporation (WI) (***)

Valley National Bancorp (NJ) (NR)

Vermont Financial Services Corp. (NR)

Volunteer Bancshares, Inc. (NR)

Washington Energy Co. (***)

Washington Mutual Savings Bank (NR)

West One Bancorp (NR)

Wetterau, Inc. (***)

Wilmington Trust Co. (***)

Wisconsin Southern Gas Co., Inc. (***)

Worthington Industries, Inc. (***)

York Financial Corp. (NR)

Zions Bancorporation (**)

Appendix D
Closed-End Funds With DRIPs

I'm sure most of you are familiar with mutual funds. These are investment companies which take in funds from many individuals, commingle the money, and buy a portfolio of stocks which they manage. There are two types of mutual funds, open-end and closed-end funds.

Open-end mutual funds have surged in popularity in the last decade. These funds provide a way for investors with limited dollars — many mutual funds have minimum investments of just $100 to $1000 — to have portfolio diversification as well as professional money management. Some of the big open-end fund families are Fidelity, Vanguard, T. Rowe Price, Scudder, Dreyfus, and Oppenheimer.

Closed-end funds are similar to open-end funds in that the funds permit investment in a basket of stocks selected and managed by an investment company. However, there are a few major differences. Open-end funds continually sell new shares to the public and redeem shares at the fund's net asset value — the market value of the firm's portfolio of stocks minus short-term liabilities. Closed-end funds, however, sell only a certain number of shares at the initial public offering, just like a stock. Once the shares are sold, the fund is "closed," and new money is not accepted.

Another major difference is that closed-end funds trade on the stock exchanges, while open-end funds do not. Because they are publicly traded, the prices of closed-end funds are set by supply and demand among various investors, just like common stocks. Thus, unlike open-end funds which always redeem shares at the net asset value, it is not unusual to see a closed-end mutual fund which is trading above or below its net asset value, and sometimes these premiums or discounts are quite large.

Analysts and academicians have explored several possible explanations for the disparity between the trading price of a closed-end fund and its net asset value. One reason is that closed-end funds have large potential tax liabilities in the form of unrealized capital gains. Therefore, this tax liability is factored into the price of the closed-end funds and thus reduces the price. Other reasons given for the disparity between a closed-end fund's price and net asset value include the potential pricing problems for fund investments that may not trade frequently (and where current prices to establish net asset value are, at best, estimates of the true value of the investment); poor diversification, as in the case of closed-end funds that invest in the stocks of a single country; and the lack of flexibility on the part of the managers because of the fixed capitalization of closed-end funds.

Regardless of the reasons, the fact is that in many instances, closed-end funds allow investors to buy a basket of stocks more cheaply than if the stocks in that basket were purchased separately.

Great, you're thinking, but what's all this have to do with DRIPs? Well, many closed-end funds offer DRIPs for their shareholders, and investing in a closed-end fund through a DRIP presents some interesting possibilities.

First, if the closed-end fund is trading at a discount to net asset value, reinvesting your dividends received from the stocks held in the closed-end fund, in effect, lets you purchase a basket of stocks at a discount. Also, keep in mind that those dividends are being earned on the full value of the assets of the fund.

For example, let's say you purchase a closed-end fund with a net asset value of $35 per share, that is trading for $25 per share—a 28 percent discount (discounts, especially during bear markets, may reach or even exceed this level). Now, the dividends on the investments in the fund come to a total of $2 per share, giving the fund a yield of 5.7 percent ($2 in dividends divided by the net asset value of $35). But remember, you only paid $25 per share for this basket of stocks that are worth $35 per share. Thus, the yield on your investment is even higher—8 percent.

Now, you reinvest the dividend via the fund's DRIP. That $2 per share in dividends is invested to purchase additional shares of the closed-end fund at a discount to the net asset value. Now, over time the closed-end fund closes the gap to a price which is a 10 percent discount to the net asset value ($31.50). You now have a gain of 26 percent on all shares purchased at $25 per share.

In addition to reinvested dividends, several closed-end funds permit optional cash payments (OCPs). If the fund is trading at a discount, these voluntary funds will, in some cases, be invested at a price which is lower than the net asset value of the fund.

How do you know if a closed-end fund is trading at discount or premium? Such information is given regularly in *The Wall Street Journal* and *Barron's.*

What are some factors to consider when investing in a closed-end fund?

- Merely because a closed-end fund is trading at a discount doesn't make it a good investment. It is important to evaluate if the fund meets your investment objective, abides by an investment strategy that makes sense to you, and fits in with the rest of your portfolio. This latter factor is crucial. For example, if your only investment is going to be a closed-end fund, it probably isn't a good idea to buy a single-country, closed-end fund.

- Never buy a closed-end fund at the initial public offering. Most closed-end funds perform poorly immediately following the initial public offering. Of course, there are exceptions. Still, you'll probably dodge a bullet or two by waiting and taking a fresh look at the find 6 months or so after it is issued.

- Avoid investing in closed-end funds that are trading at premiums to their net asset values. Remember, since closed-end funds trade on the exchanges, their prices are governed by supply and demand. If a particular sector gets hot and investors flock to the group, such as international closed-end funds in the late 1980s, these funds can trade at steep premiums. However, you wouldn't pay $25 for a $20 shirt. Why should you pay $25 per share for a basket of stocks worth $20 per share?

The closed-end funds listed here offer DRIPs. Investors should obtain prospectuses on plans of interest before investing.

1838 Bond-Debenture Trading Fund
(NYSE:BDF)
c/o Bank of New York
P.O. Box 11234, Church St. Sta.
New York, NY 10277
(212) 963-3559

ACM Government Income Fund,
Inc. (NYSE:ACG)
1345 Ave. of the Americas
New York, NY 10105
(800) 426-5523

ACM Government Opportunity
   Fund, Inc. (NYSE:AOF)
1345 Ave. of the Americas
New York, NY 10105
(800) 426-5523

ACM Government Securities Fund,
   Inc. (NYSE:GSF)
1345 Ave. of the Americas
New York, NY 10105
(800) 426-5523

ACM Government Spectrum Fund,
   Inc. (NYSE:SI)
1345 Ave. of the Americas
New York, NY 10105
(800) 426-5523

ACM Managed Income Fund, Inc.
   (NYSE:AMF)
1345 Ave. of the Americas
New York, NY 10105
(800) 426-5523

Adams Express Co. (NYSE:ADX)
c/o Bank of New York
P.O. Box 11234, Church St. Sta.
New York, NY 10249
(800) 524-4458

Allstate Muni Income Opportunities
   Trust (NYSE:AMO)
Two World Trade Center, 71st Floor
New York, NY 10048
(800) 869-3863

American Capital Bond Fund, Inc.
   (NYSE:ACB)
P.O. Box 1411
2800 Post Oak Blvd.
Houston, TX 77056
(800) 421-9696

American Capital Convertible
   Securities, Inc. (NYSE:ACS)
2800 Post Oak Blvd.
Houston, TX 77056
(800) 421-9696

American Capital Income Trust
   (NYSE:ACD)
2800 Post Oak Blvd.
Houston, TX 77056
(800) 421-9696

AMEV Securities, Inc. (NYSE:AMV)
P.O. Box 64284
St. Paul, MN 55164
(800) 800-2638

ASA Limited (NYSE:ASA)
c/o First Chicago Trust Co-NY
P.O. Box 3506, Church St. Sta.
New York, NY 10008-3506
(212) 791-6422

Baker, Fentress & Co. (NYSE:BKF)
Harris Trust & Savings Bank
P.O. Box A3309 - Dividend
   Reinvestment
Chicago, IL 60690
(312) 236-9190

Bancroft Convertible Fund, Inc.
   (ASE:BCV)
Suite 1310
56 Pine Street
New York, NY 10005
(212) 269-9236

Blue Chip Value Fund (NYSE:BLU)
Suite 1800
633 17th St.
Denver, CO 80270
(800) 288-9541

Bunker Hill Income Securities, Inc.
  (NYSE:BHL)
c/o Bankers Trust Co.
P.O. Box 9050, Church St. Sta.
New York, NY 10249
(212) 229-1290

Capital Southwest Corp.
  (NASDAQ:CSWC)
Suite 700
12900 Preston Rd.
Dallas, TX 75230
(214) 233-8242

Castle Convertible Fund, Inc.
  (ASE:CVF)
75 Maiden Lane
New York, NY 10038
(212) 806-8800

Charles Allmon Trust, The, Inc.
  (NYSE:GSO)
4405 East-West Highway
Bethesda, MD 20814
(301) 986-5866

Circle Income Shares, Inc.
  (NASDAQ:CINS)
c/o Bank One, Indianapolis
111 Monument Circle
Indianapolis, IN 46277
(317) 321-8180

CNA Income Shares, Inc.
  (NYSE:CNN)
CNA Plaza
Chicago, IL 60685
(312) 822-4181

Colonial High Income Municipal
  Trust (NYSE:CXE)
One Financial Center
Boston, MA 02111
(800) 426-3750

Colonial Investment Grade
  Municipal Trust (NYSE:CXH)
c/o Bank of Boston
P.O. Box 644
Boston, MA 02102
(800) 426-3750   (800) 442-2001

Counsellors Tandem Securities
  Fund, Inc. (NYSE:CTF)
466 Lexington Ave.
New York, NY 10017-3147
(800) 888-6878

Current Income Shares Inc.
  (NYSE:CUR)
c/o Union Bank-Los Angeles
P.O. Box 2461
Los Angeles, CA 90051
(818) 895-4560

Cypress Fund, Inc. (ASE:WJR)
1285 Ave. of the Americas
New York, NY 10019
(212) 713-2000

Dean Witter Government Income
  Trust (NYSE:GVT)
Two World Trade Ctr., 71st Floor
New York, NY 10048
(800) 869-3863

Duff & Phelps Selected Utilities
  (NYSE:DNP)
55 East Monroe St. #3800
Chicago, IL 60603
(312) 368-5510

Ellsworth Convertible Growth &
  Income Fund (ASE:ECF)
c/o The Bank of New York
P.O. Box 11002, Church Street Sta.
New York, NY 10277-0702
(800) 524-4458

Excelsior Income Shares Inc.
 (NYSE:EIS)
c/o United States Trust Co.-NY
770 Broadway
New York, NY 10007
(212) 852-3732

First Australia Prime Income Fund,
 Inc. (ASE:FAX)
c/o Boston Financial Data Services
P.O. Box 8200
Boston, MA 02266-8200
(800) 451-6788

First Boston Income Fund, Inc.
 (NYSE:FBF)
P.O. Box 1102, MS 601
Valley Forge, PA 19482-1102
(215) 648-6176

First Financial Fund, Inc.
 (NYSE:FF)
c/o Boston Financial Data Services
P.O. Box 8200
Boston, MA 02266
(800) 451-6788

Fort Dearborn Income Securities,
 Inc. (NYSE:FTD)
First Chicago Trust Co.-NY
30 West Broadway
New York, NY 10007
(800) 446-2617

Germany Fund, Inc. (NYSE:GER)
Deutsche Bank Building
31 West 52d St.
New York, NY 10019
(800) 642-0144

Global Yield Fund Inc. (NYSE:PGY)
c/o Boston Financial Data Services
P.O. Box 8200
Boston, MA 02266
(800) 451-6788

Growth Stock Outlook Trust, Inc.
 (NYSE:GSO)
4405 East-West Highway
Bethesda, MD 20814
(301) 986-5866

Hatteras Income Securities, Inc.
 (NYSE:HAT)
c/o C & S Sovran Trust Co.
P.O. Box 105555
Atlanta, GA 30348-5555
(800) 772-5564

High Income Advantage Trust
 (NYSE:YLD)
Two World Trade Center, 71st Floor
New York, NY 10048
(800) 869-3863

INA Investment Securities, Inc.
 (NYSE:IIS)
c/o Northeast Utilities Services Co.
Shareholder Services
P.O. Box 5006
Hartford, CT 06102-5006
(800) 999-7269   (203) 665-4801

InterCapital Income Securities, Inc.
 (NYSE:ICB)
Two World Trade Center, 71st Floor
New York, NY 10048
(800) 869-3863

Italy Fund Inc. (The) (NYSE:ITA)
31 W. 52d St., 11th Floor
New York, NY 10019
(212) 767-3034

John Hancock Investors Trust
 (NYSE:JHI)
101 Huntington Ave.
Boston, MA 02199
(617) 375-1760

Kleinwort Benson Australian
  Income Fund, Inc. (NYSE:KBA)
200 Park Ave.
New York, NY 10166
(800) 237-4218

Korea Fund, Inc. (NYSE:KF)
Boston Financial
P.O. Box 8200
Boston, MA 02266-8200
(617) 328-5000

Landsing Pacific Fund (ASE:LPF)
155 Bovet Rd. #101
San Mateo, CA 94402
(415) 321-7100

Liberty All-Star Equity Fund
  (NYSE:USA)
600 Atlantic Avenue
Boston, MA 02210
(617) 722-6000   (800) 542-3863

Lincoln National Convertible
  Securities (NYSE:LNV)
First National Bank of Boston
P.O. Box 1681
Boston, MA 02105
(617) 575-2000

Lincoln National Income Fund
  (NYSE:LND)
P.O. Box 1110
Fort Wayne, IN 46801
(219) 427-2056

Lomas Mortgage Securities Fund
  (NYSE:LSF)
P.O. Box 655644
2001 Bryan Tower
Dallas, TX 75265-5644
(214) 746-8240

Malaysia Fund, Inc. (NYSE:MF)
P.O. Box 1102
Valley Forge, PA 19482-1102
(617) 575-2900

MassMutual Corporate Investors
  (NYSE:MCI)
c/o First National Bank of Boston
P.O. Box 1681
Boston, MA 02105
(413) 788-8411

MassMutual Participation Investors
  (NYSE:MPV)
Bank of Boston - Dividend Agent
P.O. Box 1681
Boston, MA 02105
(617) 929-6585

MFS Multimarket Income Trust
  (NYSE:MMT)
500 Boylston St.
Boston, MA 02116
(800) 637-2304

MFS Municipal Income Trust
  (NYSE:MFM)
c/o State Street Bank and Trust
P.O. Box 366
Boston, MA 02101
(800) 637-2304

Montgomery Street Income
  Securities, Inc. (NYSE:MTS)
First National Bank of Boston
P.O. Box 1681
Boston, MA 02105
(617) 575-2000

Morgan Grenfell Smallcap Fund,
  Inc. (NYSE:MGC)
Suite 1740
885 Third Ave.
New York, NY 10022-4802
(212) 230-2600

Mutual of Omaha Interest Shares,
  Inc. (NYSE:MUO)
10235 Regency Circle
Omaha, NE 68114
(402) 397-8555

New America High Income Fund,
  Inc. (NYSE:HYB)
c/o State Street Bank & Trust
P.O. Box 366
Boston, MA 02101
(800) 426-5523

Niagara Share Corp. (NYSE:NGS)
c/o Mellon Securities
P.O. Box 470 Washington Bridge Sta.
New York, NY 10033
(201) 592-4074

Oppenheimer Multi-Sector Income
  Trust (NYSE:OMS)
State Street Bank & Trust Co.
P.O. Box 366
Boston, MA 02101
(800) 426-5523   (617) 328-5000

Pacific American Income Shares,
  Inc. (NYSE:PAI)
P.O. Box 983
Pasadena, CA 91102
(818) 584-4326

Petroleum & Resources Corp.
  (NYSE:PEO)
Suite 1140
7 Saint Paul St.
Baltimore, MD 21202
(301) 752-5900

RAC Income Fund, Inc.
  (NYSE:RMF)
P.O. Box 4000
10221 Wincopin Circle
Columbia, MD 21044
(301) 730-7222

Revere Fund, Inc. (NASDAQ:PREV)
18th Floor
575 Fifth Ave.
New York, NY 10017
(212) 661-5290

Salomon Brothers Fund, Inc.
  (NYSE:SBF)
38th Floor
7 World Trade Center
New York, NY 10048
(800) 725-6666

Scudder New Asia Fund, Inc.
  (NYSE:SAF)
345 Park Ave.
New York, NY 10154
(617) 328-5000

Source Capital, Inc. (NYSE:SOR)
c/o Manufacturers Hanover
P.O. Box 24850, Church St. Sta.
New York, NY 10249
(212) 613-7144

State Mutual Securities Trust
  (NYSE:SMS)
440 Lincoln St.
Worcester, MA 01605
(508) 852-1000

Taiwan Fund, Inc. (NYSE:TWN)
c/o State Street Bank
P.O. Box 366
Boston, MA 02101
(800) 426-5523

TCW Convertible Securities Fund,
  Inc. (NYSE:CVT)
400 S. Hope St.
Los Angeles, CA 90071
(800) 524-4458

Templeton Global Income Fund,
 Inc. (NYSE:GIM)
P.O. Box 33030
St. Petersburg, FL 33733-8030
(813) 823-8712

Thai Fund, Inc. (NYSE:TTF)
P.O. Box 1102
Valley Forge, PA 19482
(215) 648-6000

Transamerica Income Shares
 (NYSE:TAI)
Mellon Securities Trust Co.
Shareholder Investment Services
P.O. Box 444
Pittsburgh, PA 15230-0444
(800) 288-9541

Tri-Continental Corp. (NYSE:TY)
130 Liberty St.
New York, NY 10006
(212) 488-0200

USLIFE Income Fund, Inc.
 (NYSE:UIF)
c/o Manufacturers Hanover Trust Co.
Dividend Reinvestment Department
P.O. Box 24850, Church St. Sta.
New York, NY 10242
(212) 613-7147

Van Kampen Merritt Municipal
 Income Trust (NYSE:VMT)
1001 Warrenville Road
Lisle, IL 60532
(708) 719-6000

Vestaur Securities, Inc. (NYSE:VES)
Center Square West, 11th Floor
P.O. Box 7558
Philadelphia, PA 19101-7558
(215) 567-3969

Worldwide Value Fund, Inc.
 (NYSE:VLU)
P.O. Box 1476
Baltimore, MD 21203
(301) 539-3400

Zweig Fund, Inc. (NYSE:ZF)
c/o Bank of New York
Dividend Reinvestment
P.O. Box 11234, Church St. Sta.
New York, NY 10277-0734
(800) 524-4458

Zweig Total Return Fund, Inc.
 (NYSE:ZTR)
900 Third Ave.
New York, NY 10022
(212) 486-7110

Buying Treasury Securities Without a Broker

Let's face it—for some people, you'd have to hold a gun to their heads to get them to buy stocks. They just won't do it. The reasons are many:

- "I can't afford stocks." (A feeble excuse in light of the low-cost investing opportunities with DRIPs)

- "Stocks are just too volatile for me." (Again, a lame excuse if you take into account the magic of dollar-cost averaging and prudent portfolio diversification)

- "I need to generate risk-free income since I use all of the interest from my investments for living expenses." (Tough to quibble with this one)

- "I was burned by one of my broker's tips, and I'm never going to go through a broker again." (What's the name of this book?)

For these people, treasury securities hold special appeal because of their high yields and safety. Many people purchase treasuries through their brokers or local banks. But this doesn't have to be the case. There's a way to buy treasury securities without using a broker and paying commissions. But before we get into how to do this, let's define some terms for those individuals who may not be familiar with treasury securities.

Treasury Bills, Notes, and Bonds

We've all heard politicians and economists discuss the federal deficit. But it is still one of those topics that if your son saddles up and asks you to explain it, you'd probably tell him to go ask your spouse. I'll admit, it's tough to get a handle on it. But basically, the deficit represents the amount government outlays exceed revenues. Now you might wonder how the government can get away with running a deficit indefinitely while you or I would be behind bars or in bankruptcy court in no time flat. The answer is quite simple — Uncle Sam can float securities to cover the difference between revenues and outlays. The department in charge of this "debt management" is the U.S. Treasury. The Treasury raises much of its funds by selling marketable securities to John Q. Public. These securities are treasury bills, notes, and bonds, and they are sold at auctions conducted by the Treasury Department.

The major differences between treasury bills, notes, and bonds are their maturities. Treasury bills are short-term obligations with a term of 1 year or less. Treasury notes have maturities of 1 to 10 years. Treasury bonds have maturities greater than 10 years. The securities also differ in the minimum denominations in which they are issued. Notes maturing in 4 years or longer, as well as all bonds, are usually available in minimum denominations of $1000. Notes maturing in less than 4 years are issued in minimum denominations of $5000. Treasury bills are sold in minimum amounts of $10,000. One final difference is the payment of interest. Treasury notes and bonds pay interest twice a year. Treasury bills do not pay a stated interest rate. Rather, bills are sold at a discount to par, and the difference between the purchase price of the bill and the amount which the owner is paid at maturity (par) represents the interest.

Treasury securities are popular for a variety of reasons. Since treasuries are backed by the full taxing power of the federal government, the interest and return of principal are fully guaranteed. Best of all, interest earned on treasury securities is exempt from state and local taxes, although it is subject to federal income tax.

Buy Treasuries Directly From the Fed

Most investors purchase treasury securities through a broker or local bank. Purchasing fees will vary. My bank charges the following fees for purchasing a $10,000 treasury security (this is the minimum amount they will purchase):

- $55 handling and other fees
- $10 "maturity fee"
- $1 per month safekeeping fee if you want the bank to hold the security.

To put these fees in perspective, say you purchase a 5-year note. Your total fees, assuming you have the bank hold the security, would be $125 — roughly 1 1/4 percent of your investment. This isn't necessarily a huge amount, although such fees do eat away at the interest you earn on the investment.

But investors who are willing to fill out some forms and spring for some stamps can pocket these fees by purchasing treasuries directly through branches of the Federal Reserve Board (see Figure E-1).

The procedure for purchasing securities directly is simple. Treasury securities are sold via an auction process, with notices of upcoming auctions featured in *The Wall Street Journal*. Treasury bills are auctioned usually weekly, and most notes and bonds are auctioned quarterly (see Figure E-2).

Prospective purchasers may apply in person at a branch of the Federal Reserve Board if one is close to where you live or through writing to the Fed. The form used to apply is called a tender. An investor can obtain tenders from the Federal Reserve Board.

If an individual doesn't have a tender, he or she can still apply by sending a new account form (see Figure E-3) and a letter with the following information (this procedure is for purchasing notes or bonds):

- Name and address
- Telephone number
- Type and amount of securities desired
- Whether the bid is competitive or noncompetitive (I'll explain this shortly)
- Preference for form in which securities are to be issued, name(s) for registration, and the social security number(s) must be furnished
- Direct deposit information: name of purchaser's financial institution, routing number of the financial institution, account name, number and type (checking or savings)
- Purchaser's signature

Individuals should also include the payment, either in cash, certified personal check, bank check, or check issued by credit union, made payable to the Federal Reserve Bank where the information and payment are being sent (most likely the closest Federal Reserve Bank to you). On

For In-Person Visits	For Written Correspondence	For In-Person Visits	For Written Correspondence
Atlanta 104 Marietta Street, N.W. Atlanta, GA 404-521-8653 404-521-8657 (recording)	FRB Atlanta 104 Marietta Street, N.W. Atlanta, GA 30303	**Denver** 1020 16th Street Denver, CO 303-572-2477 303-572-2475 (recording)	Denver Branch FRB of Kansas City PO Box 5228 Terminal Annex Denver, CO 80217
Baltimore 502 South Sharp Street Baltimore, MD 301-576-3553 301-576-3500 (recording)	Baltimore Branch FRB of Richmond PO Box 1378 Baltimore, MD 21203	**Detroit** 160 West Fort Street Detroit, MI 313-964-6157 313-963-4936 (recording)	Detroit Branch FRB of Chicago PO Box 1059 Detroit, MI 48231
Birmingham 1801 Fifth Avenue, North Birmingham, AL 205-731-8702	Birmingham Branch FRB Atlanta PO Box 830447 Birmingham, AL 35283-0447	**El Paso** 301 East Main Street El Paso, TX Call Dallas 214-651-6362 214-651-6177 (recording)	El Paso Branch FRB of Dallas PO Box 100 El Paso, TX 79999
Boston 600 Atlantic Avenue Boston, MA 617-973-3810 617-973-3805 (recording)	FRB of Boston PO Box 2076 Boston, MA 02106	*Helena*—The Helena Branch of the Federal Reserve Bank of Minneapolis does not deal in Treasury securities. Persons in the area served by the Helena Branch should instead contact the Minneapolis office listed in this Appendix.	
Buffalo 160 Delaware Avenue Buffalo, NY 716-849-5079 716-849-5030 (recording)	Buffalo Branch FRB of New York PO Box 961 Buffalo NY 14240	**Houston** 1701 San Jacinto Street Houston, TX 713-659-4433 713-652-1688 (recording)	Houston Branch FRB of Dallas PO Box 2578 Houston, TX 77252
Charlotte 530 East Trade Street Charlotte, NC 704-358-2410 or 2411 704-358-2424 (recording)	Charlotte Branch FRB of Richmond PO Box 30248 Charlotte, NC 28230	**Jacksonville** 800 West Water Street Jacksonville, FL 904-632-1179	Jacksonville Branch FRB of Atlanta PO Box 2499 Jacksonville, FL 32231-2499
Chicago 230 South LaSalle Street Chicago, IL 312-322-5369 312-786-1110 (recording)	FRB of Chicago PO Box 834 Chicago, IL 60690	**Kansas City** 925 Grand Avenue Kansas City, MO 816-881-2783 or 2409 816-881-2767 (recording)	FRB of Kansas City Attn. Securities Dept. PO Box 419440 Kansas City, MO 64141-6440
Cincinnati 150 East Fourth Street Cincinnati, OH 513-721-4787 Ext. 333	Cincinnati Branch FRB of Cleveland PO Box 999 Cincinnati, OH 45201	**Little Rock** 325 West Capitol Avenue Little Rock, AR 501-372-5451 Ext. 288	Little Rock Branch FRB of St. Louis PO Box 1261 Little Rock AR 72203
Cleveland 1455 East Sixth Street Cleveland, OH 216-579-2490	FRB of Cleveland PO Box 6387 Cleveland, OH 44101	**Los Angeles** 950 South Grand Avenue Los Angeles, CA 213-624-7398 213-688-0068 (recording)	Los Angeles Branch FRB of San Francisco PO Box 2077 Terminal Annex Los Angeles, CA 90051
Dallas 400 South Akard Street Dallas, TX 214-651-6362 214-651-6177 (recording)	FRB of Dallas Securities Dept. Station K Dallas, TX 75222	**Louisville** 410 South Fifth Street Louisville, KY 502-568-9236 or 9231	Louisville Branch FRB of St. Louis PO Box 32710 Louisville, KY 40232

Figure E-1. Addresses and telephone numbers of Federal Reserve Banks and Treasury servicing offices. (*From Federal Reserve Book, Buying Treasury Securities*)

For In-Person Visits	For Written Correspondence	For In-Person Visits	For Written Correspondence
Memphis 200 North Main Street Memphis, TN 901-523-7171 Ext. 622 or 629 Ext. 641 (recording)	Memphis Branch FRB of St. Louis PO Box 407 Memphis, TN 38101	**Portland** 915 S.W. Stark Street Portland, OR 503-221-5932 503-221-5921 (recording)	Portland Branch FRB of San Francisco PO Box 3436 Portland, OR 97208-3436
Miami 9100 N.W. 36th Street Miami, FL 305-471-6497	Miami Branch FRB of Atlanta PO Box 520847 Miami, FL 33152-0847	**Richmond** 701 East Byrd Street Richmond, VA 804-697-8372 804-697-8355 (recording)	FRB of Richmond PO Box 27622 Richmond, VA 23261-7622
Minneapolis 250 Marquette Avenue Minneapolis, MN 612-340-2075	FRB of Minneapolis PO Box 491 Minneapolis, MN 55480	**Salt Lake City** 120 South State Street Salt Lake City, UT 801-322-7944 801-322-7911 (recording)	Salt Lake City Branch FRB of San Francisco PO Box 30780 Salt Lake City, UT 84130
Nashville 301 Eighth Avenue, North Nashville, TN 615-251-7100	Nashville Branch FRB of Atlanta 301 Eighth Avenue, North Nashville, TN 37203	**San Antonio** 126 East Nueva Street San Antonio, TX 512-978-1305 or 1309 512-978-1330 (recording)	San Antonio Branch FRB of Dallas PO Box 1471 San Antonio, TX 78295
New Orleans 525 St. Charles Avenue New Orleans, LA 504-586-1505 Ext. 293 or 294	New Orleans Branch FRB of Atlanta PO Box 61630 New Orleans, LA 70161	**San Francisco** 101 Market Street San Francisco, CA 415-974-2330 415-974-3491 (recording)	FRB of San Francisco PO Box 7702 San Francisco, CA 94120-7702
New York 33 Liberty Street New York, NY 212-720-6619 24-hour recording: 212-720-5823 (results) 212-720-7773 (new offerings)	FRB of New York Federal Reserve PO Station New York, NY 10045	**Seattle** 1015 Second Avenue Seattle, WA 206-343-3605 206-343-3615 (recording)	Seattle Branch FRB of San Francisco PO Box 3567 Terminal Annex Seattle, WA 98124
Oklahoma City 226 Dean A. McGee Avenue Oklahoma City, OK 405-270-8652	Oklahoma City Branch FRB of Kansas City PO Box 25129 Oklahoma City, OK 73125	**St. Louis** 411 Locust Street St. Louis, MO 314-444-8665 or 8666 314-444-8602 (recording)	FRB of St. Louis PO Box 442 St. Louis, MO 63166
Omaha 2201 Farnam Street Omaha, NE 402-221-5636	Omaha Branch FRB of Kansas City PO Box 3958 Omaha, NE 68102	**United States Treasury** Washington, DC Bureau of the Public Debt 1300 C Street, S.W. Washington, DC 202-287-4113 Device for hearing impaired: 202-287-4097	 Mail Inquiries to: Bureau of the Public Debt Washington, DC 20239-1000 Mail Tenders to: Bureau of the Public Debt Washington, DC 20239-1500
Philadelphia Ten Independence Mall Philadelphia, PA 215-574-6675 or 6680	FRB of Philadelphia PO Box 90 Philadelphia, PA 19105-0090		
Pittsburgh 717 Grant Street Pittsburgh, PA 412-261-7863 412-261-7988 (recording)	Pittsburgh Branch FRB of Cleveland PO Box 867 Pittsburgh, PA 15230-0867		

Figure E-1. (*Continued*) Addresses and telephone numbers of Federal Reserve Banks and Treasury servicing offices. (*From Federal Reserve Book, Buying Treasury Securities*)

The following is the current pattern of financing for marketable Treasury notes and bonds. The events are listed in the order in which they normally occur. Treasury borrowing requirements, financing policy decisions, and the timing of Congressional action on the debt limit could alter or delay the pattern. This outline is provided solely for reference and is not intended to convey information about any particular Treasury security offering. Treasury issues a press release announcing each offering. Current information on specific upcoming Treasury auctions may be obtained from a Federal Reserve Bank or Branch, from the Bureau of the Public Debt, U.S. Department of the Treasury, or from the financial press.

January:
Announce 7-year note
Auction 7-year note
Issue 7-year note
Announce 2-year and 5-year
  notes
Auction 2-year note
Auction 5-year note
Issue 2-year and 5-year notes

February:
Announce 3-year and 10-year
  notes and 30-year bond
Auction 3-year note
Auction 10-year note
Auction 30-year bond
Issue 3-year and 10-year notes
  and 30-year bond
Announce 2-year and 5-year
  notes
Auction 2-year note
Auction 5-year note
Issue 2-year and 5-year notes

March:
Announce 2-year and 5-year
  notes
Auction 2-year note
Auction 5-year note
Issue 2-year and 5-year notes

April:
Announce 7-year note
Auction 7-year note
Issue 7-year note
Announce 2-year and 5-year
  notes
Auction 2-year note
Auction 5-year note
Issue 2-year and 5-year notes

May:
Announce 3-year and 10-year
  notes and 30-year bond
Auction 3-year note
Auction 10-year note
Auction 30-year bond
Issue 3-year and 10-year
  notes and 30-year bond
Announce 2-year and 5-year
  notes
Auction 2-year note
Auction 5-year note
Issue 2-year and 5-year notes

June:
Announce 2-year and 5-year
  notes
Auction 2-year note
Auction 5-year note
Issue 2-year and 5-year notes

July:
Announce 7-year note
Auction 7-year note
Issue 7-year note
Announce 2-year and 5-year
  notes
Auction 2-year note
Auction 5-year note
Issue 2-year and 5-year notes

August:
Announce 3-year and 10-year
  notes and 30-year bond
Auction 3-year note
Auction 10-year note
Auction 30-year bond
Issue 3-year and 10-year notes
  and 30-year bond
Announce 2-year and 5-year
  notes
Auction 2-year note
Auction 5-year note
Issue 2-year and 5-year notes

September:
Announce 2-year and 5-year
  notes
Auction 2-year note
Auction 5-year note
Issue 2-year and 5-year notes

October:
Announce 7-year note
Auction 7-year note
Issue 7-year note
Announce 2-year and 5-year
  notes
Auction 2-year note
Auction 5-year note
Issue 2-year and 5-year notes

November:
Announce 3-year and 10-year
  notes and 30-year bond
Auction 3-year note
Auction 10-year note
Auction 30-year bond
Issue 3-year and 10-year notes
  and 30-year bond
Announce 2-year and 5-year
  notes
Auction 2-year note
Auction 5-year note
Issue 2-year and 5-year notes

December:
Announce 2-year and 5-year
  notes
Auction 2-year note
Auction 5-year note
Issue 2-year and 5-year notes

Figure E-2. General pattern of treasury note and bond financing by month. (*From Federal Reserve Book*)

the outside of the envelope should be written, "Tender for Treasury Notes (or Bonds or Bills)." Make sure that your payment arrives prior to the auction date listed in the paper.

The procedure of purchasing treasury bills is similar, with just a few wrinkles. Again, applications, or tenders, may be obtained at the Federal Reserve Bank. If you apply without using a tender, you should

PD F 5182
(May 1990)

TREASURY DIRECT®

**INSTRUCTIONS FOR COMPLETING
A NEW ACCOUNT REQUEST**

PURPOSE

You may use this form to establish a TREASURY DIRECT account (without purchasing securities). The Department of the Treasury will establish and maintain your book-entry account for the future deposit of securities. This form cannot be used for the purchase of securities or to request a change to an existing account.

IMPORTANT NOTE

Unless all the required information is provided legibly, there may be a delay in processing your request. To avoid delays, read the instructions carefully and **print clearly in ink only.** Where boxes are provided, enter only one letter or number in each box and leave blank spaces where appropriate.

INVESTOR INFORMATION

ACCOUNT NAME

Enter the name(s) of the owner(s) for whom the TREASURY DIRECT account will be established. Accounts may be established in the names of one or two individuals, an estate, a trust, corporation, association, natural guardian, etc.

ADDRESS

Provide a complete address, including zip code. All mailings including notices, statements and checks, will be sent to this address.

TAXPAYER IDENTIFICATION NUMBER

Provide the taxpayer identification number required on tax returns and other documents submitted to the Internal Revenue Service. For individuals, this is the social security number (SSN) of the person whose name appears FIRST on the account. The SSN of a minor or incompetent is required for accounts established in a fiduciary capacity for these individuals. In the case of a partnership, company, organization or trust, the employer identification number assigned by the IRS is used.

TELEPHONE NUMBERS

Please provide the telephone numbers (including area codes) where you may be contacted if there are questions about this request or your account.

DIRECT DEPOSIT INFORMATION

Enter the following information:
- ROUTING NUMBER (your financial institution's ABA identifying number)
- FINANCIAL INSTITUTION NAME (the name of the institution to which payments are to be made)
- ACCOUNT NUMBER (your account number at your financial institution)
- ACCOUNT TYPE (checking or savings)
- ACCOUNT NAME (the name on the account at your financial institution)

Payments to you will normally be made by direct deposit to the financial institution you designate. Payments will be made by check if a payment is due to you before we have confirmed direct deposit arrangements for your account at the financial institution. If both the TREASURY DIRECT account and the receiving financial institution account are in the names of individuals then at least one of the individuals named on the TREASURY DIRECT account must also be named on the deposit account at the receiving financial institution. The ROUTING NUMBER can be obtained from the institution or found on the bottom line of a check (see example on next page) or deposit slip. When providing your account number, please include hyphens. A hyphen is represented by the symbol ▥ .

Figure E-3. Instructions for completing a new account request. (*From Federal Reserve Book*)

PD F 5182
(May 1990)

TREASURY DIRECT®

OMB NO. 1535-0069
Expires 9-30-92

NEW ACCOUNT REQUEST

INVESTOR INFORMATION

ACCOUNT NAME

ADDRESS

CITY   STATE   ZIP CODE

FOR DEPARTMENT USE

DOCUMENT AUTHORITY

APPROVED BY

DATE APPROVED

EXT REG ☐

FOREIGN ☐

BACKUP ☐

REVIEW ☐

TAXPAYER IDENTIFICATION NUMBER

1ST NAMED OWNER ☐☐☐ - ☐☐ - ☐☐☐☐ OR ☐☐ - ☐☐☐☐☐☐☐
SOCIAL SECURITY NUMBER   EMPLOYER IDENTIFICATION NUMBER

CLASS ☐

TELEPHONE NUMBERS

(☐☐☐) ☐☐☐ - ☐☐☐☐   (☐☐☐) ☐☐☐ - ☐☐☐☐
WORK   HOME

DIRECT DEPOSIT INFORMATION

ROUTING NUMBER ☐☐☐☐☐☐☐☐☐

FINANCIAL INSTITUTION NAME

ACCOUNT NUMBER

ACCOUNT NAME

ACCOUNT TYPE ☐ CHECKING
(Check One) ☐ SAVINGS

AUTHORIZATION

I submit this request pursuant to the provisions of Department of the Treasury Circulars, Public Debt Series Nos. 1-86 and 2-86.

Under penalties of perjury, I certify that the number shown on this form is my correct taxpayer identification number and that I am not subject to backup withholding because (1) I have not been notified that I am subject to backup withholding as a result of a failure to report all interest or dividends, or (2) the Internal Revenue Service has notified me that I am no longer subject to backup withholding. I further certify that all other information provided on this form is true, correct and complete.

SIGNATURE   DATE

Figure E-3. (*Continued*) Instructions for completing a new account request. (*From Federal Reserve Book*)

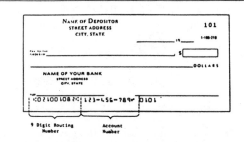

AUTHORIZATION

Sign and date the request form. Requests in the names of two individuals may be signed by either. However, if the second-named owner signs, then IRS Form W-9, signed by the first-named owner, must be submitted with the request. If the IRS has notified you that you are subject to backup withholding and you have not received notice from the IRS that backup withholding has terminated, you should strike out the language certifying that you are not subject to backup withholding.

TO SUBMIT THIS REQUEST

Submit this request to the Federal Reserve Bank or Branch serving your geographic area, or if you live in the metropolitan Washington, DC area, to the Bureau of the Public Debt, TREASURY DIRECT, Washington, DC 20239-2601.

CONFIRMATION OF THE ACCOUNT

You will receive a TREASURY DIRECT Statement of Account confirming the establishment of your account.

NOTICE UNDER THE PRIVACY AND PAPERWORK REDUCTION ACTS

The collection of the information you are requested to provide on this form is authorized by 31 U.S.C. Ch. 31 and the regulations in 31 CFR Ch. II, Subch. B, relating to the public debt. The furnishing of a taxpayer identifying number (TIN)—either a social security number or an employer identification number—is also required by Section 6109 of the Internal Revenue Code and regulations issued under that section.

The purpose for requesting the information is to enable the Bureau of the Public Debt, Department of the Treasury, and its agents to issue a Treasury security, to process securities transactions, to make payments, to identify owners and their accounts, and to provide reports to the Internal Revenue Service. The Bureau and its agents will use the information for these purposes. Furnishing the information is voluntary; however, without the information Treasury may be unable to issue a security or to conduct other transactions.

Information obtained concerning securities holdings and transactions is considered confidential under Treasury regulations (See, e.g., 31 CFR, Part 323) and under the Privacy Act and is provided only to owners of securities or their authorized representatives and is not disclosed to others unless otherwise authorized by law.

The estimated average burden associated with collection of information is 10 minutes per respondent or record-keeper and varies from 10 to 30 minutes per response, depending on individual circumstances. Comments concerning the accuracy of this burden estimate and suggestions on reducing the burden should be directed to Bureau of the Public Debt, Forms Management Officer, Washington, DC 20239-1300, and the Office of Management and Budget, Paperwork Reduction Project (1535-0069), Washington, DC 20503.

☆ U S GOVERNMENT PRINTING OFFICE 1990-279-165

Figure E-3. (*Continued*) Instructions for completing a new account request. (*From Federal Reserve Book*)

send a new account form and the same information required for notes
and bonds. In addition, you should include:

- The maturity desired — 13, 26, or 52 weeks
- The face amount of bills being purchased
- Whether you want to reinvest the funds at maturity
- Your telephone number during business hours

Payment for treasury bills may be in the form of cash; checks issued
by banks, savings and loan associations, or credit unions; certified personal checks; and matured U.S. Treasury notes or bonds. On the outside of the envelope should be written, "Tender for Treasury Bills."
Once the auction occurs, the securities that are purchased, along with
any future interest payments, are credited to the purchaser's account at
the Federal Reserve Board.

And that's all there is to it.

Competitive Versus
Noncompetitive Bidding

When purchasing treasury securities, individuals may specify if bids are
competitive or noncompetitive. Competitive bids specify the yield the
purchaser is willing to accept. With competitive bids, individuals run the
risk of paying more than the noncompetitive price if their bid is accepted. Competitive bids also run the risk of being shut out from the
auction if the bid is not accepted. Thus, it is suggested that individuals
make noncompetitive bids and accept the yield established at the auction.

For investors who want further information about treasury securities
and direct purchase through the Federal Reserve Banks, the Federal
Reserve Bank of Richmond has an informative booklet, *Buying Treasury Securities,* which explains the procedure and investment options
for individuals. A copy may be obtained at the Federal Reserve Bank of
Richmond, Public Service Department, P.O. Box 27471, Richmond, VA
23261. The price is $4.50 per copy.

Appendix **F**

DRIP
Record Book

Company Name	$ Investment W/OCP	$ Investment W/Rein. Div.	Date	Purchase Price	Shares	Fees	Date Sold	Selling Price	Capital Gain/Loss

Company Name	$ Investment W/OCP	$ Investment W/Reln. Div.	Date	Purchase Price	Shares	Fees	Date Sold	Selling Price	Capital Gain/Loss

Company Name	$ Investment W/OCP	$ Investment W/Rein. Div.	Date	Purchase Price	Shares	Fees	Date Sold	Selling Price	Capital Gain/Loss

Company Name	$ Investment W/OCP	$ Investment W/Reln. Div.	Date	Purchase Price	Shares	Fees	Date Sold	Selling Price	Capital Gain/Loss

Bibliography

Currier, Chet, and Smyth, David, *No Cost/Low Cost Investing*, Franklin Watts, New York, 1987.

Dreman, David, "Crisis Investing," *Forbes* magazine, October 22, 1990, p. 386.

DRIP Prospectus, First Commerce Corporation, 1987.

DRIP Prospectus, Potomac Electric Power, 1990.

Evergreen Enterprises, Laurel, MD, *Directory of Companies Offering Dividend Reinvestment Plans*, 1990.

Federal Reserve Bank of Richmond, *Buying Treasury Securities at Federal Reserve Banks*, 1990.

Institute of Econometric Research, *Market Logic* newsletter, pp. 6–7, October 12, 1990.

Scholes, Myron S., and Wolfson, Mark A., "Decentralized Investment Banking: The Case of Discount Dividend-Reinvestment and Stock-Purchase Plans," *Journal of Financial Economics*, 1989, pp. 7–35.

Thompson, Rex, "The Information Content of Discounts and Premiums on Closed-End Fund Shares," *Journal of Financial Economics*, pp. 151–186, 1978.

(Certain statistics were provided courtesy of Ibbotson Associates and Lipper Analytical Services, Inc.)

Index

About the Author

Charles B. Carlson has been providing profitable investment advice to individual investors for over nine years. He is the editor of *Dow Theory Forecasts*, one of the nation's oldest and most widely read newsletters for individual investors. He is also vice-president of Dow Theory Forecasts, Inc., and is a member of the Association for Investment Management and Research. Mr. Carlson, who is a Chartered Financial Analyst (CFA), writes a weekly financial column for *Editor's Copy* syndicate. He is a frequent guest expert on numerous radio and television programs.

The author of <u>Buying Stocks Without A Broker</u> invites you to try a sample copy of <u>Dow Theory Forecasts</u>

Dow Theory Forecasts investment newsletter has been serving individual investors since 1946. The weekly publication, geared primarily toward conservative and income investors, covers a variety of investment topics, such as:

1. Dividend Round-Up —
Reviews and recommendations on stocks with strong dividend records and dividend-growth prospects.

3. Analysts' Choices —
Full-page coverage of stocks picked by our analysts for best near-term performance.

2. Quarterly Utility Ratings —
A quarterly update of over 90 major electric utilities with ratings based on financial condition, regulatory climates, and dividend-growth prospects.

4. Consultation Privileges —
Full-term subscribers to *Dow Theory Forecasts* may have their stocks reviewed and investment questions answered any time at no extra cost.

Other regular features include:

- **Insider Favorites**
- **Turnaround Selections**
- **Special Situations**
- **Dividend Reinvestment Plans**

TEAR HERE

■■

Return To:
Dow Theory Forecasts, Inc.
7412 Calumet Ave.
Hammond, IN 46324-2692

FREE current issue of *Dow Theory Forecasts* for readers of this book.

Name _____
PLEASE PRINT

Address _____
INCLUDE APT.# IF APPLICABLE

City _____ State _____ Zip _____

❏ Check here if you would like to receive information on a monthly newsletter devoted exclusively to **Dividend Reinvestment Plans.**